Kurdistan in Iraq

The Kurdish-Iraqi conflict lies in the fact that Kurdistan is a nation-without-a-state and Iraq is a non-nation state, each possessing a nationhood project differing from and opposing the other. Iraqi Kurdistan is an outward looking entity seeking external patronage. Though external patronage has played a pivotal role in the evolution of the Kurdish quasi-state, a lack of positive patronage has prevented it from achieving independence.

This book looks at how the Kurdish and Iraqi quests for nationhood have led to the transformation of Iraqi Kurdistan into an unrecognised quasi-state, and the devolution of the Iraqi state into a recognised quasi-state. This is done by examining the protracted Iraqi-Kurdish conflict and by analysing the contradictions and incompatibilities between the two different nationalisms: Iraqi and Kurdish. The author explains that Kurds as a nation without a state have their own nationhood project which is in opposition to the Iraqi nationhood project. Each has its own identity, loyalty and sovereignty. The book answers the question as to how the Kurdish quest for nationhood has been treated by successive Iraqi regimes. Furthermore, it fills in the literary gaps which exist in relation to the Iraqi-Kurdish conflict by specifying and categorising the cardinal conditions that drive ethnic and nationalist conflicts which lead to the creation of separatist entities.

Drawing upon a vast amount of untapped Kurdish and Arabic primary sources, the book draws on prominent theories on nation-states and quasi-states. It will particularly appeal to students and scholars of international relations, political theory and Middle Eastern Studies.

Aram Rafaat, PhD, is a freelance researcher and educator. He has published widely in English and Kurdish and is the author of two books, *The Kurds in Post-Invasion Iraq* and *The Shiite's Position on Kirkuk and Federalism* and a number of journal articles.

Routledge Studies in Middle Eastern Democratization and Government
Edited by Larbi Sadiki,
Qatar University

This series examines new ways of understanding democratization and government in the Middle East. The varied and uneven processes of change, occurring in the Middle Eastern region, can no longer be read and interpreted solely through the prism of Euro-American transitology. Seeking to frame critical parameters in light of these new horizons, this series instigates reinterpretations of democracy and propagates formerly 'subaltern' narratives of democratization. Reinvigorating discussion on how Arab and Middle Eastern peoples and societies seek good government, *Routledge Studies in Middle Eastern Democratization and Government* provides tests and contests of old and new assumptions.

Palestine in EU and Russian Foreign Policy
Statehood and the peace process
Malath Alagha

Tunisia's International Relations since the 'Arab Spring'
Transition inside and out
Edited by Tasnim Abderrahim, Laura-Theresa Krüger, Salma Besbes and Katharina McLarren

EU Foreign Policy and Hamas
Inconsistencies and paradoxes
Adeeb Ziadeh

Politics and Revolution in Egypt
Rise and fall of the youth activists
Sarah Anne Rennick

Kurdistan in Iraq
The evolution of a quasi-state
Aram Rafaat

For a full list of titles in the series: *www.routledge.com/middleeaststudies/series/ RSMEDG*

Kurdistan in Iraq
The evolution of a quasi-state

Aram Rafaat

LONDON AND NEW YORK

First published 2018
by Routledge
2 Park Square, Milton Park, Abingdon, Oxon OX14 4RN

and by Routledge
711 Third Avenue, New York, NY 10017

Routledge is an imprint of the Taylor & Francis Group, an informa business

© 2018 Aram Rafaat

The right of Aram Rafaat to be identified as author of this work has been asserted by him in accordance with sections 77 and 78 of the Copyright, Designs and Patents Act 1988.

All rights reserved. No part of this book may be reprinted or reproduced or utilised in any form or by any electronic, mechanical, or other means, now known or hereafter invented, including photocopying and recording, or in any information storage or retrieval system, without permission in writing from the publishers.

Trademark notice: Product or corporate names may be trademarks or registered trademarks, and are used only for identification and explanation without intent to infringe.

British Library Cataloguing-in-Publication Data
A catalogue record for this book is available from the British Library

Library of Congress Cataloging-in-Publication Data
A catalog record for this book has been requested

ISBN: 978-0-8153-9333-7 (hbk)
ISBN: 978-1-351-18883-8 (ebk)

Typeset in Times New Roman
by Apex CoVantage, LLC

Contents

List of abbreviations viii
Glossary x
Introduction xi

1 Recognised and unrecognised quasi-states 1
Recognised quasi-states (RQs) and criteria for recognised quasi-states (RQC) 5
First and second criteria for recognised quasi-states (RQC-I and RQC-II) 5
Third and fourth criteria for recognised quasi-states (RQC-III and RQC-IV) 9
Unrecognised quasi-states (UQs) and criteria for unrecognised quasi-states (UQC) 12
Recognised quasi-states (RQs) versus unrecognised quasi-states (UQs) 22
States with dual sovereignty (SWDS) versus quasi-states 23

2 The context of two quasi-states in Iraq 25
Contending debate on the oppositional nature of the Kurdish and Iraqi quests for nationhood 25
Contending debate on the Kurdish quasi-state 27
Contending debate on Iraq as a quasi-state 29
Nations, nations without states, and non-nation states 30

3 The two contradictory nationhood projects in Iraq 35
Iraqi Nationhood Project and the Kurds 35
Kurdish Nationhood Project 46

4 The monarchy-Kurds relations 70
The monarchy-urban Kurds relations 73
The monarchy-aghas relations 75

vi *Contents*

*The emergence of the urbanite-*agha *coalition 77*
The KDP monopoly of Kurdish politics 80

5 The first unrecognised Kurdish quasi-state (1961–1975)   84
The emergence of the peshmerga as a unified Kurdish militia 85
The emergence of Mustafa Barzani as a charismatic Kurdish leader 85
The September revolution and the establishment of Free Kurdistan 87
The size of Free Kurdistan 88
The population of Free Kurdistan 89
Was Free Kurdistan a quasi-state? 89
Free Kurdistan from 1961–1975: the first unrecognised Kurdish quasi-state (UKQ-I) 97
Iraq from 1961–1975: a recognised quasi-state (RQ) 97

6 The case of negative patronage   102
The puzzling downfall of the UKQ-I 102
Negative patronage as the Kurds' Achilles' heel 106

7 The rise and fall of Kurdish insurgency (1976–1988)   114
The first phase: the emergence of the Kurdish insurgency (1976–1979) 114
The second phase: administrating the peshmerga controlled areas (1979–1985) 116
The third phase: the expansion of the peshmerga controlled areas (1985–1987) 118
Do the peshmerga controlled areas meet criteria for unrecognised quasi-states? 119
Kurdish insurgency and the devolution of the Iraqi state into a quasi-state 125

8 Iraq's failure to govern Kurdistan (1975–1991)   131
The Autonomous Region of Kurdistan 131
Iraqi policy: from Kurdish integration to the annihilation of Iraqi Kurdistan 134
The depopulation policy after the collapse of the Kurdish insurgency 143
The Kurds respond to the de-Iraqification policy: the uprising of 1991 143

9	**The second unrecognised Kurdish quasi-state (1992–2003)**	148
	The establishment of the Kurdistan Regional Government 148	
	The establishment of a Safe Haven 155	
	The KRI (1991–2003) as a second unrecognised Kurdish quasi-state 159	
	The case of negative patronage 159	
	Iraq between 1991 and 2003: a recognised quasi-state 163	
10	**The third unrecognised Kurdish quasi-state after the 2003 invasion**	167
	Termination of UKQ-II or a new phase of the Kurdish quasi-state? 167	
	The first criterion (UQC-I): nation-building 168	
	The second criterion (UQC-II): the militarisation of Kurdish society 170	
	The third criterion (UQC-III): Iraq as a weak parent state 172	
	The fourth criterion (UQC-IV): external patronage 173	
	Kurdish strategy to find positive patronage during and after the invasion 173	
	Iraq since 2003: a recognised quasi-state 174	
	How two quasi-states in one country hindered Kurdish integration into Iraq 178	
11	**Oil for external patronage and financial independence**	182
	From financial dependency on external patrons to revenue sharing with Baghdad 182	
	Oil for external support and positive patronage 188	
	The KRI goal: from periphery to emerging regional oil power 189	
	The failure of the financial independence policy? 191	
12	**Independence referendum and the case of negative patronage**	197
	Internal challenges 198	
	Factors behind the Kurds' move towards an independence referendum 199	
	Negative patronage as the KRI's Achilles' heel 204	

References	214
List of news and newspaper sources	243
Index	244

Abbreviations

ARK	Autonomous Region of Kurdistan
CIA	Central Intelligence Agency
CPA	Coalition Provisional Authority
CRS	Congressional Research Service
CW	Chemical Weapons
EC	Executive Council
EIA	Energy Information Administration
FFC	Fact-Finding Commission
HRW	Human Rights Watch
ICG	International Crisis Group
ICP	Iraqi Communist Party
IKF	Iraqi Kurdistan Front
INC	Iraqi National Congress
INP	Iraqi Nation-Building Project
ISIS	The Islamic State in Iraq and Syria
KDP	Kurdistan Democratic Party
KDPI	Kurdistan Democratic Party-Iran
KDS	Kurdish *De Facto Self-rule*
KLM	Kurdish Liberation Movement
KNA	Kurdistan National Assembly
KNP	Kurdish Nationhood Project
KRA	Kurdistan Revolutionary Army
KRG	Kurdistan Regional Government
KRG-ME	Kurdistan Regional Government–Ministry of Education
KRP	Kurdistan Regional Presidency
KTU	Kurdistan Teachers Union
NFZ	No-Fly Zone
NML	No-Man's Land
NNS	Non-nation State
NPC	Negative Patronage Criteria
NWS	Nation Without a State
OFFP	The Oil-For-Food Program
PCA	Peshmerga Controlled Area

PUK	Patriotic Union of Kurdistan
RAF	Royal Air Force
RCCI	Revolutionary Command Council of Iraq
RCCK	Revolutionary Command Council of Kurdistan
RI-MI	Republic of Iraq, Ministry of Information
RQ	Recognised Quasi-state
RQC	Recognised Quasi-state Criteria
SCR	Security Council Resolution
SFA	Strategic Framework Agreement
SOFA	US-Iraq Status of Forces Agreement
TAE	Traditional Autonomous Entities
TAL	Transitional Administrative Law
UKQ	Unrecognised Kurdish Quasi-state
UN	United Nations
UQ	Unrecognised Quasi-state
UQC	Criteria for Unrecognised Quasi-state
USD	United States Dollar
USSR	Union of Soviet Socialist Republics
WMD	Weapons of Mass Destruction

Glossary

Agha A Kurdish term for tribal chieftains

Amn Iraq's General Security Directorate

Anfal An Arabic term for spoils of the war, it used by Iraq for a series of major military campaigns carried out against the Kurds from 1987 to 1988

Ey Reqib A Kurdish term that literally means 'O enemy', the Kurdish national anthem is popularly known as *Ey Reqib*, which is the title of the poem used for the anthem

Jash A Kurdish derogatory term literally meaning small donkey, but popularly used to mean pro-government tribal militia

Kurdayeti A Kurdish term for Kurdish Nationalist Movement

Mujama'at An Arabic term that means collections, it used by the Iraqi government to refer to collection camps; the majority of Kurdish villagers were relocated in *Mujama'at* between 1976 and 1991

Mustashar An Arabic term that literally means adviser or consultant; it is used for a Kurdish tribal commander of a *Jash* unit

Nawroz Kurdish national day

Peshmerga A Kurdish term that means those who face death, used by Kurds for those fighting for *Kurdayeti*

Tanzimat An Arabic term used to refer to a series of reforms promulgated in the Ottoman Empire between 1839 and 1876

Introduction

On 9 April 2003, US troops advanced into Baghdad. Shortly after the entry of the US marines into the capitol city, a small crowd of Iraqis gathered in *Firdos* Square in the middle of Baghdad, where a huge statue of Iraqi President Saddam Hussein had been erected. In a highly symbolic act, a group of men climbed the statue's pedestal and attached a rope around the image of Saddam Hussein. Failing to topple the statue, the US marine armoured recovery vehicle helped Iraqi citizens pull it down. The Iraqis jumped with joy on the toppled statue, and waved the country's pre-1991 flag, signalling to the world that Americans were 'liberators' of the Iraqi people. Kurdish leaders, Masoud Barzani and Jalal Talabani, were among the first who arrived in Baghdad to participate in the work of 'rebuilding' the Iraqi state.[1] Nineteen months later, on 30 January 2005, the 'new era of democracy' commenced with the Iraqis' purple-stained fingers. They had just voted in, probably, the first free election in modern Iraq. One of the most significant parts of this development was that the overwhelming majority of the Kurds participated in the election. Another important development was the 'settlement' of the Kurdish issue in the new Iraqi constitution. On 15 October 2005, in a national referendum, the majority of Iraqis voted for the constitution, which recognised Kurdistan as a federal region run by its own regional parliament and government. The referendum also demonstrated that 80 per cent of the Kurds voted in favour of the constitution. This was taken to be proof that the Kurds supported Iraqi unity and its federal system of governance. Another important building block in the Kurds' participation in the new Iraq was the election of Kurdish president Jalal Talabani by Iraq's parliament. This was the first Kurdish president to be elected in Iraqi history and carried enormous symbolic importance.

Official Kurdish statements emphasised that Kurds chose a voluntary union with Iraq. For example, Masud Barzani, then the president of the Kurdistan Regional Government, insists that "[Kurds] have participated and contributed effectively in building a new Iraq," and "[Kurds] are one of the founders of the [new] Iraqi state."[2] He further explained that "the first two brigades of the Iraqi new army were founded by Kurdish security forces (peshmerga), while other parties were not ready to contribute in rebuilding the Iraqi army."[3] Similarly, Jalal Talabani, the former president of Iraq, insisted that 80 per cent of the Kurds voted for Iraq's constitution, and this proved that the Kurds support Iraqi unity.[4] Further, Barham

Salih[5] explained that the Kurdish leaderships' engagement in the formation of the Iraqi government is unprecedented.[6] Kurdish leaders, however, claim that their voluntary union comes with the precondition that the system of Iraq is federal.[7] In their public statements, Kurdish officials describe federalism as "the best solution for [Kurdish] issue"[8] and "one of the Kurdish top priorities".[9] At the same time they insist that federalism is "the absolute minimum the people of Iraqi Kurdistan will accept".[10] In other words, for the Kurds federalism is a *voluntary union*.[11] Furthermore, the Kurds played a tough game to enshrine their quest for autonomy under a federal system.[12] Correspondingly, many commentators argue that the Kurds in modern Iraq are pioneers of federalist thinking, and federalism's most zealous supporters.[13] This Kurdish policy, many argue, is a realistic and pragmatic policy.[14] Thus, many believe that federalism in Iraq is a Kurdish objective, and their return to Iraq and their advocacy of federalism signals Kurdish acceptance of remaining as part of the Iraqi nation.[15]

Federalism apparently became the dominant theme in Kurdish official party media and the Kurds actively participated in the reconstruction of the Iraqi state. Article 117 of the Iraqi constitution recognised the legitimacy of the KRG in a federal Iraq. Existing legislation and decrees promulgated by the Kurdistan Region of Iraq (KRI) were formally recognised in Article 141 of Iraq's permanent constitution which also favoured the KRI with revenues (Articles 106 and 121). The new Iraqi state was rebuilt on the basis of consensus, parliamentary power-sharing, and federalism. Articles 110, 111, 112, 113, 114, and 115 ratified the authority of both the KRI government and the central government. In addition to the power-sharing arrangement in some fields of authority by Baghdad and Erbil, pertinent exclusive rights were allocated to each side with the central government apportioning a degree of its sovereignty to the KRI. In post-invasion Iraq the KRI generally portrayed itself as a *de jure* federal region within Iraq. Many scholars on the Kurdish issue have argued that the KRI compromised its independent status by becoming an integral part of a federal Iraq.[16] Based on this argument one might argue that Iraq was transformed from a unitary state into a federal one, and the Kurdish quasi-state was terminated by rejoining Iraq.

The 'liberation' of Iraq from 35 years of dictatorship, the Kurds' participation in popular elections, the recognition of the federal status of the KRI, and the election of Talabani as president of Iraq resonated well with Western media outlets imagining that 'freedom' and 'justice' for the Kurds had now been established in Iraq and the Kurdish issue was settled. The dominant and popular interpretation of the Kurdish issue is that it was an issue of citizenship and human rights. All that was needed to settle the Kurdish issue was to remove the dictator, create a democratic atmosphere, include the Kurds into Iraqi state institutions, and introduce a degree of federalism to insure their control of their local affairs.

This cheerful and wishful imagining of the Iraqi functioning democracy quickly became a *faded* dream. Not only did the Kurdistan region not reintegrate into the country but Iraq itself was on the verge of dismantlement as both the US occupation and the new Iraqi rulers were challenged by a Sunni-dominated insurgency. Divided by civil war, the Shias and Sunnis were exhausted and during the first years of US occupation the Iraqi state practically collapsed. The US was the only real authority in Iraq following its occupation in 2003. For many years Iraq remained (nominally) a united country because more than 140,000 US-led coalition troops assured that this was the case. The US had the ability to dismember Iraq at will. But the US did just the opposite. The US was involved in the process of reconstructing Iraq at the expense of the independence of Kurdistan region. Initially, the US attempted to dissolve the KRG and impose a form of federalism based on 18 governorates rather than a federal system based on a plan that included the KRI as a federal region. Facing harsh rejection from the Kurds, combined with anti-American insurgencies, the Sunni-Shia civil war, and a political stalemate, the US abandoned its policy.

The unification between the Kurdistan region and Iraq, however, remained mostly nominal as reunification did not diminish KRI status or its internal sovereignty. From the Kurdish perspective, the KRI would not accept less than their existing situation. On one hand, the Kurds were relatively successful in incorporating their version of 'reunification' into the Iraqi constitution. After the invasion the Kurds insisted on the re-adjustment of the Kirkuk border and the inclusion of the population of detached districts in a referendum over the destiny of Kirkuk. Though this claim was included in Article 58 of the Transitional Administrative Law (TAL) and restated in Article 140 of the Iraqi constitution, the Iraqi government failed to implement these constitutional articles. On the opposing hand, the KRI reserved and further consolidated its *de facto* rule in the Kurdistan region. The KRG extended its authority into disputed areas that represented some 40 per cent of what the Kurds believe to be their historical homeland. To do this, the KRG used its armed forces and controlled most of the disputed areas. Following the Islamic State in Iraq and Syria (ISIS) blitzkrieg across Sunni areas and the withdrawal of the Iraqi army from Kirkuk province, peshmerga (the Kurdish army) replaced the Iraqi army and controlled significant areas of Kirkuk and Mosul provinces. Though the relationship between the Kurds and Iraqis remained calm, there were signs of cooperation between the two sides in their war against ISIS, the potential for war remains high. The threat remains as most historical conflicts between the two sides have remained unresolved; both sides own military forces and there are factions on both sides that incline towards military solutions to resolve their conflicts. On many occasions, there were standoffs between the peshmerga forces on one side and the Iraqi army and its militia on the other. The most recent series of clashes between the peshmerga and the Hashed al-Shaabi, an Iraqi militia, was in April 2016, where an open conflict broke out between the two sides in the town of Tuz Khurmatu.

In June 2014, ten years after the *Firdos* Square incident, the Iraqi army collapsed in almost the entire Sunni region of Iraq, including the two main cities of Mosul and Tikrit as a result of unrelenting ISIS attacks. The collapse of the Iraqi army resulted in the emergence of a new border between Iraq and the Kurdistan region. The KRI-Iraq border dispute and emergence of the new border was the central issue behind the contention between Baghdad and Erbil in post-invasion Iraq. The two entities were separated by clear boundaries. On 18 February 2015,

Masud Barzani visited peshmerga's frontlines against ISIS in the province of Kirkuk. In a speech to peshmerga's commandos, Barzani stated that "they [Iraqis] must know that either we will all die, or Kirkuk will never fall to the enemy ever again." Barzani emphasised that "today's reality has been achieved with precious blood and we will not tolerate any change to these borders." Terms of 'enemy' and 'border' here are clear indications as to the tense nature surrounding the Iraqi state and the new border line between Iraq and the Kurdistan region. The border conflict between Baghdad and Erbil gives the impression of being more of a dispute between two rival neighbouring quasi-states than between two regions within one country.

The Kurdish-Iraq conflict is not between a state and disadvantaged rebel or minority group, nor is it from a peripheral territory or a conflict over cultural, economic, human, and/or ethnic rights. Rather it is a conflict between two antagonistic quasi-states, each struggling to escape from its quasi-state status and be transformed into a real sovereign state at the expense of the other's sovereignty. Similar to the ongoing border dispute between two rival neighbouring states, the KRI-Iraq border dispute was the central issue behind the contention between Baghdad and Erbil. The two entities were separated by clear boundaries. To gain internal sovereignty, the KRI aimed to extend its authority into disputed areas that represented some 40 per cent of what the Kurds believe to be their historical homeland. To gain internal sovereignty, the KRG aimed to extend its authority into disputed areas that represented some 40 per cent of what the Kurds believe to be their historical homeland. To that end, the KRG unilaterally redrew the Kurdistan region's border with Iraq. The KRI's intention, in contrast, was to maintain internal sovereignty and incorporate the disputed areas into its territory. To maintain its internal sovereignty, the KRI prevented Iraq's institutions and army from entering the Kurdistan region. Furthermore, each entity was protected by two separate independent military forces. The Iraq army has over 750,000 soldiers, very few of whom are Kurds. The Kurdish armed forces number around 200,000. Of course, Iraq has no authority to command these military personnel. Moreover, the KRI has control over its own economy, military, education, and oil fields.

Conflict over external recognition of state sovereignty was another source of contentiousness between the two states. Iraq asserts that establishing international relations is its exclusive right and that Kurdistan has no right in this area since it is part of Iraq. Yet on the contrary, the KRI established both diplomatic and economic relations with foreign countries despite Iraq's opposition to achieve externally recognised sovereignty. The KRI established its representatives in dozens of countries and many countries reciprocated by establishing direct relations with the KRI by opening consulates in Kurdistan. KRI President Masud Barzani was received by heads of states of numerous countries including the US, Turkey, France, and Iran, who treated the KRI as a semi-independent entity. The latest direct military aid to Kurdish forces, the KRI-Iraq border dispute, and rows over oil shows that the conflict has remained as one of the country's most pervasive problems since the American invasion of Iraq. It also shows the nature of the Iraqi-Kurdish conflict. Thus, despite the Kurds' official statements, in the first years of the US invasion, regarding their reunification with Iraq, the US attempt to dissolve the KRI, and the recognition of the federal status of the Kurdistan region, the Iraqi government has not governed the Kurdistan region. Iraqi institutions, administration, and armed forces were not allowed to enter the region and are totally absent in Kurdistan. KRI institutions and its structure remained untouched; the Kurdistan region remained unoccupied by the US, and the Iraqi authority failed to return to and govern Kurdistan.

In fact, this was not the first time that Iraq failed to govern the Kurdistan region despite the ostensible rejoining of the Kurdish region to Iraq. On four occasions Iraq was able to recapture or return to the Kurdish region: 1975, 1988, 1991, and 2003. On all of these occasions, however, Iraq failed to adequately govern, manage, and/or to maintain its rule in the region. From 1961 to 1975 the Iraqi authority was absent in a significant part of Kurdistan, which the Kurds called Free Kurdistan. With the collapse of Free Kurdistan in 1975, Iraq regained an opportunity to rule the region. However, during the era of Free Kurdistan (1961–1975), Iraqi institutions were expelled from Kurdistan, and the Kurdish administration, institutions, and armed forces replaced them. With the collapse of Free Kurdistan, the Kurdish local administrations collapsed, leaving a void in civil administration, functional institutions, and native supporters. With this set of circumstances, Iraq's only option for maintaining its rule was to govern the region militarily. The military, however, failed to meet its obligations satisfactorily. Within one year of the collapse of Free Kurdistan, Iraq's military superiority was challenged by the peshmerga in rural Kurdistan. By the time that the Iraq-Iran war broke out, Iraq had lost military control of most parts of rural Kurdistan. Thus, Iraq did not succeed in governing the Kurdistan region administratively or militarily.

The result of Iraq's failure to govern Kurdistan from 1976 onward was that the Kurdistan region was divided into four zones, each with a different policy imposed by the central government. The policy for each zone was based on the degree of the zone's affiliation with Kurdish insurgency. The first policy offered symbolic autonomy but with a heavy military presence in the main cities and towns that were less directly affiliated with and less vulnerable to integration into Free Kurdistan. The second policy offered indirect rule through middlemen and the *Jash* militia. It was the policy for the newly created collection camps and towns that were ruled by the Kurds. From 1975 onward this zone remained under Iraq's authority but was vulnerable to be being recaptured by the peshmerga. The second policy was designed for the ethnically mixed areas that were less affiliated with Kurdish insurgency. Iraq followed the combined policies of Arabisation and de-Kurdification in this zone. They were less vulnerable to being captured by the peshmerga but insisted on being considered as an integral part of the Kurdish homeland. The fourth policy was the depopulation of rural Kurdistan that was ruled by the KQS-I until 1975 and by the peshmerga between 1980 and 1988. Iraq also followed the policy of annihilation and de-Iraqification of inhabitants of this region. By 1988 about 80 to 90 per cent of rural Kurdistan was depopulated.

The second occasion in which Iraq failed to govern the Kurdish self-ruled areas followed the collapse of the second period of Kurdish self-rule in 1988 when Iraq defeated the peshmerga and recaptured the entire Iraqi Kurdistan region. Despite its undisputed control over Kurdistan, Iraq did not attempt to reconcile with the Kurds, repopulate, or reconstruct the war-devastated rural areas. Nor did they attempt to provide services and implement a functional civil administration to the region. What Iraq did was to expand its depopulation policies to towns and collection camps that they had previously ruled indirectly. Thus, failing to govern Kurdistan between 1976 and 1991 resulted in the depopulation of two-thirds of Iraqi Kurdistan. The third occasion in which Iraq failed to govern the Kurdish self-ruled areas was after the Kurdish uprising of 1991. Iraq defeated the uprising and recaptured the main cities and towns. But it still failed to govern or maintain its authority in the region. For the first time in its history, Iraq was compelled to withdraw from all three Kurdish governorates, the region that eventually turned into the *de facto* self-rule. The final occasion in which Iraq failed to govern the Kurdish self-ruled areas was after the invasion period when the Kurds rejoined the country. In 2003 the KRI formally rejoined Iraq, an act that became constitutionally recognised and resulted in a federal and unified Iraq. The KDS established after 1991 was transformed into a more functional, progressive, and stronger quasi-state.

The main argument of this book is that both Iraq and the KRI are quasi-states; the former is a recognised quasi-state (RQ), and the latter an unrecognised quasi-state (UQ). To explain attributes that distinguish UQs from RQs, this book draws from several theories of statehood. Constitutive theory, Jackson's quasi-state theory, and Weber's legitimacy theory are used to understand RQs while declarative theory and Colsto's quasi-state theory are used to define UQs. Constitutive theory focuses on the external legal rights and duties. The key to constitutive theory is not an entity's attainment of *de facto* statehood but, rather, prior international acceptance of its asserted right to independence. Constitutive statehood is an entity that enjoys international recognition regardless of its internal reality. Thus, constitutive statehood is a juridical rather than an empirical entity. It enjoys recognition but may lack internal legitimacy. Similar to constitutive theory, for Jackson, international recognition is a precondition to recognise an entity as a state. For him, a *de facto* state which is not recognised internationally is not considered as a state. Unlike constitutive theory, however, Jackson's definition of statehood is both empirical and *de jure*. He identifies two forms of internationally recognised states: 'real' and 'quasi'. Jackson's 'real' sovereign state enjoys dual legitimacy: external, vis-à-vis other states, and internal, vis-à-vis its own citizens. Jackson's 'quasi-state' is recognised by the international community as a sovereign state, but clearly lacks internal legitimacy. However, Weber's view of statehood resembles the characteristics of empirical statehood and is useful to further understand internal legitimacy. Weber defines the state in relation to its monopolisation of the legitimate use of force. A state, according to Weber, is an entity that monopolises legitimate use of physical force within a certain territory. Hence, based on Weber's definition, an entity that lacks the monopoly on legitimate violence cannot be considered as a state. This definition of a state's claim to a monopoly on legitimate violence is used to further understand Jackson's concept of internal legitimacy and sovereignty.

Declarative theory helps in the understanding of UQs. This theory focuses on the internal factual situation. In other words, it focuses on the conditions of statehood (recognition of a state). A state, based on declarative theory, is an entity that possesses four qualifications: a permanent population; a defined territory; government; and the capacity to enter into relations with the other states. In other words, declarative theory defines an entity as a state if it possesses these qualifications, regardless of whether this entity is a member of the UN or not. Thus, declaratory statehood resembles the characteristics of the unrecognised quasi-state. Similar to UQs, declarative statehood is 'empirical' rather than 'juridical' and possesses internal sovereignty but may lack international recognition. Kolstø classifies as quasi-states those states possessing internal sovereignty but lacking international recognition.

These two sets of theory, however, fail to agree on a single and universally accepted meaning of the term quasi-state. Some scholars use different and often non-synonymous terms (such as artificial states, cleft states, failed states, rogue states, non-nation states, and pseudo-states) to describe recognised quasi-states. Other scholars use terms such as quasi-states, *de facto* states, pseudo-states, or secessionist or rebel territories for unrecognised quasi-states. Moreover, scholars on quasi-states do not agree on which type of states can be categorised as quasi-states. To overcome these generalisations and confusion, as well as to address a gap in the literature pertaining to quasi-states and drawing on these theories, this work brings in several new and original models. Two sets of criteria are introduced: one for RQs and the other for UQs. The former will be referred to as recognised quasi-state criteria (RQC) and the latter will be called unrecognised quasi-state criteria (UQC). These criteria are designed to distinguish RQs from UQs, and both from real states. Four criteria are utilised to classify recognised quasi-states. The first and second criteria of RQs pertain to the internal affairs of the state, while the third and fourth are related to the state's status vis-à-vis other states. A state that enjoys external recognition but falls within the criteria of recognised quasi-states (RQC) is considered as a recognised quasi-state. The first two criteria of unrecognised states, however, pertain to the quality of the unrecognised entities, the third criterion to the status of the parent state, and the fourth to the quality of the UQs' external patronage. If a *de facto* state, however, fails to gain international recognition but falls within these four criteria, it can be defined as an unrecognised quasi-state. Throughout this book, the status of Iraq is scrutinised in light of RQC and the KRI in light of the UQC. Other new and original models and themes that have been introduced and developed throughout the book include: the notion of the existence of two quasi-states (i.e. a recognised and an unrecognised quasi-state), the outward looking nature of the 'nations without a state', positive and negative patronages, and criteria for negative patronage.

To date, few, if any, studies have focused on the question as to whether Iraq may be considered a quasi-state and, if so, how that state of affairs impacted Kurdish integration into Iraq. *Kurdistan in Iraq: the evolution of a quasi-state* is both intriguing and extremely relevant to the debates currently taking place regarding ethno-sectarian conflict in Iraq and the wider Middle Eastern region.

Kurdistan in Iraq: the evolution of a quasi-state is the first book to dissect and discuss the diverse consequences of the evolution of the status of a nation without a state (NWS) that exists within the boundaries of a sovereign state into an unrecognised quasi-state. It is also the first to distinguish unrecognised quasi-states from recognised quasi-states and for that purpose two sets of criteria are developed for both forms of quasi-state. Moreover, the book is the first to trace the impact of an unrecognised quasi-state on the devolution of a parent state into a recognised quasi-state. The book will make a significant contribution both because these themes and models are quite original and can be applied to international relations theory, as well as because it analyses conflicts at the wider Kurdish, regional, Middle Eastern, and international levels. The model of a country of two quasi-states may offer answers not only to the protracted Kurdish-Iraqi conflict but also to internal conflicts in other countries. It may help to re-categorise many countries around the world as countries of two or more quasi-states. Cyprus is one example that can be examined to determine whether it is a country of two quasi-states: the unrecognised Turkish quasi-state and the recognised Cypriot quasi-state. Another country that needs to be evaluated is Georgia in order to understand whether it can be defined as a country of three quasi-states: the recognised quasi-state of Georgia and the two unrecognised quasi-states, Abkhazia and South Ossetia.

The model of outward looking NWSs is another that may offer the answer to internal conflicts in other countries. For example, it may offer the answer to the question of why the Kurds of Iran and Turkey have not achieved *de facto* self-rule or an unrecognised Kurdish quasi-state similar to that of the Kurds in Iraq. At the regional level, do other territorial communities, such as the Azeri and Arabs of Iran, qualify as NWSs and, if so, are they outward looking communities similar to the Kurds of Iraq? Another model developed in this book is that of positive and negative patronage. This model can be applied to the Palestinian territory, a region that is supported by many Arab and Islamic countries. In this regard one can ask, as there are Azeri and Arab states that would grant these two communities positive patronage, why have these two communities not established unrecognised quasi-states? These two examples are also useful to further research the role of negative and positive patronages in the emergence and survival of unrecognised quasi-states. The ideas of negative and positive patronage are also useful to answer the question as to why some unrecognised quasi-states (such as South Sudan, Eritrea, and East Timor) have achieved international recognition, while other quasi-states (such as the Tamils of Sri Lanka) collapsed. In between, however, are many unrecognised quasi-states that have managed to survive but failed to achieve recognition. Among these are West Sahara and the Nagorno-Karabakh Republic. These themes may also prove effective for finding a different and more appropriate solution to the Israeli-Palestinian conflict. Answering these questions not only offers a better understanding of the nature of protracted conflicts among ethno-sectarian groups but may provide a proper solution to them.

This book is the first to argue that Iraq is a country of two quasi-states and that the Kurdish-Iraqi conflict is a clash between these two quasi-states. The product of amassing a vast amount of material, as well as marshalling and organising it into a coherent analytical narrative, this book examines these two quasi-states. From 1961 onward the Kurdish-Iraqi conflict has turned into a conflict between two separate states that exist within the boundaries of one country, rather than a conflict within one nation. This book also clarifies that the devolution of Iraq from a sovereign state into a recognised quasi-state is directly related to the emergence of the unrecognised Kurdish quasi-state. It will also highlight how these dual quasi-states within the boundary of Iraq have led to many of the most deep-seated and intractable problems facing Iraq, the region, and the world today. In other words, the aim of this study is to examine the three unexplored and most challenging issues facing modern Iraq: the Kurdish and Iraqi contradictory quests for nationhood; the evolution of the status of the Kurds from being a nation without a state to a nation that is now a quasi-state; and how the Kurdish problem has caused Iraq's status to shift from what was a 'functional nation-state' and to a quasi-state.

Kurdistan in Iraq: the evolution of a quasi-state answers the question as to how the Kurdish and Iraqi quests for nationhood have led to the transformation of Iraqi Kurdistan into an unrecognised quasi-state and the devolution of the Iraqi state into a recognised quasi-state. This will be done by examining the protracted Iraqi-Kurdish conflict and by analysing the contradictions and incompatibilities between the two different nationalisms: Iraqi and Kurdish. This book explains that Kurds as a nation without a state (NWS) have their own nationhood project which is in opposition to the Iraqi Nationhood Project (INP). Each has its own identity, loyalty, and sovereignty. This study answers the question as to how the Kurdish quest for nationhood has been treated by successive Iraqi regimes. Furthermore, it fills in the literary gaps which exist in relation to the Iraqi-Kurdish conflict by specifying and categorising the cardinal conditions that drive ethnic and nationalist conflicts which lead to the creation of separatist entities.

It fills in the literary gaps pertaining to the Iraqi-Kurdish conflict by specifying and categorising the cardinal conditions that drive ethnic and nationalist conflicts, moving them towards separatist entities. This work will also address issues as to how these matters have resulted in unsatisfactory consequences for the Kurdish-Iraqi peace process in the last eight decades. This work will make sense of empirical theories on nationalism and the development of quasi-states. It will fill in the gaps in the literature pertaining to the Iraqi-Kurdish conflict by specifying and categorising the cardinal conditions that drive ethnic and nationalist conflicts, thus moving them towards separatist entities. Finally, this work will contribute to the field by providing insightful views and investigating unexamined materials written in the Arabic and Kurdish languages that relate to the issue.

In sum, this work involves a comprehensive coverage of the following issues: (1) to highlight the main principles and characteristics of the Kurdish Nationalist Movement and Iraqi nationalism; (2) to analyse the status of the Kurds and address the question as to whether the Kurdish people of Iraq comprise a nation without a state (NWS); (3) to scrutinise the status of Iraq and address the question as to whether Iraq is a non-nation state (NNS); (4) to scrutinise how the respective statuses of the Kurds and Iraqis have reshaped the nature of the Kurdish-Iraqi conflict; (5) to study factors behind the Iraqi failure to govern and integrate the Kurds into Iraq; (6) to evaluate the evolution of the Kurds from a NWS to a quasi-state; (7) to analyse the simultaneous process of (i) the development of the Kurdistan region into a quasi-state and (ii) the devolution of Iraq into a recognised quasi-state; (8) to address the challenges and obstacles that kept the Kurds from establishing an independent state; and (9) to investigate the dominant myth and symbols of nationalism and statehood in a range of schools, codes, legal and official documents, etc. These tasks are undertaken through an exhaustive study of the theoretical approaches regarding nations without states (NWSs), non-nation states (NNSs), sovereignty and recognised quasi-states (RQs), unrecognised quasi-states (UQs), and through the application of the criteria determining positive and negative patronage to quasi-states.

The book is based on a textual analysis and critical evaluation of materials relating to the Kurdish issue in Iraq, including books, journal articles, essays, official documents, and textbooks. It also draws on official statements and documents published by Iraqi and Kurdish leaders. Iraqi and Kurdish newspapers are other important sources that have contributed to the insights contained in this research: Kurdish and Iraqi political parties' programs, goals, and ideologies, as well as the ideas of the 'intelligentsia' that have been published by different institutions and articles in political party newspapers. Iraqi and the KRI constitutions, laws, decrees, and regulations are also a vital source for this study as they allow for the scrutiny of Kurdish-Iraqi relations, Iraq's Kurdish policies, and Kurdish self-rule as revealed in the state's formal documents. Official documents, issued from international organisations, particularly the UN Security Council Resolutions (SCRs), are critically reviewed. This approach enables a better understanding of the issues of sovereignty, external support, and interference, as well as the international dimension of the Iraqi-Kurdish conflict. A review of US post-invasion documents including decrees, regulations, bilateral (Iraqi-US) agreements, and public statements have also been scrutinised to add to the richness of coverage. The study draws on contributions from the theoretical debates on nationalism/quasi-states, comparative politics and ethnic groups, ethno-nationalism, nation-states, and quasi-states, as well as the empirical literature relating to Kurdish-Iraqi relations. The approach investigates these issues as they relate to the Kurds' integration/disintegration into/from the Iraqi state.

Consisting of an introduction and 12 chapters, this book considers the status of Iraq as a country of two quasi-states and the Iraqi and Kurdish counter quests for nationhood. With the exception of the first and second chapters, the book draws on the comparative-historical method to analyse Iraqi-Kurdish relations. Chapters are divided chronologically based on historical events and reflect the nature of Kurdish *de facto* self-rule that has emerged in Iraq since 1961.

The first chapter, *Recognised and unrecognised quasi-states*, conceptualises the notion of recognised and unrecognised quasi-states and in doing so introduces several new and original models. These models include the following: the country with two quasi-states; criteria for unrecognised quasi-states and criteria for recognised quasi-states; positive and negative patronages and criteria for negative patronage. These models will be used throughout the book to analyse the nature of the Iraqi-Kurdish conflict. These tasks are undertaken through an exhaustive study of the theoretical approaches regarding nations without states (NWSs), non-nation states (NNSs), sovereignty and recognised quasi-states (RQs), unrecognised quasi-states (UQs), and through the application of the criteria determining positive and negative patronage to quasi-states.

Chapter 2, *The context of two quasi-states in Iraq*, outlines the contending debate on Iraqi and Kurdish quasi-states. This chapter surveys the current literature on the Kurdish and Iraqi quasi-states and scrutinises the contending debate on the oppositional nature of the Kurdish and Iraqi quests for nationhood. Many studies have dealt with the role of good governance policies, political space, and democratisation in Kurdish integration with or secession from Iraq. This literature overlooks the contradictions between the Kurdish quest for nationhood and the Iraqi quest for a unitary state that guarantees Iraqi state sovereignty over all Iraqi territory, including Kurdistan. Scholars tend to ignore the characteristics of Kurdish quasi-states and their contribution to the reshaping of Kurdish-Iraqi relations. Many consider Iraq as a rogue state or failed state. However, the literature cannot answer the question of how and why Iraqi Kurdistan has developed into an unrecognised quasi-state.

Chapter 3, *The two contradictory nationhood projects in Iraq*, highlights the main principles and characteristics of the Kurdish Nationalist Movement and Iraqi nationalism. It explores how the status of the Kurdish people as a nation without a state (NWS) and Iraq as a non-nation state (NNS) have reshaped the nature of the Kurdish-Iraqi conflict and affected Kurdish integration or dis-integration into/from Iraq. It also addresses the developing perceptions of Kurdish and Iraqi perspectives from the formation of the Iraqi state to the present time. The chapter begins with an examination of the roots and background of Kurdish ethnic and nationalist awareness to understand how the Kurds perceive themselves. Attention is given to the literary works of several early nationalists. The chapter then delves into the Kurds' 'imagined' national identity and political culture prior to the creation of the Iraqi state, focusing on contemporary Kurdish nationalists' and historians' representations and perceptions of the Kurds. Issues addressed include to what extent Iraq could be considered as an alternative national identity for the Kurds and the development of Kurdistani identity among the Kurds. In addition, the discussion of how this background affects Kurdish integration into Iraq is explored. This chapter also examines Iraqi perceptions of Kurdish identity and nationalism. Insight into Iraq's official discourse is achieved by analysing public statements of key Iraqi officials, politicians, newspapers, and decision-makers that took place from 1921 to 2003. Special attention is given to the Ba'ath Party's perspective because they ruled Iraq for 35 years, a term longer than any other Iraqi regime. The political implications of these viewpoints are discussed and linked to the issues of the construction and justification of Iraq's nation-building project, its myth-making enterprise, and its Arabisation policies. Examination of the opposing viewpoints revealed in the Kurdish and Iraqi narratives relating to Kurdish ethnicity and nationalism will shed light on how these disparate narratives have affected Kurdish integration, or lack thereof, into Iraq.

Chapter 4, *The monarchy-Kurds relations*, investigates the internal dynamics of Kurdish society, the emergence of modern Kurdish political parties, and their ability to monopolise the Kurdish political scene during the monarchy. Three interconnected issues are covered in this chapter: first, attempts by the Kurdish Nationalist Movement (KNM) to create autonomous Kurdish political parties; second, the KNM attempt to win over the *aghas* and create a coalition of rural and urbanite Kurds; and third, the KNM monopolisation of Kurdish political life. Initially, the two phases of the evolution of the KNM are highlighted. The first phase began with World War I (WWI) and continued until the outbreak of World War II (WWII). The second phase commenced with the beginning of WWII and ended when the monarchy collapsed in 1958. Next, to determine their impact on Kurdish integration into the Iraqi state, the urbanite-*agha* relationship and the Kurdish-Iraqi relationship are explored. The KNM ability to mobilise discontented *aghas* for nationalist ends including the reformulation of the goals and ideology of the KNM is explored. Special attention is given to the role and the legacy of the Hiwa Party and its offshoots in Kurdish politics. The legacy and impact of this party on Kurdish politics is traced along with their collusion with the *aghas* to dominate the Kurdish political arena. The development of the Kurdish political parties into autonomous political entities is also investigated. Finally, in considering the monopolisation of Kurdish political life by KNM, the role of Iraq's political parties in Kurdistan is highlighted with special attention to the Iraqi Communist Party. The relationship between the status of Iraqi political parties in Kurdistan and the issue of Kurdish integration in Iraq are also highlighted.

Chapter 5, *The first unrecognised Kurdish quasi-state (1961–1975)*, focuses on Free Kurdistan, a vast area controlled by peshmerga between 1961 and 1975. Focusing first on the bases for the establishment of Free Kurdistan, two developments are scrutinised: the emergence of Kurdish militias and the unified Kurdish leadership that followed the collapse of the monarchy in 1958. Consideration is also given to Free Kurdistan, a territory controlled by peshmerga. The demographics of these areas, including the geography and population, are focused on. This is followed by the question of whether Free Kurdistan may be classified as an unrecognised quasi-state (UQ). The status of Free Kurdistan is examined in light of the four unrecognised quasi-state criteria (UQC) presented in Chapter 1. To be classified as a quasi-state, Free Kurdistan must satisfy the four criteria. The process of symbolic nation-building in Kurdistan is the first criterion to be addressed, followed by the status of Free Kurdistan in terms of the militarisation of Kurdish society. The relative weakness of Iraq as a parent state is the third criterion. To scrutinise the relative weakness of Iraq, five major wars are reviewed as the central government's attempts to recapture Kurdistan. The fourth criterion, external patronage, is briefly discussed, as this topic is covered more thoroughly in Chapter 7.

Chapter 6, *The case of negative patronage*, analyses the pivotal role that external patronage played in the emergence, survival, and collapse of the Kurdish quasi-state of 1961–1975, and examines to what extent the Iraqi state in the period concerned may be considered as a recognised quasi-state (RQ). This convoluted

Introduction xxiii

period of history cannot be understood without proper consideration of the role of regional states and superpowers in the Kurdish-Iraqi conflict. This chapter begins with a brief explanation of the importance of external patronage for UKQ-I. An examination of the Soviet Union, Israel, Iran, and the US patronages of the UKQ-I sheds light on the nature and role of external patronage in the emergence, survival, and collapse of the UKQ-I. Each case is scrutinised in light of the three criteria that determine negative patronage (NPC). These were outlined in Chapter 1. Because Iran had a profound impact on both the survival and collapse of the UK-I, its patronage is covered in greater detail. To scrutinise whether the Iraqi state was a recognised quasi-state (RQ) during the period under review, the four criteria of recognised quasi-states (RQC), outlined in Chapter 1, are applied.

Chapter 7, *The rise and fall of Kurdish insurgency (1976–1988)*, examines the nature of the Kurdish Nationalist Movement during the period encompassing 1976 to 1988 and the different phases it went through including the peshmerga controlled areas (PCA). It highlights three phases of the Kurdish Nationalist Movement from 1976 to 1988. In the first phase attention is given to the Kurdish military movement and the Iraqi reaction to the resumption of peshmerga activities on the part of the Kurds. Special focus is on Iraqi policy that was designed to depopulate rural Kurdistan. The chapter then scrutinises the second phase of the Kurdish Nationalist Movement from 1979 to 1985. While identifying the factors that contributed to the Kurds' control over part of rural Kurdistan, concentration is on the role that the Iranian revolution of 1979 and the Iraq-Iran war in 1980 played in facilitating the expansion of the Kurdish insurgency. The third phase of the Kurdish Nationalist Movement that began in 1985 is examined with attention on the collapse of the Kurdish insurgency in 1988. The chapter then traces the impact of the Kurdish insurgency on the devolution of Iraq into a recognised quasi-state (RQ). The change in Iraq's status is scrutinised in light of the four criteria of the recognised quasi-state (RQC).

Chapter 8, *Iraq's failure to govern Kurdistan (1975–1991)*, examines the impact of the unrecognised Kurdish quasi-state (1961–1975) and the Kurdish insurgency between 1976 and 1988 on Iraq's failure to adequately govern Kurdistan. The focus is primarily on Iraq's policy towards the Kurds between the collapse of the UKQ-I in 1975 and the Kurdish uprising of 1991. The aim of this chapter is threefold. The first aim is to analyse Iraq's governing policy for Kurdistan during the period 1975 to 1991. Attention is given to the Autonomous Region of Kurdistan (ARK) that was established unilaterally by Iraq following the collapse of the UKQ-I in 1975. Rights and privileges that endorsed the Kurds as well as the limitations and weaknesses of ARK are highlighted. The second aim is to trace the impact of the first Kurdish quasi-state (UKQ-I) (1961–1975) and the Kurdish rebellion (1980–1988) on Iraq's policies to govern the Kurdistan region. The chapter traces how Iraqi Kurdistan was, for all practical purposes, divided into four zones based on Iraq's governing policy of Kurdistan. Iraqi policy vis-à-vis each zone is dealt with separately. The relevance of Iraqi policy for each zone and the zone's affiliation with the UKQ-I and later the Kurdish rebellion is also concentrated on. The final section of this book examines the effects of Iraq's

xxiv   Introduction

policies on the Kurdish uprising of 1991 that eventually evolved into the Kurdistan Regional Government in 1992.

Chapter 9, *The second unrecognised Kurdish quasi-state (1992–2003)*, examines the status of the KRI and, to determine whether it was a quasi-state, the four criteria of unrecognised quasi-states (UQCs) are applied to the KRI. To answer the question of how the KRI responded to the weak parent state criterion (UQC-III), the weakness of Iraqi internal and external status in the period in question is scrutinised. The militarisation of Kurdish society (UQC-II) is then examined. Following that, the question as to what extent the KRI satisfies the criterion of symbolic nation-building (UQC-I) is reviewed. Finally, the external patronage criterion (UQC-IV) is applied to the KRI. Special attention is given to the UQC-IV. Four forms of external patronage to the Kurds are analysed including: first, Security Council Resolution 688 (SCR688) and the role of INGOs in the Kurdistan region; second, the Safe Haven (Security Zone) created by the Allied forces in 1991; third, the No-Fly Zone (NFZ) imposed on Iraq between 1991 and 2003, and fourth, Security Council Resolution 986 (SCR986), and the implementation of the Oil-for-Food Program (OFFP) in Kurdistan. The question as to whether external support was negative patronage is addressed by re-examining the four forms of external patronage (SCR688, the INGOs, Safe Haven and NFZ, and SCR986 and OFFP) in light of the identified negative patronage criteria (NPC). The answer to this question relates to the Kurds' decision to rejoin Iraq after the invasion in 2003. Finally, the question of whether Iraq was a recognised quasi-state between 1991 and 2003 is scrutinised. Iraq's status based on the recognised quasi-state criteria (RQC) explains the failure of the central government to adequately govern Iraqi Kurdistan and the failure of the Kurds to integrate with Iraq.

Chapter 10, *The third unrecognised Kurdish quasi-state after the 2003 invasion*, focuses on the KRI after the 2003 invasion of Iraq. After the US occupation in 2003, the KRI rejoined Iraq. The question is whether this process terminated the UKQ-II or whether it commenced a new phase of the pre-existing Kurdish quasi-state. The question is approached by examining the status of the KRI in light of the four unrecognised quasi-state criteria (UQC). The criteria involved in nation-building is examined (UQC-I) before focusing on the militarisation process in the Kurdistan region (UQC-II). The status of Iraq as a weak parent state of the KRI is briefly discussed (UQC-III), followed by a discussion of patronage of the quasi-state (UQC-IV). After 1961, negative patronage is the weakest point in the Kurds' successive periods of *de facto* self-rule. This chapter traces the Kurds' approach to the patronage issue after the invasion of Iraq. The Kurds' use of oil as a mechanism by which to achieve positive patronage is then highlighted. This chapter also examines Iraq during Kurdistan's post-invasion Iraq stage beginning with the recognised quasi-state criteria (RQC). Iraq's reconfiguration during the three phases of the US occupation is scrutinised. The impact of the treaties and agreements between Iraq and the US as they impacted the sovereignty of Iraq is also examined.

Chapter 11, *Oil for external patronage and financial independence*, traces the Kurds' approach to the patronage issue after the invasion of Iraq. The Kurds' use of oil as a mechanism by which to achieve positive patronage is then highlighted. The chapter suggests that a key KRI strategic objective was the achievement of financial independence and finding alternatives to negative patronage through producing and exporting oil. To achieve these goals, the KRI actively invested in its newly discovered oil wealth. The KRI provided relatively lucrative oil contracts and a friendly environment for tens of international oil companies (IOCs) as it portrayed itself as an emerging regional oil power. The KRI oil policy was formulated as oil for external support and patronage, as well as for creating an independent economy. The chapter highlights how these developments contributed to the transformation of the KRI into a developed form of quasi-statehood.

Chapter 12, *Independence referendum and the case of negative patronage*, studies the independence referendum conducted by KRI on 25 September 2017. This chapter explains that in addition to the long Kurdish aspiration for independence, there were several main factors that encouraged the KRI to move towards a referendum, including the failure of consensus that the post-2003 Iraq was built on, the Kurdish control of the disputed territories, and the rise of the Islamic State. The chapter also addresses the question of why instead of consolidating the legitimacy of KRI's status and boosting its bargaining power, the referendum backfired spectacularly and Kurds lost their control over the entire disputed areas. This chapter explains that negative patronages were the Kurds' Achilles' heel and the main reason behind the failure of the referendum.

Notes

1 USA Today, "Iraqi President Answers Questions," interviewed by Paul Wiseman <www.usatoday.com/news/world/iraq/2004-07-05-al-yawer-qanda_x.htm>, (accessed 06/06/2012).
2 "Masud Barzani: Points of disagreement with the central government", *al Jazeera*, 17/09/2008, Interviewed by Mohammad Kirishan, available at <www.aljazeera.net/NR/exeres/14863230-9624-4FE9-9656-EEB47FD9114B.htm>, (accessed 25/11/2017).
3 *Ibid*.
4 Fayad, M. Iraqi President Jalal Talabani talks to Asharq Al-Awsat, Asharq Al-Awsat, available at <www.asharqalawsat.com/english/news.asp?section=3&id=4972>, (accessed 17/09/2007).
5 Barham Salih is a senior Kurdish politician. He is the deputy general secretary of the Patriotic Union of Kurdistan (PUK), and the former prime minister of the Kurdistan Regional Government of Iraqi Kurdistan and a former deputy prime minister of the Federal government of Iraq.
6 Salih, B. (2008), "Kurds, safety valve of new Iraq," Soma-Digest, no. 4, available at <http://soma-digest.com/PDFs/soma-digest-06.pdf>, (accessed 9/06/2008).
7 Barzani, M. (2003a), "Iraqi Kurdish Claim for Federalism," *KRG*, available at <http://old.krg.org/docs/mb-federalism-kurdistan-dec03.asp>, (accessed 05/09/2010); Qubad Talabani cited in Hadi Elis, H. (2004), "The Kurdish Demand for Statehood and the Future of Iraq," *Journal of Social, Political & Economic Studies* 29(2): 202.
8 Barzani (2003a).
9 Iraqi Presidency, President Talabani: Kurds play a key role in the formation of the national unity government, Iraqi Presidency website, available at <www.iraqipresidency.net/news_detial.php?language=arabic&id=2525&type=ne>, (accessed 20/04/2008).
10 Talabani, "What the Kurds Want".

xxvi Introduction

11 *Ibid*; Chris Kutschera (2004), "An Island of Prosperity and Calm," *Middle East* 341: 42–44.
12 Chatham House (2004), "Iraq in Transition: Vortex or Catalyst?" *Chatham House*, 3, available at <www.chathamhouse.org.uk/pdf/research/mep/BP0904.pdf>, (accessed 23/05/2012).
13 Stansfield, G. (2004), "Divide and Heal," *Prospect Magazine*, no. 122, May 2006; Brancati, D. (2004), "Can Federalism Stabilize Iraq?" *The Washington Quarterly* 27(2): 11; Liam Anderson and Gareth Stansfield (2005), "The Implications of Elections for Federalism in Iraq: Toward a Five-Region Model," *Publius* 35(3): 361.
14 Gunter, M. (2004), "The Kurds in Iraq: Why Kurdish Statehood is Unlikely", *Middle East Policy* 11(1): 108; Brancati 2004: 11; Karsh, E. (2003), "Making Iraq Safe for Democracy," *Commentary* 115(4): 26.
15 For further statements by Kurdish leaders on federalism see: Talabani, Q. (2005), "What the Kurds Want," *Wall Street Journal*, Eastern Edition 246(36): 10; KRG, Kurdistan Regional Government (2003), Masud Barzani, Iraqi Kurdish Claim for Federalism, Kurdistan Regional Government, available at <http://old.krg.org/docs/mb-federalism-kurdistan-dec03.asp>, (accessed 29/01/2017); KRG, Kurdistan Regional Government, Statement by Prime Minister Nechirvan Barzani on non-implementation of the Iraqi constitution, Kurdistan Regional Government, available at <www.krg.org/articles/article_detail.asp?LangNr=12&RubricNr=24&ArticleNr=13950&LNNr=28&RNNr=70>, (accessed 07/07/2008).
16 Brancati 2004: 11–12; Galbraith, P. W. (2006), "Kurdistan in a Federal Iraq," *The Future of Kurdistan in Iraq*, B. O'Leary, J. McGarry K. and Salih (eds.), Philadelphia, PA: University of Pennsylvania Press: 268–281: 169; Gunter, M. M. (2008), *The Kurds Ascending: The Evolving Solution to the Kurdish Problem in Iraq and Turkey*, New York: Palgrave Macmillan: 20–22; Natali, D. (2010). "Kurdish Quasi-State: Development and Dependency," *Post-Gulf War Iraq*, New York: Syracuse University Press: 110.

1 Recognised and unrecognised quasi-states

There is no single and universally accepted meaning of the term quasi-states. On one hand, different and often non-synonymous terms are used by scholars to describe some recognised and unrecognised states around the world. For example, concepts such as quasi-states, artificial states, cleft states, failed states, rogue states, non-nation states, and pseudo-states are used for recognised quasi-states, and terms such as quasi-states, *de facto* states, pseudo-states, and secessionist or rebel territories are used for unrecognised quasi-states. On the other hand, scholars on quasi-states do not agree on which form of states can be categorised as quasi-states. For example, a quasi-state in Jackson's model is a state that is internationally recognised as a sovereign state, but clearly lacks the internal legitimacy. For him, a *de facto* non-sovereign state which is not recognised internationally does not fit in this category.[1] In contrast, for Kolstø, Kosienkowski, Caspersen, Steinsdorff, and Fruhstorfer, states that lack international recognition but enjoy internal legitimacy are quasi-states; and those that enjoy such recognition but lack internal legitimacy are failed states.[2] Thus, the term quasi-state, in its classical use, remains vague and problematic; some scholars use the term exclusively to refer to recognised, and others to unrecognised, quasi-states.

This study attempts to tackle the terminological confusion which developed in the study of quasi-states in two ways. First, fundamental distinctions between the two types of states, and between them and other political entities, including real severing nation-states or states with dual sovereignty (SWDS), will be highlighted. Second, using the Iraqi and Kurdistan regions as case studies, new criteria which go beyond the traditional understanding of the quasi-states and statehood are created. This work provides two sets of criteria, and this allows a clear line to be drawn between these entities. Criteria for RQs and UQs are designed to distinguish RQs from UQs and the two forms of states from SWDS. This distinction between the three forms of states helps to illustrate the ambiguities surrounding the concept of quasi-states. It also can be seen as an attempt to standardise and re-categorise these different entities in a manner which reinforces their contemporary significance to our understanding of the quasi-states.

Theories regarding states and quasi-states need to be examined in order to explore the behaviour of the KRI and Iraq. In this regard, Weber's and Smith's perspectives of state are relevant. States, according to Smith and Weber, are autonomous institutions in a given territory, monopolising "coercion and extraction" (Smith), and/or "the legitimate use of force" (Weber).[3] However, in their respective definitions the international status of the state is unknown. Therefore, three other theories (namely, the declarative, the constitutive, and Jackson's quasi-state theory) may be used to complement the Weber-Smith theory in order to bring about a fuller and more nuanced understanding. These theories may be useful to explain attributes that distinguish states from other political entities and to explain the similarities and differences between unrecognised quasi-states (UQs) and recognised quasi-states (RQs).

The declarative theory is useful to further understand UQs, and the constitutive and Jackson's theories to recognise RQs. The declarative theory suggests that a state must meet four criteria specified in the Montevideo Convention, adopted in 1933 by the International Conference of American States. The first qualification is a permanent population linked to a particular territory. The second and third qualifications are a defined territory and a government that exercises its powers on it. The forth qualification is the ability to enter into relations with other states. The three forms of states – UQ, RQ, and SWDS – all meet all declarative criteria. The three groups of states are similar in terms of their claim to sovereignty and administrative monopoly over a territory with fixed population and demarcated boundaries. The three forms of states, however, differ in their ability to enter into relations with other states. Both SWDS and RQ enjoy complete relations with international community. Though UQs are not recognised as part of the international state system, many UQs have managed to establish low-key bilateral relations with several states and informal contacts with regional organisations. For example, Taiwan, the Kurdistan region, Palestine, Northern Cyprus, and Somaliland established their representatives in dozens of countries and many countries reciprocated by opening consulates in these 'countries'. Being established for more than two decades, many quasi-states have demonstrated their capabilities for acting within the international arena.

The declarative theory qualifications, however, are key attributes that distinguish states from other political entities. These criteria are indicators of the existence of a state in practical terms and are preconditions for statehood and its primary foundation. Establishing maintaining authority and administrative monopoly over a territory and people is closely connected to the formation of territorial states. Without a territory, a government, a permanent population, and relations with the outside world, a state or any political entity, sovereign or non-sovereign, cannot be imagined. One would have to include all these qualifications in order to be able to talk about any kind of regime in the first place. The declarative statehood, in fact, is an 'empirical' rather than 'juridical' statehood. In other words, criteria presented by the declarative theory are prerequisites of the existence of statehood, rather than the quality of the state. Highlighting their empirical status, many UQs reference the declarative doctrine to legitimise their claims for recognition as a *de jure* state and international recognition.

In contrast to the declarative theory, the constitutive theory defines statehood as a juridical rather than empirical entity. Oppenheim, one of the earliest theorists of the constitutive theory, suggested that "a new state before its recognition cannot claim any right which a member of Family of Nations has." He also emphasised that "through recognition only and exclusively a state becomes an international person and a subject of international law".[4] Thus, the constitutive theory focuses on the external legal rights and duties. The fundamental assumption of the constitutive theory is that states are international legal persons with defined rights, privileges, duties, and immunities. In other words, states are subject to international law and statehood is contingent on recognition from other states. Recognition by other states becomes a precondition of statehood and an entity is only considered as a state if it is recognised as sovereign by other states.

There is a key difference between the declarative and the constitutive theories; the former focuses on the conditions of statehood (recognition of a state), while the latter focuses on the conditions of recognition (recognition as a state). According to the declarative theory, a sovereign state can exist without being recognised by other sovereign states. For the adherents of the constitutive theory, states do not exist in international law until recognised. The declaratory theory focuses on the internal factual situation, namely: territory, population, government, and relations. For the constitutive theory, by contrast, an entity can be considered as a state without these requirements as long as it is recognised by other states.

Despite fundamental differences between the constitutive and the declaratory schools, the two theories are relevant to the question of the RQ and the UQ and help to understand the distinction between the two forms of quasi-states. The constitutive statehood is similar to recognised quasi-states and the declaratory statehood resembles the characteristics of the unrecognised quasi-state. An RQ is an entity which enjoys international recognition but fails to function as a nation-state and develop the necessary infrastructure capacity. Similarly, the key to the constitutive theory is not an entity's attainment of *de facto* statehood, but rather, prior international acceptance of its asserted right to independence. A constitutive statehood is based on the international recognition and disregards the internal reality. By the same token, the main characteristics of the declarative statehood are the same for UQs. A declarative statehood is an entity that has successfully established a set of institutional forms of governance and maintained an administrative monopoly over a territory with demarcated boundaries. Its status, however, has not been sanctioned by international law. In other words, UQs resemble normal states, but they lack international recognition. The declarative theory of state defines an entity as a state if it possesses a permanent population, a defined territory, government, and the capacity to enter into relations with the other states.

The two theories are also useful to redefine the real sovereign nation-state. Since both the declarative and the constitutive views are theories of statehood, both theories are complementary to each other. In fact, a real sovereign state is the state that meets the definitions of both declarative and constitutive theories of statehood. The constitutive statehood enjoys recognition but may lack capabilities, whereas the declarative statehood possesses capabilities but may lack recognition. The nation-state or a state with dual sovereignties (SWDS) enjoys both international recognition and internal capabilities. Accordingly, a SWDS enjoys all qualifications of the declarative and the constitutive theories. A SWDS is a person of international law with a defined territory, a permanent population, a government, and a capacity to enter into relations. This state enjoys a clear recognition as sovereign by other states and the international community. In other words, a real state is both a legitimate and a legal entity. The legitimacy of a real state is driven from the established internal capability and its legality comes from the legal prerogatives of sovereignty.

In his development of quasi-states theory Jackson re-identified state and sovereignty. He argues that not all existing states in the world are 'real' states. Jackson identifies two forms of states: 'real' and 'quasi'. A positively sovereign government, according to Jackson, is one which possesses rights of non-intervention and the wherewithal to provide political goods for its citizens. Put another way, the responsibility of a sovereign government is both external to other sovereign states and internal to its citizens.[5] Hence, a sovereign state enjoys double sovereignty: external, vis-à-vis other states, and internal, vis-à-vis its own citizens. Jackson classifies external sovereignty as a negative aspect of sovereignty and internal sovereignty as a positive form of sovereignty. Negative sovereignty, for Jackson, is the legal foundation upon which formally equal states fundamentally rests. It can therefore be defined as freedom from outside interference: a formal-legal condition. The positive aspect of sovereignty, however, presupposes capabilities which enable governments to be their own masters. Negative sovereignty is a formal and legal condition that is endowed by the international community. Positive sovereignty is not a legal but a political attribute.[6] In other words, international community provides governments with negative sovereignty through the act of general recognition, while positive sovereignty depends on the action and resources of internal governments and their populations.

A real sovereign state is a state that enjoys double sovereignties, organised domestic reality and not merely by international law. A quasi-state, in contrast, is a state in which "its sovereignty is derived not internally from empirical statehood but externally from the state-system whose members have evidently decided and are resolved that these jurisdictions shall not disappear." Therefore, the quasi-state is upheld by an external covenant among sovereign states. Because this form of statehood enjoys an internationally guaranteed independence, it does not require positive sovereignty.[7] Hence, quasi-states, from Jackson's perspective, are states that only enjoy external (negative) sovereignty but lack the internal (positive) sovereignty.

Jackson's theory, however, is inadequate. One of the main weaknesses of Jackson's theory is that positive sovereignty is an absolute rather than a relative concept. On one hand, no state enjoys ultimate positive sovereignty and no state totally lacks it. On the other hand, there is a huge difference between a state that totally lacks internal sovereignty and that ultimately enjoys it. The internal legitimacy of many developed European states, according to Jackson, demonstrates real sovereignty, though they are rejected by many minority groups. Similarly, many post-colonial states that Jackson classifies as quasi-states enjoy some form of internal legitimacy and support at least by a faction of society. For example, the

Iraqi state enjoyed internal legitimacy vis-à-vis its Sunni community until 2003, and its Shia community after the invasion. Put another way, no state around the world totally lacks or totally enjoys internal support and legitimacy. In addition, states differ in their capacities, state-structures, and abilities to deliver services and goods to their constituencies.

Recognised quasi-states (RQs) and criteria for recognised quasi-states (RQC)

To overcome these generalisations and confusion, and drawing on Smith's and Weber's definitions of state, this work introduces four criteria that a recognised state must satisfy to qualify as a quasi-state. To distinguish a state that meets these criteria from a 'real' sovereign state, it will be called a recognised quasi-state (RQ); and criteria that have been used to classify such a state will be referred as recognised quasi-state criteria (RQC).

The first criterion of a quasi-state is a state that exercises the illegitimate use of force and that violates, instead of imposes, the rule of law and threatens some of its citizens. For the purpose of this study, this criterion will be referred to as (RQC-I). The second criterion is a state that loses monopoly over the legitimate use of force in a given territory. This also includes the state's failure to collect taxes or to deliver public services to all or a portion of its population in a given territory. This criterion will be referred to as (RQC-II). Another criterion is the case of a state that is too weak to confront a separatist region without external support. Due to its weakness, the state seeks external patronage from a stronger state to enable it to challenge the separatist region. This criterion will be identified as (RQC-III). The final criterion is a state that, in addition to lacking internal sovereignty, suffers violation of its sovereignty from external powers. This criterion will be referred to as (RQC-IV). Criteria RQC-I and RQC-II pertain to the internal affairs of the state, while RQC-III and RQC-IV are related to the state's status vis-à-vis other states. A state that enjoys external recognition but fulfils these four criteria will be classified as a recognised quasi-state (RQ).

First and second criteria for recognised quasi-states (RQC-I and RQC-II)

The first two criteria are interconnected so that one criterion leads to another. Therefore, it will be useful to scrutinise RQC-I and RQC-II at once. Jackson suggests that internal sovereignty is an 'empirical' rather than 'juridical' aspect of statehood and falls within the internal affairs of the state. International society can only provide governments with legal status through the act of general recognition.[8] It is the citizens of the state, rather than the international community, that endow the state and its rulers with domestic authority and power. This endowment represents the marks and merits of empirical statehood. Internal sovereignty is a function of the state's ability to protect its citizens and to provide other services, such as health and education. In many ways, Jackson's understanding of internal sovereignty is similar to Max Weber's definition of internal legitimacy. Weber defines the state in relation to its monopolisation of the legitimate use of force. A state, according to Weber, is an entity that "successfully lays claim to the monopoly of legitimate physical violence within a certain territory".[9] Two key variables in Weber's statehood are the state's monopoly on force and the legitimate use of it. The question is who determines whether the state's use of force is legitimate or not. Weber suggests that legitimacy can be achieved if the state manages to maintain its control over the means of violence and its ruler enjoys traditional authority, charisma, and legality.[10]

Two important conclusions may be drawn from Weber's definition of the state and legitimacy. First, the state's monopoly of the use of force is conditional and subject to the legitimised use of force, and the legitimacy of the government is a precondition for the legitimacy of government-sanctioned violence. Second, Weber's criteria for the legitimacy of the state are more aligned with the internal affairs of the state rather with its international status. Control over the means of violence, traditional authority, charisma, and legality are internal characteristics of the state. Simply put, for Weber, the provision of security to citizens is synonymous with the notion of legitimacy of the state. Thus, in Jackson's thesis, internal sovereignty is intimately related to the notion of internal legitimacy in Weber's theory of the state. In fact, sources of internal sovereignty in Jackson's model are the same as legitimacy in Weber's thesis, namely the population under the state's jurisdiction. In other words, the state that possesses internal legitimacy also enjoys internal sovereignty.

The difference between Weber's and Jackson's definition of state is that Weber's state is empirical rather than juridical, *de facto* rather than *de jure*, while Jackson's state is both empirical and *de jure*. However, both emphasise that internal legitimacy is an 'empirical' rather than 'juridical' aspect of statehood. Weber defines empirical statehood primarily in terms of its ability to monopolise the legitimate means of force. Jackson suggests that the international recognition of an entity is not enough to consider it as a real state; an entity can only be considered as a state if it enjoys external and internal sovereignty. The state that lacks internal sovereignty is not a state but rather is a quasi-state. By implication, the state that lacks internal legitimacy is a quasi-state. Thus, the Weberian criteria of statehood, namely the state's monopoly on legitimate violence, is identical to Jackson's understanding of internal or positive sovereignty.

Legitimacy of the state falls within its internal affairs and relies on a positive attitude of the state. It pertains to the relations between state and society, particularly the relations of power within society. Legitimacy is based on a specific conception of how the state and society are linked and how the state's authority is justified. In addition, legitimacy is rendered by citizens through their adherence to those laws that change legal prescription into legal practice. In other words, legitimacy of a state is equivalent to the acceptance of its authority among citizens in a given society or territory. If the state's power is exerted through voluntary compliance the state is legitimate and, therefore, lacks legitimacy when it exerts power through coercion.[11] The state is also legitimate if citizens accept it as the ultimate political authority in their territory. In other words, a state is considered legitimate if those subjected to it consider it so. Thus, legitimacy is the empirical rather than the juridical attribute of statehood. It concerns the relations between the state and society and how the two are linked. Legitimacy depends on people's beliefs, perceptions, and expectations, and these characteristics are influenced by both the relationship between the state and society and the capability and characteristics of the state. To be legitimate, the state must gain recognition as the highest political authority from the majority of the population under its jurisdiction. The legitimacy of the state constitutes the belief that there are adequate reasons to voluntarily obey its commands. Such a belief depends on there being some kind of consent among all those who are under its jurisdiction that the state treats them fairly and provide them with security and other services. This consent is possible if three conditions are fulfilled. First, the political and security needs of the state must be similar to those of the population. The second condition is an established rule of law that protects and reconciles the security needs of the state and population. The final condition is the adherence of both the state and population to the rule of law.

Legitimacy and the legitimate use of violence are complementary. On one hand, the legitimacy of the state is situated in its ability to monopolise the legitimate use of violence. On the other hand, the legitimacy of the government is a condition for the legitimacy of violence. Both the legitimacy of state and its monopoly of the legitimate use of force depend on the subordination of violence to the rule of law. The rule of law can be defined as a situation in which "the state only subject the citizenry to publicly promulgated laws, that the state's legislative function be separate from the adjudicative function, and that no one within the polity be above the law."[12] Civilians in an area of conflict may obey the commands of authorities voluntarily if the rule of law: protects fundamental rights; supports the rights of citizens; subordinates the exercise of power to a legal and rational framework; subordinates violence to decision-making; holds government accountable and limits its powers; allows checks and balances on control over the use of violence; only permits selective rather indiscriminate violence; and subordinate rulers to the rule of law.

Establishing and maintaining the rule of law, and subordinating the rulers and citizens to it, is a precondition for the legitimacy of the state. There are several ways in which the effective application of the rule of law contributes to the establishment of legitimacy. First, while the rule of law allows the state to maintain its control over the means of violence, it also restrains it from enforcing commands through coercive measures. Second, if the population believe that the rule of law is on their side and protects their fundamental rights, they will accept the state as a fair administrator of justice and the protector of their fundamental rights. Third, the effective application of the rule of law subordinates both the state and the citizens to the rule of law. Rules that allow for an orderly process of change that makes violence unnecessary are crucial for the legitimacy of the state. This is because such rules improve the perception among the population, including those in contested territories, regarding the legitimacy of the state. When violence becomes unnecessary, the state's power can be exerted through voluntary compliance. Accordingly, when the state is perceived as legitimate, its monopolisation of the legitimate use of force is rarely challenged. Thus, on one hand, the effective application of the rule of law subordinates both the state and the citizens to the rule of law. On the other hand, adherence to and implementation of the rule of law increase the state's legitimacy and its monopoly over the use of force. By the same token, failure to implement the rule of law undermines the legitimacy of the state and its monopoly over the use of force.

There are two interconnected consequences of the state's insubordination to, or the absence of, the rule of law. The first is that in the absence of the rule of law, rulers are not restrained from extreme use of violence against the people who challenge the state's legitimacy. If a state's noncompliance to the rule of law is combined with intense conflict and widespread violence, the state may resort to the indiscriminate use of violence against a general population. To establish permanent control over a contested territory, many states commit genocide, ethnocide, or ethnic cleansing against the civilian population in secessionist territories. The second consequence is that the extreme and indiscriminate use of violence not only undermines the legitimacy of the state-sanctioned violence but also the legitimacy of the state itself. In this context, illegitimacy of the state and its use of force reproduce one other. On the one hand, the more the state frequently and violently targets civilians in the area of conflict, the greater the risks of losing its legitimacy. Civilians in the area of conflict challenge the legitimacy of the choice of war, the legitimacy of the means adopted within war, and ultimately the legitimacy of the state. On the other hand, in the absence of the state's legitimacy, coercion becomes commonplace. The state adopts violent responses to challenges in secessionist territories and relies upon increasing levels of repression in order to maintain its control and to survive. Consequently, in secessionist territories, where the population is convulsed by internal violence, the state is considered to be the illegitimate political authority.

Since legitimacy relies on a positive attitude of the state, the sympathy or neutral attitude of the population in the contested territories towards the state changes to a hostile one, and loyalties shift away from the state towards the separatist leaders. Populations in these contested territories increase their challenge to the state and its rules. As a result, secessionist movements gain more legitimacy, loyalty, and support from local citizens. In such an environment, the state cannot effectively claim to have a monopoly of force throughout the contested territory. The state is no longer able to maintain control without resorting to violence. The more the regime loses its legitimacy, the more it resorts to violence. Accordingly, instead of fulfilling its responsibility to protect society and its members from internal and external threats, the state emerges as the main threat to the population in secessionist territories. This means the state loses its position as a political authority within the territory of conflict and its monopoly on legitimate violence. This would have three interconnected consequences on the internal sovereignty of the state. First, the provision of security is fundamental for the state's legitimacy. By losing its monopoly over the means of force, the state loses the significant elements of legitimacy and becomes illegitimate in the hearts and minds of its citizens. Second, the state's loss of internal legitimacy and monopoly on violence enables secessionist groups to establish an effective monopoly on force within significant territories and populations. Citizens then naturally turn more and more to territorial and community loyalties and transfer their allegiances to rebellion and secessionist movements and their leaders. The absence or weakness of the central authority helps secessionist and rebellion groups to expand their control over regions and subregions. They also build up their own local administration, security apparatuses, and even a form of international relations. Thus, the third consequence is that, by losing its position as a political authority in the secessionist region, the state loses its internal sovereignty, at least in the regions under the control of rebels.

The question that is addressed in this chapter is whether the state that loses its monopoly on violence in a contested territory still can be considered as a real or sovereign state. Weber's definition of the state is useful in answering this question. Weber emphasises that "the state is held to be the sole source of the 'right' to use violence."[13] In a separate work, Weber suggests that "the right to use physical violence is attributed to any and all other associations or individuals." This right, however, is conditional and "only to the extent that the state for its part permits this to happen".[14] In situations where a secessionist movement's monopolies of force exist over a contested territory and its population, the state cannot any more lay claim to a monopoly on legitimate violence within that territory. In many countries (such as Iraq, Syria, Cyprus, Georgia, Yemen, and Somalia), secessionist movements have established their *de facto* permanent control over contested territories. Secessionist movements thereby not only challenge the state, but also carve out areas of monopolistic control for themselves which results in the state losing control over a certain portion of the country. Thus, secessionist movements undermine the essential criterion of statehood, namely the monopoly on force. The state that loses its monopoly on force cannot be considered as a proper or real state. Therefore, if a state loses its control and monopoly on the legitimised use of violence over a territory, it satisfies the second criterion of a recognised quasi-state (RQC-II). In many cases, the state not only loses its ability to act as a protector of the fundamental rights of the population and their security, but also turns into an enemy of the people within secessionist territories. If a state turns from a protector into an enemy to part of its population, it satisfies the first criterion of recognised quasi-states (RQC-I).

Third and fourth criteria for recognised quasi-states (RQC-III and RQC-IV)

So far, this study has addressed the situation where the state loses its internal sovereignty and monopoly over the legitimised use of force to an internal actor, mostly secessionist movements. Criteria RQC-III and RQC-IV are designed to describe the situation in which the state loses its internal sovereignty and monopoly over the legitimate use of violence towards a foreign state. The third criterion is the case of a state that is too weak to confront a separatist region without the direct military involvement of another country. The state that seeks external patronage from and the military involvement of a stronger state in its internal affairs, in order to enable it to confront the internal challenges of the separatist region, meets the third criterion (RQC-III). The fourth criterion (RQC-IV) is a situation in which, in addition to lacking internal sovereignty, a state suffers violation of its sovereignty from external powers (e.g. direct occupation, imposed no-fly zones, the presence of foreign military forces on its soil, or subjected to international sanctions).

Though the difference between the first two criteria (RQC-I and RQC-II) and the criteria III and IV is clear, the two sets of criteria are interlaced and one reproduces the other. It is the state's lack of legitimacy and internal sovereignty that facilitate the military intervention of a foreign country. As was a case with the first and second criteria of the recognised quasi-states, the third and fourth criteria are also established on the notion of internal legitimacy and sovereignty. As discussed earlier, the Weberian definition of a state's claim to a monopoly on legitimate violence is identical to the concept of internal or positive sovereignty. Whether the source of violation of the state's internal legitimacy and sovereignty is external or internal, the result is the same: the state lacks the criteria of Weberian statehood (i.e. monopoly on violence) and Jackson's real state (internal sovereignty).

Many states, however, only meet the first and second criteria (RQC-I and RQC-II), and so cannot be considered as quasi-states. The state may lose its supreme status and, therefore, lose its internal sovereignty over part of its territory, but may mostly stay independent from foreign influences if there were no foreign troops on its soil. In the context where the state loses its monopoly of force to an internal actor, which is usually a non-state actor, the state may still maintain, or at least claim, its external sovereignty. Many states have temporarily or permanently lost control of part of their territories (e.g. China lost Taiwan; Russia lost its former Soviet republics; and for a while it lost Chechnya). Russia and China, however, cannot be considered as quasi-states, despite their loss of sovereignty over a part of the land that traditionally was under their jurisdiction. When both internal non-state actor and external state actors are involved, the state loses both supremacy within one of its territories and its independence from foreign influences. Hence, RQC-III and RQC-IV are crucial to distinguish states that possess dual sovereignties, such as Russia and China, from recognised quasi-states from states that lack these features. To be considered as a quasi-state, in addition to the first two criteria, the state must also meet the two other criteria, namely, RQC-III (state invites foreign troops to face internal challenges) and RQC-IV (state cannot prevent foreign military presence in its territory). The state meets criterion RQS-III if the foreign military involvement of the foreign country on its land is at its request. In this case, military bases are mostly established in areas under the host state's control, as in the case of the Syrian army in Lebanon in the 1980s, Coalition forces in Iraq following the emergence of the Islamic State (ISIS), and Russian forces in Syria since 2015. The targeted state, however, meets the RQC-IV criterion if foreign troops violate its sovereignty unilaterally. In this case, the foreign troops are usually stationed in areas under the control of secessionist groups as in the case of Turkish forces in northern Cyprus and Russian bases in the Crimea region of Ukraine.

Internal (positive) sovereignty is distinct from (external) negative sovereignty in that the former is empirical and therefore is a relative sovereignty, while the latter is *de jure* and therefore is an absolute sovereignty. The internal sovereignty of statehood is relative in two senses. First, the empirical statehood may be still far from complete and remains to be built. In other words, it may change with time. Second, empirical statehood may fail in a certain region, mostly secessionist regions, but operate satisfactorily in the rest of the country. In contrast to internal sovereignty, negative sovereignty "is the legal foundation upon which a society of independent and formally equal states fundamentally rests". Therefore, it is an absolute condition "in the sense that it is not dependent on any conditions other than the compact itself which does not require positive action but only observance and forbearance".[15] In other words, non-intervention and negative (external) sovereignty are two aspects of the same entity.

With negative sovereignty, states are blessed with the right of independence and non-intervention. The presence of foreign troops, whether with the permission of the state or without, results in the state's loss of its absolute rights and, therefore, its external sovereignty. The presence of the foreign military, whether it be at the request of the host country or unilaterally, usually works in favour of the foreign country and undermines the host state's sovereignty. Even if these foreign troops were invited by the host state (RQC-III), the host state cannot claim sovereignty over all its territories. The foreign troops usually operate semi-autonomously, which means the host state cannot impose effective and complete control over foreign military bases that have been established within its territory. This semi-autonomous status of the foreign military facilitates its interference in the internal affairs of the targeted state and, ultimately, may lead to greater violence of sovereignty and more acts of intervention. Moreover, the intervention of foreign troops in the host country's affairs at the latter's request means that the host state is too weak to maintain its integrity and internal sovereignty without this external patronage. To survive as an integrated country, the host state mostly relies on a patron state and, thus, loses those rights that have been guaranteed by international law: namely, independence, non-intervention, and equality with other states.

If foreign troops enter into a state's territory unilaterally to support secessionist movements, as in the case of the Turkish invasion of Northern Cyprus and Russia in Crimea, the targeted state meets the fourth criterion (RQC-IV). This unilateral intervention is the most obvious form of violation of the target state's negative sovereignty. The principle of sovereignty of the state clashes with the unilateral presence of foreign troops. By interfering militarily, the perpetrator state violates a key rule of the negative sovereignty right, namely non-intervention. Failing to prevent foreign military entrance into its territory, the targeted state no longer can lay claim to unchallenged territorial sovereignty. The presence of the foreign troops, which usually results in further undermining of the targeted country's internal security, means that the targeted state cannot defend its land, maintain control over its own territory, or provide security and basic protection to its own citizens. In such a situation, the state not only loses its monopoly over the legitimate use of force but ultimately loses its legitimacy. Jackson defines negative sovereignty as a "freedom from outside interference".[16] Hence, the presence of foreign militaries results in the state's loss of its distinctive rights as an independent and sovereign state, that is, freedom from outside interference.

This study examines the status of Iraq in different periods in light of the four recognised quasi-state criteria (RQC) presented earlier in this chapter. To be classified as a recognised quasi-state, the state must satisfy these four criteria. This study applies the four criteria of RQC to ascertain whether Iraq could be classified as a recognised quasi-state (RQ) in the period under consideration. All four criteria used to determine RQ status must be met in order for Iraq to qualify as a recognised quasi-state.

Unrecognised quasi-states (UQs) and criteria for unrecognised quasi-states (UQC)

Jackson's theory suffers another crucial deficiency. His theory pertains only to those quasi-states that lack internal (positive) sovereignty and fails to address unrecognised quasi-states (i.e. those entities that enjoy internal sovereignty but lack international recognition). Similar to Jackson, Kolstø distinguishes those states that enjoy dual sovereignty from those lacking internal sovereignty and those lacking international recognition.[17]

One significant weakness found in Kolstø's treatment of Jackson's quasi-state theory is that a state that lacks internal sovereignty, but has been recognised by the international community, cannot be considered as a quasi-state. Kolstø classifies this entity as a failed state. In Kolstø's model, states that lack international recognition but enjoy internal legitimacy are quasi-states; and those that enjoy such recognition but lack internal legitimacy are failed states. This classification is an over-generalisation for two reasons. First, the concept of failed state, developed by the Fund for Peace, uses 12 indicators to identify a failed state. These are: mounting demographic pressures; massive movement of refugees and IDPs; legacy of vengeance – seeking group grievances; chronic and sustained human flight; uneven economic development along group lines; sharp and/or severe economic decline; criminalisation or delegitimisation of the state; progressive deterioration of public services; widespread violation of human rights; security apparatus as a state within a state; rise of factionalised elites; and intervention of other states or external actors. On one hand, recognised quasi-states (RQs) do not necessarily meet all of these conditions; therefore, they may not be considered as failed states. On the other, most countries around the world, with or without internal sovereignty, to some degree share some of these characteristics.

Second, The Failed States Index (2009) has labelled the overwhelming majority of states around the world as potentially failed states. The Failed States Index 2009 and The Failed States Index (2010), as examples, presented a list of 177 countries (almost all the countries around the world) and categorised them into 'extreme', 'most', 'middle moderate', and 'less failed' states. The Failed States Index mechanism for identifying 'failed states' has been criticised for painting the majority of countries around the world with the same brush. Call, for example, objects to such a generalisation, stating that: "It is silly to say that Colombia, North Korea and Somalia are any more equivalent than are Belgium, Bolivia and Burma, all of which at least share [the characteristic of] ethnic separatist movements." Call, however, more accurately defines the failed state concept. He explains that the failed-state concept refers to wholly collapsed states, where no authority is recognisable either internally to a country's inhabitants or externally to the international community. In the case of failed states, however, the state collapse is often so thoroughgoing that the external power is required to exert authority simply to avoid calamity. In the late twentieth century, this situation occurred over a sustained period only in Somalia, from 1991 until roughly 2004. Hence, there is a great difference between a failed state and a recognised state that lacks internal legitimacy. In contrast to failed states, quasi-states that enjoy external recognition are not 'collapsed' and they still enjoy external recognition by the international community as well as internal recognition by part of its population.

Kolstø, however, correctly classifies those states that lack international recognition, but enjoy internal sovereignty, as quasi-states. For Kolstø a political entity that enjoys internal legitimacy and lacks external legitimacy must fulfil three criteria to be classified as a quasi-state: (1) "Its leadership must be in control of (most of) the territory it lays claim to"; (2) "it must have sought but not achieved international recognition as an independent state"; and (3) "to eliminate a whole spate of ephemeral political contraptions, those that have persisted in this state of non-recognition for less than two years [are excluded]."[18] Kolstø's criteria fail to establish themselves for several reasons. First, the criterion that its leadership must be in control of (most of) the territory it lays claim to is problematic. Not only non-recognised states, but also many sovereign states around the world fail to control most of the territory to which they lay claim. Moreover, most separatist regions share territory with parent states and have mixed ethnic and/or religious communities that both the parent state and the separatist entity lay claim to. A striking example is Kirkuk and other disputed areas in Iraq; both Kurdish and Iraqi sides claim Kirkuk as an integral part of their respective territories. Similar examples may be found among many quasi-states as well. The second criterion is also vague and over-generalised. Any separatist region, whether its leaders control their territory or not, may seek international recognition as an independent state. The 'two years' criterion is not helpful for understanding the nature of a separate entity. It is not time, but rather the issue of internal legitimacy, financial resources, external support, and balance of power with the parent state that propel a separatist region into quasi-statehood.

Kolstø tackles a question that may be used as a criterion to classify a separatist entity as a quasi-state when he asks how and why they survive and why some survive longer than others. Here we see that the questions of survivability and viability of a *de facto* state may be used as a threshold measure of quasi-statehood. In this sense, Kolstø argues that five factors can be identified that contribute to the viability of unrecognised quasi-states. These factors are "symbolic nation-building; militarisation of society; the weakness of the parent state; support from an external patron; and lack of involvement on the part of the international community".[19] The first four factors, in one way or another, relate to the same patterns of a 'real' state as much as they are factors pertaining to the survivability and viability of a quasi-state. Therefore, I will use these four factors as criteria to classify unrecognised entities as quasi-states.

The first criterion (UQC-I): nation-building process

The first factor that may be used as a criterion for classifying unrecognised entities as quasi-states is the nation-building process. The nation-building process pertain soft aspects of state consolidation, such as the development of a common national identity among the inhabitants through education, symbols, rewriting of history, and the revival of traditions and national customs.[20] Any real sovereign state is involved in a wide range of nation-building processes. If a semi-independent separatist region is involved in a nation-building process, it thereby plays the same role as an independent state in this regard. When only a recognised quasi-state exists within a country, the issue of integration of all segments of society and the improvement of the system of governance is more likely than in the case where two quasi-states co-exist within a country. In the case of one quasi-state there is only one nation-building and state-building process, though such a process may be challenged by a portion of that state's inhabitants. The process of nation-building, in that case, is unbalanced and the process does not happen simultaneously and at the same pace in all parts of the country. The process may fail, but the state-directed nation-building project is the only dominant process.

In the case of two quasi-states (i.e. an unrecognised and a recognised quasi-state) within the boundaries of one country, there are two necessarily oppositional state- and nation-building projects transpiring simultaneously. Two different (and usually oppositional) identities and loyalties make each state- and nation-building project counterproductive and in opposition to the success of the other. In such dual quasi-states, two rival forces vie for power and seek to monopolise the exercise of violence in the secessionist territory. Two separate systems of army recruitment and two armed forces are active in defending their respective territories, and two entities push their respective legitimacies on the other. There is a *de facto* boundary that separates the two states in which the institutions of the recognised quasi-state are absent in the areas of the unrecognised quasi-state. The separatist unrecognised entity finds it easy to portray the parent state as its main occupier and threat. This perception was a useful and powerful tool by which to motivate secessionist unification and nationalistic sentiments. In a country of one recognised quasi-state, the process of integrating the inhabitants of different territories and ethnic/national backgrounds is more likely than in a country with two quasi-states. Thus, the degree of the *de facto* state's involvement in the nation-building process is considered as the first criterion (UQC-I) by which to classify a separatist entity as a quasi-state.

The second criterion (UQC-II): the militarisation of society

The militarisation of society may be used as a criterion for classifying unrecognised entities as quasi-states. The militarisation of society is not only a contributing factor to the survival of the quasi-state but also a trait of the UQ. State formation, in the case of the UQ, is more a revolutionary than evolutionary process. UQs emerge out of a violent struggle for secession and independence. This process requires a breach of orthodoxies of territorial integrity and the taboos of secession. They tend to be involved in a considerably larger number of interstate disputes than RQs and real sovereign states. Therefore, militarisation becomes not only a protective measure but a method to create a balance of power with the parent state. The militarisation of society does not necessarily mean that the UQs' armed forces are very large. Though they need a strong military capability, compared to their parent states, most UQs do not have a large military.

Militarisation in the UQs, however, could be understood primarily in terms of the militarisation of all aspects of society rather than numbers of armed personnel. Military spending is one form of the militarisation of the UQs. Most UQs are examples of making states by making war. UQs, however, are not protected by the international system; they rely on military, which makes war a constant possibility. To survive, UQs devote a disproportionate share of the nation's resources to military expenditure. The need for a high military capability requires allocation of the large part of their resources to their armed forces. Rising military spending needs the diversion of funds from development projects and basic civil services to military. This means inadequate spending on non-productive infrastructures; military highways; construction of fortifications, armours, and other military equipment; and weapon accumulation. And all of this at the expense of other productive infrastructure: public goods, infrastructure, welfare, education, and health. This process often associates with the rise of paramilitary groups and the diffusion of small arms and light weapons.

Another dimension of the militarisation of society is militarisation of politics. Military leaders of the UQs became powerful political actors. Most of the UQs are established via military means. UQs lack negative sovereignty and international protection. This state of non-recognition reshapes the role of armed forces in several ways. First, armed forces possess a crucial role in the survival of the UQs. Second, the military becomes the most influential institution in UQs. Third, the armed forces of UQs are often highly politicised. This essential role of the armed forces may lead to further legitimising militarism and militarisation of the political environment. Participating in the 'liberation war' becomes the criteria for gaining access to political power, and the armed forces of UQs are highly politicised. Moreover, wars of independence elevate the status of military leaders within the social and political life of UQs. In the post-conflict settings, political processes such as elections and institutionalisation of the state can serve as a mechanism to militarise politics. Institutions of war that characterise the period of secessionist struggle are transformed into new political and social structures. The attitude towards military leaders, veterans, ex-combatants, and warriors remains supportive, and many people perceive their abuse of power to be deserved.

The 'post-liberation' situation encourages the transformation of militias and militarised organisations into political parties. In fact, to the extent that powerful military leaders perceive that they have the option to operate as politicians, the chances of the transformation from a military organisation to a competitive political party are increased. The post-secession situation may also increase the opportunity for military leaders to transform their influence into political power and control local political bodies. For many voters, the transformation of military organisations into effective political parties means that their vote must be given to those powerful leaders who are capable of defending the country. Consequently, indisputably charismatic military leaders rise to power, enjoy a prominent role in every aspect of political life, gain high political office, and enjoy great social renown.

Militarisation of urban space is another form of militarisation of society in the UQs. For many reasons, the UQs turn into uncivil places. First, unlike RQs that are protected by international state systems and the military, UQs have to manage without international protection. Attempting to compensate for the shortage of negative sovereignty and the lack of international protection, UQs continue to provide civic defence. Second, because their survival depends fundamentally on military strength, most of the post-secession UQs experience the rise of paramilitary groups and the diffusion of small arms and light weapons. During the war of secession, individuals and different sections of society often find it necessary to participate in the secessionist war and to protect their homeland. Consequently, the larger fraction of the population possesses weapons and receives training for military conflicts. In most UQ societies, civilians (including teenagers, junior soldiers, and all sorts of irregulars) have access to weaponry. They buy cheap weapons and small arms such as grenades, land mines, and, particularly, light machine guns.

Third, for the UQ rulers, the external threat is greater than the internal threats. Most UQs are under the constant threat of re-invasion by their parent states and remain highly suspicious of their parent states. Other UQs are often in direct armed conflict with their parent states. Moreover, enjoying legitimacy and popular support, rulers in the UQs find that no significant internal threat exists. Therefore, governments of UQs are unwilling to disarm civilians and collect those arms that are mostly pointed outward at foreign powers rather than inward. Fourth, leaders of UQs find their rule is more secure in the militarised society. The leadership of UQs finds it easier to derogate civil rights whenever necessary. In the militarised society, there are ready justifications and even 'legal grounds' to suspend civil rights and to suppress opponents.

The militarisation of urban space may also come in the form of the establishment of military bases around cities; the establishment of military checkpoints along the administrative border; the construction of military highways; construction of fortifications; and establishment of new military installations. In many cases villages along the border are forcibly evacuated and road and rail blockades are imposed by the UQ authorities. Military convoys regularly travel between cities. The dispatch of peacekeeping forces in disputed areas often contributes in the further militarisation of the urban spaces.

Another aspect of the militarisation of society in the UQs is the combination of militarism with business. Three factors may result in the militarisation of the economy. First, lacking the *de jure* status, UQs are mostly maintained by military means. Being a secessionist unit, the establishment of a UQ is resisted forcibly by a central government. Parent states attempt to crush secessionist movements through military force. UQs, therefore, would feel obliged to militarise. In the event of a new outbreak of war, the loyalty and experiences of the veterans would be in very high demand. Coupled with their military power and having benefited from the revolutionary legitimacy, the veterans and warriors expect moral and financial compensation. Such a socio-political context helps military leaders to transform their influence into economic power. Second, the state of non-recognition and lack of international relations results in the flourishing of the black market trade in UQs. Smuggling of the military equipment and weaponry is highly profitable trade. Inventing every possible subterfuge to secure financial resources, trade with neighbouring countries is often arranged without paying production taxes or tariffs. Luxury goods, mainly cigarettes and alcohol, can be brought in for resale or export. Domination of such a trade may allow royal leaders to secure sufficient revenue for governing the country. Third, military leaders often control shady business structures of their territories. UQs' military capabilities are a function of illegal imports and clandestine military training. Combining politics with business, military leaders control these shady business structures. They establish a monopoly over lucrative trade (often smuggling trade) such as cigarettes and gasoline. Consequently, military leaders often take over areas of the economy and became competitive business figures, and this may result in the militarisation of economic and social life.

Another form of the militarisation of societies in UQs is the militarisation of the collective consciousness of society. Residents of the UQs feel that war may break out again at any time. UQ authorities play on their population's fears by inducing a permanent-siege mentality within the UQ. With population war experiences becoming an important part of the national discussion, state media broadcasts patriotic programs, dance, song, and poetry, which continues to glorify their war for independence and liberation. Rulers of the UQs often resort to militarised language to produce their narratives with frames and metaphors from the UQ-parent state conflicts. Vocabularies dominate the culture and range from the language used to describe those who live 'over there' to the occupier of the homeland. Examples of the militarised vocabularies are clashes, skirmishes, violent confrontations, human crime, national treason, battle, and wars of liberations. This language is repeatedly used to signify the status of the UQ as a separate country with its fixed border. Thus, the military is another common feature of separatist quasi-states and sovereign states. Accordingly, the militarisation of society is the second criterion (UQC-II) that may be used to classify a separatist region as a quasi-state.

The third criterion (UQC-III): weak parent state

The third factor that may be used as a criterion for the formation of quasi-states is the weakness of the parent state. Kolstø emphasises that "the parent state of most quasi-states is a weak state, in political and institutional as well as in military terms."[21] Military strength and weakness, however, are relative measures. In addition to the military balance of power between the parent and separatist region, the parent state politically and militarily is a weak state. So the balance of power favours the quasi-state as it keeps the parent state at bay. This factor is based on the comparison between the parent state, which is at the same time a recognised state, and the separatist region. Therefore, a separatist region is strong enough to be compared to, and at the same time challenge, the parent state.

The term 'parent state' refers to political units that have international legal recognition but are unable to exercise authority over a particular region of their territory. The failure to exercise authority by the central government over all parts of the country means that the coexistence of a *de facto* state and a parent state within a country is expected. The criterion of weak parent states is designed to answer questions related to relations between parent states and their separatist territories. Many factors may account for a parent state to be weak and such weaknesses propel the following questions: Why do some *de facto* states evolve to the quasi-state status while others are not? Why do some of these UQs manage to survive without international support and recognition while some fail to exist? Why have some UQs successfully obtained independence with very little opposition and others have failed to transform into sovereign statehood? Why are some cleft states protected from fragmenting and others not? Why is the status of all recognised entities protected as members of the international community? Why can some countries successfully protect their territorial integrity while others cannot? The questions raised here will not only help in understanding the difference between long-term survival or failure of a *de facto* state but also the difference between unrecognised quasi-states and other forms of *de facto* states. The prospects for UQs hinge generally on two things: their survival and their ability to develop into *de jure* entities. UQs exist and survive by virtue of the UQ-parent state balance of power. The weakness of the parent state is one of the main contributing factors for the emergence of the UQs and their development into sovereign states. The weakness of the parent state creates an internal circumstance which makes it easier for quasi-states to emerge, survive, and eventually develop into a *de jure* entity.

The category of weak parent state covers a variety of cases and cannot be defined by a single variable. A careful assessment of several manifest indicators may provide evidence for the weakness of the parent state. What makes parent states different from non-parent states or nation-states is the degree of nation-building process, territorial control, effective administration and bureaucratic functional governance, strength of its armed forces, and sufficient economic resources. While most parent states lack sufficient military capability, effective government structures, and sufficient economic resources, non-parent states or nation-states perform well in all these indicators. Non-parent states possess control over their territories and their territorial integrity and monopolisation of the legitimate use of force are rarely challenged. The people of these states possess a strong sense of cohesion, cultural harmony, and a shared history. Non-parent states enjoy legitimacy in the eyes of most of their citizens and their minority groups are less inclined towards territorial claims and do not threaten the territorial integrity. This form of state rarely faces demands for territorial secession from the territorial communities. Instead, elites in most regions continue to seek autonomy within the state. The central government faces pressure to reform its basic institutional ties between the central and regional governments. Demands for regional autonomy are far more common than those for independence. Territorial demand, however, is limited to the equal distribution of power and economy. For example, residents of a certain territory may call for control over the appointment of local officials and for a larger share of the revenues. Political and military leaders of these states usually respond to those demands with negotiation rather than coercion. As demands for regional autonomy have been far more common than those for independence, the probability of separatist rebellions and widespread violence remains low. The main characteristic of the non-parent state is that the struggle of the ethno-nationalist or socio-political groups is regulated by rule of law which takes place within the state and not outside of it.

Many parent states, by contrast, possess all necessary ingredients of weak states in terms of lacking military capabilities, ineffective government structures, insufficient economic resource, heterogeneous society, and an uncompleted nation-building process. In addition, many parent states lack bureaucratic functional governance. Though parent states may provide reasonable public goods for the dominant ethnic group in the mainland, they often fail to supply inhabitants of the separatist region with the basic essential services needed for decent livelihood. The lack of basic social amenities may propel the separatist region to rebel against the central government and the inhabitants of the secessionist territories are often regarded as the enemy by their parent states.

Most parent states suffer the absence of material resources and lack sufficient economic resources and a robust economy. Parent states experience secessionist and often civil wars, as well as spend most of their funds on updating military arsenal. Therefore, providing public goods to inhabitants of the separatist regions becomes less and less of a priority. They lack enough capital resources necessary for maintaining road or rail access to distant districts and for providing proper health and education to inhabitants of the separatist regions. Insufficient economic resources may lead to the weakness of the parent state in several ways. First, impoverishment potentially undermines the legitimacy of the state. Second, lack of enough resources makes reintegration of little interest to separatist territories. This is because a weak economy of the parent state means there is little to offer to the separatist region and its population to rejoin the parent state. Third, a secessionist *de facto* state survives because the parent state fails to mobilise resources to suppress the secessionist movements successfully. If the parent state has abundant resources, it may be difficult for a separatist region to have its way. Iraq and Nigeria are good example of this scenario. The oil boom in Iraq and Nigeria in the late 1960s and early 1970s had a significant role in the collapse of the Kurdistan Region of Iraq in 1975 and Nigeria's Biafra region in 1970. Accordingly, weak parent states are far more vulnerable to disintegration compared to non-parent states.

The military weakness of the parent state reveals its inability to prohibit the formation of the *de facto* self-rule in one or more of its separatist regions. The extent of a state weakness can be measured by how much of the country's territory is controlled by the central government and by how nominal or contested the parent state's authority is over the separatist territory. Though, in theory, weak parent states enjoy a monopoly of legitimate force within their borders, they often cannot control their borders and their authority over sections of territory is almost absent. One of the state's prime functions is to prevent any loss of their territories. Maintaining the separatist territory under control would be militarily and financially imprudent. Furthermore, most parent states lack the capacity to channel social tensions, regulate conflicts, and control their territory and borders. This failure facilitates the widespread internal insurgent movement directed against the government. Failing to contain armed revolts led by separatist movements may result in loss of territory to the separatists. This helps separatists to use the region as safe havens and as a base for their attacks. Such inability to prevent the emergence of a separatist movement which may implicitly result in cross-border invasions and infiltrations often lays ground for foreign intervention in the internal affairs of the parent state. The intervention of a stronger state usually has a severe impact on the disintegration of the weaker state and strengthens the statehood of the separatist regions. As a result of the loss of legitimacy of the state over significant parts of the population, the already weak parent states are likely to become even weaker. Thus, the physical absence of the state in certain regions of the country becomes a distinguished characteristic of the parent states.

The uncompleted nation-building process is another weakness of the parent states. Unlike non-parent states, many parent states are weak and heterogeneous in nature. In most cases, two or more territorialised ethno-religious groups exist within their borders. These groups lack a shared culture, common ancestor, and history. Societies in these states suffer primordial cleavages and cultural fragmentation. Never integrated into the state in the first place, territorial and separatist groups reject the legitimacy of central rule in their territories. In other words, most parent states suffer the failure of the nation-building process and thereby lack internal legitimacy and socio-political cohesion. The state itself is perceived as illegitimate in the eyes of a large number of the inhabitants of the separatist territories. By explicitly dishonouring the legitimacy of the parent states, minorities' demands are mostly for the purpose of independence. The emergence and survival of UQs can be attributed to the failure of the nation-building process of weak parent states.

The immediate consequence of this weakness could be the demise of parent states as functioning states. Given the structural, financial, and militarily weakness of the parent state, it can easily fragment and collapse, as well as prepare the ground for the emergence of the *de facto* separatist regions. These weaknesses are major factors and a precondition for the emergence and survival of the UQ. The degree of the UQ's success can be measured by the extent of its parent state's weaknesses. The disorganised and fragmented nature of weak states lays the ground for some *de facto* semi-independent entities to evolve enough to be considered as quasi-states. In other words, without the dissolution of weak parent states, it may prove a Herculean task for *de facto* groups to evolve into a quasi-state. In some sense the separatist region is equivalent to its parent state. Through the weakness and strength of the parent state, one can imagine the weakness and strength of the *de facto* independent state. Therefore the character of a weak parent state may be a third criterion for classifying the separatist entity as a quasi-state (UQC-III).

The fourth criterion (UQC-IV): positive and negative patronage

The fourth factor that may be used as a criterion for classifying the quasi-state is external patronage. Most quasi-states are dependent upon support from an external patron. Such a patron, however, fulfils the same role as the international community does vis-à-vis failed states. External patronage is therefore another similarity between unrecognised quasi-states and recognised states. Accordingly, a separatist entity's ability to find external patronage may be considered as the fourth criterion (UQC-IV) by which to qualify as a quasi-state. Thus, in this work, to be classified as a quasi-state, a *de facto* self-rule of a secessionist territory must satisfy these four unrecognised quasi-state criteria (UQC): (1) a symbolic nation-building process (UQC-I); (2) a militarisation of society (UQC-II); (3) a weak parent state (UQC-III); and external patronage and support (UQC-IV).

Positive and negative patronage

Kolstø does not recognise different forms of patronage. Highlighting the patron state's agenda, he suggests that the patron states use the quasi-states as political instruments "to put pressure on the parent states and, generally, to project power into the region". Putting pressure on the parent state and projecting power into the region are probably common agendas of all patron states. However, it is not the only reason behind the patronage project. Patron states may also be motivated by the fact that the ethnicity and the nationality of the client population is the same as the patron state. They may also be motivated by irredentist agendas, such as historical claim of the separatist territory. Accordingly, the nature of external patronage may be categorised according to the motivations and agendas of the patron state. There are two forms of external patronages: positive and negative. I distinguish the two forms by applying three criteria.

The first criterion used to determine whether an example of external patronage is negative or positive is the ethnic and cultural identity of the patron and client states. In negative patronage, populations of the patron and client states do not share the same ethnic or cultural identity. I refer to this criterion as the first negative patronage criterion (NPC-I). In positive patronage, however, the population shares the same ethnic background and the population of the client state is a natural extension of that of the patron state. In many cases the patron state has historically claimed separate territory of the client state as part of its homeland. Hence, in positive patronage, supporting and consolidating ethnic, cultural, and territorial rights of the client region are the main reasons behind the patron state's willingness to provide assistance. In negative patronage, however, such motivation is absent. Rather, a patron state is mainly motivated by issues other than the identity of the client state. The second negative patronage criterion (NPC-II) is that the patron state is not motivated by the interests, rights, and/or identity of the client state. The third criterion for determining the positive or negative status of patronage is whether the patron state is willing to recognise the independent state. In positive patronage, the client state's independence and the consolidation of its political, cultural, and economic status strengthens the internal and external position of the patron state. In negative patronage the independence of client states may jeopardise the patron's interests. Thus, the third negative patronage criterion (NPC-III) is the fact that the patron state does not seek the client's independence and is not willing to recognise the independent status of the client state. In positive patronage, however, the patron state supports and often recognises the independence of its client state.

Positive patronage-client relations are based on good will, long-term interests, and the principal values of the patron state and longstanding patronage. For the client state it is a reliable and indispensable source of external support and is therefore considered as positive patronage. While negative patronage is a tactical, short-term measure of limited support, it is usually a no-win policy for the client and it often ends up with the patron state using the client state as a bargaining chip. It is an unreliable source of external support and therefore is considered as negative patronage. Turkey's, Serbia's, and Armenia's patronage of North Cyprus Turks, Republika Srpska in Bosnia, and Nagorno Karabagh in Azerbaijan are a few examples of positive patronage. The form of patronage that has been offered to the Iraqi Kurds by Iran in 1961–1975, and Turkey and the US in the 1990s, are examples of negative patronage. External patronage is negative if it fulfils three negative patronage criteria (NPC): (1) the populations of the patron and client states do not share the same ethnic or cultural identity (NPC-I); (2) the patron state is not motivated by the interests, rights, and/or the identity of the client state; and (3) the patron state does not seek the client's independence and is not willing to recognise the independence of the entity.

Recognised quasi-states (RQs) versus unrecognised quasi-states (UQs)

There is strong evidence that explain why the two forms of quasi-states, the recognised and unrecognised, should be differently defined. The difference between the RQs and the UQs goes beyond the issue international recognition. The first significant difference between the two entities is that a RQ is a *de jure* state while a UQ is a *de facto* state. RQs are constitutionally independent in a formal way, while UQs are informal but with more of a substantive condition. The second key difference between the two quasi-sates is that UQs are more coherent domestically with fewer civil conflicts compared to RQs. Compared to RQs, the UQs enjoy broader popular support and their governance is more effective. Another difference is that a RQ is a juridical entity that suffers a crisis of legitimacy and a UQ is an empirical entity that suffers the crisis of legality.

RQs are accepted as wholly legal international personalities and function as such, but they lack capabilities and have failed to take such effective control over their territory. RQs exist because of their formal acceptance by the international community rather than their internal legitimacy. UQs, by contrast, enjoy legitimacy from the vast majority of the population at home, but lack recognition. They have perceived illegal personalities by the international community. Most UQs have shown their ability to take effective control of a territory and population, as well as to establish an efficient government. Though both UQs and RQs attempt to escape their quasi-statehood status, they follow different methods for that end. UQs use the internal legitimacy that they have established to promote their status to a legal entity. The RQs, by contrast, view their legal status of sovereignty and recognition as a contributing factor to promote the legitimacy that they failed to establish. Thus, both RQs and UQs are by-products of the new sovereignty regime.

The final striking difference between the two forms of quasi-states is that the UQ is a case of the secession process but the RQ is that of decolonisation. Unlike RQs, which are the by-product of the self-determination process, the claim of self-determination by the UQs, is perceived to be outside the framework of decolonisation. No UQ are a case of decolonisation. UQs are cast within a context of secession and separatism and not decolonisation. The international society denies the *de jure* status of the UQs for three reasons. First, historically, the right to self-determination was confined to the colonial territories and this right has not gone beyond the decolonisation context. Second, the international community deals with the principle of self-determination as that of the sanctity of existing territorial borders. Therefore, secession, especially a unilateral secession, is perceived as an illegitimate process. Third, the majority of states around the world perceive secession as a threat to their fundamental interests. Thus, the international community resists any attempt to sanction self-determination through secession from a recognised state. The denial of the right of self-determination is the main reason behind the survival of RQs to integrate countries and failure of the UQs to promote to a *de jure* status. Accordingly, a UQ is a result the existing entity in which an empirical statehood in large measure is built, on one hand, and the unwillingness of the international system to condone secession on the other.

States with dual sovereignty (SWDS) versus quasi-states

A 'real' sovereign state enjoys dual sovereignty: external, vis-à-vis other states, and internal, vis-à-vis its own citizens. If an internationally recognised state lacks internal sovereignty and falls within the criteria of recognised quasi-states (RQC), it is considered as a recognised quasi-state (RQ). If a *de facto* state, however, fails to gain international recognition but falls within the criteria for unrecognised quasi-states (UQC), it may be classified as an unrecognised quasi-state (UQ). These theoretical discussions will be used throughout the book to analyse the nature of conflict.

Notes

1. Jackson, R. H. (1993), *Quasi-States: Sovereignty, International Relations and the Third World*, Cambridge: Cambridge University Press: 153.
2. Kosienkowski, M. (2013), "Is Internationally Recognised Independence the Goal of Quasi-States? The Case of Transnistria," *Moldova: In Search of Its Own Place in Europe*, Natalia Cwicinskaja and Piotr Oleksy (eds.), Bygdoszcz: Epigram: 55–65; Caspersen, N. (2011), *Unrecognized States: The Struggle for Sovereignty in the Modern International System*, Chichester: Wiley-Blackwell: 337; Fruhstorfer, A. (2012). "Post-Soviet De Facto States in Search of Internal and External Legitimacy. Introduction," *Communist and Post-Communist Studies* 45(2): 117–121.
3. Smith 2009: 49; Weber, M. (1997), *The Theory of Social and Economic Organization*, New York: Free Press: 156.
4. Lassa Oppenheim and Ronald Roxburgh (1920), "Recognition of States as International Persons," *International Law: A Treatise*, Sir Ronald Roxburgh (ed.), Clark, NJ: The Lawbook Exchange, Ltd. : 135; for the new edition see: Oppenheim, Lessa (2005), *A Treatise*, Ronald F. Roxburgh (eds.), 3rd edition, Clark, NJ: The Lawbook Exchange Ltd.
5. Jackson 1993: 28–30.
6. *Ibid.*: 21–29.
7. *Ibid.*: 179.
8. Jackson 1993: 153.
9. Weber (1994), *Political Writings*, Peter Lassman, Ronald Speirs (eds.), Ronald Speirs (trans.), UK: Cambridge University Press: 310–311.
10. Max Weber's Complete Writings on Academic and Political Vocations/Edited and with an Introduction by John Dreijmanis; Translation by Gordon C. Wells: 156–157; Weber, Max (1964), *The Theory of Social and Economic Organization*, Talcott Parsons (ed.), New York: Free Press: 130–131.
11. Dominique Darbon, Stein Sundstøl Eriksen, Ole Jacob Sending, Report for the OECD DAC International Network on Conflict and Fragility Final version The Legitimacy of the State in Fragile Situations, Prepared by Séverine Bellina, Institute for Research and Debate on Governance – IRG, February 2009; McCullough, A. (2015), The Legitimacy of States and Armed Non-state Actors: Topic Guide. Birmingham, UK: GSDRC, University of Birmingham.
12. Rosenfeld, M. (2001), "The Rule of Law and the, Legitimacy of Constitutional Democracy," Jacob Burns Institute for Advanced Legal Studies, No. 36, available at < https://cardozo.yu.edu/sites/default/files/Rule%20of%20law.pdf> (accessed 03-05-2016).
13. Max Weber's Complete Writings on Academic and Political Vocations/Edited and with an Introduction by John Dreijmanis; Translation by Gordon C. Wells: 156–157; Weber 1964: 130–31.
14. Max Weber, *Political Writings*: 311.
15. Jackson 1993: 27.
16. *Ibid.*: 27.
17. Kolstø, P. (2006). "The Sustainability and Future of Unrecognized Quasi-States," *Journal of Peace Research* 43(6): 725.
18. *Ibid.*: 725–726.
19. *Ibid.*: 729.
20. *Ibid.*: 730.
21. Kolstø 2006: 732.

2 The context of two quasi-states in Iraq

Many studies have dealt with good governance policies,[1] political space,[2] democratisation,[3] and the Kurdish integration with or secession from Iraq. However, little attention has been given to the question of the significance of Kurdish and Iraqi counter quests for nationhood and the evolution of Kurdish nationalism into a quasi-state and its influence on Kurdish integration into Iraq. Few, if any, studies have focused on the question as to whether Iraq may be considered as a quasi-state and, if so, how that state of affairs impacted Kurdish integration into Iraq. The debate relating to the Kurdish-Iraqi conflict is categorised into three types: the oppositional nature of the Kurdish and Iraqi quests for nationhood, the unrecognised Kurdish quasi-state, and the recognised Iraqi quasi-state.

Contending debate on the oppositional nature of the Kurdish and Iraqi quests for nationhood

Analyses of the relations between the Kurds and the state of Iraq have often focused on Iraqi nationalism as the factor to be explained. Davis and Yaphe have argued that Iraq has already achieved nation status.[4] However, this Iraq-centric perspective fails to explain the nine decades of ongoing Kurdish-Iraqi conflict and the enduring clash between Shia and Sunni Arabs. Davis insists that the current ethno-sectarian violence in Iraq is a direct result of America's invasion.[5] In contrast, Dodge argues that the Iraqi predicament is rooted in both the British (in the 1920s and 1930s) and the US (post-2003) failure to create the elements that would enhance state-building in Iraq.[6] The concept of 'political space' is another relevant variable that sheds light on this issue. Natali argues that the extent of ethnicisation of Kurdish national identity is a result of the political space character of the state.[7] Iraq's current political predicament, its ethno-sectarian conflict, and the desire by the Kurds for their own ethnic-based organisations are the result of discrimination by Sunni-Arab rulers.[8] According to this reasoning, if the Kurds were accorded more suitable political space, they might leave their secessionist dreams and develop an enduring loyalty to the Iraqi state.[9] Bozarslan argues that providing more acceptable political space may not terminate the conflict, but discrimination may provoke a shift from peaceful interaction to a more violent expression by the Kurdish opposition.[10] Similarly, Gurr and Harff state that discrimination encourages ethnic groups to organise for action against the source of discrimination.[11] Nevertheless, they acknowledge that the most serious political grievance of the Kurds is not discrimination in the usual sense but, rather, involves restrictions on their efforts to express and pursue their ethnic interests.[12] In this sense, regardless of the extent of political space, the Kurds are likely to remain a politically active ethnic group.

Another relevant variable that aids our understanding of the Iraqi-Kurdish conflict is ethno-political conflict. Gurr views ethno-political groups as identity groups whose ethnicity has political consequences.[13] Scarritt depicts the Kurds and their ongoing agitation for independence as an ethno-political conflict. He points out that the grievances, clash of identities, and violence are three main characteristics of ethno-political conflicts.[14] The ethno-political approach, however, fails to adequately describe the current Kurdish conflict because the theory ignores the size and character of the ethnic group and does not take into account the various underlying causes and unique demands of this people. Gurr and Harff have refined a model of ethnic conflict based on group demands and goals of statehood, economic autonomy, and political power-sharing. Their model applies to four important types of contenders: ethno-nationalists, ethno-classes, indigenous peoples, and communal contenders. They used the Kurds as their case study and defined them as ethno-nationalists. However, their analytical work is based on the assumption of the superiority of Iraqi civic-nationalism over Kurdish ethnic-nationalism. Their work also excludes the fact of Kurdish intermittent self-rule since 1961 and all the experience and history that the self-rule period involved.

Other studies, such as Cottam and Cottam and O'Leary, classify Iraq as a non-nation state (NNS).[15] Both studies assert that the identity and comparison patterns of an NNS produce deeper conflicts and greater violence than they do in nation-states. Cottam and Cottam outline three significant scenarios of NNSs. First is intensity of group identity; second is the lack of a common identity; and third is the weakness of the notion of citizenship.[16] O'Leary attributes most of the violence of the Iraqi-Kurdish conflict, including the slaughter of the Kurds by the Ba'ath regime, to the status of Iraq as an NNS.[17] However, like ethno-nationalist models, the NNS model was built in abstraction without regard to the fact of Kurdish controlled territories since 1961. The model also ignores the question as to why the establishment of the Kurdish quasi-state after 1991 culminated in the most peaceful period in Iraqi-Kurdish relations in history.

There are several gaps in the literature relating to the nature of the Iraqi-Kurdish conflict. It overlooks the contradictions between the Kurdish quest for nationhood and the Iraqi quest for a unitary state that guarantees Iraqi state sovereignty over all Iraqi territory, including Kurdistan. The study also fails to explain how these contradictions affect the peace-building process in the post-invasion period of Iraq. It ignores the evolution of Kurdish nationalism into a quasi-state. Finally, less attention tends to be paid to the status of Iraq either as a parent state to the separatist region of Kurdistan or as a quasi-state that lacks internal and/or external sovereignty.

Contending debate on the Kurdish quasi-state

Most studies dealing with the Kurdish quasi-state concentrate on factors that contribute to either the survival of or the decline of the Kurdish *de facto* state. Scholars tend to ignore the characteristics of this *de facto* state and their contribution to the reshaping of Kurdish-Iraqi relations. They also tend to ignore the process of Kurdish integration into Iraq. The existing approaches may easily be categorised into five types: (1) the geopolitical approach, (2) internal divisions focus, (3) the international factors approach, (4) the institutional designs model, and (5) the humanitarian aid approach.

The first model suggests that the Kurdish desire to secede is blocked by implacable opposition from large, hostile neighbours.[18] This model is based upon two geopolitical facts. First, Kurdistan is landlocked and surrounded by neighbouring states that refuse to countenance an independent Kurdish state. This makes a potential Kurdish state dependent on its neighbours and vulnerable to embargos and blockades.[19] Second, the dispersal of the Kurdish population throughout four countries and the irredentist nature of Kurdish separatist movements give the Kurdish problem a transnational character.[20] Believing that an independent Kurdish state would threaten their territorial integrity, proponents of this approach argue that an independent Kurdish state cannot survive because the surrounding countries with substantial Kurdish minorities would not hesitate to intervene and even invade Kurdistan, if necessary, to keep them from gaining full independence. Thus, a contested secession would be a recipe for suicide.[21] This model, however, is based on the assumption that the Kurds, as a peripheral ethnic minority, would be passive, vulnerable, and unable to defend themselves, if attacked.

The geopolitical approach, however, fails to consider three interconnected issues. First, since 1961, Kurdish nationalistic fervour has helped to move the Kurdistan region into quasi-state status. The Kurdish quasi-state has managed to survive for over two decades. Second, the Kurdistan region has developed its oil sector and transformed Kurdistan into one of the richest regions in terms of oil wealth in the world. In this sense, the Kurdistan region has moved from the sidelines of regional activity to the very centre of regional economics and politics. Third, as a result of this shift in the status of the Kurdistan Region of Iraq (KRI), the balance of power between the KRI and neighbouring states has shifted from hostile interactions to interdependence and cooperation. Taken together, these three factors have raised the probability of Kurdish independence becoming a reality.

The second model suggests that intra-Kurdish divisions are the main cause of the failure of the Kurds to achieve statehood. Mack argues that Kurdish internal struggles are the most immediate danger to their security and future development.[22] These internal struggles have caused the collapse of the *de facto* Kurdish state in the 1990s, and undermined the Kurds' quest for independence and statehood.[23] Highlighting the impact of the Kurdish internal conflict on their failure to achieve statehood, Chorev argues that the Kurds have no worse enemies than themselves.[24] This model, however, undermines the reunification and reconciliation process between the Kurdish factions in post-invasion Iraq. Another central issue that this approach ignores is the administrative divisions of Iraqi Kurdistan. While it has a unified administration, parliament, and institutions, the KRG administers less than two-thirds of the region that the Kurds believe historically belongs to Iraqi Kurdistan. The province of Kirkuk, however, remains outside the KRG administration altogether. The approach also ignores the question as to how this administrative division has led to the border dispute between the Erbil and Baghdad, and how this dispute has been dealt with. It seems like a conflict between two separate states, the KRI and Iraq, rather than a conflict within one nation. Finally, this model fails to trace the links between internal Iraqi divisions (i.e. the Sunni-Shia conflict) and their impact on further strengthening the Kurdish quasi-state.

The third model suggests that the Kurdish conflict is an international issue and that the future of the KRI depends significantly on international elements.[25] This approach is based on two assumptions. One assumption is that the region occupied by the Kurds straddles four countries and is therefore a transnational issue with serious implications for the Kurds' neighbours. An independent Kurdistan would threaten the territorial integrity and stability of these pre-existing neighbouring states, and so disrupt the international system.[26] Consequently, within the state-centric international system, any border change becomes a call to action for the international community.[27]

Another assumption is based on the fact that the Kurdish question is the historical result of complex international power-plays in the region since WWI.[28]

Gurr and Harff maintain that the international factors that determine the future of the KRI are beyond the Kurds' control.[29] Relationships between Kurdish and international movements are characterised as an imbalance against and subordination of the Kurds. Whether the Kurds secede from or remain a part of Iraq depends on their understanding and recognition of these international factors.[30] One contradiction inherent in this model is that while it emphasises the international nature of the Kurdish conflict, at the same time it claims that the Kurds themselves are minor players. It also overlooks the fact that Kurdish nationalism has propelled the Kurdistan region into a quasi-state. The quasi-state status of Kurdistan is partially a result of the Kurds' ability to destabilise the region due to its international role. Iraq is also a victim of international interference, and this has enlarged the capacity for manoeuvres by the Kurdish quasi-state to improve its status and survivability. This is evidenced by UN Resolution No. 688 of 5 April 1991 and the confirmation of a subsequent Kurdish Safe Haven which culminated in the present Kurdish quasi-state.

The fourth model, the institutional design approach, suggests that whether the Kurds remain in Iraq depends heavily on the institutional design of the Iraqi state.[31] This approach can further be categorised into (a) Iraq/state centrists and (b) consequentialists. The Iraq/state centrists stress integrative mechanisms that encourage de-ethnicisation and fragmentation of Kurdish politics.[32] These integrative mechanisms include the cross-ethnic electoral system, the banning of Kurdish parties, and an 18-province territorial federation.[33] The consequentialists claim that the Kurds' quest for self-determination may be satisfied while avoiding the unwanted consequences of secession. This can be met by a multi-national federation with proportional representation and territorial and cultural autonomy for key nationalities.[34] However, given the current quasi-state status of the KRI and the internal divisions within Iraq, this raises questions as to who would implement such models, by what means they would do so, and what the costs and risks would be.

The fifth model is the humanitarian aid approach. This model was advocated by Natali and presents a more realistic analysis on the Kurdish quasi-state entity that emerged after the second Gulf war. She correctly defines the *de facto* Kurdish self-rule in the 1990s as a quasi-state. She defines quasi-state as political entities that have internal but not external sovereignty. These political entities seek some form of autonomy or independence.[35] Her basic thesis is that the emergence, survival, and development of the Kurdish quasi-state are attributed to external humanitarian aid programs offered and provided to the Kurds. This humanitarian and external aid, furthermore, determined the extent of the economic, social, and political achievements and therefore the nature of the Kurdish entity. Viewing it this way, she suggests three phases of development in Kurdistan based on external assistance, namely: (1) emergency relief phase (1991–1996); (2) Oil-for-Food Program (OFFP) phase (1996–2001); and (3) democracy mission phase (2003-present).[36]

Natali's thesis, however, has several weaknesses. First, for Natali it was the nature of the type of foreign aid offered to the Kurds that determined the extent of sovereignty and leverage of the Kurdish quasi-state entity. Hence, internal sovereignty of the quasi-state was provided by external patronage rather than from the internal legitimacy provided by the Kurdish population to the *de facto* state. Second, by attributing the nature and survivability of the Kurdish quasi-state to external humanitarian aid, Natali overlooks other forms of patronage such as diplomatic, political, military, and logistical support. By the same token, Natali disregards other important factors that contributed to the survivability and development of quasi-states such as the military capability of the quasi-state, the internal legitimacy that leaders of the quasi-state enjoy among its population, the weakness of the parent state and its unpopularity in the separatist region, and finally the ability of the quasi-state to perform the state- and nation-building process in which it provides basic service and protection to its population. Third, Natali deals with the Kurdish quasi-state of the 1990s as a separate abstraction taken from the history of the Kurdish controlled areas experiment that they enjoyed during the 1960s, 1970s, and 1980s. Thus, the literature on the Kurdish quasi-state suffers from several major gaps in coverage.

Contending debate on Iraq as a quasi-state

Little scholarship, if any, has been devoted to the state of Iraq as a quasi-state. For many scholars the functionality of Iraq as a sovereign nation is an open question. Two prominent approaches in the literature pertain to the status of Iraq as a 'real' nation-state. The first approach portrays Iraq as a rogue state and the second as a failed state. Scholars of comparative politics and policy analysts often refer to Iraq as a 'rogue state' though they disagree on the definition and usage of the rogue state concept.[37] Princeton University defines the rogue state as that which does not respect other states in its international actions.[38] In contrast, Rose defines rogue states as those that possess the power and credibility to engage in behaviour that sharply conflicts with the net interests of international society as defined by major powers.[39] Three most commonly invoked criteria used to define rogues are (1) states that work for WMD proliferation, (2) support for terrorism, and (3) those that violate human rights.[40] Thus, the more common understanding of rogue states portrays them as violating international norms.

Regardless of whether Iraq qualifies as a rogue state, the definition of 'rogue' has little relation to the issue of sovereignty, which is a qualification of the quasi-state. 'Quasi-state' refers to either the lack of internal sovereignty vis-à-vis the state's population or the lack of external sovereignty vis-à-vis the international community. Abuse of human rights refers more to the character of the regime while sovereignty refers to the inherent power of the state to function autonomously. With the installation of a new democratic regime, the issue of human rights abuse and even support for terrorism would be expected to be terminated. Terminating abuse itself would not normally change the status of the state in terms of sovereignty. Iraq is a striking example that illustrates this situation. Under Saddam Hussein, especially during the 1980s, Iraq fulfilled all three criteria: the regime abused human rights; it supported terrorism; and it obtained and used WMD, such as chemical weapons. Interestingly, the rogue concept has widely been applied to Iraq during the period between the second Gulf War and the US invasion in 2003. Iraq improved its behaviour in all three respects after the invasion. However, post-invasion Iraq is less sovereign and more aptly fits the definition of 'quasi-state' than the pre-invasion Iraq under Saddam.

The second approach to Iraq as a quasi-state in the body of literature considers Iraq as a 'failed state'. Many in this camp argue that Iraq is one of the world's prominent failed states.[41] The Fund for Peace's Failed State Index presented in 2009 and in 2010, for example, ranks Iraq as the world's sixth and seventh most failed states, respectively.[42] Definitions of failed states vary, but the most accurate definition comes from Call, who refers to such as wholly collapsed states. In such a state no authority is recognisable either internally to a country's inhabitants or externally to the international community.[43] In the case of failed states, Fukuyama insists that the outside power is forced to exert authority simply to avoid calamity.[44] The failed state by definition has lost both external and internal sovereignty. In quasi-state theory, however, the state lacks one of its sovereignty types. Since 1932 when Iraq achieved independence from the British, this situation existed for only one year when the Iraqi state collapsed completely during the occupation of Iraq in 2003. Therefore, the literature on failed states does not aid the understanding of Iraq as a quasi-state. This book analyses, develops, and applies quasi-state theory in order to scrutinise the quasi-state status of Iraq.

Nations, nations without states, and non-nation states

The existing approaches to the Iraqi-Kurdish conflict can be categorised into three major types: (1) primordial (ethno-symbolic), (2) instrumental, and (3) constructive. The primordialist approach takes the view that the Kurds identify themselves according to clans, language, or regional divisions.[45] This approach draws on the primordialist theoretical orientation, which attaches a high value to historical continuity, group sanctions, and social solidarity as determinants of human behaviour. The second approach considers the role of the Kurdish leadership in reshaping Kurdish-Iraqi relations. It is widely understood that in the interests of securing their vital interests and to avoid the costs of secession, Kurdish leaders have not promoted the vision of a separate state.[46] This view is compatible with instrumental theory, which posits that politicians benefit from calculated behaviour, from the manipulation of nationalist appeals, and from the struggle over resources. The third approach emphasises that Kurdish identity has emerged and evolved over time, first from religion to ethnicity and then to 'Iraqiness' during the monarchy. Later, ethnic elements re-emerged in response to discriminatory policies directed against the Kurds by central governments.[47] This approach may be categorised as 'constructivist' and emphasises that collective and ethnic identities are socially constructed, fluid, and endogenous.

It must be noted that, however, none of these three approaches adequately describes the situation of the *de facto* Kurdish self-rule that has been established since 1961. Moreover, all three are inadequate to provide a comprehensive theoretical framework for understanding these issues. To fill this gap, prominent theories on ethno-nationalism and scholarly treatises that deal with the concepts of nations, states, and quasi-states are drawn on to build a new theoretical framework. This new theoretical framework is relevant to the question of Kurdish and Iraqi counter quests for nationhood and the status of the Kurdish controlled territories since 1961, though intermittently, as a quasi-state.

Gurr's and Harff's theory of ethnic-mobilisation and ethno-nationalism can be used as a foundation to explain the Iraqi and Kurdish counter quests for nationhood. Gurr and Harff define ethno-nationalism as "relatively large and regionally-concentrated ethnic groups that live within the boundaries of one state or of several adjacent states; their modern political movements are directed toward achieving greater autonomy or independent statehood."[48] Three key variables are used by ethno-nationalists to make their cases: (1) ethnic group, (2) region, and (3) political agenda. In their work on ethnic conflicts, Gurr and Harff used the Kurds as a case study to test their theory on ethno-nationalism.[49] In doing so, they categorised Kurds as 'ethno-nationalists'. Accordingly, the Kurds emerged as a territorial ethnic group directed politically towards building a nation-state in their traditional homeland.

For Smith, nations are territorialised communities that feel a strong attachment to their respective territories.[50] In Smith's definition of nations, three dimensions can be found: (1) territory, (2) community, and (3) attachment to homeland (identity). McDowall's approach to the national identity of the Kurds is useful when analysing the Kurdish case. He states that Kurdistan is both a practical and a mythical territory that exists in the minds of most Kurds as the basis of their conceived national identity.[51] Three criteria used for defining the Kurds' status by McDowall are: (1) Kurdistan as a territory, (2) Kurds as a community, and (3) Kurdistan as an identity. By combining Smith's theory and Gurr's and Harff's theory, a useful formula is found to define the Kurds: the Kurds are a territorialised community that is politically bent on building a nation-state, and that community makes its territory the basis of its identity. Two more pertinent theories are Anderson's "imagined community" and Guibernau's "nation without a state" (NWS). For Anderson, a nation is an imagined political community with finite boundaries and limited sovereignty.[52] Anderson's imagined political community presents a useful tool for understanding the Kurds' self-identification as a nation. It also integrates well with Smith's notion of territorial identity and Gurr's and Harff's political agenda attributed to the Kurds. Anderson's notion of sovereignty, though limited, is that of a sovereign state, and therefore goes beyond the Kurds' current status.[53]

Guibernau's NWS concept is a useful alternative. He suggests that "nations, which in spite of having their territories included within the boundaries of one or more States, by and large do not identify with them." Moreover, nations "maintain a separate sense of national identity generally based on a common culture, history, attachment to a particular territory and the explicit wish to rule themselves".[54] Guibernau's criteria for nations without states incorporate both Smith's criteria of nation and Gurr's and Harff's criteria of ethno-nationalism. These are: community (nation), territory, identity, and desire for self-rule. In other words, the NWS refers to a nation that lacks a state and that is politically directed towards creating such a state. Guibernau's theory, however, fails to distinguish between those states that include NWSs from those that do not. Cottams's theory of nation-states and non-nation states (NNSs) is useful for the research questions posed by this book. Their definition of nation-states is states which a nation should be based on.[55] Using these criteria, a state that is not based on a nation is a non-nation state. Hence, Anderson's theory, Guibernau's explanation of a NWS, and Cottams's approach to NNSs provide guidelines for analysing the oppositional nature of the Kurdish quests for nationhood versus Iraq's status as a nation-state. In sum, the Kurdish-Iraqi conflict lies in these two entities' respective statuses as a nation without a state in the case of Iraqi Kurdistan and a non-nation state in the case of Iraq. Each possesses a nationhood project that differs from and opposes the other's to the extent that Iraq is unwilling to accommodate the Kurdish Nationhood Project (KNP) and the Kurds are unwilling to accept the Iraqi Nationhood Project Project (INP).

Notes

1. Brinkerhoff, D. W. and J. B. Mayfield (2005), "Democratic Governance in Iraq? Progress and Peril in Reforming State-Society Relations," *Public Administration and Development* 25(1): 59–73.
2. Natali, D. (2000), "Manufacturing Identity and Managing Kurds Iraq, Turkey, and Iran: A Study in the Evolution of Nationalism," Ph.D thesis, University of Pennsylvania.
3. Anderson, L. and G. Stansfield. (2005), *The Future of Iraq: Dictatorship, Democracy, or Division?* New York: Palgrave Macmillan.
4. Davis, E. (2005), *Memories of State: Politics, History, and Collective Identity in Modern Iraq*, Los Angeles, CA: University of California Press: 276; Yaphe, Judith S. (2004), *Iraqi Identity After the Fall of Saddam*. Middle East Institute, available at <www.mideasti.org/publications/publications_transcripts.php>, (accessed 01/09/2009).

5 Davis, E. (2004), " Democracy's Prospects in Iraq," *American Diplomacy* 9(3).
6 Dodge, T. (2006), "Iraq: the Contradictions of Exogenous State-Building in Historical Perspective," *Third World Quarterly* 27(1): 187–200; 187–188.
7 Natali 2000: 3.
8 Wimmer, A. (2004), "Democracy and Ethno-Religious Conflict in Iraq," *Survival* 45(4): 112; Al-Janabi, M. (2004), *Al-Iraq wa Mu'asarat al-Mustaqbal (Iraq and Future Convoying)*, Damascus: Dar al-Mada.
9 Natali 2000: 77–79.
10 Bozarslan, H. (1996), "Kurds: States, Marginality and Security," *Margins of Insecurity: Minority and International Security*, C. Sam Nolutshungu (ed.), New York: University of Rochester Press: 113.
11 Gurr, T. R. and B. Harff. (2004), *Ethnic Conflict in World Politics*. Boulder, CO: Westview Press: 103.
12 *Ibid.*: 109.
13 Gurr, T. R. (2000), *Peoples Versus States: Minorities at Risk in the New Century*, Washington, DC: United States Institute for Peace Press: 5.
14 Scarritt, J. R. (2008), "Ethnopolitics and Nationalism," *Politics in the Developing World*, P. Burnell and Vicky Randall (eds.), Oxford: Oxford University Press: 115.
15 Cottam, M. L. and Cottam, R. W. (2001), *Nationalism & Politics: The Political Behavior of Nation States*, Boulder, CO: Lynne Rienner Publishers: 197; O'Leary (2007), "Nationalities, Oil, and Land: Kirkuk and the Disputed Territories," Paper for Conference at Chatham House, London, UK, 19/12/2007.
16 Cottam and Cottam 2001: 197.
17 O'Leary 2007.
18 Dawisha, A. (2005), "The Prospects for Democracy in Iraq: Challenges and Opportunities," *Third World Quarterly* 26(4–5): 723–737: 725; O'Leary, B. (2009), *How to Get Out of Iraq with Integrity*, Philadelphia, PA: University of Pennsylvania Press: 137.
19 Barkey, H. J. and E. Laipson (2005), "Iraqi Kurds and Iraq's Future," *Middle East Policy* 12(4): 70; Ackerman, S. (2006), "Good Actors – The Kurds' Cunning Plan," *New Republic* 235(4): 1–10: 16; O'Leary 2009: 137.
20 Ayoob, M. (1995), *The Third World Security Predicament: State Making, Regional Conflict, and the International System*, Boulder, CO: Lynne Rienner Publishers: 51; Bozarslan 1996: 107.
21 Gunter, M. M. (1996), "The KDP-PUK Conflict in Northern Iraq," *The Middle East Journal*: 229; Ackerman 2006: 16; O'Leary 2009: 149.
22 Mack, D. L. (2007), "The United State Policy and the Iraqi Kurds," *Kurdish Identity: Human Rights and Political Status*, C. G. MacDonald and Carole S. O'Leary (eds.), Gainesville, FL: University Press of Florida: 118.
23 Chorev, M. (2007), "Iraqi Kurdistan: The Internal Dynamics and Statecraft of a Semi-state," *Al Nakhlah*; Lawrence, Q. (2008). *Invisible Nation: How the Kurds' Quest for Statehood is Shaping Iraq and the Middle East*, New York: Walker Publishing Company: 87.
24 Chorev 2007
25 Bozarslan 1996: 107; Gurr and Harff 2004: 126.
26 Bozarslan 1996: 107; Gunter 1996: 239; Gurr and Harff 2004: 119; Moore, M. (2006), "The Ethics of Secession and Postinvasion Iraq," *Ethics & International Affairs* 20(1): 64.
27 Bozarslan 1996: 110.
28 *Ibid* : 203.
29 Gurr and Harff 2004: 126.
30 *Ibid* : 151, 163; Moore 2006: 57.
31 Weinstock, A. B. (2005), "Using Institutions to Moderate Separatist Tendencies: A Focus on Iraqi Kurdistan," Masters thesis, Massachusetts Institute of Technology: 21; Simonsen, S. G. (2005), "Addressing Ethnic Divisions in Post-Conflict Institution-Building: Lessons from Recent Cases," *Security Dialogue* 36(3): 306.

32 Wimmer, A. (2004), "Democracy and Ethno-Religious Conflict in Iraq," *Survival* 45(4): 111; Dawisha 2005: 72; Brancati, D. (2006), "Decentralization: Fuelling the Fire or Dampening the Flames of Ethnic Conflict and Secessionism?" *Decentralization and Ethnic Conflict International Conference* 60(3): 654.
33 Dawisha and Dawisha 2003; Simonsen 2005: 305.
34 O'Leary 2009: 149.
35 Natali 2010: xxv.
36 *Ibid.*: 2010: xxix–xxxiii.
37 see Hoyt, P. D. (2000), "'Rogue States' and International Relations Theory," *Journal of Conflict Studies* 20(2); Eland, I. and Lee, D. (2001), "The Rogue State Doctrine and National Missile Defense," *Foreign Policy Briefing* (2): 9; Stromseth, J. E. (2003), "Law and Force After Iraq: A Transitional Moment," *American Journal of International Law:* 628–642: 636; Dueck, C. (2006), "Strategies for Managing Rogue States," *Orbis* 50(2): 230.
38 Princeton University. (2010), "Wordnet," Princeton, NJ.
39 Rose, J. (2011), "Defining the Rogue State: A Definitional Comparative Analysis Within the Rationalist, Culturalist, and Structural Traditions," available at <http://jpi-nyu.org/wp-content/uploads/2011/02/Defining-the-Rogue-State-.pdf >, (accessed 23/1/2014): 12.
40 (Klare 1996; Tanter 1999; Hoyt 2000).
41 Baker 2003; Bilgin and Morton 2004: 169–180; Brooks 2005: 1164; Fukuyama, F. (2005), "Stateness First," *Journal of Democracy* 16(1): 84.
42 Fund for Peace (2011), "The Failed States Index 2010," available at <www.fundforpeace.org/global/?q=fsi-grid2010>, (accessed 22/10/2015); Fund for Peace (2011), "The Failed States Index 2009," available at <www.fundforpeace.org/global/?q=fsi-grid2009>, (accessed 20/10/2015).
43 Call, C. T. (2008), "The Fallacy of the 'Failed State," *Third World Quarterly*, 29(8): 1492.
44 Fukuyama 2005: 86.
45 For example see: Bruinessen, M. V. (1986), "The Kurds Between Iran and Iraq," *MERIP Middle East Report* 141: 16; Wimmer 2004.
46 For example see: Moore, M. (2006), "The Ethics of Secession and Postinvasion Iraq," *Ethics & International Affairs* 20(1): 57; Chorev 2007: 7; O'Leary 2009: 143.
47 Natali, D. (2005), *The Kurds and the State: Evolving National Identity in Iraq, Turkey, and Iran*, New York: Syracuse University Press.
48 Gurr and Harff 2004: 23.
49 *Ibid.*: 19.
50 Smith, A. D. (2009), *Ethno-Symbolism and Nationalism: A Cultural Approach*, London: Routledge: 49.
51 McDowall, D. (2004), *A Modern History of the Kurds*. London: IB Tauris: 3.
52 Benedict Anderson (1991), *Imagined Communities: Reflections on the Origin and Spread of Nationalism*, New York: Palgrave Macmillan: 6.
53 *Ibid.*: 7.
54 Guibernau, M. (1999), *Nations Without States: Political Communities in a Global Age*, Cambridge: Polity Press: 125.
55 Cottam and Cottam 2001: 197.

3 The two contradictory nationhood projects in Iraq

An examination of the Iraqi and Kurdish nationhood projects shows that the Kurdish-Iraqi conflict lies in these two entities' respective statuses as a nation without a state (NWS in the case of Iraqi Kurdistan) and a non-nation state (NNS in the case of Iraq). Each of these two entities possesses a nationhood project that differs from and opposes the others to the extent that Iraq is unwilling to accommodate the Kurdish Nationhood Project (KNP), and the Kurds are unwilling to accept the Iraqi National Project (INP). The aim of the INP is to create a homogeneous and overarching Iraqi identity. To achieve such a homogenous identity, the INP was centred on two principles. The first was the abnegation of the Kurdish ethnic, national, and territorial identities in order to solidify one nation-state. The second principle was the Arab identity and the unitary integrity of Iraq. The KNP, by contrast, is based on the creation of a homogeneous Kurdistani identity and a sovereign independent Kurdish state. The Kurdish project is built on the perspective that the Kurds are a nation and eligible to establish their nation-state on their traditional homeland of Kurdistan. The Kurds constitute an NWS and their project is to establish an independent Kurdish nation-state in their historical homeland in present-day northern Iraq. Since the early years of the establishment of the Iraqi state, Kurdish nationalism with its nationhood project has become the main obstacle to the success of the INP. The irreconcilable and oppositional nature of the respective Kurdish and Iraqi nationhood projects were the main reasons underlying the Iraqi-Kurdish conflict, the emergence of three successive Kurdish (Kurdish quasi-states) since 1961, and the devolution of Iraqi status into a recognised quasi-state.

Iraqi Nationhood Project and the Kurds

Iraq's nationhood project has several ramifications. The first is the denial of Kurdish self-representation as a separate nation. Since the creation of the modern state of Iraq in the 1920s, in addition to the Arab identity of the country, the Iraqi Nationhood Project focus has been on the abnegation of Kurdish ethnicity and identity, assimilation of the Kurds into Arab society, the criminalisation of the Kurdish Nationalist Movement, and the delegitimisation of its nationhood project.

The abnegation of Kurdish ethnicity

One of the main elements of the Iraqi Nationhood Project was the abnegation of Kurdish ethnicity. Though Kurdish identity has been constitutionally recognised for decades, the separate ethnic identity of the Kurds was denied. The Kurds were commonly viewed as an ethnic minority inhabiting Arab land and perceived as potential Arabs. During the era of the monarchy, Iraq's mainstream media and state discourse officially refrained from using the words 'Kurds', 'Kurdish people', or 'ethnic Kurds'.[1] The Kurds were re-categorised as 'Kurdish elements' or 'northerners'.[2] After the monarchy, Iraqi official discourse and media outlets followed their predecessors' policies, denying the Kurdish people's separate national identity and their distinct ethnic heritage. One exemption, however, was Abd al-Karim Qasim, who seized power in a 1958 coup d'état and remained Iraqi prime minister until his death in 1963. He initially offered a degree of recognition to Kurdish rights. For example, he stated that Iraq is not only an Arab state, but an Arabo-Kurdish state. As a gesture to his belief that Iraq is an Arabo-Kurdish state, he introduced an article to the Iraqi constitution. Article 3 stated that "Arabs and Kurds are considered partners in this homeland." He also placed a yellow sun on the Iraqi national flag and a Kurdish dagger. Moreover, it was under Qasim's rule that, for the first time, a Kurdish party, namely the KDP, was officially licenced. However, he changed his discourse following the Kurdish rebellion in September 1961 to the extent that he denied the ethnic identity of the Kurds. He stated that the Kurds were not a nation or an ethnic group, and the term 'Kurd' historically had been used for Persian nomads.

Components of Iraqi ethno-symbolism include: the Arab and Islamic identity of the country, a shared Arabic-Islamic culture, and the integrated history associated with Mesopotamia and Islamic civilisation. The Iraqi Nationhood Project emphasises Iraqi identity, which rests on the idea that Iraqis are the direct descendants of the Sumerian, Babylonian, Assyrian, and Arab peoples. The Iraqi approach of reviving their ethnic past was designed to eliminate the Kurdish Nationhood Project and to impose its nationhood project on the Kurds. For example, while Kurds trace their origin back to the Medes, Qourties, and other Zagrossian ancient groups, Iraqi history textbooks describe these groups as invaders, barbarians, uncivilised, and the destroyers of the Mesopotamian civilisation. A similar trend was evident in the post-invasion Iraqi state. For example, the Iraqi textbook for year 10, while glorifying the Arabic, Islamic, and Mesopotamian civilisations and emphasising the Arab and Islamic identity of Iraq, avoids mentioning any trace of civilisations that prove the historical existence of the Kurds in Iraqi Kurdistan. The textbook even teaches most old towns and cities in Iraq and other Arab countries but avoids mentioning ancient Kurdish cities such as Kirkuk and Erbil. Similarly, *Principles of geography*, a textbook for year 10 emphasises the old civilisations of Mesopotamia and avoids mentioning any trace of the historical and/or the geographical existence of the Kurds in Iraq.[3] The Iraqi textbook for year 9 emphasises that Iraq has five great, proud, and distinct civilisations, which developed into the Sumerian, Akkadian, Babylonian, Assyrian, and Arab Islamic civilisations.[4] Though the

Iraqi textbooks do not demonise the Zagrossian civilisation, as has been a norm in the pre-invasion Iraq, they ignore the existence of these civilisations in today's Kurdistan region. Moreover, the Iraqi textbooks glorify Islamic conquests and the process of Arabisation and Islamisation of the conquered people.[5]

The Iraqi textbooks don't recognise the existence of the Zagrossian civilisation and overlook the existence of the Kurds in today's Iraq. It is noteworthy to mention that it is rare to find the terms 'Kurds', 'Kurdish', or 'Kurdistan' in most Iraqi textbooks in post-invasion Iraq which pertain to the study of Iraqi history, geography, culture, and society.[6] One exception is *The modern and contemporary history of the Arab countries*. The mention of the Kurds in this textbook, however, comes within the framework of the eternal existence of the Iraqi nation and motherland and its indivisible unity. The textbook explain how the Zahab Treaty signed between the Ottoman and Safavids in 1639 resulted in the division of many Kurdish tribes. The textbook, however, emphasises that what happened in 1639 was the division of the Iraqi soil and the loss of part of Iraqi land to Iran.[7]

Re-tribalisation of Kurdish society

The monarchy followed a conciliatory policy towards Kurdish landlords, religious leaders, and tribal leaders (hereafter *aghas*),[8] as well as attempted to reinstate their power and authority within Kurdish society. Initially, the British mandate passed separate legislation for the tribal areas that remained as law throughout the monarchy.[9] The British aim of these laws was to undo the detribalisation process of the *Tanzimat* reforms that were initiated by the Ottoman authorities and re-establish the tribal system.[10] These policies favouring traditional strata over the urban Kurds continued until the Kurdish uprising in 1991. The British and Iraqi re-tribalisation policy was strategically calculated. The Ottoman *Tanzimat* reforms of the nineteenth century were only partially implemented in Kurdistan.[11] After the creation of Iraq, the *aghas* still dominated Iraqi Kurdistan socio-economically and kept their privileged position in the local power structure. In contrast to the Arabised Kurds, they were an integral and essential part of the social, economic, and cultural life of rural Kurdistan. The status of the *aghas* put them in a highly awkward position. The state's interference in the daily life of the *aghas* might imply the loss of their socio-political power. The *aghas*, however, showed their staunch resistance to Iraqi penetration into their local communities and defended their semi-independent status. Tribal resistance to Iraqi centralisation policies had often resulted in tribal rebellions, as it did with the Barzani revolt of the early 1930s. This resistance presented a serious obstacle to the Iraqi state-building process and Iraq's goal to integrate the Kurds into the Iraqi state. Therefore, the eradication of the *aghas*' social and cultural base was vital for the state-building process and maintenance of Iraq's integrity. Baghdad, however, adopted a policy of reinstating the *aghas*' socio-political base.

By securing the *aghas*' loyalty, Baghdad aimed to gain support and legitimacy in the Kurdish countryside and limit the impact of the Kurdish Nationalist Movement. In other words, the policy of indirect rule in tribal areas was designed to pacify a significant part of Kurdish society, isolate Kurdish nationalism, and gain a modicum of legitimacy of Iraqi rule in Kurdistan. To that end, Iraq followed the policy of indirect rule in rural areas of Kurdistan. The *aghas* were one of the most influential groups in Kurdish society at that time. Accommodating the *aghas* was not perceived as a threat to Iraq's integrity. In order to gain legitimacy within Kurdish society, Baghdad followed the policy of accommodating them and offered them a modicum of autonomy and sovereignty. Iraq ceded sovereignty to the *aghas* in many crucial areas such as taxation, maintaining armed forces, and handling judicial issues. This policy was carried out by both the monarchy from 1925 to 1958 and the Ba'ath regime from 1968 to 2003. Tribal communities were permitted to maintain their *de facto* autonomy in rural Kurdistan during the monarchy. The *agha*, as head of the tribe, enjoyed undeniable authority over his areas of responsibility. The status that Kurdish tribes enjoyed can be described as tribal autonomy. These autonomous tribes possessed traditional boundaries that separated one from another. The area of an autonomous tribe was equal to that of a tribe's territory. Many autonomous tribes had an area that was equal to that of a state the size of Lebanon. For example, in the early 1930s, Sheikh Ahmed Barzani administered an area of 10,000 square kilometres.[12] The status of tribal communities was especially evident in their right to maintain their militias. Even during the mandate era, the *aghas* received arms and ammunition from the British.[13] In the early 1930s, for instance, the Jaf tribe alone had more than 2,500 militants and the confederation of Barzani under Sheikh Ahmed had 10,000 fighters.[14] These militias were under the direct command of their *aghas* and were not organised by or administered from Baghdad. Hence the state ceded its right to monopolise the legitimate use of force in Kurdistan.

Jurisdiction was another area in which tribal communities enjoyed autonomy. Tribes were excluded from the jurisdiction of Iraqi courts; the absolute jurisdictional authority was given to the *aghas*. The head of the autonomous tribes retained the right to settle civil and criminal cases including land and other local disputes of the community.[15] Fiscal autonomy was another sign of the autonomous status of the tribes. In tax affairs, certain *aghas* whose tribes enjoyed autonomy retained dual rights: on the national level they enjoyed special tax benefits while on the local level they extracted taxation rights.[16] Tribes also retained the right to regulate commercial affairs in their areas. The Iraqi state gave up many important symbols of sovereignty including the monopoly of the legitimate use of force, governmental jurisdiction, and the power to collect taxes from Kurdistan. The majority of tribal communities (whether a single tribe or a confederation of tribes) enjoyed a degree of administrative autonomy.

In the 1980s, Iraq allowed indirect rule in the collection camps (*Mujama'at*) and towns of Kurdistan. This indirect rule took several forms. First, the conscription system was replaced by the *Jash* system. The tribal system was revived in Kurdistan and almost all tribes were organised into one or more battalions with the *aghas* appointed as commanders. Each Kurdish tribe was organised into one battalion or more, and in principle, each battalion constituted some 1,000 irregular troops. The tribal chieftains (*aghas*) were appointed as commanders of their respective units and granted the title of *mustashar* (consultant). Baghdad conceded a degree of sovereignty to the *aghas* who acted as middlemen between the *Mujama'at* and the populated towns and state. They were responsible for the local security of their areas.

Assimilation and Arabisation of the Kurds

Another significant element of the INP is the assimilation and Arabisation of the Kurds. This policy was designed to create a homogeneous and overarching Iraqi identity. This was often done by forcibly assimilating the Kurds into Arab society and/or crafting an Arab identity for them. The Kurds were viewed as 'prospective Arabs' by successive Iraqi regimes. The 'rediscovery' of Kurdish Arab origins was used to constrain the Kurds' self-representation as a separate nation. Sati' al-Husri, who is considered as a father of pan-Arab nationalism and the engineer of the Iraqi education policy, laid the theoretical foundation for the systematic Arabisation of the Kurds. His Arabisation project was based on two pillars: 'finding' the Arab origin of the Kurds and legislating their forced Arabisation. According to him, an Arab was one who inhabited Arab lands and spoke Arabic regardless of origin or race. From his viewpoint Iraq was an Arab country, and since many Kurds do indeed speak Arabic, Arab identity extended to them as well regardless of ethnic origin, self-identification, or cooperation.[17] Abd al-Salam Arif, Qasim's successor, revived al-Husri's ideologies and conducted a propaganda campaign that reconstructed the Arab origins of the Kurds. Several books were published during his rule including al-Fil's, which emphasised the Arab origin of the Kurds who supposedly immigrated from the Arabian Peninsula to their present homeland.[18]

When the Ba'ath came to power in 1968, the policies of Kurdish assimilation and denial of Kurdish identity continued. Constructing a convincing myth of the Arab origins of the Kurds became a permanent enterprise in the official Ba'ath agenda that controlled Iraq between 1968 and 2003. According to senior Ba'ath leader and historian Hani al-Fukaiki, establishing Arab roots for the Kurds was one of the primary missions of the party since its beginning.[19] In his research on the Arab origins of the Kurds, Ba'ath researcher Naji Maruf provided detailed information on the 'Arab background' of the Kurds.[20] In 1989, the Ba'athist-affiliated *al-Watan al-Arabi* magazine published two so-called scientific research articles that purported to 're-discover' the Arab roots of all Kurdish tribes.[21] These articles were translated into Kurdish and published by the state-owned magazine *Roshinbiri Nwe*.[22] They emphasised the superiority of the Arabs as a nation vis-à-vis the Kurds, who supposedly lacked a distinct ethnic heritage. The belief in the existence of Arab elements among the Kurds was concocted to superimpose Arab identity upon the Kurdish identity.

From the Ba'ath Party's perspective, the Kurds are potential members of the Arab ethno-cultural community. According to Article 10 of the Ba'ath constitution, "an Arab is anyone that lives in or wants to live on Arab lands, secure affiliation with the Arab nation and whose language is Arabic.[23] Thus, the three Ba'athist criteria for being 'Arab' was (1) one's ability to speak Arabic, (2) living on Arab land, and (3) affiliating with the Arab nation. These criteria deserve further investigation. Language was the first Ba'athist criterion for being considered as part of the Arab nation. How this criterion was meant to assimilate the Kurds is clearly described by Khayrullah Tulfah.[24] He emphasised that anyone who dwelled within the Arab homeland and can speak Arabic is an Arab regardless of ethnic origin or desire. Since the creation of Iraq in the 1920s, the Arabic language has been the compulsory language of instruction in all schools and levels of study in Kurdistan. Though often only partially carried out, at least until 1991, most Kurds who attended public schools or served time in compulsory military service were considered to be bilingual. Since they spoke Arabic, they were counted as potential Arabs.

The second Ba'athist criterion for being considered as part of the Arab nation was living on Arab land. According to Article 7 of the Ba'ath constitution, "the Arab homeland was a stretch of land inhabited by the Arab nation that extended between the Taurus Mountains and the mountains of Bstquih and the Gulf of Basra."[25] Accordingly, Iraqi Kurdistan was indisputably 'Arab land'. It is noteworthy that not only the Ba'ath constitution, but all Iraqi constitutions ratified between 1958 and 2003, emphasised (i) the Arab identity of Iraq and (ii) Iraq is part of the 'greater Arab nation'.[26] Thus, as residents of 'Arab land', the Kurds met the second Ba'athist criterion for being considered 'Arab'.

The third Ba'athist criterion for being considered 'Arab' was one's affiliation to the Arab nation. Michel Aflaq (1910–1989), the founder of the Ba'ath Party, the founding father of Pan-Arabism, and the mentor of Saddam Hussein, left a significant mark in this regard. In Aflaq's attempt to find a theoretical basis for the Arab origin of the Kurds, he categorised minorities into two groups: (1) those with distinctive and clear ethnic characteristics, and (2) those with no specific characteristics. The former was comprised of 'special nations/ethnic groupings' (al-Qawmiya al-Khasa) and the latter was comprised of non-ethnic/national groups. According to Aflaq's schema, to be considered as a 'special ethnic/national group' the group must possess its own land, history, and civilisation. Since the Kurds had lived on Arab land within Arab society for centuries, they failed the test of 'possessing their own land'. He also argued that there had not been a single Kurdish rebellion in history.[27] Aflaq stressed that these people lived within and were integrated into Arab society while defending Arab land. Therefore, he claimed, the Kurds had no unique history but shared history in common with the Arabs. Accordingly, the Kurds failed to create their own civilisation, but instead accommodated to Arab civilisation and adopted its values as their own.[28] Thus, for Arab nationalists, the Kurds were neither a special nation/ethnic group nor a nation different from the Arab nation.[29] Aflaq concluded that because of their deep integration into and intermingling with Arab history and participation in Arab glories, the Kurds gained a special status. This meant that the Kurds were Arab Muslim citizens like other Arab Muslims and there was no difference between them. Simply put, the Kurds are Arabs.[30]

On many occasions Saddam Hussein made claims similar to those of his mentor, Aflaq. He stated that the "[Arabs and Kurds] are Iraqis and they belong to the Arab nation's tradition, heritage, glory and honour, and they look forward to carrying out their role honourably in the service of the Arab nation."[31] In 1979, Hussein stated that to be a Kurd did not contradict being part of the Arab nation.[32] Hence the Kurds were Arabs by nature of their ability to speak Arabic, their residency on Arab land, and their affiliation with the Arab nation, as claimed by Arab nationalists. Thus, ever since its foundation, the Ba'ath Party attempted to legitimise the assimilation, accommodation, and Arabisation of the Kurds.

Several Ba'ath policies derived from the stylised imagined idea of the Arab origin of the Kurds. The first was the forced assimilation of the Kurds through the 'nationality correction' policy. In 1977, after almost a decade of Ba'athist totalitarian rule in Iraq, Aflaq assessed the Arabisation process. He conceded that some minorities inhabiting Arab land had retained their Arab identity, while other segments of the population had not been fully integrated into the Arab nation.[33] Following his direction, several Kurdish religious groups and tribes were forced to change their identities to 'Arab'. Consequently, in an official statistic that was published in 1977, these groups had been officially and forcibly registered as Arabs. The main target of this process was the non-Muslim Kurdish religious groups such as Yezidis, Kakays, and Christians.[34] Arab identity was also superimposed upon Kurdish tribes inhabiting mixed areas such as the Shabaks, Gargars, Salayi, Gezh, Palani, and Kikan.

By 2001 the correction of ethnicity or nationality became Iraq's official policy. The Revolutionary Command Council (RCC) officially introduced the 'nationality correction' code which supposedly 'corrected' the ethnic identity of the Kurds and other minorities.[35] These minorities were ordered to avow that they had been mistakenly registered as non-Arabs and that they now wished to reclaim their Arab origins.[36] Although the policy was designed for all non-Arab minorities of Iraq, it was used primarily against the Kurds.[37] By 2001, one-third of the Kurds lived in areas and cities that were ruled by the Iraqi government; therefore at least one-third of the Kurds had faced these measures. Harsh punishment including confiscation of lands and properties, deportation, displacement, and imprisonment was applied to those unwilling to change their identities.[38] Prior to this, another decree was issued by the RCC in 1988 that prohibited the Arabs from changing their ethnic identity to Kurdish or any other identity. In addition to the rejection of one's appeal to change his/her nationality from Arabic to Kurdish, the resistor could face at least one year of imprisonment for not changing his/her identity to Arab.[39] Thus, one of the main ramifications of the Iraqi Nationhood Project was the denial of the Kurds' self-representation as a separate nation and/or separate ethnic group.

Post-invasion Iraqi nation-builders followed their predecessor in considering the Kurdish land as an Arab land. Textbooks present a prime example in this regard. The grade 8 Iraqi textbook, for example, describes the greater Arab homeland in the same way as it has been described by Article 7 of the Ba'ath constitution. Similar to the Ba'athist constitution, the textbook emphasises that the Arab homeland starts with the Torus and Zagros mountain ranges that extend between the Iraqi border with Iran and Turkey. The Kurdistan region's lakes, mountains, and valleys were used as examples to explain different geographical aspects of the Arab homeland.[40] Thus, based on post-invasion Iraqi textbooks, the Kurdistan region is part of the greater Arab homeland.

By considering the Kurdistan region as part of the Arab homeland, post-invasion Iraqi textbooks carefully avoid using the term 'Kurdistan region'. Instead, the term '*Shimal al-Iraq*' (northern Iraq) is used for that region. Post-invasion Iraqi textbooks in this regard borrowed from the Ba'ath-era textbooks the term '*Shimal al-Iraq*' (northern Iraq) to describe or indicate cities, towns, rivers, and mountains of the Kurdistan region.[41] *The geography of the Arab homeland*, a textbook for grade 8, is an example that uses the topography, natural resources, and agricultural products of the Kurdish region as examples of the richness of the Arab homeland. Explaining the tobacco product in the greater Arab homeland, the textbook highlights that:

> Tobacco is grown in areas where water is available during the summer season. It is cultivated in northern Iraq, especially in Sulaimania area and in the region of Latakia and Tartus in Syria and in the north of Tunisia, on the slopes of a mountain in Lebanon and Jordan. The total production of tobacco is about 59,000 tons which is used in cigarettes industry.[42]

Thus, post-invasion Iraqi students are taught that, similar to Latakia and Tartu of northern Tunisia and the mountain regions of Lebanon and Jordan, northern Iraq is also part of a greater Arab homeland and its agricultural production is viewed as part of the richness of the Arab homeland. By using the term 'northern Iraq' for the Kurdish region, the textbook denies the separate status and identity of that region. Instead, the Kurdistan region is viewed as an integrated part of Iraq and therefore part of the greater Arab homeland.

Another example of identifying the Kurdistan region as northern Iraq and part of the greater Arab homeland by post-invasion Iraqi textbooks is *Natural geography* for grade 11, which focuses on the natural geography of the greater Arab homeland. On many occasions, the textbook uses the term 'northern Iraq' to explain some aspects of the Arab homeland's natural geography. For example, when explaining how the Earth's motion has contributed to the formation of the Arab homeland, the textbook states that ground motions are torsional or refractive, which may be represented by former valleys that contained concave folds, as is the case in the valleys and Sindi Shahrazour and Ranya in northern Iraq.[43] The map of the greater Arab homeland, taught in post-invasion Iraqi textbooks, shows the similar vision of the Ba'ath Party of the greater Arab homeland borders which include the Zagrossian and Torous ranges (i.e. the entire Kurdistan region is considered as part of the Arab homeland). Similarly, the lakes of Dukan and Darbandikhan in Sulaimania, and the oil fields of Kirkuk, are used as examples of the richness of the Arab homeland in terms of natural resources.[44] Avoiding the use of 'Kurdistan region', describing the region as northern Iraq and part of the Arab homeland, means that despite the dominance of Shias in post-invasion Iraq, the Iraqi Nationhood Project has basically remained the same since the 1920s, namely the integrity, unitary, and Arab identity of the country. It also means that the post-invasion nation-builders follow their predecessors' strategies of denying the existence of a separate identity of the Kurdistan region, and of imposing the Iraqi and Arab identity on the region.

The Iraqi textbooks also emphasise the existence of Iraq as an administration unit throughout the Ottoman era. *The modern and contemporary history of Arab countries*, a textbook for year 12 students, is an example. The book teaches that the loyalty of Iraqi people to Iraq goes back many centuries. For example, it emphasises that during the Ottoman era, the Iraqi people's loyalty was to Iraq and not to the Ottomans.[45] Emphasising the deep-rooted loyalty to the country during the Ottoman era, the book suggests that only those *Walies* (governors) of Iraq who were successful were chosen by Iraqi people and whose loyalty was to Iraq rather than to the Ottoman Sultans. The book also teaches that Iraq, including the Kurdistan region, had always been a united country and that the division of Iraq was created by the Ottomans in 1864, when the country was divided into three *Wilayet* (governorates) of Mosul, Baghdad, and Basra. Despite this administrative division, Baghdad remained the capitol city of Iraq. Though intermittently, both Mosul and Basra *Wilayets* were reporting to Baghdad rather than to Istanbul.[46] Whether these teachings of Iraqi history are facts or fictions is irrelevant; they show the nature of the Iraqi Nationhood Project in post-invasion Iraq and its denial of the status of the Kurds as a separate national and territorial group.

Delegitimisation and criminalisation of Kurdish nationalism

Another ramification of the Iraqi Nationhood Project was the delegitimisation and criminalisation of Kurdish nationalism. Iraq's strategy was to eliminate the Kurdish Nationhood Project and to impose its nationhood project on the Kurds. Since the early years of the creation of Iraq in the 1920s, the Kurds' quest for nationhood with a separate territory was rejected, suppressed, and criminalised as the Kurdish plotters conspired with the enemies of the Arab nation. The Kurdish issue was perceived as a security issue and threat to the very nature and existence of the Iraqi state. Under the monarchy, Kurdish nationalist claims were perceived as part of a British conspiracy against the Iraqi state and its Arab identity. This was the main discourse of both pro- and anti-British Iraqi politicians.[47] Others, however, described the Kurdish revolts as communist movements.[48] Post-monarchy regimes followed the same norm. Qasim, for example, maintained that "all previous Kurdish revolts in Iraq were instigated by imperialism".[49] In 1966, President Abdul-Salam Arif of Iraq called the leader of the Kurdish rebellion (1961–1975), Mustafa Barzani, a "puppet of imperialism".[50]

The Ba'ath Party further developed this notion and adopted it as its official stance when dealing with the Kurdish issue. Aflaq, for instance, argued that while the Kurds were part of the Arab nation, the Kurdish patriotic movement should be considered as a legitimate and original part of the Arab revolution against imperialism. According to his ideals, the Arabs emerged as nationalists and a patronising 'big brother', while the Kurds were portrayed as dwellers of the Arab homeland. Therefore, the Kurds' only right or purpose was to be Iraqi patriots and defend the Arab nation and cause.[51] According to this view, the Kurdish patriotic movement of Iraq should not be seen as contradictory to the Arab revolution. If it were, it would require an imperialistic interpretation to discredit it. Aflaq further insisted that Kurdish nationalist and ethnic movements only began when Western imperialism entered the Arab homeland. He insisted that Kurdish nationalism was an imperialist legacy; the distinctiveness of Kurdish ethnicity, language, and history was also seen as an imperialist project designed to divide Arab countries.[52] Thus, Ba'athist discourse reconstructed binary nationalisms by superimposing a 'superior Arab nationalism' as a historical fact and by portraying the 'artificial' and 'treacherous' Kurdish Nationalist Movement as a counterfeit movement created by imperialistic forces against the Arab nation.

The Kurdish Nationalist Movement rejected the Iraqi patriotic and pan-Arab nationalist principles and ideals, and instead developed their own Kurdish brand of nationalism and patriotism. Kurdish nationalism, as will be explained, remained the main challenge to Iraqi integrity and its Arab identity. The hegemonic discourse of the Iraqi state involved the accusation of the Kurds as being in diabolical alliance with enemies of the Arab nation, namely, imperialism, Zionism, and Iran.[53] The Iraqi mainstream media and official discourse often refrained from identifying or mentioning the Kurdish parties or leaders by name. Whenever the Kurdish question was mentioned in Iraqi state discourse, Kurdish nationalists were portrayed as traitors, agents of imperialism, plotters, conspirators, collaborators with the enemy, criminals, and saboteurs. The areas controlled by Kurdish rebellions were described as 'pocket[s] of foreign agents', 'the other Israel', 'the second Israel', and/or 'the offspring of treachery'.[54] Viewed this way, the war against Kurdish nationalism became associated with the Arab war against imperialism and Zionism.[55] Thus, another policy that derived from the Iraqi Nationhood Project was the criminalisation of the Kurdish Nationalist Movement due to its supposedly imperialist backing.

Elimination of Kurdish nationalism

Another set of policies was the physical elimination of the Kurdish Nationalist Movement. Since the very beginning, Kurdish nationalism challenged the state-sponsored nation-building process, the legitimacy of Baghdad's authority in Kurdistan, and the integrity of Iraq. To contain Kurdish nationalism, all successive Iraqi regimes followed policies of exclusion, suppression, and criminalisation of Kurdish nationalism. Throughout the mandate and monarchy periods, all political parties of the urban Kurds had been banned. The Kurds were also prevented from founding democratic institutions, Kurdish cultural associations, and civil society trade unions, as well as from offering free elections.[56] The Kurds were thus deprived of the legal political channels and proper venues of expression of their ideas. The Kurdistan region was also largely excluded from the economic, political, and military institutions of Iraq.

Iraq has often accused the Kurds of being traitors, clients of Iraq's enemies, imperialists, Zionists, pro-Iranian, and other denigrating names. During the early years of the monarchy, the Kurds were accused of being agents of colonialism. The 'Kurdish question' is portrayed as being created by the British to weaken Iraq and its national unity.[57] Not only Kurdish rebellions, but many Kurdish MPs who accepted the Kurdistan region as being part of Iraq faced these accusations after making relatively moderate demands. Kurdish leaders appealed to the Iraqi prime minister in 1945 to explain how the conspiracy theory was used by different Iraqi rulers in their dealings with the Kurds. They complained that:

> When [pro-Nazi] Rashid Ali's government declared war on the British, every nationalist Kurd was regarded as a British spy and agent by that government. Later, when things returned to normal, the Kurds were accused of harbouring Nazi ideologies and of being of German origin.[58]

Iraqi historians and officials accused Kurdish nationalists during the 1930s of being encouraged by Germany. It was claimed that the Hiwa Party, a Kurdish nationalist organisation established in 1939, was created by the British and that Barzani had 'special relations' with the British.[59] These accusations were made despite British participation in suppressing the Barzani rebellions of 1931–1932 and 1943–1945.

Referring to the Kurds as puppets of the 'imperialists' was part of the post-monarch political discourse and the accusation has been used by all successive Iraqi governments. The Ba'ath Party described the Kurdish rebellion of 1961–1975 as a reactionary and imperialistic insurgency encouraged by imperialist circles. The Ba'ath insisted that the Barzani anti-revolution (i.e. Ba'ath rule) did not result from Barzani's personal decision but was a major attack of the imperialists and Zionists against the Iraqi state. The aim of the Kurdish insurgency, according to the Ba'ath Party, was to drain, weaken, destroy, or subjugate Iraq to American imperialism. The Ba'ath also insisted that Iraq's war against the Kurds was a fight against reactionary insurgency and Zionist imperialists who supported Barzani.[60]

The Iraqi perception of the Kurds as plotters, conspirators, and enemies of the Arab nation justified sustained state-sponsored violence and militaristic strategies against the Kurds. The Kurdish issue was perceived as a security threat to the very nature of the Iraqi state. To contain this threat, state violence and militaristic strategies levelled against the Kurds prevailed and became an important part of Iraq's Kurdish policy. The state-sponsored military violence against the Kurds came in the form of the genocidal operation known as the *Anfal* operations. It involved the gassing of civilians, destruction of over 4,000 Kurdish villages, displacement and resettling of 1.5 million Kurds, and depopulation of 45,000 out of 75,000 square kilometres of Kurdistan.[61] Kurdish-Iraqi relations were dominated by constant, systematic, and widespread violence by the Iraqis. The Iraqi perception of the Kurds as plotters, conspirators, and enemies justified this sustained violence and unrelenting oppression. These elements of the Iraqi Nationhood Project show the irreconcilable and oppositional nature of the respective Kurdish

46 *The two contradictory nationhood projects*

and Iraqi nationhood projects. They are also important contributing elements to the constant state of conflict between Iraq and Kurdistan and the evolution of a separate Kurdish Nationhood Project.

Kurdish Nationhood Project

Kurdayeti was constructed with the perspective that the Kurds as a people could qualify for, but are deprived from, achieving nation-state status. The Kurdish Nationhood Project (KNP) was designed with nationhood status and an independent state in mind. Kurdish nationalism and its national project emphasised several fundamental principles.

A separate collective memory

One significant element of the KNP is the rediscovery of a form of ethnosymbolism that differentiates them from Iraq and contradicts the Iraqi official national narratives. As explained previously, the INP emphasised integrated history associated with Mesopotamia and the Islamic civilisation. To deconstruct the Iraqi official narratives, however, the Kurds promoted a self-image that emphasised their shared culture, a common myth of ancestry, and an integrated history associated with the Zagrossian territory that stretched into antiquity. Based on the Kurdish narrative, the Kurds share a distinctive culture, a common myth of descent (ancestry), and an integrated history associated with Kurdistan. Kurdish nationalism emphasises that the Iraqi Kurds and Arabs never shared a common memory, ancestry, culture, language, history, territory, or national identity. The Kurds are a distinct people who shared a culture, possessed a common myth of descent (ancestry), and had an integrated history associated with Kurdistan. Kurdish scholars argue that the Kurds, as an identifiable ethnic group, have existed for more than 2,500 years under related names such as Kardu, Karda, Kurti, Qurtie, Cordueni, and Gordyeni. The Kurds also suggest that the ethnogenesis of the Kurdish people is believed to have started as early as 2500–1000 BC and the Kurdish language as an independent language goes back to at least 700–300 BC. From their perspective, the Kurds belong to a pure racial stock and the phenomenon of miscegenation has not significantly affected them, as it has other ethnic groups.[62]

Kurdish nationalists have revived and sustained their pre-Islamic myths of the construction of the Kurdish nation. For example, the symbol of the sun of Mithraism and Zoroastrianism has been adopted as the Kurds' national symbol and is placed in the centre of the Kurdish flag.[63] Legislation no. 14 of the Kurdistan National Assembly (KNA) in 1999 ratified the Kurdistan national flag that "reflected the feats and glories, the history and struggle and aspirations of its people".[64] According to the legislation, the Kurdistani flag reflects the pride and dignity of that people and symbolises the home of that people. Article 6 ordered the Iraqi flag to fly alongside the Kurdistani flag on occasions where required, and only after the recognition of the Kurdish right of federalism. The Kurdistani flag was a symbol of the status of the Kurds as a separate nation (rather than a minority within Iraq), with its own history that goes beyond the borders of the Iraqi state. According to the legislation, the flag's red colour "symbolise[d] the martyrs of the Kurdish liberation movement". The Kurdish flag represented and continues to represent for the Kurds one of the most important symbols of the nation-building process and the crafting of a separate identity for Kurdistan.

Another important symbol of the nation-building process is the Kurdish national day *Nawroz*. In 1997, the Kurdistan National Assembly (Parliament of Kurdistan Region) in its Legislation no. 2 promulgated *Nawroz* as the Kurds national holiday. *Nawroz* is another pre-Islamic myth. It represents the myth of the Kurds' victory over tyranny in 700 BC.[65] It also represents both the Kurdish New Year and calendar. *Nawroz* has been accepted throughout greater Kurdistan as their national day. In 1958, *Nawroz* was even recognised by the central government as a national holiday, albeit by a different name.[66]

Another important symbol of the Kurdish Nationhood Project is the Kurdish national anthem, known in Kurdish as *Ey Reqib*. The Kurdish national anthem was first created and adopted by the Kurdish Republic of Mahabad in Iranian Kurdistan in 1946.[67] The KRG described *Ey Reqib* as "a mirror of the thoughts and the conscience of all segments and strata of the Kurdistani nation".[68] Moreover, *Ey Reqib* emphasises that "We [Kurds] are the children of the Medes and Cyaxares,[69] Both our faith and religion are our homeland." Hence, similar to the sun of Zoroastrianism represented in the Kurdish flag, by tracing Kurds to the Medes and Zagrossian civilisations, *Ey Reqib* abnegated any Kurdish relations to Iraq.

The establishment of the Median Empire in 700 BC is the start of the Kurdish calendar.[70] The Kurds' belief that they are the offspring of the Medes[71] and the heirs of the Median legacy is emphasised in the Kurdish national anthem. Finally, the legend of Kawa the Smith and his 'victory' over Zuhak's tyranny[72] have inspired the Kurdish struggle for freedom and independence.[73] This past glory of the pre-Islamic Zagrossian civilisation is firmly rooted in the Kurds' common memory. A popular belief among Kurdish scholars is that their origins date to ancient times and refer to those who lived in the Zagros-upper-Mesopotamian region since antiquity.[74] The KNM ceaselessly sustained the pre-Islamic myths to homogenise mentalities and to construct an overarching identity for the Kurdish nation.

Kurds' interpretations of the major historical events of the twentieth century also negate the Iraqi narratives. One of the most significant historical events in contemporary Iraq is the 1920 revolution against the colonial power. The revolution has become the founding myth for Arab Iraqis and has rendered their myth and imagination. However, scholars of the Kurds portrayed the revolution as Iraqi-Arab revolution and not a Kurdish one. By contrast, the uprising of 6 September 1930 in the city of Sulaimani became a national myth for Kurdish nationalists. On 6 September 1930, mass demonstrations had been arranged in Sulaimani, a Kurdish city. Some 60 protestors were killed by the Iraqi police, and tens were either wounded or arrested.[75] The uprising known as 'the Dark Day of September Sixth' is a milestone in the Kurdish Nationhood Project in contemporary Iraq. Many famous and well-respected Kurdish poets of the time wrote poems for the uprising.[76] In addition, *The new and modern history*, a textbook for year 12 Kurdistan region students, describes the Dark Day as a modern-day symbol of Kurdish resistance and victimisation.[77] Thus, on the one hand, the Kurds have retained their own symbols, memories, myths, and values. On the other hand, the Iraqi state has failed to homogenise the country's population and to unify them around shared values, symbols, myths, and memories based on Mesopotamian and Islamic mythology.

Kurdistan as a separate imagined national identity

The KNP was constructed with the perspective that Kurdistan and Iraq comprise two separate homelands and Kurdistan has been a separate national identity throughout its history. To deconstruct the Iraqi official narratives, Iraq is portrayed as though it never served as the national identity for the Kurds. The identity of the Iraqi has been 'artificially' imposed upon the Kurds and it is wholly and unequivocally unacceptable. Kurdistan is represented as an 'authentic' national identity and as central to their imagined and real national identity. Kurdish nationalism emphasised that the Kurdish homeland had never been part of Iraq prior to the creation of the modern state of Iraq. Kurdistan as the national identity of the Kurds precedes the creation of the modern Iraqi state. Prior to the creation of the state of Iraq, Kurdistan was a well-established national territory of the Kurds and their national identity was Kurdish.

The first generation of Kurds in the new Iraqi state inherited and transferred the ideals of the Kurdish nation and the Kurdistani national identity from one generation to the next. In 1931, Sheikh Mahmud wrote that the Kurds lived on their own land and that southern Kurdistan had never been part of Mesopotamia or a part of Arab land and territories.[78] He also labelled the Iraqi state and government as an Arab state and government and the Iraqi army as an Arab army.[79] Similarly, in 1931, Tofiq Wehbi stated that southern Kurdistan was the historical homeland of the Kurds, which had never been part of Arab land, and which had never been ruled by Arabs – even during the caliphate period.[80] He insisted that the annexation of Kurdistan to Iraq was illegitimate and unjustified. He protested against identifying the Kurds as Iraqis, explaining that it would be as wrong to identify them as Iraq as it would be to identify an Irish person as 'English'.[81] More than eight decades later, Jalal Talabani[82] reiterated the League of Nations Commission's claims that Kurdistan had never been part of Iraq and the Arab part of Iraq did not encompass Kurdistan. He further argued that, at the Paris Peace Conference, the separate homeland of Kurdistan received similar treatment and equal status as Arabia, the Arab homeland, and Armenia.[83] He also pointed out that in all Ottoman documents and early Arab geography textbooks that had been used in Egyptian schools, Kurdistan was shown as a separate country from Iraq. For Talabani, 'Iraq' was a strange and unknown name for the inhabitants of Kurdistan and the Kurdish people in Iraq were part of the Kurdistani nation.[84]

The two contradictory nationhood projects 49

Kurdistan has always been identified as a separate geographic and political entity in Kurdish political party literature and official documents. In 1960, *Khabat* newspaper, the mouthpiece of the Kurdistan Democratic Party (KDP), published an article suggesting that historically the term 'Iraq' was used to describe a land much smaller than what is known today as Iraq.[85] *Khabat* further explained that Kurdistan had never been part of Arab land, and the part annexed to Iraq is part of Kurdistan. *Khabat* stressed that the term 'Iraq', as a political entity, was formed after WWI by forcible annexation of 'Southern Kurdistan to Iraq by the British'. From *Khabat's* perspective, Iraq consisted of 'Southern Kurdistan and the Arab part, Mesopotamia'. Finally, *Khabat* re-emphasised that only the Arab part of Iraq is part of the greater Arab homeland, and the Kurdish part was a part of the greater Kurdistan region.[86] This view is shared by most Kurdish nationalists.[87] Kurdistan is considered by the KLM to have always been a separate homeland from Arab Iraq.

Moreover, Kurdish historians and scholars insist that the term 'Iraq' had been used historically for two different, albeit adjacent, regions. The term Iraq-i Arabi or Iraq al-Arab had been used to refer to a region in modern southern Iraq. The term Iraqi-Ajami or Iraq al-Ajam, which means 'non-Arab Iraq', was used to describe modern southern Iran. The Kurds also argue that contemporary northern Iraq was referred to as *Bilad al-Akrad* ('the land of the Kurds') and in later centuries as *Kurdistani Jenubi* (southern Kurdistan).[88] According to Izady, the land of the Kurds has been called 'Kurdistan' for nearly a millennium.[89] Nebez, however, states that the first map that shows 'Bilad al-Kurd', or the land of the Kurds, goes back to 1073.[90] *The new and modern history*, a textbook for year 12 Kurdistan region students, emphasises that contemporary northern Iraq was referred to as *Bilad al-Akrad* ('the land of the Kurds') and in later centuries as *Kurdistani Jenubi* (southern Kurdistan).[91] When the Iraqi state was created, these geographical, territorial and administrative separations still applied. The commission that was founded by the League of Nations to determine the statutes of Mosul *Vilayet* or 'Kurdistan' discovered that historically modern Iraq was comprised of and known by three different regions: Arab Iraq, al-Jezire, and Kurdistan. They also found that throughout history the inhabitants of Kurdistan never considered themselves to be Iraqi, nor were they ever known or referred to as Iraqi.[92] Thus, from the Kurds' perspective, the Kurdish homeland had never been part of Iraq or a part of an Arab land and/or territory, and 'Iraqi' had never served as the national identity of the Kurds prior to the creation of the modern state of Iraq. Kurdistan and Iraq consisted of two separate homelands: the Arab part of Iraq was part of the greater Arab homeland and Iraqi Kurdistan was part of the greater Kurdistan region.

The Kurds perspective that Kurdistan as the national identity of the Kurds precedes the creation of the modern Iraqi state is supported by the work of several primordial nationalists. Sharafkhan Bitlisi's book, *Sharafname*, written in 1597, offers a history of the Kurdish ruling families that goes back for centuries. Bitlisi's work presents the first documented conscious use of the term 'Kurd' by the Kurds themselves. His book, written to present the Kurdish case to neighbouring

50 *The two contradictory nationhood projects*

nations, has revived and sustained the medieval myths in order to construct a distinct origin of Kurdish ethnicity and to demonstrate the uniqueness of Kurdish identity.[93] Bitlisi's historical inquiry is confined to the Kurdish people and includes all Kurds, regardless of geographic distribution, political orientation, administrative status, loyalties, dialects, and religion. His 'others' include Arabs, Turks, Persians, and Armenians.[94] Thus Bitlisi distinguished clear boundaries of inclusion and exclusion.

Bitlisi is probably the first Kurd to associate the term 'Kurd' with a geographical territory. For him, Kurdistan referred to a territory that belonged to ethnic Kurds irrespective of political and/or administrative boundaries. He confidently outlines the boundary of Kurdistan:

> The boundaries of the Kurdish land begin from the sea of Hurmiz [the Persian Gulf] and stretch on an even line to the end of Malatya and Marash [south of today's Turkey]. The north of this line includes Fars, Iraq-i Ajem [southern Iran], Azerbaijan, Little and Great Armenia. To the south, there is Iraq-i Arab [southern Iraq], Musul and Diyarbakir.[95]

Thus, for Bitlisi, Kurdistan is the defined homeland of the Kurds. Kurds easily can claim that the imagined national identity of the Kurds existed long before the creation of Iraq.

Nearly a century later, in 1695, Ahmedi Khani's Kurdish romantic epic, *Mem û Zîn*, made an even clearer boundary of inclusion versus exclusion that was motivated by his extreme feelings and consciousness of 'Kurdishness'. Khani hails the Kurds as a visible tower among the Georgians, Arabs, Turks, and Persians.[96] More than being distinct from these 'other' nations, Khani portrays the Kurds as surrounded, targeted, and even oppressed by the Turks and the Persians. He represents the Kurds as being at war with these nations and complains about the Kurds' failure to establish an independent state. He explicitly calls the Kurdish rulers 'princes' that must unite, select a king among themselves and establish a united Kurdish state. Khani instructs the Kurdish rulers to unify in order to reverse the subjugated status of the Kurdish people, and instead to subjugate the Turks and Persians to the Kurds.[97]

Two important figures of the nineteenth century are Sheikh Ubeydeulla-i Nehri and Haji Qadri Koyi. In 1880, Nehri led the largest movement in Kurdish history by joining together the Kurds of the then-Ottoman and Persian Kurdistan area. He depicted the inhabitants of Kurdistan as a nation apart. He also suggested that Kurdish customs, beliefs, and religion were different from that of the Arabs, Turks, and Persians, and therefore they should enjoy an independent state.[98] Haji Qadri Koyi (1817–d. 1892), a nationalist poet of the late nineteenth century, draws on Bitlisi's vision of a Kurdish national identity and Khani's call for an independent state in his nationalist poems. However, unlike Khani, Koyi's vision and call to unify in order to establish a Kurdish state was not limited to Kurdish rulers; it was directed to ordinary Kurds as well.[99] The great respect that the Kurds have maintained for Bitlisi, Khani, Nehri, and Koyi as pioneers of Kurdish nationalism remains to the present day.

Koyi presented a similar description, though better detailed geographical boundaries of Kurdistan. He also provided an estimated area of the Kurds' land.[100] In a memorandum to the Versailles Peace Conference in 1919, Sharif Pasha, the head of Kurdish delegation, presented a map of 'greater Kurdistan' for the proposed independent Kurdish state.[101] It is noteworthy that, under the name of 'Kurdistan', the first Kurdish newspaper was founded in 1898. Hence, a building block of the Kurds' nationhood project is that, prior to the creation of the Iraqi state, Kurdistan was represented as a separate territory with a well-established 'imagined' national identity.

Hence, historically and geographically speaking, from the Kurds' perspective, both today's Kurdish and Arab regions of Iraq were and are considered as two separate territories. Iraqi identity and nationalism was an alien phenomenon to the Kurds, artificial and externally imposed, and therefore it was rejected.

Kurdistan as a separate political entity

Another element of the Kurds' nationhood project is that Kurdistan is considered to have been a political entity throughout history. Kurdish historians insist that Kurdistan as a separate administrative unit goes back to the Umayyad era in the eighth century.[102] Other Kurdish historians and scholars suggest that the term 'Kurdistan' was used both as a territorial and administrative-political unit by the Seljuks in the twelfth century.[103] Bitlisi used the term *Welati Kurdistan* (the country of Kurdistan) in his referral to the homeland. Although he recognised that Kurdistan was divided among many Kurdish principalities, he dealt with Kurdistan as one homeland and presented each principality as part of the whole political system of Kurdistan.[104] He categorised three systems of governance in Kurdistan. The first system was the era of the sultans and kings, whose rule and status parallel that of the Arab and Turkish caliphs. The second category was the Kurdish rulers, whose rule was equivalent to a state but did not claim independence. These rulers maintained their own armies and currencies, and their names are mentioned in *Khutba* (Friday prayers).[105] According to the Islamic faith, only the name of the caliph or the head of state should be mentioned in Friday's prayer. They didn't pay tribute to the sultan and there were no Ottoman fiefdoms that required an army to protect. The entire revenue of the principality was granted to the prince himself and Ottoman armed forces did not exist in areas under the principalities' rule.[106] This category was probably the most common and long-lasting form of governance in Kurdistan. The third category, according to Bitlisi, was the princes' rule. The prince was the head of a confederacy of tribes and submitted taxes to either the Ottoman or Safavid empires.[107]

The official Ottoman documents of the sixteenth, seventeenth, and nineteenth centuries demonstrate that Kurdistan was an administrative unit called *Wilayet-i Kurdistan*, the province of Kurdistan. This *Wilayet* (*Vilayet*) included vast areas of Kurdistan territory with Diyarbakir (a Kurdish city in modern southeast Turkey) as its centre.[108] During this period, both Mosul and Shehrizor, two provinces of Kurdistan, reported to the governor of Diyarbakr, rather than to Baghdad or Istanbul.[109] For centuries the term 'Kurdistan', both as a territory and as an administrative-political unit, "[was] in circulation and readily used in the official sources and documents of the Ottomans".[110] Prior to the collapse of the Ottoman Empire and the creation of the new Iraq, the Ottomans dealt with the Kurdish and Arab regions separately. From the mid-sixteenth century until the mid-nineteenth, the Ottomans followed two systems of governance: one indirect and nominal rule of Kurdistan, and the other a direct rule of Baghdad, Basra, and elsewhere. The Kurds enjoyed semi-independence and were governed by Kurdish principalities. Furthermore, from the sixteenth to the nineteenth centuries, the term 'Kurdistan' commonly denoted an administrative unit with Diyarbakr as its capitol; all other *Wilayets* of Kurdistan reported to it.[111] In contrast, the Ottomans that ruled the region until WWI never dealt with Iraq as a single administrative unit. By the mid-nineteenth century, however, the last five principalities had been destroyed by both the Iranian state and the Ottoman Empire. Despite the success of the Ottomans in abolishing the Kurdish emirates, they never succeeded in imposing a direct central administrative authority upon Kurdistan. Until WWI and the collapse of the Ottoman Empire, the tribal chiefs and religious *sheikhs* imposed their authority on Kurdish society; they filled the local power vacuum and became the spokesmen for the Kurds as a whole.[112]

Prior to its formal annexation to Iraq in 1925, Kurdistan was dealt with by the colonial powers as a separate entity. While the British occupied Iraq and imposed direct colonial rule in Iraq for several years (with Kirkuk as an exemption), Kurdistan never had such an experience. In fact, the British made "a clear-cut political and administrative distinction between Southern Kurdistan and Iraq".[113] They proposed an autonomous Kurdistan region and even recognised the authority of Sheikh Mahmud as a *Hukmdar* (ruler).[114] For several years, the Kurds enjoyed a degree of administrative, economic, and security self-rule, albeit intermittently. Sheikh Mahmud founded his first government in October 1918 that lasted until June 1919. In 1922, the second Kurdish government was formed and he proclaimed himself king of Kurdistan. The British role in Kurdistan was confined to that of providing political and administrative advice to Sheikh Mahmud.[115] Despite the fact that the British removed both governments, "British officials in London and the Middle East often referred to the autonomous entity as the 'Kurdish state'."[116] It is noteworthy that after the creation of Iraq, the term 'Southern Kurdistan' was still commonly used by British officials and scholars at least until the mid-1940s.[117] Thus, another substantial element of the Kurds' nationhood project is that, for many centuries, until the annexation of Kurdistan to Iraq, Kurdistan enjoyed a form of self-rule that contributed to its political culture.

Autonomous political parties

Another distinguishing characteristic of the KNP is its capability to establish autonomous political parties. The term 'autonomous political parties' is used to describe the status of the post-WWII Kurdish political parties, especially the KDP, the Patriotic Union of Kurdistan (PUK), and other smaller Kurdish parties. For several reasons, these parties that functioned outside the state control may be considered autonomous. One reason to describe as 'autonomous political party' is that these parties were founded and operated outside state control. Their goals, functions, and ideology were not necessarily compatible with Iraqi legislation or regulations. Moreover, their programs were, in fact, independent of and antagonistic to the state's constitution, laws, and ideology. Though apparently clandestine and outlawed, they acted relatively free of constraints and were even able to monopolise politics in rural areas of Kurdistan. This is due to the fact that in these areas the government's interference and authority was either absent or too weak to restrict or terminate their activities.

Kurdish nationalism experienced several phases of development. The first phase may be considered as a transitional period in which the Kurds found themselves with new boundaries and under the new authority of a hitherto fellow-subjugated nation. This phase was characterised by the proliferation of political parties, a state of non-cooperation between the urbanites and the *aghas*, the fragmentation of Kurdish political parties, and the lack of a unified Kurdish front. Despite these weaknesses, Kurdish nationalism was able to challenge the Iraqi nation-building process in Kurdistan. First, Kurdish nationalist sentiments emerged as a dominant ideology among the urbanites. Second, Kurdish nationalism departed from its tribal and traditional sphere and organised itself into a modern political structure. Third, all first-generation political parties were based on and associated themselves with Kurdistani rather than Iraqi identity. These parties were separate from and antagonist towards Iraqi political parties.

Another reason to describe Kurdish parties as 'autonomous' is their ability to institutionalise the KNM. For example, possessing *de facto* political status, the KDP felt confident enough to institutionalise the KNM through the establishment of Kurdish popular (youth and professional) organisations. These organisations were affiliated with Kurdish nationalism and independent from their Iraqi counterparts or state-licenced NGOs.[118] In 1952, for example, the Kurdistan Women's Union (KWU) was founded by the female members of the KDP. Advocating for an autonomous Kurdistan, the KWU actively participated in Kurdish struggle. Thus, KWU goals went far beyond the limits of defending the rights of Kurdish women, and thereby put women on the frontlines of Kurdish politics.[119] Another example of institutionalisation of the KNM was the Kurdistan Teachers Union (KTU), founded in 1952. The KTU insisted that the foundation of the General Directorate of Education for Kurdish Studies (GDEKS) includes all Kurdish areas.[120] Founded in 1952, the Kurdistan Student Union (KSU) was another organisation that pushed for a separate national identity from Iraq.[121]

Kurdish nationalism operated in the rural areas and in the founding of a Safe Haven and power base in rural areas, whereas the *aghas* enjoyed *de facto* self-rule and the Iraqi administration was either absent or weak. In other words, Kurdish political parties were autonomous and founded and operated outside state control. Throughout the last century, Kurdish nationalism dominated Kurdish politics and the Iraqi political parties were absent in Kurdistan. Kurdish nationalism was unified and organised into autonomous political parties that dominated the political sphere and operated freely in rural Kurdistan. They were well supported and protected by tribal militants. Being autonomous, Kurdish parties developed topics such as Kurdistani identity; the Kurdish nationhood; Kurdish history; distinct Kurdish culture, language, and customs; reviving common memories; and the glorification of Kurdish heroes and martyrs. These themes dominated all Kurdish political party discourses. For many decades, these discourses were re-emphasised daily through several radio stations belonging to Kurdish political parties, and tens of weekly, monthly, and periodical publications.[122] Thus, the KNM created Kurdish political parties as autonomous political entities outside of Iraqi control and monopolised the political sphere in Kurdistan. Advocating for the Kurdish quest for nationhood, *Kurdayeti* challenged the Iraqi quest for a unitary state that insisted upon Iraqi state sovereignty over all of Iraq.

Iraq as occupier of Kurdistan

The perception of Iraq as an Arab occupier has dominated Kurdish nationalist literature throughout the last century. Kurdish political rhetoric abounds with terms such as 'the occupier regime of Iraq' and 'the occupiers of Kurdistan', which are used as descriptors of the four countries that have incorporated parts of greater Kurdistan into their state territory. This notion has dominated Kurdish nationalist literature.[123] Similarly, post-monarch Kurdish nationalists have portrayed Iraq as the occupier of Kurdistan.[124] Rejecting the legitimacy of Iraqi rule over Kurdistan, Jalal Talabani insisted that the Kurds did not agree to be part of Iraq. Rather the League of Nations was responsible for authorising the Iraqi army to occupy Kurdistan.[125] The Patriotic Union of Kurdistan (PUK)[126] and the Kurdistan Toilers League (*Komalla*)[127] referred to the Iraqi army in Kurdistan as the occupation army.[128] The internal political program put forth by the first and second PUK General Congresses depicted Kurdistan as an occupied and divided country and the Kurds as a subjugated nation divided into several parts.[129]

The occupation of Kurdistan and the assimilation of the Kurds was a dominant part of Iraqi political culture. For example, Sabir, a well-respected Kurdish intellectual, posited that the Kurds were forced to be 'Iraqi' via an occupation of the Kurdistan region through tyranny and terror. The reciprocal role of the occupied and occupier was the bond that connected 'Southern Kurdistan' to Iraq.[130] Kurdish Islamists shared the perception with the nationalist and leftist Kurds that the central government was the 'occupier'. For example, Osman Abd al-Aziz, the leader of the Islamic Movement in Iraqi Kurdistan, blamed the 'occupiers of Kurdistan' (i.e. Iraq, Iran, Syria, and Turkey) for the division and subjugation of the Kurdish nation.[131] Textbooks of the Kurdistan region often describe Iraq as an occupier of Kurdistan. For instance, *The new and modern history*, a textbook for year 12 Kurdistan region students, describes Kurdistan as an 'occupied country' and the Kurds as 'a subjugated nation'.[132] Thus, a significant feature of the Kurdish Nationhood Project was the portrayal of Iraq as the occupier of Kurdistan.

The Kurdish Liberation Movement

Another distinguishing feature of the Kurdish Nationhood Project is the Kurds' perception of its nationalist movement as a 'liberation movement'. Since the 1940s, the 'liberation of Kurdistan' from 'Iraqi occupation' was an objective of both autonomous and separatist-minded Kurdish nationalists. The Kurdish struggle has been glorified as a Kurdish Liberation Movement (KLM). This vision has dominated most Kurdish political parties' discourses and the majority of them have identified themselves as part of the KLM. For example, in a memorandum to the UN dated 18 January 1946, the Kurdish Rizgari Party[133] stated that its duty was to achieve the liberation and sovereignty of the Kurdish nation.[134] The constitution of the Freedom Committee, a front founded by Kurdish officers who joined the Barzani uprising of 1945 and the Hiwa Party,[135] stipulated that their party's goals were "to liberate Iraqi Kurdistan by political means".[136] The KDP also followed the same line of thinking during the monarchy.[137]

Major post-monarch Kurdish political parties adopted the same principles of the liberation movement. For example, the KDP, which has dominated Kurdish politics since its establishment in 1946 until the present, emphasised that it is a pioneer and leader of the KLM.[138] Similarly, in 1992, the PUK, which has also played a dominant role since 1976, stressed that it is the revival and leader of the KLM.[139] The Kurdistan Toiler League, *Komalla*, claimed that it is at the forefront of the KLM.[140] The Kurdistan Democratic Popular Party (1979–1992) is another that identified itself as part of the KLM.[141] The Iraqi Kurdistan Front (IKF)[142] insisted that its role was to lead the Kurdish Liberation Movement.[143] The term 'Kurdish Liberation Movement' is enshrined in the KRI's constitution, referred to in Kurdish literature, and common in Kurdish political discourse. The preamble to the Draft Constitution of the Kurdistan Region glorifies "the Kurdish liberation movement" as a movement "for our freedom, for the defense of our dignity, and the protection of our nation".[144] Albeit intermittent, the Kurds have imposed their *de facto* self-rule on wide areas of the Kurdistan region since 1961, and referencing these areas as liberated or Free Kurdistan dominated political discourse.[145] In the same way, the terms 'non-liberated' or 'occupied' have been used to refer to such areas as Kirkuk, which is controlled by the Iraqi government. Thus, the portrayal of the KLM as a liberation movement is deeply rooted in Kurdish political culture.

In many ways, the Kurds' belief of being a liberation movement has reshaped Kurdish-Iraqi relations, as well as the process of Kurdish integration into the country, in many ways. First, the Kurds used the self-declared liberation movement to refute Iraq's policy of delegitimisation, and further criminalisation of Kurdish political parties. Second, the liberation movement provided the KLM with a basis by which to legitimise and mobilise the Kurdish populace. Third, by pointing out Iraq's occupier status, the Kurdish parties undermined the legitimacy of the central government's rule in Kurdistan among the Kurds. Fourth, categorising the Kurdish-Iraq relationship as that of 'liberator versus occupier' motivated the Kurdish Nationhood Project and elevated the probabilities of its survival. This

56 *The two contradictory nationhood projects*

is because the KLM used the struggle against 'occupy Iraq' as a fertile ground to recruit Kurds into its ranks. Hence, the dichotomy in use by KNM of 'Kurdistani liberators' versus 'Iraqi occupiers' exposed the oppositional nature of the Kurdish and Iraqi nationhood projects.

Search for outside protection from internal exploitation

Rejecting the legitimacy of Iraqi authority in Kurdistan for the past 80 years, the Kurds have been in an almost constant quest for an outside source of protection. Iraq's leaders, likewise, have constantly accused the Kurds of conspiring with the enemies of the Arabs/Iraqis. Between 1925 (the year Iraqi Kurdistan was first annexed to Iraq) and 1932 (the year of Iraq's independence), the Kurds sought British and League of Nations' protection. During that period, regardless of their demands, most pro- and anti-colonial Kurds considered the British as their main security against Iraqi oppression. This is evident in that the Kurdish MPs in the Iraqi parliament were viewed as advocates of British interests against Iraq's interests. Their pro-British stance, however, was based on trusting British 'good faith' to protect them. A striking example in this regard is a petition written by six Kurdish MPs to Britain in 1928 requesting both protection and self-rule for the Kurds.[146]

Following the independence of Iraq in the 1930s, the Kurds' nationalist stand shifted from a pro-British to an anti-imperialist position. Such change did not result in rapprochement of the Kurdish nationalists and Iraqi rulers, however. Their oppositional status was augmented to the extent that their inherent rivalry developed into a military confrontation that would last for decades. A supreme irony is that the same Kurdish rebels who fought the British and Iraqis also sought British protection. Sheikh Mahmud and Mustafa Barzani, who were in constant rebellion against the British, preferred British rule over that of the Iraqis. In two separate memoranda, both leaders demonstrated their willingness to obey the British rather than the Iraqis.[147] From 1930 to 1932, Kurdish leaders and different segments of Kurdish society presented dozens of petitions to the League and often to the British seeking support. Kurdish demands ranged from autonomy to the independence of Kurdistan; but in either case, the Kurds insisted on Britain or League of Nations' protection from the exploitation of Iraq.[148] Between 1940 and 1958, Kurdish nationalists unsuccessfully pursued another method which was to communicate with various international bodies and leading statesmen. Jwaideh reviewed 24 letters,[149] and Andrews documented 20 letters, notes, and memoranda that were presented by Kurdish nationalists to foreign powers.[150] They found that the Kurds' demands ranged from protection and minority rights to the right of self-determination and full independence.

The Kurds' search for outside protection during the monarchy became part of their political culture and was adopted by future generations of Kurdish nationalists and intellectuals. Since the establishment of the first Kurdish quasi-state in 1961, the Kurds continued searching for a regional state or a superpower to serve as patron. During this period the Kurds received political, logistic, military, and financial support from other states. The Kurds established relations with whoever was willing to offer them assistance, regardless of their stand on Iraq or even the Kurdish case itself. For example, at different times, the Kurds found support from Iraq's traditional enemy, Israel, as they did in the 1960s. They found support from the Kurds' traditional enemy, Turkey, in the 1990s and from both the Kurds' and Iraq's traditional enemy, Iran, from the mid-1960s to the end of 1980s. They found support from the US in the 1970s and the 1990s. Explaining the Kurds' eagerness for outside assistance, Mustafa Barzani stated that the Kurds were "blind beggar[s]" who were "incapable of seeing who was pressing a gold coin into their palms".[151] However, only during the 1991 Kurdish mass exodus could they gain any sort of international protection. This was granted in SCR688 and the subsequent establishment of the Kurdish Safe Haven of 1991 that incidentally culminated in the present *de facto* Kurdish state.[152] After the US invasion and its negotiation with the Iraqi government over the status of the US forces in Iraq, it was apparent that while the Iraqis preferred the withdrawal of all American forces, the Kurds called on the US to establish a permanent military base in Kurdistan.[153] Rejecting the legitimacy of Iraq's rule in Kurdistan, the Kurds were less inclined to negotiate with Iraq to attain political and cultural rights within Iraq's boundaries. Thus, another feature of the Kurdish Nationhood Project was its outward search to find external patronage and support for attaining Kurdish demands.

Self-governance and indirect rule

Another element of the Kurdish Nationhood Project is the deeply rooted culture of self-governance and indirect rule. Centuries of Kurdish self-governance and semi-autonomy have shaped the Kurdish way of life and contributed to its political culture and belief system. The creation of the modern and highly centralised Iraqi state in the 1920s put the Kurds at a crossroads. To establish a strong centralised Iraqi nation-state, Iraq's rulers thought they had to eliminate Kurdish political traditions. Most Kurds expected their relative independence to be respected if they were going to accept externally imposed governance. The expectation of being free from direct rule of the central government was evident in the political behaviour of almost all segments of Kurdish society. This expectation applied to all Kurds: tribal or urban, modern or traditional, pro-Iraqi or rebel, whether irredentist or autonomously inclined. In the early 1930s, the Barzani Kurds rebelled in reaction to the central government's policy of imposing direct rule and interfering in the local affairs of the Barzan district of Kurdistan.[154] From 1944 onward, traditional segments of Kurdish society began to play significant roles in the KLM. The military and proto-nationalist tribal leaders, such as Sheikh Ahmed Barzani in 1932, Mustafa Barzani in 1942–1945, and Sheikh Mahmud during WWII, ranged between fiscal autonomy, cultural rights, and administrative autonomy. The demands of the moderate wing of the *aghas* (Kurdish tribal leaders) were limited to a few cultural and economic rights.

One prominent figure of tribal leaders was Mustafa Barzani. His principles and programs were an extension of the political culture that had dominated Kurdish society for centuries, namely the culture of principalities. Barzani's call for administrative autonomy under British protection later evolved into demands for an autonomous Kurdistan that cooperated with Baghdad. Barzani was accepted as a nationalist leader of the Kurds, especially after his participation in the Republic of Mahabad of Iranian Kurdistan, in 1946–1947, and his exile in the Soviet Union. Throughout the twentieth century, the Barzanis remained in a state of rebellion against practically all successive Iraqi regimes. From 1946 onward, the Barzanis joined the Kurdish nationalist movement. Close to the Barzan district, leaders of the Lolan, Zibari, and Herki tribes cooperated with all successive Iraqi regimes.[155] Their cooperation was attributed to the central government's compromise to allow these tribes to manage their own local affairs. The cooperation between the central government and leaders of these tribes began from the first years of incorporating Kurdistan into Iraq, and it continued throughout the monarchy and republican eras up to the present day. The main factor that contributed to the tribal rebellion or cooperation was the central government's policy of direct and indirect rule in tribal areas of Kurdistan. All successive Iraqi regimes, from King Faisal to Saddam Hussein, ceded the pro-centrist government segment of Kurdish society a limited sovereignty and permitted local autonomous cantons based in tribal confederations.

The political culture of self-governance is reflected in the Kurdish political discourse and literature throughout the last century. For example, in its founding statement, the KDP called for federalism for Kurdistan.[156] However, from 1961 onward, the party's primary goals were democracy for Iraq and autonomy for Kurdistan.[157] The PUK, a coalition of several organisations that was founded in 1975, followed a similar pathway. For many years, the PUK's primary goal was the achievement of democracy for Iraq and real autonomy for Kurdistan.[158] In other words, all Kurdish parties that accommodated the tribal leaders, including the Azadi Committee, KDP, and the *Shoreshgeran*,[159] called for autonomy. Those that remained exclusively urban, such as *Tekoshin*, *Shoresh*, and *Komalla*,[160] called for independence. Hence, another element of the KNP was the deeply rooted culture of self-governance and indirect rule. This political culture is ingrained in the KLM and serves to challenge Iraqi rule and its centralisation policy as it applies to Kurdistan.

Kurdish right of self-determination

The Kurds of Iraq portray themselves as a nation eligible for and capable of self-determination and the establishment of their own independent state. Being part of Iraq is perceived as a usurpation of their inherent rights as a nation. Therefore attaining the right of self-determination has become a common goal of most Kurdish political parties. For many Kurds attaching Kurdistan to Iraq against its will meant the usurpation of their right of self-determination. Prior to the League of Nations' decision to annex Kurdistan to Iraq, many treaties and declarations provided for Kurdish self-determination. US President Woodrow Wilson's famous Fourteen Points, declared on 8 January 1918, is a prime example.

President Wilson not only promoted the principles of self-determination, but he also aided and abetted the Kurdish hope to attain such a right. In Point 12, Wilson declared that "other nationalities which are now under Turkish rule should be assured an undoubted security of life and an absolutely unmolested opportunity of autonomous development."[161] The Paris Peace Conference held in 1919, an international conference in which a Kurdish delegation was represented, produced another international document that supported the principle of self-determination for the Kurds. Other international documents are Articles 61 and 63 of the Treaty of Sèvres (1920), which clearly proposed an independent Kurdish state.[162]

The commonly held belief among the Kurds was that their right of self-determination was recognised in the Treaty of Sèvres and they were thus entitled to practise such self-determination. Thus, the Kurds' hope to attain autonomy and independence has been formally substantiated. However, these promises have never come to fruition; the Kurds were left without a state as they became a minority in the newly created state of Iraq. Many Kurds understood their right of self-determination to be usurped by the British and League of Nations. Most political parties, personalities, and institutions in the last century described the annexation of Kurdistan to Iraq as a clear violation of the Kurds' right of self-determination. For example, in the 1940s, the Rizgari Party stated that the awarding of Kurdistan to Iraq ultimately led to the denial of self-determination for the Kurds.[163] The Kurdistan Toilers League (*Komalla*), another influential political party, described the attachment of Kurdistan to Iraq as a usurpation of the Kurds' right of self-determination.[164] In 1988, Talabani, then secretary general of the PUK, held that the process was a clear violation of the Kurds' right to self-determination.[165] He stated that the Kurdish question was a direct result of the usurpation of the Kurds' right to self-determination. In 1992 the Kurdistan National Assembly (parliament) stressed that the Kurds were entitled to practice their right of self-determination, but international interests have prevented them from carrying out this right. Hence, for the majority of Kurdish nationalists, being part of Iraq was equivalent to the usurpation of their right of self-determination.

The denial of the Kurds' right to self-determination cut so deeply that it bred discontent, disorder, and rebellion throughout the years of the last century. The solution to the Kurdish question based on their right of self-determination became the theme of prominent Kurdish parties. As early as the 1930s, Tawfiq Wahbi, the authorised representative of many Kurdish organisations and leaders, called for the right of self-determination.[166] A decade later the Rizgari Party demanded "full natural rights and full opportunity to self-determination" for the Kurds.[167] The more conservative KDP, which demanded autonomy until 1992, also emphasised the Kurds' right to self-determination. Attaining self-determination became the main article of the party program since its 11th conference in 1993.[168] Self-determination became the theme of the PUK since 1985.[169] The IKF stated that a lasting and just settlement of the Kurdish question rests on the attainment of the right of self-determination.[170] Consequently, Kurdish history in Iraq has been characterised by the domination of Kurdish nationalist parties that put the achievement of self-determination at the top of their agendas. Hence, the Kurdish demand for self-determination has historically been a fundamental principle of *Kurdayeti* and its nationhood project. It is probably correct to say that the failure of Kurdish integration into the Iraqi state was due to their unending quest for self-determination. However, it is incorrect to say that Kurdish self-determination is equivalent to the creation of an independent Kurdish state.

Voluntary unification with Iraq

Another significant future of the Kurdish Nationhood Project in modern Iraq is their call for voluntary union with Iraq. Historically, the right of self-determination has not gone beyond the decolonisation context. The international community does not allow minority nations that already belong to a 'sovereign' state to have self-determination. The Kurds' demand for such a right has been challenged by the international community itself, and this denial has been justified by the principle of state sovereignty and integrity, guaranteed by international law principles such as the UN Charter. In the case of the Kurds, this challenge is further complicated by the fact that the Kurds are divided among four sovereign states. This means that in addition to the opposition by the international community to the dismemberment of these sovereign states, these four countries individually and collectively oppose the formation of a Kurdish independent state that would threaten each of their states' territorial integrity. Therefore, it has become extremely difficult for the Kurds to attempt to secede based on the principle of national self-determination no matter how enshrined the principle is in international documents.

Because an independent Kurdistan may not survive, many Kurdish mainstream leaders no longer aspire for independence. A union based on volunteerism is seen by the Kurds as a more realistic and pragmatic policy and remedy to arbitrary annexation and the usurpation of their right of self-determination. Since the 1960s, many Kurds have replaced the precarious goal of an independent Kurdistan with the desire of autonomy or a federalist system based on the voluntary union of the Kurds and Arabs. For example, in 1986, the PUK, then the largest Kurdish party in Kurdistan, called for a voluntary union based on the right of self-determination within a federal and democratic Iraq.[171] The collapse of the Iraqi state in 2003 was a historical opportunity for the Kurds to declare their independence. However, Jalal Talabani and his PUK party, which previously had actively proclaimed 'self-determination' as the party's main theme, rejected the opportunity to pursue independence. During this opportune time, it stated that an independent Kurdish state "could not survive because neighbouring Turkey, Iran and Syria would close their borders". He advocated remaining within Iraq as being "in the interests of the Kurdish people".[172] Masud Barzani, the president of the KDP and the Kurdistan region, insisted that the Kurds had the right of self-determination. However, he explained that a Kurdish state was a claim of suicidal nationalists.[173] It appears that these two leaders' concerns related to the survivability of the Kurdish state, rather than their loyalty to Iraq. Therefore, both appear to be content to remain in a federal Iraq.

Through its first political program ratified in 1946, the KDP is probably the first political party that called for the voluntary unification between the Kurds and Arabs as an alternative to forced amalgamation.[174] In 1956, the Iraqi Communist Party, under the Kurds' influence, proclaimed Kurdish internal sovereignty based on a voluntary and fraternal unification.[175] During the 1970s negotiations between the Kurds and Iraq over autonomy for Kurdistan, the Kurds insisted on the voluntary unification of the Kurdistan region with Iraq. The IKF that was ratified by eight Kurdish parties states that Kurdistan Front's goal is to attain the right of self-determination for the Kurdish people and to achieve a voluntary and free union between the Kurdish and Arab nations within an independent and democratic Iraq.[176] Thus, the Kurds' notion of self-determination seems to be predisposed more to voluntary union, rather than separatism, for pragmatic reasons.

In summary, Iraqi Arabs and Kurds are two separate nations with two distinct nationhood projects, whose goals run in opposition to that of the other. The Iraqi Nationhood Project emphasises the unitary integrity of Iraq, including the Kurdistan region, as its historical Arab homeland. The Iraqi nation-building project aims to create one homogenised and unified Iraqi nation through the abnegation of Kurdish ethnicity and identity, the criminalisation of Kurdish nationalism, and the delegitimisation of its nationhood project.

The Kurds' project, in contrast, is to establish an independent Kurdish nation-state in its historical homeland in present-day northern Iraq. The Kurdish Nationhood Project is based on the creation of a homogeneous Kurdistani identity and a sovereign independent Kurdish state. The two nationalisms shared neither common ground nor the intention to accommodate each other. Iraq's perception of the Kurds as plotters, conspirators, and enemies of the Arab nation justified sustained state-sponsored violence and militaristic strategies against the Kurds – from Iraq's perspective. For decades, the Kurds remained in a state of rebellion against practically all successive Iraqi regimes. Military movement was introduced into the Kurdish nationalism modus operandi of resistance to fulfil its nationhood project and to challenge state 'oppression'. Consequently, the oppositional nature of Kurdish and Iraqi nationalisms, their respective nationhood projects, and their exclusive visions were important contributors to the tension that existed between two nationalisms that existed at the expense of the other.

Notes

1 Sharif, A. S. T. (2007), *Al-Jamiyat wal-Munadhamat wal-Ahzab al-Kurdiya fi nisf al-Qirn: 1908–1958 (Associations, Organisations and Kurdish parties in half a century 1908–1958)*, Sulaimaniya, Iraq: Dar al-Sardam: 183.
2 Talabani, J. (1970), *Kurdistan wa al-Haraka al-Qawmiya al-Kurdiya (Kurdistan and the Kurdish Nationalist Movement)*, Baghdad: Al-Nur: 179; Kosrat (1985), "Keshey Kurd le Eraqda" (The Kurdish Question in iraq), *Kurdayeti* 3(1): 38–64: 50; Sharif 2007: 183.
3 Republic of Iraq – Ministry of Education (2016), *Principles of Geography for Grade Ten*, Baghdad: Ministry of Education: 6–8.
4 Republic of Iraq – Ministry of Education (2015), *National and Social Education for Grade Eight*, Baghdad: Ministry of Education: 53.

62 The two contradictory nationhood projects

5 Republic of Iraq – Ministry of Education (2015), *The Arab and Islamic History for Grade Eight Schools*, Baghdad: Ministry of Education: 67–72.
6 For example see: *The Islamic Arabic History for Year Eight*, Baghdad: Ministry of Education.
7 Republic of Iraq – Ministry of Education (2015), *Modern and Contemporary History of the Arab Countries for Grade Twelve Schools*, Baghdad: Ministry of Education.
8 Landlords are not necessarily affiliated with tribes. *Agha* is a tribal leader and *sheikh* is a religious leader. For the sake of brevity they are categorised here as *aghas*.
9 Bruinessen, M. V. (1992). *Agha, Sheikh, and State: The Social and Political Structures of Kurdistan*, London: Zed books: 190; Lukitz, L. (1995), *Iraq: The Search for National Identity*, London: Frank Cass & Co. Ltd.: 211.
10 Lukitz 1995: 211; Fuccaro, N. (1997), "Ethnicity, State Formation, and Conscription in Postcolonial Iraq: The Case of the Yazidi Kurds of Jabal Sinjar," *International Journal of Middle East Studies* 29(4): 559–580: 563.
11 *Tanzimat* refers to a "series of reforms promulgated in the Ottoman Empire between 1839 and 1876 under the reigns of the sultans Abdülmecid I and Abdülaziz. Heavily influenced by European ideas, these reforms were intended to effectuate a fundamental change of the empire from the old system based on theocratic principles to that of a modern state," (Encyclopedia Britannica (2012), "Tanzimat," *Encyclopedia Britannica*, available at <www.britannica.com/EBchecked/topic/582884/Tanzimat>, (accessed 03/06/2012).
12 Ali, O. (2003), *Dirasat fi al-Hereke al-Taharruriye al-kurdiye al-Ma'asre 1833–1946 (A study of the contemporary Kurdish liberation movement)*. Erbil, Iraq: al-Tafsir: 575.
13 Bruinessen 1986: 16; Fuccaro 1997: 563; Natali 2000: 69; McDowall 2004: 180.
14 Ali 2003: 529, 567.
15 Bruinessen 1992: 190; Natali 2005: 30, 79.
16 Bruinessen 1992: 78; Natali 2005: 30.
17 Al-Husri, S. (1967), *Mudhakarati fi al-Iraq 1921–1927 (My Memoir in Iraq 1921–1927)*, Beirut: Dar al-Tali'a; Al-Husri, S. (1985), *Abhath Mukhtare fi al-Qawmiya al-Arabiya (Selected Essays on Arab Nationalism)*, Beirut: Dar al-Mustaqbal al-Araby: 157.
18 Al-Fil, M. R. (1965), *Al-Akrad fi Nadhar al-'Ilm (The Kurds in the Eyes of Science)*, Najaf, Iraq: Maktaba al-Adab.
19 Al-Fukaiki, H. (1993), *Awkar al-Hazima: Tajrubati fi Hizb al-Ba'th al-Iraqi* (The Den of Defeat: My Experience in the Iraqi Ba'th Party), London: Riad El-Rayyes, 76.
20 Maruf, N. (1979), *Arrube al-Ulama al-Mansubin ila al-Alacamye fi bilad al-Rum w al-Jazire w Shehrezur we Azerbaijan (The Arab Origin of Islamic Scholars in the Rum Land, Al-Jazira and Azerbaijan)*, Third Edition, Baghdad: Wazara al-Fnun wal-Thaqafa al-Iraqiya: 97–100.
21 "'Hadhihi al-'Ashaer al-Kurdiyya Aslihn Arabiyun (The Origin of these Kurdish Tribes is Arab)", *Al-Watan al-Arabi* 14/07/1989; "Hadhihi al-'Ashaer al-Kurdiyya Aslihn Arabiyun (The Origin of these Kurdish Tribes is Arab)," *Al-Watan al-Arabi* 21/07/1989.
22 Roshinbiri News (1989), "Em Hoze Kurdane le Bnecheda Arab" (These Kurdish tribes are originally Arabs). *Roshnbiri News* no. 124. Baghdad
23 ABSP, (Arab Ba'ath Socialist Party). (2007), "Dastur Hizb al-Ba'ath al-Arabi al-Ishtraki (The Constitution of the Arab Ba'ath Socialist Party)," *Shabaka al-Basrah*, available at <www.albasrah.net/ar_articles_2007/0307/dstor-b3th_070307.htm>, (accessed 09/08/2012).
24 Khayrullah Tulfah was defence minister, senior Ba'athist leader, and uncle, father in law and mentor of former president Saddam Hussein.
25 ABSP 2007.

26 For example, see Article 2 of the Iraqi Interim Constitution-1958; Article 1 of the Iraqi Interim Constitution-1964; Article 1 of the Iraqi Interim Constitution-1968; and Article 5 of the Interim Constitution of Iraq-1990.
27 Aflaq, M. (1987), *Fi Sabil al-Ba'ath (On the Way to Resurrection)*, Vol. 5, Baghdad: Maktab al-Thaqafah wal-Ilam al-Qawmi: 219–220.
28 *Ibid.*: 219–220.
29 *Ibid.*: 220.
30 *Ibid.*: 37, 133.
31 Cited in Bengio, O. (1979–1980), "Iraq," *Middle East Contemporary Survey; (CD-ROM Version), vol. I–XVIII*, O. Bengio (ed.), The Moshe Dayan Center for Middle Eastern and African Studies. Tel Aviv University, Tel Aviv, Israel, 2000: 501–534: 512.
32 Al-Thawra 23/02/1979.
33 Aflaq: 1987: 220.
34 Mina, A. Q. (2012), *Amni Stratiji Iraq w Sekuchkay Ba'siyan: Tarhil, Ta'rib, Tab'ith (Iraq's security strategy and the Ba'thists' tripod: Displacement, Arabization and Ba'thification)*, Suleimaniya, Iraq: Kurdistan Centre for Strategic Studies: 246–247.
35 The Revolutionary Command Council (*Majlis al-Qyade al-thewre*) chaired by Saddam and all its members were senior Ba'ath and almost exclusively Sunnis. It was the highest authority institution in Iraq and his decrees were dealt with as constitutional decrees.
36 *Al-Waqai' al-Iraqiya* 17/09/2001.
37 Burns, J. F. (2002),"Kurds Must Endure Iraq's 'Nationality Correction," *The New York Times*, available at <www.nytimes.com/2002/08/11/world/kurds-must-endure-iraq-s-nationality-correction.html>, (accessed 08/09/2012).
38 Mohammad, K. I. (2006), *Al-Qadhiye al-Kurdiye fi Iraq wjud am Hadud? (Is the Kurdish issue in Iraq the Issue of Presence or Border?)*, Erbil, Iraq: Salahaddin University: 220–230.
39 *Al-Waqai' al-Iraqiya* 12/12/1988.
40 Republic of Iraq – Ministry of Education (2015), *Jughrafiat Alwatan Alearabii Lilsafi Alththani Almutawasit (The Geography of the Arab Homeland for the Second Intermediate Grade)*, Baghdad: Ministry of Education: 4–17; 45–46; Natural Geography Grade 11: 20.
41 For example see: *The Geography of the Arab Homeland for the Second Intermediate Grade*: 60; Natural Geography Grade 11: 20.
42 *The Geography of the Arab Homeland for the Second Intermediate Grade*: 60.
43 Natural Geography Grade 11: 20.
44 *Ibid.*: 46.
45 *The Modern and Contemporary History of Arab Countries 2015*: 7–16.
46 *Ibid.*: 16.
47 Emin 2000: 24.
48 Barzani, M. (2003b), *Mustafa Barzani and the Kurdish Liberation Movement*, New York: Palgrave Macmillan: 176.
49 Cited in Jawad, S. N. (1990), *Al-Iraq wal-Masa'ala al-Kurdiya (Iraq and the Kurdish Question)*, London: Dar al-Laam: 176.
50 For example see: Al-Jamhurriya 13/02/1966.
51 Aflaq 1987: 38.
52 *Ibid.*: 37–38, 142, and 219.
53 See: ABSP 1983: 45; Aflaq 1987: 142; Hussein 1998: 48–49.
54 See: al-Ghamrawi 1967: 394; al-Taghalubi 1967; Al-Hayat 16/03/1970; al-Jamhuriya 13/09/1983; Hawkari 24/03/1988, 28/04/1988, 18/08/1988; Rengin 1988; Al-Barak, F. (1989), *Mustafa al-Barzani: Al-Istura wa al-Haqiqa (Mustafa Barzani: The Myth and the Reality)*, Baghdad, Iraq: Dar al-Sh'un al-Thaqafiya al-'Amma: 48; *Al-Iraq Newspaper*18/03/1993.

55 ABSP 1983: 58.
56 Talabani 1970: 179; Lukitz 1995: 11; Farouk-Sluglett, M. and P. Sluglett (2001), *Iraq Since 1958: From Revolution to Dictatorship*, London: IB Tauris: 80; Natali 2005: 44.
57 Zhiyan 28/08/1930; Sluglett, P. (1976) *Britain in Iraq: 1914–1932*, Beirut: Ithaca Press for the Middle East Centre: 25.
58 For the full text of the letter see Andrews, D. (1982), *The Lost Peoples of the Middle East: Documents of the Struggle for Survival and Independence of the Kurds, Assyrians, and other Minority Races in the Middle East*, Salisbury, NC: Documentary Publications: 7.
59 Al-Barak 1989: 35; Jawad 1990: 2.
60 ABSP 1983: 56–57.
61 Graham-Brown, S. (1999), *Sanctioning Saddam: The Politics of Intervention in Iraq*, London: IB Tauris: 214; McDowall 2004: 360; Gull, M. O. (2007), *Jenosidy Geli Kurd (The Genocide of the Kurdish People)*, Erbil, Iraq: Aras Publisher: 57.
62 Entessar, N. (1984), "The Kurds in Post-Revolutionary Iran and Iraq," *Third World Quarterly* 6(4): 911–933: 914.
63 Mithraism and Zoroastrianism were two dominant religions of the Kurds prior to the Islamic conquering. The two religions have undoubtedly exerted a powerful influence on the Kurdish culture until the present day. For further information see: Nebez, J. (2004), *The Kurds: History and Kulture*, London: WKA Publications: 10.
64 KNA, Kurdistan National Assembly (1999), Qanun 'Alam Eqlim Kurdistan al-Iraq Raqam 14 li-Sinna 1999 (Law of the flag of the Kurdistan Region of Iraq, Resolution no 14 of the Year 1999), *Al-Waqai' al-Iraqiya (Iraqi Official Gazzeta)*.
65 KNA, Kurdistan National Assembly (2004), 'Qarar raqam 2 li-Sinna 1997 (Resolution no. 2 for the Year 1997)', *al-Waqai' al-Iraqiya, Iraqi Official Gazzeta*.
66 *Al-Waqai' al-Iraqiya* 30/08/1958.
67 Aydin, D. (2005), "Mobilizing the Kurds in Turkey: Newroz as a Myth," Masters Thesis, Middle East Technical University: 35, 69.
68 KRG, (1997), "Ala u Srwdi Nishtimani" (The Flag and National Anthem), available at <www.krg.org/articles/detail.asp?lngnr=13&smap=03010100&rnr=168&anr=16877>, (accessed 12/07/2013).
69 Cyaxares was the first king of Medes.
70 KRG-ME, Kurdistan Regional Government–Ministry of Education (2004), *Babaten Komallayati Pola Penje Saratayi (Societal Topics for the Grade Five Primary School)*, Erbil: Kurdistan Region.
71 Medes were ancient Indo-European people who flourished from the eighth to the sixth centuries BCE. Under King Cyaxares, the Medes joined forces with the Babylonians and destroyed the Assyrian Empire in 612 BCE. The Medes then established a large but short-lived empire of their own over areas that are now in western Iran and northern Iraq.
72 The Blacksmith Kawa is a legendary Kurdish folk hero who rebelled against a tyrant and defeated the ruthless ruler Zohhak (or Dahak), who had been feeding the brains of young men to two giant serpents' heads growing from his shoulders.
73 KRG-ME, *Babaten Komallayati Pola Penje Saratayi*, 68.
74 For example see: Talabani 1970: 140; Mirawdeli, K.(1993), "The Kurds Political status and Human Rights," paper presented at The Kurds Political status and Human Rights Conference, Georgetown, Washington, DC; Mukiryani, K. (2008), *Serdemani Zmani Kurdi w Komele Zmanani Erani (Stages of Kurdish Language and the Iranian group of languages)*, Erbil, Iraq: Aras Publishers: 25; Miran, R. (2009), *Etnografya w Yeketi Etniki Kurd (Ethnograpy and the Unity of the Kurdish Ethnicity)*, Erbil, Iraq: Aras Publications: 53; Shamzini, A. (2006), *Jwlanaway Rizgari Nishtimani Kurdistan (The Kurdish National Liberation Movement)*, Fourth edition, Sulaimaniya, Iraq: Senteri Lekolinewey Strategi Kurdistan: 23.
75 Emin 2000: 66–68.

76 For example see: *Diwani Bekas* (2000), Ashna, O. (eds.), *Kurdistan Region*, Erbil: Aras Publication: 15–16; *Diwani Piremerd u Pedachuneweyeki Nwey Zhyan u Berhemekani (Divan of Piremerd and a Revision of his Life and Writings)*" 2002. Erbil, Kurdistan Region: Aras Publishers.
77 For example see: Talabani 1970: 108; KRG-ME, (Kurdistan Regional Government–Ministry of Education), (2008), *Mezhwi Nwe w Hawcharkh Poli Dwazdahami Amadayi Wejayi (New and Modern History for Grade Twelve High School – Humanities)*, Beirut, Lebanon: Al-Mustaqbal Press, 2008), 156–157.
78 For the full text of Sheikh Mahmud's letter, see Emin 2000: 197–200.
79 *Ibid.*: 197–200.
80 Tofiq Wehbi, an Ottoman officer, was a well-respected Kurdish scholar and nationalist. He was the governor of Sulaimani province in the early 1930s and was authorised by Kurdish leaders to represent them in correspondence with the international community.
81 Emin 2000: 197–200.
82 Jalal Talabani was the founder and secretary general of the Patriotic Union of Kurdistan (PUK) and the former president of Iraq (2005–2014).
83 The Paris Peace Conference was held by Allied victors in 1919 to discuss, among other issues, the future of the Ottoman Empire.
84 Talabani, J (2004), *Gft u Goyeki Ciddi Legel Subhi 'Abdulhamid u Hawrekani (A serious dialogue with Subhi 'Abd al-Hamid and his colleagues)*, Sulaymania, Kurdistan Region: Sharewani Slemani: 48.
85 The article was written by Ibrahim Ahmed, the Party's general secretary.
86 *Khabat* Newspaper, "The Mouthpiece of the Kurdistan Democratic Party," 09/10/1960.
87 Talabani 1970: 6–7; Mella, J. (2000), *Kurdistan w al-Kurd: Watan Masruq we Mughtasab we Muqasm; Umma mustbide w Sajine wa Bila Dawla (Kurdistan and the Kurds, a Stolen and Divided Homeland, a Nation Enslaved, Imprisoned and Without a State)*, Third edition, London: Jamiaat Gharb Kurdistan; KNA, Kurdistan National Assembly (2007), *'Mezhwi Koni Kurdistan', (The Ancient History of Kurdistan)*, available at <www.krg.org/articles/detail.asp?lngnr=13&smap=03010600&rnr=173&anr=22043>, (accessed 12/11/2014).
88 Talabani 1970: 210; KRG-ME 2008: 184.
89 Izady, M. R. (2004), "Between Iraq and a Hard Place: The Kurdish Predicament," in *Iran, Iraq, and the Legacies of War*, Lawrence G. Potter and Gary G. Sick (eds.), New York: Palgrave Macmillan: 95.
90 Jamal Nebez is a reputed Kurdish linguist, mathematician, and writer, as well as the founder of the National Union of the Kurdish Students in Europe (NUKSE).
91 KRG-ME 2008: 184. Also see Talabani 1970: 210.
92 Talabani 1970: 210; Hussein, F. (1997), *Mushkilet al-Mosul (The Mosul Problem)*, Baghdad: Matba'at Eshbiliya.
93 Bitlisi, S. (1860), *Sharafname*, Petersburg: Dar al-Taba'a Ekadimiyah Impratoriya: 8–18.
94 *Ibid.*: 14.
95 *Ibid.*: 1860: 23–24.
96 Khani, A. (1968) *Mem u Zin (Mem and Zin)*, Third edition, Hewler, Iraq: Chapkhaney: 43–44.
97 *Ibid.*: 43–45.
98 See Abu-Bakr, A. O. (2005), *Kurd u Kurdistan le Komalla Wtareki Mezhwiyda (Kurds and Kurdistan in Some Historical Articles)*, Erbil, Iraq: Mukiryani: 13.
99 Koyi, H. Q. (2004), *Diwani Haji Qadri Koyi" (Divan of Haji Qadri Koyi)*, Stockholm: Nefel: 75,109, 113.
100 *Ibid.*: 122.
101 For the full text of the memorandum see Sherko, B. (1986), *Keshay Kurd: Mezhwi nwe u Estay Kurd (Kurdish Question: Old and Present History of the Kurds)*, trans. by Muhammad Hama Baqi, Kurdistan: Shahid Ja'far Press: 138–150.

66 The two contradictory nationhood projects

102 *Serjem Berhemi 'Abdulaziz Yamulki (The Collection of Writings from 'Abd al-'Aziz Yamulki)*, (Sulaimani, Kurdistan Region, Binkey Zhin, 1997), 40; Miran 2009: 92.
103 Hassanpour, A. and S. Mojab (2005), "Kurdish Diaspora," *Encyclopedia of Diasporas: Immigrant and Refugee Cultures Around the World*, Melvin Ember, Carol R. Ember and Ian Skoggard (eds.), New York: Springer.
 Seljuks were Turkish dynasties that ruled Asia Minor from the eleventh to the thirteenth centuries; they successfully invaded Byzantium and defended the Holy Land against Crusaders.
104 Bitlisi 1860: 19–30.
105 *Ibid.*: 8–9.
106 Bruinessen, M. V. (1999), "The Kurds and Islam," *Islamic Area Studies Project*, Tokyo, Japan: [publisher Unknown].
107 Bitlisi 1860: 8–9.
108 Çakar, E. (2002), "According to the Qanunname of Sultan Suleyman I: The Administrative Divisions of the Ottoman Empire in 1522," *F.U. Sosyal Bilimler Dergisi* 12(1): 281; Özoğlu, H. (2004), *Kurdish Notables and the Ottoman State: Evolving Identities, Competing Loyalties, and Shifting Boundaries*, Albany, NY: State University of New York Press: 159; Cuthell, D. (2004), "A Kemalist Gambit: A View of the Political Negotiations in the Determination of the Turkish-Iraqi Border," *The Creation of Iraq, 1914–1922*, Reeva Spector Simon and Eleanor H. Tejirian (eds.), New York: Columbia Press: 82.
109 Cuthell 2004: 82.
110 Özoğlu 2004: 164.
111 Çakar 2002: 281; Özoğlu 2004: 159; Cuthell 2004: 82.
112 Bruinessen 1999; Tejel, J. (2008), *Syria's Kurds: History, Politics and Society*, London: Routledge: 96.
113 Eskander, S. (2000), "Britain's Policy in Southern Kurdistan: The Formation and the Termination of the First Kurdish Government, 1918–1919," *British Journal of Middle Eastern Studies* 27(2): 161.
114 Sluglett 1976: 116: Olson, R. (1987), "The Second Time Around: British Policy Toward the Kurds (1921–22)," *Die Welt des Islams* 27(1/3): 91–102: 101; 116; Fieldhouse 2002: 34; Eskander 2000: 163; Emin 2000: 198, 313.
115 Kirisçi, K. and G. Winrow (1997), *The Kurdish Question and Turkey: An Example of a Trans-State Ethnic Conflict*, London: Frank Cass & Co. Ltd: 84; Eskander 2000: 141–143, 163; Qadir, A. M. (2007), *Mawqif Majlis al-Nawab al-Iraqi mn al-Qadhiya al-Kurdiya fi al-Iraq 1925–1945 (The Position of the Iraqi Parliament on the Kurdish Question 1925–1945)*, Sulaimaniya, Iraq: Binkey Zhin: 19, 46–47.
116 Eskander 2000: 141.
117 E.g. see, Edmonds, C. J. (1928) "Two More Ancient Monuments in Southern Kurdistan," *The Geographical Journal* 72(2): 162–163; Rajkowski, R. (1946), "A Visit to Southern Kurdistan," *The Geographical Journal* 107(3/4): 128–134: 128–134.
118 Talabani 1970: 102.
119 KDP, Kurdistan Democratic Party (2011), "Kurdistan Women Union" (KWU), available at <www.kdp.se/?do=women, (accessed 08/09/2012).
120 Khabat Newspaper, "The Mouthpiece of the Kurdistan Democratic Party," 31/08/1959, 14/09/1959.
121 Khabat Newspaper, "The Mouthpiece of the Kurdistan Democratic Party," 13/10/1960, 21/10/1960.
122 E.g. see: KDP-PC, Kurdistan Democratic Party-The Preparatory Committee (1979), *Tariq al-Haraka al-Taharruriye al-Kurdiye: Taqim Thawra Aylul wa barnamj al-Jadid lil-Hizb al-dimuqrati al-Kurdistani (The Path of the Kurdish Liberation Movement: The Evaluation of the September Revolution and a New Political Program of the Kurdistan Democratic Party)*, Publisher unknown; *Komalla Magazine* (1981), "Organi Komallay Ranjderani Kurdistan," (The Review of the Kurdistan Toilers

League, 1(9); Komalla Magazine (1982b), "Organi Komallay Ranjderani Kurdistan," *The Review of the Kurdistan Toilers League* 2(3); Komalla, Komallay Renjderani Kurdistan (1983), *Eraqcheti Dagirker u Borzhwazi Kurdistan(The Iraqism of the Occupation and Kurdistan's Bourgeoisie), Blawkrawekani Komallay Renjderan*; Komalla Magazine (1987), "Organi Komallay Ranjderani Kurdistan," *The Review of the Kurdistan Toilers League* 3(6); Rebazi Nwe 1982; Peshang newspaper 1982, Kurdistan Democratic Popular Party, no. 1; Khabat Newspaper, The Mouthpiece of the Kurdistan Democratic Party 1988.

123 'Yadi Roley Nebez Pesheway Netewey Kurd' (In the Memory of a Brave Son and the Leader of the Kurdish Nation,' Rizgari Magazine), 7(1952); Nida Kurdistan (1956), "Fi sabil tawhid al-Haraka al-Thawriyya fi Kurdistan al-Iraq" (For the revolutionary movement in Iraqi Kurdistan), *Nida Kurdistan Magazine*, Baghdad.

124 Komalla Magazine 1981; Komalla Magazine 1981; Ibrahim Jalal (1984), *Komallay Renjderani Kurdistan bo Kurdistaniye (The Reason for the Kurdistaniness of the Kurdistan Toilers League*, Kurdistan: Chapkhaney Shehid Ibrahim Ezzo; Talabani, J. (1988), *Hawla al-Qadhiyya al-Kurdiyya (About the Kurdish Question)*, Kurdistan: Chapkhaney Ibrahim Ezzo: 25; Sabir, R. (2005), *Iraq: Dimokratizekrdn yan Helwashandnewe? (Iraq: Democratisation or Dismemberment?)*, Kurdistan Region, publisher unknown: 47.

125 Talabani 1988: 25.

126 The Patriotic Union of Kurdistan is one of the largest political parties in Kurdistan. It has played a dominant role in Kurdish politics since 1976.

127 The Kurdistan Toilers League (*Komalla*), was the largest faction within the PUK and an influential political party in the 1980s.

128 For the PUK see: PUK, Patriotic Union of Kurdistan (1988), "Rageyandini Mektebi Syasi Yeketi Nishtimani Kurdistan' (A Statement by the Politboro of the Patriotic Union of Kurdistan)," available at <www.sbeiy.com/UserFiles/File/NewFiles/Beyani%20Anfal.JPG>, (accessed 12/12/2014).
For Komalla see: Komalla Magazine 1982b.

129 PUK, Patriotic Union of Kurdistan 1988: 21; Patriotic Union of Kurdistan (2001), *Bername u Peyrewi Nawkhoy Yekei Nishtimani Kurdistan: Pesend Krawi Yekemin Kongrey Gshti 2001 (The Constitution of the Patriotic Union of Kurdistan: Ratified in the Eleventh General Congress 2001)*, Kurdistan Region, Publisher unknown: 18.

130 Sabir 2005: 47–55.

131 Ahmed, A. M. (2008), *Mamosta 'Ali 'Abdul-'Aziz Temenek Xizmet le Bizavi Islamida (Islamic Scholar 'Abd al-'Aziz and an age of Islamic Movement)*, Kurdistan Region, Publisher unknown: 84.

132 KRG-ME 2008: 179–181.

133 Parti Rizgari Kurd (the Kurdish Liberation Party) was founded in 1944 with the goal of establishing an independent Kurdish state. It was one of the main factions that participated in the establishment of the KDP in 1946.

134 For the full text of the memorandum see Andrews 1982: 43–45.

135 In 1943, Mustafa Barzani began a revolt against the monarchy regime. The rebellion collapsed in 1945. The Hiwa Party, one of the most influential Kurdish political parties during the monarchy, was established by a student from the Kirkuk Intermediate School in 1939.

136 Jwaideh, W. (2006), *The Kurdish National Movement: Its Origins and Development*, Syracuse, NY: Syracuse University Press: 233.

137 Nida Kurdistan 1956.

138 Kurdistan Democratic Party (1979), *Tariq al-Haraka al-Taharruriyya al-Kurdiyya: Taqim Thawra Aylul wa Barnamj al-Jadid li-l-Hizb al-Dimuqrati al-Kurdistani (The Path of the Kurdish Liberation Movement: The Evaluation of the September Revolution and a New Political Program of the Kurdistan Democratic Party)*, Iraqi Kurdistan, Publisher unknown: 14–15; KDP, Kurdistan Democratic Party (2004),

68 *The two contradictory nationhood projects*

"Al-Mnhaj wa-l-Nidham al-Dakhili, (The Platform and Internal System)," *Kurdistan Democratic Party*, available at <www.kdp6.com>, (accessed 04/01/2015).
139 PUK, Patriotic Union of Kurdistan 1988: 22.
140 Komalla Magazine 1987: 32.
141 The party was founded in 1979 by Sami Sinjari, the former vice prime minister of the KRG. *see: Peshang Newspaper* 1982: 28.
142 In 1987, eight Kurdish parties united under the Iraqi Kurdistan Front, the IKF, and acted as the overarching umbrella for all Kurdish militant groups. The new IKF, with its 15,000 to 20,000 peshmerga forces, was further consolidated. Following the withdrawal of Iraq, the IKF moved swiftly to fill the vacuum in the region. Following the Kurdish uprising in 1991, the IKF controlled most of Iraqi Kurdistan. To achieve internal legitimacy, the IKF planned elections for 19 May 1992.
143 IKF, Iraqi Kurdistan, Publisher unknown (1988), *Mithaq wa-l-Nidham al-dakhili li-Jabha al-Kurdistaniya (The Charter and Program of Iraqi Kurdistan Front)*, Iraqi Kurdistan Front.
144 'Draft Constitution of Kurdistan Region, Kurdistan Parliament – Iraq, 2009, available at <www.perleman.org/default.aspx?page=Constitution&c=Constitution-Kurdistan>, (accessed 07/09/2014).
145 Komalla Magazine 1981; *Regay Rizgari*, Yeketi Shorishgeriani Kurdistan's Magazine (1985), "Shorish le Pilanekani Dwzhmn be Heztre (Revolution Is Stronger than the Enemy's Conspiracy)," (3); *Khabat* Newspaper (1988), "The Mouthpiece of the Kurdistan Democratic Party,"; *Khabat Newspaper* (2002), "The Mouthpiece of the Kurdistan Democratic Party,"; PUK, Patriotic Union of Kurdistan (1986), *Haqiqa al-Mwaqif al-Itihad al-watani al-Kurdistani' (Facts About Positions of the Patriotic Union of Kurdistan)*, (Iraqi Kurdistan, Shahid Jaf'ar; Patriotic Union of Kurdista (1992), *Bername u Peyrewi Nawkhoy Yeketi Nishtimani Kurdistan: Pesend Krawi Yekemin Kongrey Gshti 1992 (The Constitution of the Patriotic Union of Kurdistan: Ratified by the First General Congress*, Kurdistan Region, Publisher unknown: 18–19; Barzani, M. (2002), *Barzani wa-l-Haraka al-Taharruriyya al-Kurdiyya (Barzani and the Kurdish Liberation Movement)*, Erbil: Kurdistan Region, Aras Publications: 39; Talabani 2004: 64; KDP, Kurdistan Democratic Party 2004.
146 See Zhiyan 11/04/1929; Emin 2000: 32–34.
147 See Bois, T. (1966), *The Kurds*, M. W. M. Welland (trans.), Beirut: Khayats: 152; Sluglett 1976: 183; Ali 2003: 603–604.
148 See Zhiyan 21/07/1930; Emin 2000: 251–315.
149 Jwaideh 2006: 273–275.
150 Andrews 1982.
151 Randal, J. C. (1997), *After Such Knowledge, What Forgiveness? My Encounters with Kurdistan*, New York: Farrar, Straus and Giroux 1997: 189.
152 Security Council Resolution 688 (1991), "The United Nations Security Council," 05/04/1991, available at <www.casi.org.uk/info/undocs/gopher/s91/5>, (accessed 27/09/2012).
153 Jam, K. (2007), "Talabani Calls for US Military Base in Kurdistan," *The Kurdish Globe* (115): 7; Khalil, L. (2009), *Stability in Iraqi Kurdistan: Reality or Mirage?* Washington, DC: Brookings Institution: 14.
154 Barzani 2003b: 11–45; McDowall 2004:180; Jwaideh 2006: 219–229.
155 Bruinessen, M. V. (1992), *Agha, Sheikh, and State: The Social and Political Structures of Kurdistan*, London: Zed books: 172.
156 Mustafa, N. (2004), *Chend Laparayak la Mezhwi Rojnamawani Kurdi (Some Pages in the History of Kurdish journalism*, Kurdistan Region, Publisher unknown: 188; Sharif 2007: 187–188.
157 Barzani 2003b: 209.
158 Rebazi Nwe 1982.

159 *Yeketi Shoreshgerani Kurdistan* (the Revolutionary Union of Kurdistan), popularly known as *Shoreshgeran*, was one of the two factions within the PUK, established in the mid-1980s.
160 In the middle of the 1940s, the leftist Kurds created their own Marxist organisation, *Tekoshin*, that later became the *Shoresh*.
161 For the full text of Woodrow Wilson's Fourteen Points, see *American History*, available at <www.hbci.com/~tgort/14points.htm>, (accessed 11/05/2015).
162 For the articles of the Treaty of Sèvres, see WWI Document Archive, available at <http://wwi.lib.byu.edu/index.php/Section_I%2C_Articles_1_-_260>, (accessed 07/2014).
163 See Andrews 1982: 45.
164 Komalla 1983: 4.
165 Talabani 1988: 6–7, 1970: 210.
166 Emin 2000: 287–296.
167 Cited in Andrews 1982: 44.
168 KDP 1993; 2004; 2010.
169 PUK 1986: 16; 1993: 5; 2001: 18.
170 IKF 1988.
171 PUK 1986: 16.
172 Cited in "Kurdish Independence Just a Dream, Talabani Tells Turkey," *Reuters*, 16/03/2009, available at <www.reuters.com/article/2009/03/16/idUSLG519166>, (accessed 11/06/2012).
173 Barzani, M. (2005), "A Kurdish Vision of Iraq," *The Washington Post*, available at <www.washingtonpost.com/wpdyn/content/article/2005/10/25/AR2005102501390.html>, (accessed 03/04/2013).
174 See Emin 2004: 188; Sharif 2007: 229.
175 Ahmed 2006: 140; Sharif 2007: 232.
176 IKF 1988.

4 The monarchy-Kurds relations

Modern Iraq was created by the British after the fall of the Ottoman Empire and placed under the League of Nations mandate in 1921. Initially, the newly created state of Iraq did not include the former Ottoman province of Mosul, the area that constituted the Kurdish region. While the British occupied Iraq and imposed direct colonial rule in Iraq for several years (with Kirkuk as an exemption), Kurdistan never had such an experience. The colonial power dealt with Kurdistan as a separate entity and made a clear-cut political and administrative distinction between Kurdistan and Iraq. The British proposed an autonomous Kurdistan region and even recognised the authority of Sheikh Mahmud as its *Hukmdar* (ruler).[1] For several years, the Kurds enjoyed a degree of administrative, economic, and security self-rule, albeit intermittently. Sheikh Mahmud founded the first Kurdish government in October 1918 that lasted until June 1919. In 1922, he formed the second Kurdish government and proclaimed himself king of Kurdistan.[2] During that period, the British role in Kurdistan was confined to that of providing political and administrative advice to Sheikh Mahmud.

By the end of 1922, Britain shifted its policy from supporting Kurdish self-rule to incorporating their region to Iraq. The British were committed to building a strong Iraqi state, and the policy of privileging the Iraqi centre over the Kurdish periphery. Kurdish self-rule posed a challenge to British imperial priorities and a direct threat to the state-building project that tied Iraqi and British interests together. At this point it was clear that Britain was willing to sacrifice the Kurds and had a vested interest in the attachment of Kurdistan to Iraq and the establishment of a strong, centralised government. To contain Kurdish opposition to attaching Kurdistan to Iraq, the British made generous promises. In December 1922, the British and Iraq issued a joint declaration and offered the Kurds the opportunity to establish an autonomous Kurdistan if the Kurds first agreed to be part of Iraq. The British and League of Nations also promised an administrative autonomy under mandate protection for 25 years, in return for Kurdish support for the annexation of the province of Mosul (Kurdish region) to Iraq.

To determine the future of the Kurdish region, the League of Nations, established the Fact-Finding Commission (FFC) in September 1924. The mission of the FFC was to find out whether the people of Kurdistan were Turks or Iraqis. A nominal referendum of Mosul was arranged by the League of Nations in 1925 and the commission declared that the desires expressed by the population were more in favour of Iraq.[3] From the very beginning, Kurdish leaders rejected the legitimacy of the League of Nations' decision to authorise Britain to force Kurdistan to join Iraq. In a letter to the League he stated that their decision was a grave injustice that harmed the moral status and reputation of the League.[4] By 1926, the British, Iraq, and the League of Nations reneged on their promises to protect the Kurds and to guarantee some form of Kurdish self-rule. By 1930, the British announced unconditional support for Iraq's entry into the League of Nations without any formal safeguards in place for the Kurds. For many decades, the British clearly showed their commitment to maintaining the unity of the Iraqi state.

Forcing the Kurds to stay in Iraq, the British contributed directly and played a main role in the defeat of all Kurdish rebellions in Iraq between the two World Wars. The Royal Air Force (RAF) suppressed the Kurdish government under the leadership of Sheikh Mahmud. The British destroyed the Kurdish government of Sheikh Mahmud and occupied its capitol in 1923. The RAF then helped the new Iraqi army put down revolts led by Sheikh Mahmud from 1924–1927 and 1931–1932. The British also played a key role in preventing Sheikh Mahmud from reviving his movement during WWII. In addition to the presence of the British army and its direct involvement, British forces encouraged and supported the Iraqi state in attacking Sheikh Mahmud's forces and declaring martial law in Kurdistan in 1943. The Barzan revolt of 1932 was defeated only with the help of British troops and an extensive RAF bombing campaign. Later in 1936, the RAF participated in the suppression of another Barzan rebellion led by Khalil Khoshewi. In 1943 when Mustafa Barzani began his second revolt, the British moved its forces to Kurdistan to fight against him. In 1945, following the defeat of the Iraqi army, the RAF bombarded the Barzan region, the heartland of the rebellions, and their villages. Thus, for decades the imbalance of power between the Kurds and Iraqis was buttressed by the military support of Britain for Iraq against the Kurds.

Following Iraqi independence and its membership in the League of Nations in 1932, the international community treated the Kurdish issue as an internal affair of the Iraqi state. Iraq adopted the policy of 'Iraqisation' of the Kurds through introducing the concepts of 'Iraqi subjects' (*Re'aya*) or describing them as a 'race' or 'linguistic minority', rather than a distinct nation or ethnic group which the Kurds considered themselves to be. Iraq's mainstream media and state discourse officially refrained from using the words 'Kurds', 'Kurdish people', or 'ethnic Kurds'. The Kurds were re-categorised as 'Kurdish elements' or 'northerners'. Baghdad confidently took an uncompromising stand towards Kurdish nationalism and was unwilling to accommodate their aspirations. Kurdish nationalism was perceived as a serious threat to the integrity of Iraq. Kurdish nationalism was delegitimised and even criminalised. Iraq's leaders constantly accused the Kurds of conspiring with the enemies of the Arabs/Iraqis. Though the colonial power had a decisive role in the suppression of the Kurds, Iraqi official discourse and media outlets represented Kurdish nationalism as part of the British conspiracy against the Iraqi state and its Arab identity. Kurdish political parties were frequently referred to as puppets of the 'imperialists' and the accusation was used by both pro- and anti-British Iraqi politicians.

From Kurdish nationalists' perspective, attaching Kurdistan to Iraq against its will meant the usurpation of their right of self-determination. Prior to the League of Nations' decision to annex Kurdistan to Iraq in 1925, many treaties and declarations provided for Kurdish self-determination. President Woodrow Wilson's famous Fourteen Points, published in 1918, promoted the principles of self-determination and the Kurds' independent state.[5] The Paris Peace Conference held in 1919, an international conference in which a Kurdish delegation was represented, produced another international document that supported the principle of self-determination for the Kurds. Articles 61 and 63 of the Treaty of Sèvres clearly proposed an independent Kurdish state.[6] These promises, however, have never come to fruition; the Kurds were left without a state as they became a minority in the newly created state of Iraq.

Kurdish nationalists perceived the attachment of Kurdistan to Iraq as an imperialistic process that usurped the Kurds' right of self-determination. Equating the process of incorporation of Kurdistan into Iraq to usurpation of their right of self-determination has become a shared vision of most Kurdish political parties as well as individuals. Iraq was viewed as an 'occupier' and Kurdistan was seen as an occupied homeland. Attaining the right of self-determination has become a common goal of most Kurdish political parties during the monarchy era. For instance, Tawfiq Wahbi, the mayor of Sulaimaniya in the early 1930s, called for the right of self-determination.[7] In the 1940s, both the Rizgari Party[8] and the *Yeketi Tekoshin*[9] advocated Kurds the right to self-determination for the Kurds and the establishment of an independent Kurdish state.[10] Kurdish history in Iraq has been characterised by the domination of Kurdish nationalist parties that put the achievement of self-determination at the top of their agendas. The failure of Kurdish integration into the Iraqi state was mostly due to their unending quest for self-determination.

To earn legitimacy in Kurdish society and to make a claim at the League of Nations that the Kurds were adequately represented, the monarchy regime relied on the Arabised Kurds and ex-Ottoman Kurdish officers (hereafter Arabised Kurds).[11] This segment of Kurdish society was the only group that inclined towards accommodating the Kurds and advocated for the 'Iraqi-first' identity policy. Arabised Kurds lacked Kurdish nationalist sentiments and were the first among the Kurdish population that openly identified as Iraqis and declared their loyalty to the newly created state. Accommodating this group was not perceived as a threat to Iraq's integrity. Bakir Sidqi, an Arabised Kurd who replaced the old cabinet of pan-Arabs in a coup d'état on 30 October 1936, is an example. As an Arabised Kurd and advocate of the Iraqi-first policy, he attempted to identify with the Iraqi state.[12] Like many other Arabised Kurds, however, Sidqi was motivated by his personal interests and Iraqi nationalism rather than Kurdish nationalism. Between the 1920s and the early 1940s, the Arabised Kurds actively participated in the Iraqi state-building process. Most Kurdish deputies and ministers were from this group and four Arabised Kurds served as prime ministers.

Accommodation of Arabised Kurds, however, neither had significant impact on the perceived legitimacy of Iraqi authority in Kurdistan, nor did it aid Kurdish integration into Iraq. Though the Arabised Kurds were Kurdish by origin, they belong to families that migrated to Arab areas of Iraq, mostly to Baghdad, during the last part of the nineteenth century. Most Arabised Kurds were not residents of Kurdistan and they had little influence on Iraqi-Kurdish relations. Arabised Kurds were assimilated into Arab society and were Arab in sentiment rather than Kurdish. They rarely claimed their Kurdish origin and had little, if any, Kurdish nationalist feelings. They had little contact with the Kurdish community and had a weak political and social base and support among the Kurds. They were perceived by many Kurds as proxies for British and Iraqi rulers.

The inclusion of Arabised Kurds into Iraqi politics cannot be considered as an accommodation to Kurdish society. By the early 1940s, Kurdish resentment and feelings of alienation had increased, resulting in the emergence of new a wave of Kurdish nationalism. Baghdad's reliance on the Arabised Kurds to earn legitimacy in Kurdish society failed. In desperation Baghdad began to search for a better alternative to reliance on Arabised Kurds to strengthen their standing within Kurdish society. Two influential segments of the Kurdish population that played critical roles during the monarchy in Iraq were urban nationalists (hereafter urbanites) and traditional tribal leaders. The regime applied different policies to each segment of the population. The monarchy followed a conciliatory policy towards Kurdish landlords, religious leaders, and tribal leaders, as well as attempted to reinstate their power and authority within Kurdish society.

The monarchy-urban Kurds relations

Urbanites were pioneers and advocates of Kurdish nationalism. They were by-products of the modernisation process of the Ottoman *Tanzimat* reforms that began during the second half of the nineteenth century. Urbanites were educated by the educational system of the Ottoman Empire and later by the monarchy. The urbanites of Kurdistan were aware of modern political ideologies and witnessed the development of Arab and Turkish nationalisms into strong political movements. They, however, showed little, if any, loyalty to Arab nationalism in Iraq and they did not seek a role within the Iraqi state structure. Aiming to play a political role of their own, from the very beginning the urbanites challenged the state-sponsored nation-building process in the Kurdistan region. Likewise, the majority of the urbanite Kurds rejected membership within the Iraqi political parties and alternatively created their own nationalist parties such as Hiwa, Rizgari, the Kurdistan Democratic Party (KDP), and the Kurdistan branch of the Iraqi Communist Party with leftist and nationalist orientations.

The Kurdish urbanites were influential segments of Kurdish society. Several striking examples demonstrate the urbanites' leadership role in Kurdish society. In Sulaimaniya, for example, the city's notables and intelligentsia arranged mass demonstrations in September 1930. Tens of protestors were killed by the Iraqi police and tens were either wounded or arrested.[13] The September demonstration known as 'the Dark Day of September Sixth' was considered by modern Kurds to be a milestone in the Kurdish Nationalist Movement. The uprising turned into a modern-day symbol of Kurdish resistance and victimisation.[14] Urbanities also demonstrated their ability to challenge the Iraqi nation-building process. For example, they succeeded in convincing the Kurdish masses to elevate *Nawroz*, a pre-Islamic myth, to a Kurdish national day, thus replacing Iraq's national day which celebrated the founding of the Iraqi army. From 1940 onward, *Nawroz* was popularly celebrated in Iraqi Kurdistan as the Kurdish national day.[15] In fact, not only in Iraqi Kurdistan but throughout greater Kurdistan, *Nawroz* has been accepted as Kurdish national day. Since 1958, *Nawroz* has been recognised by the Iraqi central government as a national holiday.[16] The urbanites emerged as a driving force to threaten the legitimacy of Iraqi rule in the Kurdistan region and the integrity of the Iraqi state.

To constrain the urbanites' role, Baghdad followed a policy of exclusion and suppression against them. Throughout the mandate and monarchy periods, all political parties of the urban Kurds had been banned. The Kurds were also prevented from founding democratic institutions, Kurdish cultural associations, and civil society trade unions, as well as from offering free elections.[17] Iraq has often accused the Kurds of being traitors, clients of Iraq's enemies, imperialists, Zionists, and other denigrating names. They have used these accusations to justify their rejection of the Kurds and even to perpetrate wars against the Kurds. During the early years of the monarchy the Kurds were accused of being agents of colonialism. The 'Kurdish question' is portrayed as being created by the British to weaken Iraq and its national unity.[18] Iraqi historians and officials accused Kurdish nationalists during the 1930s of being encouraged by Germany. It was claimed that the Hiwa Party, a Kurdish nationalist organisation established in 1939, was created by the British and that Barzani had 'special relations' with the British.[19] These accusations were made despite British participation in suppressing the Barzani rebellions of 1931–1932 and 1943–1945.

The monarchy's policies of exclusion and repression of urbanites proved to be counterproductive. The policy resulted in the decrease of the legitimacy of Iraq's authority in the Kurds' eyes. Kurdish nationalists rejected Iraqi rule in Kurdistan and portrayed Iraq as an occupier rather than legitimate ruler. The perception of Iraq as an Arab occupier has dominated Kurdish nationalist literature. Kurdish political rhetoric abounds with terms such as 'the occupier regime of Iraq' and 'the occupiers of Kurdistan'. The Kurdish Rizgari Party, for example, emphasised that its duty was to achieve the liberation and sovereignty of the Kurdish nation.[20] The Hiwa Party stressed that its goal is to liberate Iraqi Kurdistan by political means.[21] The KDP also followed the same line of thinking during the monarchy.[22] By pointing out Iraq's occupier status, the Kurdish parties undermined the legitimacy of the central government's rule in Kurdistan among the Kurds. Categorising the Kurdish-Iraq relationship as that of 'liberator versus occupier' motivated Kurdish nationalism and elevated the probabilities of its survival. The struggle against 'occupy Iraq' was used as a fertile ground to recruit Kurds into its ranks.

Rejecting the legitimacy of Iraqi authority in Kurdistan, the Kurds have been in an almost constant quest for an outside source of protection. Between 1925 and 1932, the Kurds sought British and League of Nations' protection. Regardless of their demands, most pro- and anti-colonial Kurds considered the British as their main security against Iraqi oppression. From 1930 to 1932, Kurdish leaders and different segments of Kurdish society presented dozens of petitions to the League and often to the British seeking support. Kurdish demands ranged from autonomy to the independence of Kurdistan; but in either case, the Kurds insisted on Britain or League of Nations' protection from the exploitation of Iraq.[23] Between 1940 and 1958, Kurdish nationalists unsuccessfully pursued another method, which was to communicate with various international bodies and leading statesmen. Tens of letters, notes, and memoranda were presented by Kurdish nationalists to foreign powers. Their demands ranged from protection and minority rights to the right of self-determination and full independence. The Kurds' search for outside protection during the monarchy became part of their political culture and was adopted by future generations of Kurdish nationalists and intellectuals. From the Kurdish perspective, the search for outside protection was a legitimate reaction to internal exploitation by Kurdistan's occupiers. The Kurds' constant search for outside support was considered by the Iraqi officials a violation of the country's sovereignty.

The monarchy-*aghas* relations

For many centuries, Kurdistan enjoyed a form of self-rule that contributed to its political culture. Kurdistan as a separate administrative unit goes back to the Umayyad era in the eighth century. During the Ottoman era (1453–1920), the empire followed an indirect and nominal rule in Kurdistan. The Kurds enjoyed semi-independence and were governed by Kurdish principalities. The Ottoman *Tanzimat* reforms of the nineteenth century were partially implemented in Kurdistan.[24] Centuries of Kurdish self-governance and semi-autonomy have shaped the Kurdish way of life and contributed to Kurdistan's political culture and belief system. After the creation of Iraq, the *aghas* still dominated Iraqi Kurdistan socio-economically and kept their privileged position in the local power structure. They were an integral and essential part of the social, economic, and cultural life of rural Kurdistan. *Aghas* expected their relative independence to be respected if they were going to accept externally imposed governance.

The status of the *aghas* put them in a highly awkward position. The eradication of the *aghas*' social and cultural base was vital for the state-building process and maintenance of Iraq's integrity. The state's interference in the daily life of the *aghas* might imply the loss of their socio-political power. The *aghas*, showed their staunch resistance to Iraqi penetration into their local communities and defended their semi-independent status. Tribal resistance to Iraqi centralisation policies had often resulted in tribal rebellions, as it did with the Barzani and *yazidis* revolts of the early 1930s. This resistance presented a serious obstacle to the Iraqi state-building process.

76 The monarchy-Kurds relations

To assure their loyalty and cooperation, both the British and Iraq had to acknowledge and support their local authority, albeit at the expense of state sovereignty. Initially, the British mandate passed separate legislation for the tribal areas that remained as law throughout the monarchy. The British aim of these laws was to undo the detribalisation process of the *Tanzimat* reforms that were initiated by the Ottoman authorities and re-establish the tribal system. Similarly, Baghdad adopted a policy of accommodation and maintained the Kurdish tribal system. These policies favouring traditional strata over the urban Kurds continued until the last years of the monarchy.

The Iraqi state gave up many important symbols of sovereignty including the monopoly of the legitimate use of force, governmental jurisdiction, and the power to collect taxes from Kurdistan. *Aghas* maintain their right to appoint their leaders. Baghdad had little say in appointing the head of the tribal community. In most cases, the tribal community rejected the government's candidate for heading the community, as was the case with the Jaf tribe.[25] The *agha*, as head of the tribe, enjoyed undisputed authority over its areas of responsibility. Many *aghas* governed a territory that was equal to that of a state the size of Lebanon. For example, in the early 1930s, Sheikh Ahmed Barzani administered an area of 10,000 square kilometres.[26] The status of tribal communities was especially evident in their right to maintain their militias. Even during the mandate era, the *aghas* received arms and ammunition from the British.[27] In the early 1930s, for instance, the Jaf tribe alone had more than 2,500 militants and the confederation of the Barzan under Sheikh Ahmed had 10,000 fighters.[28] These militias were under the direct command of their *agha* and were not organised by or administered from Baghdad. Jurisdiction was another area in which traditional communities enjoyed autonomy. Tribal areas were excluded from the jurisdiction of Iraqi courts and the absolute jurisdictional authority was given to the *aghas*. The head tribes retained the right to settle civil and criminal cases, including land and other local disputes of the community. In tax affairs, certain *aghas* whose tribes enjoyed autonomy retained dual rights: on the national level they enjoyed special tax benefits while on the local level they extracted taxation rights. Though theoretically the monarchy was a centralised state, an unspoken system of semi-decentralisation and indirect rule had been arranged in many parts of Kurdistan. This indirect rule in rural Kurdistan has reshaped Kurdish-Iraqi relations in modern Iraq.

The British and Iraqi re-tribalisation policy was strategically calculated. The monarchy lacked suitable governmental apparatuses and administrative control over Kurdistan. It also failed to gain sufficient support in Kurdistan to carry out their national plan. In the years following WWII, these difficulties were compounded by the establishment of a coalition by right wing urban nationalist Kurds and many discontented *aghas*. Within this unfavourable context, reinstating the power and authority of the *aghas* was not perceived as a serious threat to the integrity of Iraq. The majority of the *aghas* focused principally upon land ownership and they were therefore not motivated by notions of Kurdish nationalism that might jeopardise their tribal interests. The *aghas* who were motivated by Kurdish nationalism adopted a minimalist approach to Kurdish rights. Their demands ranged between cultural rights and fiscal and administrative autonomy. The monarchy *agha* policy, therefore, was a double-edged sword. While it provided a scope of indirect rule and tolerance for the Kurdish culture, the policy reinforced the fragmentation of Kurdish society and kept the Kurds under the state's control.

The emergence of the urbanite-*agha* coalition

WWII impacted the political atmosphere of Kurdish society significantly. WWII led to the diminution of the British influence in Iraq and this further exacerbated internal Iraqi conflicts. On 1 April 1941, Rashid Ali al-Gaylani, a pan-Arabist and pro-Nazi Sunni Arab politician, led a military coup against the pro-British regime of Iraq. Though toppled by the British, the coup revealed the rise of pan-Arabism and the manipulation of power politics in Iraq. This increased the *aghas*' feeling of vulnerability due to the potential threat to the survival of their tribal autonomous entities. This anxiety was made evident by the rebellion of Sheikh Mahmud, Barzanis, and many tribes against the government. Due to increasing pressure from state elites, both traditional and urbanite Kurds found it necessary to cooperate and became less isolated from one another compared to their relations in the early 1930s. In this manner, the decline of the British presence facilitated the cooperation between Kurdish urbanites and *aghas*; the al-Gaylani coup, coupled with the effects of WWII, resulted in the diminishment of the British role in Iraq. After their withdrawal from Iraq, their ability to suppress and subvert any Kurdish rebellions diminished.

In addition to the ascendency of pan-Arabism, many factors created a fertile ground for the revival of *Kurdayeti* after WWII. Among other factors that played a crucial role in breathing life back into Kurdish nationalism were the decolonisation process, the emergence of a new independent state, and the rise and fall of the first Kurdish republic of Iranian Kurdistan. The widespread use of radio and other telecommunications resulted in the spread of modern ideals such as communism, Nazism, liberalism, and democracy. Consequently, the newly educated generation of *aghas* exposed to modern ideals and politics and it indicated their willingness to participate in Kurdish nationalism. Two examples are Bahaddin Nuri, the former secretary of the Iraqi Communist Party, and Jalal Talabani, then a member of the KDP politburo. This provided an opportunity for the traditional Kurdish tribal leadership to join forces with the urban nationalist movement. Mustafa Barzani, who joined the Kurdish nationalist during his exile in Sulaimaniya (1933–1943), is an example that shows that the two strata were more apt to cooperate than they were during the first wave of reawakening. By now, the urban Kurds were no longer the single body to represent Kurdish nationalism. The cooperation of the two strata resulted in an unprecedented revival of Kurdish nationalism among traditional and urban Kurds. Both nationalist *aghas* and the urbanites extended their popularity and authority beyond their respective territories.

The Hiwa Party may be considered as a pioneer of the urban-tribal elites' coalition. In 1944, for the first time in modern Kurdish history, the Hiwa Party organised both urban and tribal communities within one political party, namely the

Azadi Committee. By 1944, the Hiwa Party was dissolved and two years later, on 16 August 1946, the KDP was established as a coalition of leftists, army officers, city nobles, and dominant tribal leaders. The ex-members of the Azadi Committee and the Hiwa Party took the leadership role of the new party and wrote its constitution.[29] The party became a broader coalition of tribal leaders, leftists, city notables, and dominant tribal leaders such as Barzani and Sheikh Latif. In other words, the KDP adopted the policy of incorporating both urbanites and *aghas* into one political party. The KDP adopted the principle of dual leadership (*aghas* and urbanites) of the party. Rafiq Hilmi, the leader of the Hiwa Party, introduced the idea of dual leadership, civil and militant, for the Kurdish Nationalist Movement.[30] The militants were exclusively tribal and with the officers, but the urbanites were more civil. By implication, the Hiwa's call consisted of nothing more tribal and urban leadership. This perspective was adopted by the Azadi Committee. While offering the chairmanship of the party to Barzani as tribal leader, all its central committee members were from the officers.[31] It is worth noting that, apart from Barzani, all leadership members were also members of the Hiwa. Similar principles were followed in the establishment of the Iraqi KDP. This was evident in the fact that Barzani and the army officers were in Mahabad when they initiated the establishment of the KDP. They also formalised the silent understanding to allocate the positions of the president and secretary within the KDP evenly to tribal and urban elites. The tribal leaders guaranteed the nomination of the party's presidency and the urbanites retained the positions of secretary and political bureau of the party. Barzani, Sheikh Latif, and Kaka-Zyad, three of the most significant figures within Kurdish tribal society, were appointed as the party's president and deputies, respectively. The KDP remained one of the main political parties that dominated the Kurdish political sphere since its establishment in 1946. Though in a different form, the dual leadership is still followed by the KDP today. The president of the party is dedicated to the Barzani family, with Masud Barzani as the president. His nephew, Nechirvan Barzani, is its vice president, and the secretary of the party and the majority of its politburo are allocated to non-Barzanis of whom most are members of the urban elite.

Urbanites introduced the militaristic rebellion as a method to achieve nationalist goals. The tribal or semi-tribal wing of the Azadi and the KDP (including leader Mustafa Barzani) originated from the rural regions and had a warrior background. They preferred to draw on military methods to oppose the Iraqi authority in Kurdistan. The Iraqi authority itself had a military mentality as a consequence of the army's role which was evident in a series of military coups that transpired between 1937 and 1941. The Hiwa approached Barzani to confront this development through the creation of an armed force. Consequently a militia of some 4,000–5,000 persons was established.[32] Hence, for the first time, *Kurdayeti* in Iraq established an organised military force. In the following decades the tribal and rural leaders retained the military wing of the KDP.

Urbanites also invested tribal revolts for the nationalist agenda and the redirection of tribal unrest to a nationalist rebellion. Urban nationalists were disappointed at the failure to achieve Kurdish rights through peaceful and political means. In a letter to Barzani, Rafiq Hilmi expressed the nationalists' disappointment at being deprived of legal channels to express nationalist sentiments. He suggested that a successful nationalist movement required a military and a political wing. Viewed in this way, Hiwa perceived the second Barzani revolt (1943–1945) as an opportunity to invest in both political and nationalist goals. The rebellion initially began as a tribal insurgency against increasing governmental interference in the Barzani tribal affairs and its main goals and demands were exclusively tribal. Iraq appointed Majid Mustafa, a Kurdish minister in Baghdad, as the government's representative to negotiate on its behalf with the Barzanis. Mustafa was an independent personality who established a close relationship with the clandestine Hiwa.

Not impressed with the urbanites' style of nationalism, the traditional communities' demands were mostly concerned with tribal interests and local community affairs. Therefore, on the one hand, in order to bring the rural communities into the Kurdish nationalist struggle, Hiwa, through Azadi, offered significant concessions based on nationalist principles, such as abandoning irredentism and secessionism. Hiwa minimalised its nationalist goals to more closely meet tribal concerns that centred on fiscal, cultural, and administrative autonomy. Urbanites abandoned their goal of the liberation of greater Kurdistan and the establishment of a united Kurdish state and confined their goals to the liberation of Iraqi Kurdistan. On the other hand, Mustafa Barzani elevated his tribal demand to nationalist rights on behalf of the wider Kurdish community. Barzani proposed to negotiate with Baghdad in April 1944. As a leader of the Barzan rebellion, and with the encouragement of the army officers, Barzani replaced his tribal demands with moderate Kurdish rights.[33] Barzani summed up his claims as follows: organising the Kurdish provinces and districts in Iraq within one administrative unit. This unit was to be administered from Baghdad through a Kurdish minister in the Iraqi government. A Kurd was to be appointed as deputy minister in each ministry. The Kurdish administration would retain decision-making authority over cultural, economic, and agricultural affairs, while security issues would remain with the central government.

As pointed out, many tribes enjoyed a modicum of autonomy and retained the right to bear arms, collect taxes, and administer their local affairs. Most tribes, however, resented interference in their internal affairs by a Kurdish political party as much as that by the central government. That is why the *aghas* were not attracted to the Kurdish political parties or their nationalist ideologies until WWII. Two factors encouraged the *aghas* to adopt a more conciliatory attitude. First, the developments related to WWII reshaped state-*agha* relations. The autonomous status of traditional communities was not officially organised or constitutionally recognised. The lack of official status deprived these traditional communities of the ability to institutionalise or to find a network of collaborators or central command. Therefore, their very survival depended on the weakness of the central government and the influence of the British in the country. However, since WWII, British influence declined and pan-Arab and centrist ideologies ascended among the leadership in Iraq. Accordingly, the main threat to the Traditional Autonomous

Entities (TAE) did not come from the Kurdish party; rather it came from Baghdad, which was eager to consolidate its control over all parts of Iraq.

Kurdish nationalists' (especially Hiwa and KDP) policy was to include the *aghas* into its ranks, thus bringing the urban and tribal elites of Iraqi Kurdistan together in one coalition. This step had three important messages for the *aghas* and the traditional communities. First, it meant that the KDP would accommodate tribal and the rural populations' interests. Second, it showed the party's willingness not only to accept members from all segments of tribal communities, but also to provide a position within the Kurdish movement that matched their socioeconomic status. Though the KDP diminished the *agha* power base by emerging as an additional new player in Kurdish rural society, it was compensated by offering the *aghas* political status. For the traditional stratum, the KDP provided an opportunity to retain its role in Kurdish politics. Third, the KDP's willingness to establish direct and conciliatory relations with traditional communities meant that the party would refrain from interference in their internal affairs. Fourth, the KDP offered a potential counterbalance against both the Iraqi state and the left wing of the Kurdish Nationalist Movement. These factors merged the moderate urbanites and *aghas* into a conciliatory, if not a common, front.

A common urban-tribal front resulted in the change of the balance of power in favour of Kurdish nationalism. The coalition of the *aghas* and urbanites resulted in the emergence of Kurdish political parties as modern and autonomous political entities. The most significant consequence of this development was that the rural areas were opened up for urban activities. Through incorporating the *aghas*, the KDP became the first nationalist party to establish a base in the Kurdish rural areas. At the same time the traditional elites found a leadership role and representation in a nationalist party. Thus, the KDP not only spoke on behalf of the urban nationalists, but also represented the tribal and rural communities. Consequently, the Kurdish nationalists penetrated the rural areas of Kurdistan, areas that had not been penetrated by any Kurdish or Iraqi political parties up to that time.

The KDP monopoly of Kurdish politics

The establishment of a common front between the tribal and urban communities strengthened the Kurdish Nationalist Movement significantly. From the 1940s onward, the hitherto fragmented feudal leadership of Kurdish society was replaced by a unified nationalist leadership outside of Iraqi state control. Until 1940, Kurdish nationalists failed to unify its ranks and leadership. However, initiated by the Hiwa Party, the dual leadership facilitated the KDP's ability to establish a unified leadership centred on the legendary personality of the Kurdish leader Mustafa Barzani. Thousands of Iraqi Kurds, mostly under the leadership of Mustafa Barzani, participated in the establishment and defence of the Republic of Mahabad. He was exiled to the Soviet Union following the collapse of the Republic. Now as a national hero who defended the Kurdish republic and was exiled for the Kurdish cause, Barzani assumed leadership of the Iraqi Kurds. The KDP literature considered Barzani to be a symbolic hero of the Kurdish Nationalist Movement and could find no one of his stature to replace him. Despite his exile for 12 years (1946–1958), the KDP did not search for a leader to replace Barzani. Barzani's charismatic personality enabled *Kurdayeti* to challenge the impact of the Iraqi personalities on ordinary Kurds.

By the end of the 1940s, Kurdish nationalists enjoyed a safe haven in rural areas and their activities were no longer monitored or restricted by Iraqi security forces. Though apparently clandestine and outlawed, the KDP acted relatively free of constraints and even monopolised Kurdistan's political sphere. Most Iraqi political parties, nearly a dozen pan-Arab or Iraqi-first types, failed to find enough Kurdish followers to create an organisational base in Kurdistan. The ICP, however, was an exception. The party that emerged as a major Iraqi force in the 1950s and early 1960s was the only Iraqi party that created an organisational base in Kurdistan. The Kurds' attraction to the ICP was significant enough that in the 1950s and 1960s the Kurds constituted more than 31 per cent of the party's central committee and 35–40 per cent of party membership.

The autonomous environment that the KDP enjoyed enabled the party to publish its clandestine publications and establish its popular organisations. The KDP was founded and operated outside state control and the legal system of Iraq, and it had no permission or licence.[34] Its goals, functions, and ideology were not necessarily compatible with Iraqi legislation or regulations. Its programs were, in fact, independent of and antagonistic to the state's constitution, laws, and ideology. Though limited, Kurdish nationalists were still free in their relations with the outside world, especially with fellow Kurds in Iran. During the Iraqi monarchy, many semi-nomadic Kurds still followed their traditional summer practice of travelling to the highlands of Iranian and Turkish Kurdistan. This also provided freedom of movement for nationalists to cross borders into and from Iranian Kurdistan. Kurdish leaders in Iran and Iraq frequently took refuge on the opposite side of the border. Within this relatively free and uncontrolled environment, the KDP established relations with the Kurds from elsewhere – far from the eyes of the central government of Iraq. For example, the Hiwa Party had a significant role in the establishment of the *Komallay Jyanewey Kurd* (the Kurdish Renaissance League in 1943), which later developed into the Kurdistan Democratic Party-Iran (KDPI). In August 1944, Kurdish nationalist leaders from Turkey, Iran, and Iraq met and signed a mutual support pact.[35] Moreover, when the Republic of Mahabad was declared in 1946, tribal militants under the leadership of Mustafa Barzani and military officers from Iraqi Kurdistan formed the most effective wing of the new republic's military.

By the early 1950s, the KDP felt confident enough to institutionalise the nationalist movement through the establishment of the Kurdish youth and professional organisations. In 1952, for example, three popular organisations were founded to institutionalise the Kurdish Nationalist Movement: Kurdistan Women's Union (founded by the female members of the KDP), the Kurdistan Teachers Union, and the Kurdistan Student Union. Other popular organisations that were founded to institutionalise *Kurdayeti* were the Youth Union of Kurdistan, the Islamic Scholars

Union of Kurdistan, and the Writers League of Kurdistan. These organisations were territorially (Kurdistan) based unions that emphasised separate national identities, namely Kurdistani identity.

The Iraq monarchy was so weak in Kurdistan that it failed to impose its authority in rural areas. Consequently, the *aghas* successfully resisted the penetration of Iraqi state institutions into their areas. What further worsened the Iraqi position in Kurdistan was that Kurdish nationalists were already active and in a dominant position. Official Iraqi state mechanisms and organisations by which the Iraqi nation-building project could operate were absent in Kurdistan. That is why all Iraqi regimes, beginning with the monarchy and ending with Saddam, depended on the *aghas* for support to impose their rule in Kurdistan. With the failure of the Iraqi nation-building project, coupled with the absence of grass-roots supporters of the Iraqi state in Kurdistan, the Kurdish population found a voice in their nationalist parties, especially the KDP. Thus, Kurdish nationalism was unified and organised into autonomous political parties that dominated the political sphere and operated freely in rural Kurdistan. They were well supported and protected by tribal militants.

Notes

1. Sluglett 1976: 116: Olson 1987: 101; 116; Fieldhouse 2002: 34; Eskander 2000: 163; Emin 2000: 198, 313.
2. Sheikh Mahmud, fought for Kurdish independence from 1919 to 1932.
3. League of Nations 1925: 88.
4. Emin 2000: 197–200.
5. For the full text of Woodrow Wilson's Fourteen Points, see *American History*, available at <www.hbci.com/~tgort/14points.htm>, (accessed 12/12/2014).
6. For the articles of the Treaty of Sèvres, see *WWI Document Archive*, available at <http://wwi.lib.byu.edu/index.php/Section_I%2C_Articles_1_-_260>, (accessed 10/09/2014).
7. Emin 2000: 287–296.
8. For the full text of the Rizgari Party's statement see Andrews 1982: 45.
9. The *Yeketi Tekoshin* (hereafter *Tekoshin*) was established in 1944 and later turned into the Communist Party of Iraqi Kurdistan, which was popularly known as *Shoresh*.
10. Yeketi Tekoshin 1944: 8–11.
11. The Arabised Kurds were a group of Iraqi politicians who were Kurdish by origin and belonged to families that migrated to Arab areas of Iraq, mostly to Baghdad, during the last part of the nineteenth century. As many of them belonged to Kurdish noble or high-class families, they entered the Ottoman education and political system. However, this group was assimilated into Arab society and they played a vital role in Iraqi politics. Some were motivated by personal interests and Iraqi nationalism rather than Kurdish interests and nationalism.
12. Bill 1969: 58; Freij, H. Y. (1993), "Kurdish Nationalism," *The Muslim World* 83(3–4): 326; Lukitz 1995: 80.
13. Emin 2000: 66–68.
14. For example see the textbook for grade 12 in the Kurdistan region: KRG-ME 2008: 156–157.
15. Bnkey Zhin (2012), *Nawrozi Rojaneki Rabrdu (Nawroz of the Old Days)*, Suleymaniya, Iraq: 7.
16. *Al-Waqai' al-Iraqiya* 30/08/1958.

17 Talabani 1970: 179; Lukitz 1995: 11; Farouk-Sluglett and Sluglett 2001: 80; Natali 2005: 44.
18 Zhiyan 28–08–1930; Sluglett 1976: 25.
19 Al-Barak 1989: 35; Jawad 1990: 2.
20 For the full text of the Kurdish Rizgari Party see Andrews 1982: 43–44.
21 Jwaideh 2006: 233.
22 Rizgari 1952.
23 Zhiyan 21–07–1930; Emin 2000: 251–315.
24 *Tanzimat* refers to a "series of reforms promulgated in the Ottoman Empire between 1839 and 1876 under the reigns of the sultans Abdülmecid I and Abdülaziz. Heavily influenced by European ideas, these reforms were intended to effectuate a fundamental change of the empire from the old system based on theocratic principles to that of a modern state" (Encyclopedia Britannica).
25 Ali 2003: 568.
26 Ali 2003: 575.
27 Bruinessen 1986: 16; Fuccaro 1997: 563; Natali 2000: 69; McDowall 2004: 180.
28 Ali 2003: 529; 567.
29 Emin 2004: 186.
30 For the full version of the letter in English, see Barzani (2003b: 74). For the Arabic version see Sharif (2007: 164–165).
31 Qaftan, K. (2003), *Al-Intifadhat al-Barzaniya: Safhat mn Tarikh al-Haraka al-Taharruriya al-Kurdiya fi Nisf al-Awal mn al-Qrn al-Ishrin (The Barzanis' uprisings: Pages in the History of the Kurdish Revolutionary Movement During the First Half of the Twentieth Century)*, Erbil, Iraq: Aras Publisher: 86; Shamzini 2006: 286.
32 Borovali, A. F. (1987), "Kurdish Insurgencies, the Gulf War, and Turkey's Changing Role," *Journal of Conflict Studies* 7(4): 31; Qaftan 2003: 83.
33 Emin, N. M. (1997b), *Penjekan Yektri Deshkenin: Diwi Nawewey Rwdawekani Kurdistani Iraq le Newan 1979–1983 (Fingers that Crush Each Other: Political Events in Iraqi Kurdistan from 1979–1983)*, Berlin: Postfach: 49: Shamzini 2006: 284.
34 Talabani 1970: 88.
35 Eagleton, William, Jr. (1963), *The Kurdish Republic of 1946*, London: Oxford University Press: 36.

5 The first unrecognised Kurdish quasi-state (1961–1975)

Post-monarchical developments in Kurdish affairs may not be adequately understood apart from the second phase of Kurdish nationalism (1939–1958). In fact, the post-monarch Kurdish *de facto* state is a natural extension of that phase of Kurdish nationalism. During the monarchy, Kurdish landlords, religious leaders, and tribal leaders (hereafter *aghas*)[1] enjoyed a modicum of autonomy which guaranteed them a form of *de facto* autonomy in many areas.[2] Kurdish nationalism enjoyed many elements necessary to establish *de facto* self-rule including territory, an autonomous political party, and access to weaponry and a militia. In terms of territory, Iraqi rule was either weak or absent in rural Kurdistan especially in rural areas. Despite Iraq's refusal to recognise or licence Kurdish political parties, as well as its attempt to suppress their activities, it failed to prevent their domination in the Kurdish political sphere or infuse Iraqi conditions and principles into their constitutions and political programs. With the exception of the ICP, none of the Iraqi parties managed to establish a power base in Kurdistan. Many tribes that enjoyed TAE were permitted to have their own militias. These militias were under the direct command of their *aghas* and Baghdad had no control over them. These factors facilitated the emergence of Kurdish nationalism as a dominant force in Kurdistan. The collapse of the monarchy in 1958 and the power vacuum left in Kurdistan offered a golden opportunity for Kurdistan to promote its nationhood project and establish its *de facto* self-rule.

On 14 July 1958, the Hashemite monarchy was toppled by the Free Officers. Coup leader Abdul-Karim Qasim assumed control and declared Iraq to be a republic. The coup brought about a power vacuum in Kurdistan as Baghdad's status deteriorated further. Though challenged by new rulers, the *aghas* retained their modicum of autonomy in daily affairs. The local militia that remained under the *aghas*' control became the foundation for the newly organised peshmerga forces and enabled a unified leadership to emerge. The KDP, which monopolised politics in Kurdistan, strengthened its firm grip on Kurdish politics even more. While it was recognised as a legal political party by Baghdad, it operated freely in both the rural areas and the city centres. The next sections highlight how these new circumstances helped the Kurdish nationalists to expand and transform TAE into a semi-institutionalised *de facto* autonomy.

The emergence of the peshmerga as a unified Kurdish militia

One significant consequence of the 1958 coup was the emergence of a unified Kurdish army known as the peshmerga. Similar to the tribal militias, the peshmerga acted outside of Iraqi state control. Unlike the tribal armed men, however, the peshmerga was not commanded by the tribal leaders; rather they served under the command of the KDP and Barzani. In 1958 Barzani single-handedly recruited more than 2,000 soldiers to fight under his command.[3] Though this armed force seemed relatively small, it was one of the best organised forces outside of the state command. Its strength was so remarkable that Qasim pleaded for Barzani's aid in 1959 to crush the pan-Arab coup of al-Shawaf in Mosul. Barzani responded by sending more than 5,000 Kurdish fighters to suppress the rebellion and to defend Qasim.[4] The latter also supported Barzani's forces with 1,000 machine guns and an ammunition stockpile.[5] Though Qasim's support of Barzani's forces was symbolic for the most part, it gave recognition and legitimisation to the Kurdish militia by Qasim. Thus another autonomous entity was added to the pre-existing entities that developed in the Kurdistan region after the monarchy. As explained later, within a few years, the peshmerga became a formidable armed force that dominated a significant part of Kurdistan.

The emergence of Mustafa Barzani as a charismatic Kurdish leader

After the 1958 anti-Hashemite coup, both the KDP and Barzani continued to gain strength and popularity. Soon after Barzani's return from exile, his charismatic style of leadership allowed him to monopolise the role as undisputed authority in Kurdistan. Despite his popularity and claim to be the sole leader of all Iraqis, Qasim initially dealt with Barzani as the leader of the Kurds. Several factors were behind Qasim's recognition of Mustafa Barzani as the undisputed leader of the Kurds in Iraq. One of Qasim's weaknesses was that as an army officer he lacked his own party to rely on. Support among a political party, particularly within its leadership, would have compensated for this weakness. As explained previously, the political power base in Kurdistan was monopolised by the KDP and the Iraqi political parties were practically non-existent in Kurdistan. Therefore, to establish his authority in Kurdistan and to legitimise his rule among the Kurds, Qasim persisted in searching for an alliance with Barzani.

Traditionally Iraq's rule in Kurdistan was bolstered by two sources of power: an alliance with traditional social leaders and Iraq's security forces. Qasim, however, failed to avail himself of these two bases of power. Qasim thought to undermine the power of the *aghas* as part of his confrontation with old monarchy rivals.[6] After the 1958 coup, the security forces lost their dominant position in Kurdistan. Moreover, Qasim's rule was threatened by the pan-Arab movement that was sympathetic to Jamal Abdul-Nasir and represented by his deputy and successor Abdul-Salam Arif. Within these circumstances, Barzani's support for Qasim was indispensable. As the president of the KDP, Barzani secured the loyalties of the KDP for Qasim. Finally, Barzani was simultaneously an opponent of the monarchy and the pan-Arab nationalists. Barzani's animosity towards pan-Arabism was perceived by Qasim as a counterweight to the Arab nationalists.

Initially Qasim plied Barzani with financial largesse and weapons, in addition to granting him a licence for state-sanctioned violence. In return, Barzani helped to suppress anti-Qasim resistance among rebel Kurdish tribal leaders and Arab nationalists. Barzani played a significant role in crushing the pro-Hashemite Kurdish tribal leaders as well as the pan-Arab rebellion that took place in Mosul in March 1959.[7] Barzani helped to secure the loyalties of the Kurds in general and the KDP, the dominant political party in Kurdistan, in particular. He also proved to be a useful tool for the Iraqi regime to crush plots or forces directed against the latter. Being the head of the KDP and the Kurds' strongest leader, Barzani emerged as an ideal leader on whom Qasim could rely. Despite his self-proclamation as the sole leader of Iraq, Qasim ceded some of his sovereignty to Barzani. This caused others to view Barzani as the second most powerful personality in Iraq after Qasim, with an undisputed grip on Kurdistan.[8] Thus, Barzani emerged as a rare leader with the ability to challenge the state's sovereignty in Kurdistan. Moreover, he reserved the right to make war on his tribal rivals at will, with or without Qasim's sanction. He also managed to unify the Kurdish ranks by attracting both the tribes and the city folk with his charisma. Consequently, he became the absolute leader within the KDP with veto power and the right to change its leadership at his discretion.

As early as 1959, the KDP under his leadership called for an autonomous region for the Kurds.[9] Qasim, of course, refused to consider Kurdish claims of autonomy. Towards the end of 1960, Barzani sought to establish diplomatic relations with foreign countries on behalf of the Kurds. In late 1960, Barzani received an official invitation from the USSR to visit Moscow. He met with top Soviet officials, including Nikita Khrushchev, the president of Soviet Union, and while there he requested Soviet aid for the Kurds. The Soviets showed their willingness to support the Kurds and with their financial support the Kurds could prepare to buy weaponry and begin their rebellion.[10] With this new balance of power, Barzani thought to further consolidate his grip on Kurdistan. He used a 'stick and carrot' policy to control the Kurdish tribes and urbanites as well as to enhance his authority in Kurdistan. Barzani began touring Kurdistan to garner support among nationalist, tribal, and local leaders in preparation for an inevitable conflict, after which he successfully went on the offensive against those who refused his leadership. By the beginning of 1961 it was clear that Barzani was successful, especially when he defeated the pro-Qasim tribal leaders.

By 1961, Barzani succeeded in building an armed force of 5,000 to 7,000 fighters under his command.[11] At the same time, Qasim lost popularity and control in Kurdistan. In addition to lacking a grass-roots organisation in Kurdistan, Qasim initially failed to gain tribal leaders' support for his regime. What made the situation increasingly awkward for Qasim was that since 1958 the Iraqi army's strength waned in Kurdistan. The Kurdish movement compelled Qasim to dispense with most of the Kurdish officers in the Iraqi army. Barzani's status was further consolidated due to the financial aid and ammunition received from the USSR, grass-roots organisations loyal to the KDP, and token recognition from Qasim. At this stage, Qasim perceived Barzani to challenge his popularity, state sovereignty, and Iraq's integrity. By now it appeared that Barzani was the only leader of the KDP and the only political party to survive Qasim's reign. Consequently, Barzani emerged as an intolerable challenge to Qasim who imposed his authority on a significant part of Kurdistan.

The September revolution and the establishment of Free Kurdistan

On the eve of the Kurdish rebellion of 1961, Barzani and the KDP presented themselves as what Masud Barzani, the president of the KDP, called a state within a state.[12] Relations between the Kurds and the central government deteriorated to the point where Kurdistan was headed towards a revolt. Expecting a confrontation, both sides prepared for armed conflict. The gesture that kicked off the Kurdish revolt in the summer of 1961 was Barzani's expulsion of Iraqi forces from many areas in Kurdistan that resulted in further consolidating his authority. In mid-July 1961, Barzani's forces seized strategic passes and bridges and attacked pro-Iraqi tribal leaders.[13] The pro-Qasim Kurdish tribal militias had been defeated by the more unified Barzani forces. In September, an armed rebellion broke out throughout the mountainous regions of Kurdistan. This revolt is known as the September revolution in Kurdish literature. By the middle of 1962 the Kurdish rebels controlled the whole Kurdish region on the Iraqi-Iranian and Iraqi-Turkish borders. Within months the official Iraqi presence disappeared in most of the Kurdish countryside.[14] The Iraqi army, however, retained control of the main cities and highways. Its activities in Kurdistan were restricted almost exclusively to bombing raids on Kurdish villages.

The 'September revolution' is a turning point in modern Iraqi-Kurdish relations. The first and the most important consequence of the Kurdish revolt was carving out a territory that would comprise most parts of rural and mountainous Kurdistan. This Kurdish controlled area is popularly known as Free Kurdistan or Liberated Territory (hereafter Free Kurdistan). These terms are used interchangeably in Kurdish political discourse and indicate the areas that the Kurdish 'liberators' freed from Iraq.[15] The terms also suggest that the Kurds in Iraq live in a state of constant rebellion since only a portion of Iraqi Kurdistan is 'liberated'; the rest is still under the Iraqi 'occupation'. The territory over which the Kurds established their rule stretched from the corner of the Iraqi-Syrian-Turkish border to the edge of Khaneqin on the Iranian border. Despite Iraq's attempt to recapture these areas and the Kurds' struggle to control the rest of the Kurdish region, neither side succeeded in their attempts. For 14 years (1961–1975), the Kurds maintained *de facto* autonomy in a large area of Kurdistan.

The size of Free Kurdistan

It is difficult to provide an accurate size of Free Kurdistan. In the first year of the revolt (1961–1962), Kurdish rebels controlled most parts of the Kurdish region on the Iraqi-Iranian and Iraqi-Turkish borders. However, the details of the Free Kurdistan area have remained vague up to this point. In 1974, the peshmerga controlled a border of about 725 kilometres, including the entire Iraqi-Turkish frontier and 488 kilometres of the frontier with Iran.[16] Within a year or so the Kurds had further consolidated their hold on Iraqi Kurdistan and advanced south towards Khanaqin, the last Kurdish town inside Iraq on the Iraq-Iranian frontier. The most accurate estimate of the length of the self-ruled territory, however, could be described as a crescent of land running 480 kilometres in length.[17] This arc stretched from Khaneqin, the last Kurdish town in the southeast, to Zakho, the last Kurdish town in the northwest on the Turkish and Syrian border.

The depth of the territory that comprised the Free Kurdistan area poses another question. This is because, on one hand, Iraqi rule was confined to the principal towns of Kirkuk, Sulaimaniya, Erbil, and Duhok, and the Kurdish countryside remained controlled by the peshmerga.[18] On the other hand, Kurdish rule had reached as far as the Kurdish rural areas of Mosul, Erbil, and the Kirkuk plains, tens if not hundreds of kilometres from the Iranian and Turkish borders. The most widely accepted figure for the width of the area of Free Kurdistan was 110 kilometres.[19] Accordingly, the total area of Free Kurdistan was some 54,000 square kilometres. This figure is close to that provided by the Kurds. Mustafa Barzani on many occasions claimed to have 'liberated' 65,000 square kilometres.[20] Though not official, another estimate of the Free Kurdistan area was as much as 30,000 to 40,000 square kilometres.[21] Based on the above estimates, the size of Free Kurdistan may be estimated at over 35,000 square kilometres.

Another dispute involved the ratio of Free Kurdistan to the total Kurdish territory in Iraq. Catudal suggests that the Kurds established virtual autonomy over about three-quarters of Iraqi Kurdistan.[22] O'Balance insisted that the Kurds controlled half of Iraqi Kurdistan, a figure based on the belief that the total area of Iraqi Kurdistan was around 80,000 square kilometres.[23] Although none of the main Kurdish cities had been located in Free Kurdistan, many Kurdish districts and sub-districts and almost the entire rural area of Kurdistan were ruled by the Kurds. The Kurdish semi-independent region with its special administration lasted for 14 years. Interestingly, the area of the KRI in post-invasion Iraq was approximately 40,643 square kilometres, an area roughly equal to that of Free Kurdistan. This area also approximated 9 per cent of the total land area of Iraq, which is 437,400 square kilometres. Thus, for 14 years, the Kurds controlled a Free Kurdistan area roughly equal to the combined size of Israel, Lebanon, and Cyprus.

From 1965 onward, larger cities and towns in the Kurdistan region were only nominally ruled by Baghdad. The Free Kurdistan authority had stretched to the main Kurdish cities that remained under government rule, and its representatives were more active than those from the government. The influence of Free

Kurdistan was such that it extracted contributions from the population of these areas. Moreover, it instructed inhabitants of these areas to deal only with Free Kurdistan officials and not with the Iraqis.[24] Finally, some city centres outside Free Kurdistan control, especially in the Kirkuk and Sulaimaniya districts, were dominated by Jalal Talabani's faction that broke away from the KDP and founded an alliance with the government of Iraq in 1966. Thus the area of Free Kurdistan combined with areas under their indirect rule was much larger than those Kurdish areas under the control of the government of Iraq.

The population of Free Kurdistan

In the absence of an official census, it is difficult to provide an accurate accounting of the Free Kurdistan population. However, several indicators allow a reasonable estimate to be made. The first indicator is that, in addition to many districts, the Free Kurdistan area included almost the entire rural area of Kurdistan. By ascertaining the approximate size of the rural population, one can estimate the number of Free Kurdistan residents. By the 1960s and 1970s the majority of Kurds inhabited rural areas. In the early 1960s rural inhabitants constituted 80 per cent of the total Kurdish population.[25] In 1977, two years after the recapture of Free Kurdistan by Iraq, 51 per cent of the population of Iraqi Kurdistan was considered to be rural.[26] The population of rural Kurdistan, however, was much higher in the period in question. This is because by 1977 the region underwent a process of urbanisation and deported a large percentage of the rural population. The Free Kurdistan population constituted at least half of the total Kurdish population in Iraq.

The second indicator of the true population of Free Kurdistan was that the Kurds represented some 20 per cent of the entire population of Iraq. Considering that over half of the Kurdish population were inhabitants of Free Kurdistan, one can say that from 1961 to 1975 at least 10 per cent of the total Iraqi population lived in these areas. In the first half of the 1960s, Iraq had a total of 6.75 million people.[27] Accordingly, in the first four years of the establishment of Free Kurdistan, the total Kurdish population in Iraq was around 1.5 million. A reasonable estimate of the population of Free Kurdistan may be said to be over 700,000. Others estimate that by 1965 the population of Free Kurdistan was one million.[28] This number rose to 1.2 million in 1969[29] and around 1.5 million by 1974.[30] Thus, prior to its collapse in 1975, Free Kurdistan consisted of an area of over 35,000 square kilometres and a population of around 1.5 million. This significant population and sizable geographic area supplied both the human and financial resources for the survival of Free Kurdistan for 14 years. The immediate question, then, is whether Free Kurdistan may be considered as a quasi-state.

Was Free Kurdistan a quasi-state?

Chapter 2 developed four criteria by which to classify *de facto* self-rule of separatist regions as unrecognised quasi-states. The four criteria were: (1) symbolic nation-building; (2) the militarisation of society; (3) the weakness of the parent state; and (4) support from an external patron. This section examines the status of Kurdish self-rule based on these four criteria.

State-building process

Before examining the nation-building process, it is necessary to analyse the state-building process. State-building is the 'hard' aspect of state construction, while nation-building pertains to the 'soft' aspects of state consolidation. There, is however, a relationship between the two. On the one hand, successful nation-building depends upon successful state-building. In fact, the state-building process is a precondition of the nation-building process. On the other hand, the consolidation of the state depends on the successful nation-building process. Based on the dependent relationship of the state and nation-building processes, our first concern must be the areas that are involved in the state-building process during the period in question. Similar to the state-building process elsewhere, state-building in Free Kurdistan concerns institutional, economic, and military groundwork.

The first pillar, institutional aspects of state-building in Free Kurdistan, would include such things as the institutional and administrative mechanisms of the Revolutionary Command Council of Kurdistan (RCCK), the Executive Council (EC), and the institutionalisation of military forces. One important step towards the state-building process and the establishment of Free Kurdistan was the RCCK. The expulsion of Iraqi institutions from Free Kurdistan resulted in a power vacuum. To fill this power vacuum and govern the region, the KDP established a legislative and executive council. From 1964 onward the Kurds began to constitutionalise and institutionalise their *de facto* rule in Free Kurdistan. In October 1964 the KDP under Barzani held a popular congress to establish the laws and rules for governing the region. The first and most important institution was the RCCK, founded in 1964.[31]

An examination of the structure, authority, and goals of the RCCK clearly demonstrates that the Kurds intended to build a state structure similar to that of the Iraqi state. It was comprised of 63 members from all religious sects, classes, and ethnic groups of Kurdistan, including peasants, chieftains, peshmerga soldiers, senior KDP members, two Christians, a Jew, and one Turkman.[32] Similar to the Revolutionary Command Council of Iraq (RCCI), the RCCK was a non-elected body and the highest institutional authority in Free Kurdistan. The Kurdish Council ratified its own constitution known as the Constitution of the Revolutionary Command Council of Kurdistan.[33] Article 2 of the constitution promulgates that its decrees should be dealt with as constitutional decrees in Kurdistan. Under Article 4, the Kurdish Council was authorised to lead the revolution, enact laws and regulations, and administer the affairs of the Iraqi Kurdistan region including political, military, economic, administrative, judicial, and other affairs. The president of the RCCK was to be the head and his authority was incontestable, similar to that of the president of the RCCI. Furthermore, according to Article 11, the head of the Kurdish Council enjoyed the right to appoint and dismiss members of the Executive Office and army commanders and to endorse the RCCK laws and resolutions. The most sensitive responsibility of the Kurdish Council president was the right to make peace or declare war after consultation with the majority members of the Kurdish council. Article 4 of the constitution stipulated that the Kurdish Council enjoyed the power to ratify a constitution and to enact resolutions and legislation, a power similar to that of the Iraqi RCC. With 63 members from all echelons of society, the RCCK acted more like a Kurdish parliament and was more inclusive than the RCCI.

Another important step towards the state-building process and the establishment of *de facto* autonomy in Free Kurdistan was the establishment of the Executive Council in 1964. Article 6 of the constitution empowered the Kurdish council to establish an Executive Council. The Executive Council took responsibility for carrying out the executive decisions of the Kurdish Council (Article 8). Based on Article 6, the Executive Council was comprised of nine members, all of whom were elected by and within the Kurdish council, and was headed by a secretary. The Executive Council had nine departments including the peshmerga, financial, administrative, justice and judiciary, health, security, and internal affairs. Although the head of each department was also a member of the RCCK, they were dedicated to the Executive Council (Article 6). Like the Iraqi Council of Ministries, under the RCCI, the Executive Council was supervised by the RCCK.[34] The Executive Council was a governing body that possessed the power and authority to administer Free Kurdistan. It was also entrusted with responsibility to implement the rules and laws promulgated by the Kurdish Council (Article 8). The Kurdish administration organised public works projects such as road building, schools, hospitals, and sanitation. It provided mail services, printed newspapers, and released communiqués. Thus, the mission of the Executive Council was the same as that of any council of ministries and it functioned as a ministerial council in all but name.

The next most important body was the governorate (provincial offices). This office was akin to that of a local government. Although none of the governorate centres of Kurdistan were under Kurdish control, significant portions, if not most, of the Kurdish governorates including many districts were under their control. To govern these areas, Free Kurdistan was administratively divided into five governorates: Sulaimaniya, Erbil, Kirkuk, Mosul, and Duhok. Each governorate had its own governor, judicial system, and financial administration.[35] These administrations were based on Iraqi governorates. A governor was appointed as the head of each governorate. The administration of each district constituted a three-member committee consisting of a senior KDP member, a representative of the peshmerga forces, and a representative of the people. The mayors of both districts and sub-districts were appointed by the RCCK.[36] Thus, similar to any other states, Free Kurdistan achieved a degree of institutionalising its self-rule in Free Kurdistan.

The second pillar of state-building in Free Kurdistan pertained to economics. Free Kurdistan managed to create a semi-independent economy through the collection of taxes. A 10 per cent income tax was imposed on inhabitants of Free Kurdistan. Additionally, Free Kurdistan authorities extracted contributions from Kurds of areas under Iraqi rule.[37] The vital role of tax collecting derived from the symbolic importance of Kurdish sovereignty in Free Kurdistan. The power of tax collection partly contributed to the survival of Free Kurdistan in the face of constant war. Free Kurdistan was under a harsh Iraqi economic blockade and was in the hinterland and in Iraq's most backward industrial region. Despite that, tax collection provided the economic power to guarantee Free Kurdistan self-sufficiency. Kurdistan was Iraq's main granary and produced as much as half of Iraq's agricultural output and half of its wheat needs.

The third pillar of the state-building process in Free Kurdistan was establishment of an armed force. The establishment and institutionalisation of the Kurdish armed forces were some of the foci of Free Kurdistan. In 1962, only few months after the 'September revolution', the Kurdistan Revolutionary Army (KRA) was formed with the express purpose to institutionalise Kurdish society and peshmerga forces. This administrative body was headed by a Revolutionary Council and was comprised of popular Kurdish intelligentsia such as Jalal Talabani and Ibrahim Ahmed. This collective decision-making body unified the peshmerga and consolidated Kurdish forces. Together the KRA and the Revolutionary Council transformed the leadership from the old class of tribal leader to urban intelligentsia. The role of the army in Kurdish society was crucial to transform the hitherto unorganised Kurdish fighters into a sophisticated and educated army. The top echelon of the KRA to the smallest unit was organised by the KDP.

Institutionalisation of the armed forces was a top-down process including the general command, chief of staff, and four army divisions distributed according to province and each consisting of several brigades. Kurdistan was divided into four provinces: Mosul, Sulaimaniya, Erbil, and Kirkuk.[38] Each provincial division was divided into a number of subdivisions, almost one for each district and sub-district, and each of these were organised in several army units known as '*Hez*'. The Kurdistan Revolutionary Army (KRA) consisted of 18 *Hez*. Each of them consisted of numbers of battalions (totalling 65). Each battalion consisted of 120 peshmerga soldiers (i.e. '*Liq*'), and each *Liq* consisted of 10 peshmerga (i.e. '*Dasta*').[39] Another step towards the institutionalisation of the armed forces was the establishment of the Kurdish Intelligence Agency (*Parastin*) in 1967. Having financial resources at its disposal, this unit was responsible for gathering and interpreting intelligence information about Iraq and other countries. In sum, similar to other functioning states, Free Kurdistan developed the institutional, economic, and military apparatuses of a functional quasi-state. Similar to any unrecognised quasi-state (UQ), the Kurdish *de facto* state had many symbolic attributes of statehood.

Symbolic nation-building

The Kurds' relative success in governing the region included the establishment of the executive and legislative bodies that facilitated the nation-building process. During 1961–1975, more than two dozen publications were published, including daily, weekly, and monthly newspapers and magazines. Similar numbers of various types of newspapers and magazines were published in areas dominated by

Baghdad. Kurdish books that reflected different aspects of Kurdish history, geography, and politics were also published. Historians published their interpretations of Kurdish history and culture and the Kurdish language experienced a revival. The *de facto* state had a radio station that deeply impacted the Kurdish national consciousness. Another step on the path to nation-building was the consolidation of territorial identity through the republishing of maps. The map of greater Kurdistan, similar to that presented to the Paris Conference in 1918 by the Kurdish delegation, was published by the KDP.[40] The Kurdish national day was another important symbol of nation-building. Inherited from earlier generations of Kurdish nationalists, *Nawroz* was adopted by Free Kurdistan as the Kurdish national day. The flag was another important symbol of nation-building.[41] Free Kurdistan used the same Kurdish flag that was inherited from earlier generations of Kurds in the Republic of Mahabad of Iranian Kurdistan.[42] The national anthem is another important symbol of nation-building. Free Kurdistan adopted the anthem of the Republic of Mahabad, known as *Ey Reqib*. The anthem was sung at the start of each school day in Free Kurdistan.[43] Thus, the process of nation-building in Free Kurdistan fully meets the first criterion of the UQC-I.

The militarisation of Kurdish society

The second criterion by which to classify a separate region as a quasi-state is the militarisation of society. This factor also helps to explain the failure of the Iraqi state to re-impose its authority on Kurdistan and attempt to reintegrate the Kurdish population into Iraq, especially from 1961 to 1975. Scrutiny of the military strength of Kurdistan during that period reveals that Iraqi Kurdistan was indeed a militarised society. In September 1961, the Kurdish revolt began with only 5,000 to 7,000 fighters.[44] However, within a year, the Kurds developed and organised 15,000 to 20,000 trained peshmerga soldiers. These trained forces were also supported by 20,000 irregular troops (partisans, local reserves, and tribal warriors).[45] Thus, in the first year of its creation, Free Kurdistan was protected by 30,000 to 40,000 armed men. By 1963, the number of trained peshmerga soldiers increased to 20,000 to 25,000.[46] Rotating and local reserve forces were strengthened as thousands of Kurdish draft dodgers, officers, and soldiers deserted from the Iraqi army and joined the Kurdish revolt. Irregular troops were estimated to number as many as 40,000.[47]

By 1974, the fighting Kurdish forces doubled and reached 100,000 personnel. This army was comprised of 50,000 to 60,000 trained peshmerga soldiers and 40,000 to 50,000 Kurdish partisans and irregulars.[48] As mentioned, the population of Free Kurdistan was estimated at around 1.5 million. Accordingly, there was one fighter for every 15 inhabitants of Free Kurdistan. It is noteworthy that the total Iraqi armed forces were estimated at 30,000 to 40,000 in 1963 and around 140,000 in 1975.[49] The Kurdish armed forces were nearly half as large as the Iraqi army in 1963 and as many as two-thirds in 1975. They were also larger than the armies of many independent countries. The Kurdish forces were strong enough to protect the region from recapture by Iraq and remained this strong until the collapse of Kurdish rule, an event that resulted from the Iraqi-Iranian/ Algeria Agreement of 1975. Thus, Free Kurdistan was one of the most militarised societies in the world. Accordingly, the militarisation process that Free Kurdistan undertook from 1961–1975 fulfilled the second criterion (UQC-II) for classifying a separatist region as a quasi-state.

The relative weakness of the parent state

The third criterion by which to classify a *de facto* self-ruling entity as a quasi-state is the relative weakness of the parent state and its failure to recapture the secessionist region (UQC-III). Despite semi-constant military conflict, Iraq failed to terminate this quasi-state and never succeeded in imposing its full authority in the region. Scrutinising the military confrontations during this period reveals the relative weakness of Iraq as a parent state of Free Kurdistan. Iraq's weakness is evident in that, from 1961 to 1975, Free Kurdistan survived almost daily skirmishes and five major Iraqi wars perpetrated on it by Iraq. To understand the balance of power between Free Kurdistan and Iraq, a review of these five wars is necessary. The first major war that Iraq perpetrated on Free Kurdistan began directly after the Kurdish revolt in September 1961 and lasted until February 1963. Initially, Iraq had deployed some 30,000 troops in an unsuccessful attempt to recapture Free Kurdistan.[50] On the eve of the fall of Qasim in February 1963, eight of 12 Iraqi army divisions and 10,000 pro-government militias (*Jash*) were involved in the fight against Kurdistan.[51] The first Iraqi-Kurdish war ended at the same time Qasim's regime ended in 1963, and Free Kurdistan remained outside of Iraqi control.

The second major Iraqi-Kurdish war started in June 1963. Following the coup that was arranged by a pro-Ba'ath Party junta against Qasim on 8 February 1963, the Kurds declared a ceasefire and started negotiating with the new Iraqi regime. However, by June 1963, negotiations had collapsed and the new regime launched a new offensive in Kurdistan that resulted in the outbreak of what may be considered as the second phase of the Iraqi-Kurdish war. This phase of war lasted only four months, though 75 to 80 per cent of the Iraqi army was involved.[52] Moreover, thousands of Ba'athist militia and pro-government tribal Kurds (*Jash*) engaged in unsuccessful combat operations to recapture Free Kurdistan. Another important event in the second war was the participation of 5,000 Syrian troops in battle that reinforced Syrian air forces with heavy artillery. The Syrians opened a front against the Kurds from Zakho to Duhok on the Syrian-Iraqi border.[53] The Syrian participation in the Iraqi-Kurdish war demonstrated the strength of the peshmerga and the scale of the battle. It also revealed the inability of Iraq, despite deploying 80 per cent of its army, to defeat the Kurds and to recapture Free Kurdistan. The severity of the combat can also be seen in the number of casualties: 600 to 700 Iraqi troops.[54] Like the first Iraqi-Kurdish war, this phase ended with another coup against the Ba'athists in November 1963 that was led by Arif, the president of Iraq. The coup resulted in the collapse of the first Ba'athist rule in Iraq. The Kurds maintained their control of Free Kurdistan.

The third major Iraqi-Kurdish war started in April 1965. The Kurds relished in Arif's successful coup that was followed by another truce signed in February 1964 by Arif and Barzani. The negotiations that took place in this peace process lasted only a few months. From mid-October onward, the Iraqi army and the peshmerga began to experience skirmishes. By spring 1965, both sides prepared for war and in April 1965 the third round of the Iraqi-Kurdish wars began that lasted until January 1966. Nine out of 12 Iraqi army divisions launched a major offensive along the 400 kilometres of the Iraqi-Kurdish front.[55] The total Iraqi force was estimated at 50,000 troops, supported by aircraft and artillery.[56] Though Egypt did not participate directly in the Kurdish-Iraqi war, it sent 12,000 troops to support Iraq.[57] After seven months of conventional fighting (April 1965 to January 1966), both sides were greatly harmed. On the Kurdish side, around 750 villages had been destroyed and nearly 200,000 villagers displaced.[58] The Kurds, however, inflicted serious casualties on the Iraqi army and destroyed an entire brigade in one battle.[59]

The last round of war in May 1966 was considered to be a Kurdish victory that forced Iraq to temporarily change its Kurdish policy. This was evident in the June Declaration by Prime Minister 'Abd al-Rahman al-Bazzaz. A 12-point peace program outlined in June 1966 gave hope for a peaceful settlement.[60] However, opposition from the Iraqi armed forces made it impossible to implement the June agreement. As in the previous period, this phase of war was followed by a period of sporadic fighting and stalemate. This affair of 'no peace no war' continued until the fall of Arif's regime in a coup arranged by the Ba'ath. As it was during other phases of war, Iraq's supremacy in the number of armed forces, air force, and heavy artillery, as well as its stronger economy, was offset by other factors. First, the Kurds' familiarity and control over the Iranian and Turkish borders earned them popular support. Second, the Iraqi army only had control over the main roads during daylight hours, while the peshmerga retained control over the same roads during the night. The peshmerga demonstrated their long reach by attacking Iraqi forces in cities such as Sulaimaniya, Erbil, and Kirkuk. On many occasions, they shelled and blew up the vulnerable Iraq Petroleum Company's installations, thereby impeding the flow of petroleum from Kirkuk.[61] Consequently, as in previous wars, the Iraqi forces failed to recapture Free Kurdistan.

The fourth major Iraqi-Kurdish war began in April 1969. The new Ba'athist regime that came to power in July 1968 by means of a coup launched the war to recapture several strategic towns within Free Kurdistan. The new Iraqi regime deployed pro-Iraqi militias and all 12 army divisions that amounted to 60,000 troops.[62] The onslaught against the Kurds in the fourth war alone required 30 per cent of the total Iraqi budget or over $1 billion.[63] The Kurds, however, resisted Iraq and demonstrated their ability to protect their territory and to challenge government forces. Lacking the power to suppress Free Kurdistan, Iraq was compelled to negotiate another ceasefire. After months of bloody fighting, Iraq offered the Kurds autonomy in 1970 and both sides came to an agreement in March. The settlement, known as the 'March Manifesto' or 'March Agreement', accommodated significant Kurdish national desires as it implicitly recognised Kurdish self-rule not only in Free Kurdistan, but also in many larger Kurdish cities outside

Kurdish control.[64] Thus, the Kurds enjoyed a good deal of autonomy between 1970 and 1974 and they controlled and administered more territory than they held in the 1960s.

The fifth major Iraqi-Kurdish war started in the spring of 1974. The March Agreement of 1970 provided a roadmap for implementing self-rule, or Kurdish autonomy, within four years. However, a stalemate resulted between Iraq and the Kurds over border issues and the nature and character of the proposed Kurdish autonomy. Once again, tensions eventually erupted into heavy fighting in 1974, and the fifth Iraqi-Kurdish war broke out. The fifth war lasted 12 months, but it was the most decisive. Iraq deployed a massive force of 90,000 to 120,000 troops, backed by 20,000 policemen. Baghdad also deployed tens of thousands of militiamen, 20 battalions of mobile artillery including 800 to 1,200 tanks, the entire air force of 11,000 men, and several hundred planes. When the fighting began, Barzani had 50,000 to 60,000 peshmerga fighters and 50,000 irregulars to call on.[65] As in previous wars, this offensive turned out to have disastrous consequences for both Kurds and Iraq. It is estimated that during 12 months of fighting, the Iraqi army suffered 17,000 casualties; 2,000 peshmerga were killed and thousands were wounded.[66] Kelidar argues that the human cost of this war was much higher. Iraq sustained more than 60,000 casualties; of 600,000 displaced Kurds, 250,000 of them had fled to Iran.[67] He also estimates the cost of the fifth war was estimated at $4 billion. This is almost half of the Iraqi budget and it constituted a costly drain on Iraq's national resources.

Despite the enormous costs in terms of finances and human capital, the fifth war resulted in the same pattern of stalemate that occurred in previous wars. The Iraqi army launched bombing raids against civilian targets and showed their superior fire power. Iraq also imposed an economic blockade on Free Kurdistan. This phase of war ended with the collapse of Free Kurdistan in March 1975. However, the main reason behind the collapse of Free Kurdistan was not the superiority of the Iraqi army. On the eve of the collapse of Free Kurdistan, there were no signs of defeat in the Iraqi attack and Iraq seemed to be under unprecedented pressure. More than anything, this state of affairs pointed out the weakness of the Iraqi state. Up to this point, Iraq could be considered as a weak parent state that failed to recapture Free Kurdistan for more than 14 years. In view of these facts, the *de facto* Kurdish self-rule fully satisfied the third criterion (UQC-III) for classifying the separatist region as an unrecognised quasi-state (UQ).

The external patronage factor

The fourth criterion required to qualify as a *de facto* self-ruling quasi-state is the extent of external patronage and support given it. As is detailed in the next chapter, Free Kurdistan enjoyed significant external support from several states. In 1961, the Soviet Union offered financial support and this continued until 1972. From the mid-1960s to 1975, Israel provided military, financial, and logistical support. The US offered support from 1972 to 1975. However, Iran's patronage and support were the most important both in terms of quantity and duration of patronage. The extent of patronage offered the Kurds was significant enough that Free Kurdistan survived for 14 years. Free Kurdistan enjoyed external support and patronage, thus fulfilling the fourth criterion of unrecognised quasi-states (UQC-IV).

Free Kurdistan from 1961–1975: the first unrecognised Kurdish quasi-state (UKQ-I)

Between 1961 and 1975, Free Kurdistan met all of the qualifications to qualify as a *de facto* independent quasi-state. Because it was the first Kurdish quasi-state in modern Iraq, it will be referred to as the first unrecognised Kurdish quasi-state (UKQ-I) from this point on. The impact of the UKQ-I on Kurdish integration into Iraq is significant. For 14 years half of the Kurdish population was administered by this quasi-state and experienced a separate state system. The population had no experience with Iraqi rule. Most of the populace in the parts of Iraqi Kurdistan that remained under Iraqi rule were motivated by and supportive of the UKQ-I. Free Kurdistan became a safe haven for thousands of young Kurds who refused to serve in the central government's army. For 14 years, most Kurds ruled by the UKQ-I did not serve in the Iraqi army and they did not pay taxes to the central government. They were not educated in Iraqi schools and they were impervious to the Iraqi media. They did not avail themselves of the Iraqi judicial system. The Kurds of Free Kurdistan were not protected by the Iraqi army, which presented a real threat to them. The influence of this quasi-state went far beyond Free Kurdistan. Most Kurds under Iraqi control were directly or indirectly mobilised and influenced by the UKQ-I. In sum, the inhabitants of Free Kurdistan were, for all practical purposes, citizens of a separate state. Thus, the existence of the Kurdish quasi-state remained the main obstacle to Kurdish integration into the Iraqi state.

Iraq from 1961–1975: a recognised quasi-state (RQ)

This section examines the status of Iraq in light of recognised quasi-state theory. It applies the four criteria of RQC to ascertain whether Iraq could be classified as a recognised quasi-state (RQ) in the period under consideration. All four criteria used to determine RQC must be met in order to qualify as a recognised quasi-state. The first criterion is a state that violates, rather than imposes, the rule of law and threatens some of its citizens (RQC-I). Though Iraq officially asserted that it attempted to re-impose order and legitimate authority in this region, in many ways it both violated Iraqi and international rules and laws as it threatened the population of Free Kurdistan. During the 14 years of Kurdish quasi-state existence, Iraq inflicted five major wars on Free Kurdistan. In these wars, civilians were indiscriminately targeted by Iraq, particularly by its air forces. In the first phase of the Iraqi-Kurdish war alone (1961–1963), over 1,000 Kurdish villages were seriously damaged or destroyed, mostly by Iraqi air attacks. In addition, 80,000 civilians were displaced, thus becoming homeless. The second round of war (June to November 1963) resulted in more than 25,000 predominantly civilian casualties, 875 demolished Kurdish villages, and hundreds of thousands of displaced Kurds.

98   The first unrecognised quasi-state

In the third Iraqi-Kurdish war (April 1965 to January 1966), the Iraqi state posed a great threat to the Kurdish population and clearly violated international rules. Seven months of conventional fighting (April 1965 to January 1966) was a major disaster for the civilian Kurds. It resulted in the displacement of 200,000 villagers and the destruction of approximately 750 villages. In the fourth round of the Iraqi-Kurdish war in April 1969, approximately 300 Kurdish villages were damaged and more than 30,000 people joined the ranks of the internally displaced. In the final round of the war, 600,000 civilians were displaced from which 250,000 fled to Iran.[68] Thus, during this period, the Iraqi state was the main threat to Kurdish civilians. This meets the criterion of RQC-I.

The second criterion of an RQs (i.e. a state that loses its monopoly of the legitimate use of force in a given territory) applied to Iraq during this period. This involved losing control of one or more of its territories (e.g. a separatist region) or losing its monopoly on the legitimate use of force in a territory. As explained, for 14 years, Iraq had lost control of more than 35,000 square kilometres of its territory. The third criterion (RQC-III) (i.e. a state that seeks external patronage from a stronger state because it cannot confront the separatist region on its own) applies to Iraq during this period. Despite the Iraqi deployment of two-thirds of its armed forces, Iraq failed to recapture Free Kurdistan. Iraq also faced difficulties holding its grip on the Kurdish areas that remained under its control. From 1965 onward the Kurds had more influence on that region than did Iraq.

The Kurdish war contributed to regime changes in the central government on many occasions. It is not coincidental that the fall of Qasim's regime in 1963, the first Ba'athist regime in 1963, and Arif's regime in 1968 followed their failures to recapture Free Kurdistan. Iraq often attempted to find military support from a regional power or superpower after failing to recapture Free Kurdistan. In 1963, for example, Iraq appealed to Syria for support. In response, Syria sent two brigades totalling 5,000–6,000 troops and Egypt sent 12,000 troops to support Iraq. The USSR also participated in the Iraqi war against the UKQ-I. Prior to the Soviet-Iraq alignment of 1972, the Kurds capably protected their quasi-state. After the 1972 Soviet-Iraq agreement, however, the Soviets restructured and expanded their Iraqi military capabilities. In 1974, the Soviet army, mostly Soviet generals and pilots, participated directly in the Iraqi-Kurdish war. They piloted the Mig-23, one of the most advanced Russian jets to bombard Kurdish positions.[69] The consequences of Soviet support to Iraq and its impact on the balance of power in the fifth war on Kurdistan in 1975 was crucial. With significant foreign assistance, Iraq managed to contain Kurdish progress and recapture some areas claimed by the Kurds as part of their homeland. Failing to confront the Kurds on its own power and seeking outside support was another facet of the Iraqi regime that qualified as the third criterion of recognised quasi-states (RQC-III).

The fourth criterion (RQC-IV) emphasises the violation of a state's sovereignty by external powers as a result of foreign military forces on its soil. As outlined previously, there were significant numbers of Syrian, Egyptian, and Russian security forces in Iraq. In Kurdistan, Israeli security elements and hundreds, if not thousands, of Iranian commandos were on the ground especially during the final war in 1974–1975. These Iranian forces entered Free Kurdistan with heavy and sophisticated artillery and they participated directly in the Kurdish war against Baghdad.[70] Thus, during the period in question, there was a semi-permanent foreign military presence in Iraq often at the request of the Iraqi state (Egypt, Syria, and the USSR); or they were there outside of Iraqi control (i.e. Israeli and Iranian troops). Therefore, Iraq satisfies the fourth criterion (RQC-IV). From 1961–1975, Iraq possessed all criteria that a recognised state had to meet to be considered as a recognised quasi-state. During this period in question, Kurdistan also established its first unrecognised quasi-state qualification (UKQ-I).

In sum, Iraq's wars on Kurdistan resulted in tens of thousands of casualties among civilians and the displacement of hundreds of thousands of Kurds. By targeting civilians in an indiscriminate manner, the Iraqi state threatened part of its own population and violated Iraqi and international law. Therefore, the first criterion (RQC-I), which is a state that violates its rules and/or threatens its own citizens, was satisfied by Iraq. Second, Iraq lost control over Free Kurdistan for 14 years, thus satisfying RQC-II. Third, in the period under review, Iraq, on numerous occasions, resorted to outside support, including Syria, Egypt, and Russia, to confront the UKQ-I. Therefore, the third criterion (RQC-III), the seeking of external military support from a stronger state to challenge a separatist region, was satisfied by Iraq. Fourth, during this period Iraq failed to prevent the presence of foreign (i.e. Israeli and Iranian) military forces on its soil. Therefore, the qualification of the fourth criterion (RQC-IV), the violation of a state's sovereignty by external powers outside of its control through foreign military forces on its soil, was satisfied by Iraq. Thus, Iraq satisfied all criteria that qualified it to be classified as a recognised quasi-state. In sum, from 1961 to 1975, Iraq may be redefined as a country of two quasi-states: the recognised quasi-state of Iraq and the unrecognised Kurdish quasi-state.

Notes

1 Landlords are not necessarily affiliated with tribes. *Agha* is a tribal leader and *sheikh* is a religious leader. For the sake of brevity they are categorised here as *aghas*.
2 As explained in Chapter 4, the Tribal Autonomous Communities (TAE) enjoyed a modicum of autonomy and retained the right to bear arms, collect taxes, and administer their local affairs.
3 Jawad 1990: 54.
4 Jwaideh 2006: 283.
5 Rubin, A. H. (2007), "Abd al-Karim Qasim and the Kurds of Iraq: Centralization, Resistance and Revolt, 1958–63," *Middle Eastern Studies* 43(3): 353–382.
6 *Ibid.*: 354.
7 McDowall 2004: 304; Rubin 2007: 355–356; Nuri, F. (2007), *Bzavi Barzani (The Barzani Movement)*, Erbil, Iraq: Aras Publisher: 256.
8 Al-Barak 1989: 157; Jawad 1990: 53; Al-Botani, A.F.A.Y. (2001), *Watha'q 'an al-Haraka al-Qawmiya al-Kurdiya al-Taharruriya: Mulahadhat Tarikhiya wa Dirasat Awaliya (Documents on the Kurdish Nationalist Liberation Movement: Historical Observations and Primary Studies)*, Erbil, Iraq: Dazgay Mukiryani: 70; McDowall 2004: 307.
9 Jawad 1990: 286–289; Al-Botani 2001: 68.

100 The first unrecognised quasi-state

10 Barzani 2002: 12, 22.
11 Schmidt D. A. (1962), "Warn U.S. to Give Them Aid or They Will Ask the Soviets," *The New York Times*, 10/09/1962; Mella 2000: 111; Nuri 2007: 283.
12 Barzani 2002: 8.
13 O'Balance, E. (1973), *The Kurdish Revolt: 1961–1970*, London: Faber and Faber, Ltd. Publishers: 47; McDowall 2004: 310.
14 O'Balance 1973: 90; Al-Botani 2001: 92; Barzani 2002: 73; McDowall 2004: 310.
15 For example see: *Komalla Magazine* (1981), "Organi Komallay Ranjderani Kurdistan," (The Review of the Kurdistan Toilers League; Kurdayeti 1985; PUK 1986: 7; Khabat (1988), *Hawla al-Qadhiye al-Kurdiya (About the Kurdish Question)*, Ibrahim Ezzo; Barzani 2002: 39; Shamzini, A. (2006), *Jwlanaway Rizgari Nishtimani Kurdistan (The Kurdish National Liberation Movement)*, Fourth edition. Sulaimaniya, Iraq: Senteri Lekolinewey Strategi Kurdistan: 281.
16 Schmidt, D. A. (1974), "Kurdish Leader, Facing Possible Civil War, Looks to West for Support," *The New York Times*, 01/04/1974; Al-Botani 2001: 92.
17 O'Balance 1973: 90; Catudal, H. M. (1976), "The War in Kurdistan: End of a Nationalist Struggle?" *International Relations* 5(3): 1029.
18 Kinnane, D. (1964), *The Kurds and Kurdistan*, Oxford: Oxford University Press: 71; Catudal 1976: 1030; Al-Botani 2001: 92.
19 O'Balance 1973: 90; Catudal 1976: 1029; Al-Botani 2001: 92.
20 Hiro, D. (1989), *The Longest War: The Iran-Iraq Military Conflict*, London: Routledge: 16.
21 Schmidt 1962, "Warn U.S. to Give Them Aid or They Will Ask the Soviets," *The New York Times*, 10/09/1962; Vanly, I. C. (1992), "The Kurds in Syria and Lebanon," *The Kurds: A Contemporary Overview*, London: Routledge: 155, 209; Bakhash, S. (2004), "The Troubled Relationship: Iran and Iraq, 1930–1980," *Iran, Iraq and the Legacies of War*, Lawrence G. Potter and Gary G. Sick (eds.), New York: Palgrave MacMillan: 19; Muheddin, W. O. (2006), *Danusanekani Bzwtnewey Rizgarixwazi Netewey kwrd u hkwmetekani Eraq 1921–1968 (Negotiations of the Kurdish Liberation Movement with Iraqi Governments 1921–1968)*, Sulaimaniya, Iraq: Centeri Lekolinewey Strategi Kurdistan: 329.
22 Catudal 1976: 1030.
23 O'Balance 1973: 157.
24 Kinnane 1964: 74; Jawad 1990: 135; Rubin 2007: 370.
25 Nebez, J. (2001), *Kurdistan w Shorishekey (Kurdistan's Revolution)*, Erbil, Iraq: Aras Publishing House: 245.
26 Marr, P. (1985), *Modern History of Iraq*, Boulder, CO: Westview Press: 285.
27 Naamani, I. T. (1966), "The Kurdish Drive for Self-Determination," *Middle East Journal* 20(3): 279–295; 279; Rubin 2007: 355.
28 Nebez 2001: 162; Bakhash 2004: 19; Muheddin 2006: 329; Nuri 2007: 315.
29 *The New York Times*, 30/12/1969; O'Balance 1973: 157.
30 Vanly 1990: 180.
31 See: Al-Botani 2001: 311–313; Barzani 2002: 149–152.
32 Nebez 2001: 162; Qadir 2007: 63.
33 For the full text of *The Constitution of the Revolutionary Command Council of Kurdistan* in Arabic, see Barzani 2002, Appendix no. 19: 510–516.
34 Barzani 2002: 150.
35 Catudal 1976: 1030; Barzani 2002: 150.
36 O'Balance 1973: 125; Barzani 2002: 150.
37 O'Balance 1973: 64; Rubin 2007: 370.
38 Barzani 2002: 150–151.
39 Emin 1997: 65.
40 Barzani, A. (2011), *Al-Haraka al-Taharruriya al-Kurdiya: Wa Sira'a Qwa al-Aqlimiya we Al-Dawliya (The Kurdish Liberation Movement and the Regional and International Conflict)*, Geneva, Switzerland: Dar al-Nashir Haqaiq al-Mashriq: 53.

41 Alakom, R. (2007), *Kurderna Fyrtio är i Sverige 1965–2005 (The Kurds Forty Years in Sweden 1965–2005)*, Serkland: Stockholm: 149.
42 Dizeyi, M. (2001), *Ahdath A'aserteha" (Events that I Witnessed)*, Erbil, Iraq: Dar Aras lil-Taba'a wal-Nashir: 143; Nuri 2007: 261.
43 The author witnessed such an event.
44 Schmidt, D. A. (1962), "Warn U.S. to Give Them Aid or They Will Ask the Soviets," *The New York Times*, 10/09/1962; Mella 2000: 111.
45 Schmidt, D. A. (1964), "Kurdish Rebels and Iraq Agree to Cease Fighting," *The New York Times*, 11/02/1964; Lortz, M. G. (2005), "Willing to Face Death: A History of Kurdish Military Forces, the Peshmerga, from the Ottoman Empire to Present-Day Iraq," Masters thesis, Florida State University: 40.
46 Schmidt, D. A. (1963), "Kurds Try to Foil Iraqi Army Drive," *The New York Times*, 02/08/1963; O'Balance 1973: 85, 104; Vanly, I. S. (1990), "Kurdistan in Iraq," *People without a Country: The Kurds and Kurdistan*, Chaliand, G. (ed.), Michael Pallis (trans.), London: Zed Press: 155; Nisan, M. (2002), *Minorities in the Middle East: A History of Struggle and Self-Expression*, Jefferson, NC: McFarland & Company, Inc: 43.
47 *Ibid.*
48 Vanly 1990: 155; Farouk-Sluglett and Sluglett 2001: 337, 168; McDowall 2004: 337.
49 Vanly 1990: 182; Mella 2000: 111.
50 Mella 2000: 111.
51 Al-Botani 2001: 135.
52 Nuri 2007: 303.
53 O'Balance 1973: 107; Jawad 1990: 84; 99; Mamikonian, S. (2005), "Israel and the Kurds (1949–1990)," *Iran and the Caucasus*: 394.
54 Nebez 2001: 156.
55 Catudal 1976: 1030; McDowall 2004: 317.
56 According to McDowall 2004: 310, the total Iraqi armed forces that participated in this round of war were as many as 100,000 troops.
57 Nebez 2001: 172; Barzani 2002: 328.
58 McDowall 2004: 319.
59 Jawad 1990: 128; Nebez 2001: 145.
60 For the full Arabic text of Bazzaz's program, known as the June 29th declaration, see Sharif (1978: 183–189).
61 Catudal 1976: 1032; Natali 2000: 54; Nuri 2007: 286, 346.
62 O'Balance 1973: 151; Borovali 1987: 34; Nebez 2001: 192.
63 O'Balance 1973: 157.
64 For the full Arabic text of the March Manifesto, see Sharif (1978: 206–222).
65 Catudal 1976: 1024; Vanly 1990: 181–182; Farouk-Sluglett and Sluglett 2001: 169; McDowall 2004: 337.
66 Minorities at Risk Project (2004), "Chronology for Kurds in Iraq," available at <www.unhcr.org/refworld/docid/469f38a6c.html>, (accessed 11/04/2014).
67 Kelidar, A. (1992), "The Wars of Saddam Hussein," *Middle Eastern Studies* 28(4): 789.
68 Adelman, Howard (1992), "Humanitarian Intervention: The Case of the Kurds," *International Journal of Refugee Law* 4(1): 4–38.
69 Catudal 1976: 1036.
70 Tomasek, R. D. (1976), "The Resolution of Major Controversies between Iran and Iraq," *World Affairs* 139(3): 206–230; 221; Farouk-Sluglett and Sluglett 2001: 170; Bakhash 2004: 20.

6 The case of negative patronage

Chapter 5 highlighted the emergence of the first unrecognised Kurdish quasi-state. It explained that within a 14-year period, Iraq launched five failed major military campaigns against Free Kurdistan that were designed to recapture it. The fifth war on Kurdistan lasted one year and ended in March 1975 with the sudden and total collapse of the UKQ-I. The Kurds lost control of Free Kurdistan as the KDP, other UKQ-I institutions, and the 100,000-man Kurdish armed forces collapsed. After 14 years, the Iraqi army entered Free Kurdistan for the first time.

The puzzling downfall of the UKQ-I

The collapse of the UKQ-I, along with the recapture of Free Kurdistan by the parent state, is unparalleled. Kolstø outlines the three methods by which a parent state may successfully reabsorb a secessionist region. It may do so by (1) peacefully offering a "higher standard of living for the quasi-state population in [the] case of reunification"; (2) offering a political solution and achieving a mutual agreement between the leaders of both sides that is facilitated by federal power; and (3) recapturing the territory through military conquest.[1] The Kurdish case, however, did not fit into any of these categories. First, the collapse of the UKQ-I did not result from a shift of Kurdish loyalty to the Iraqi-state.

Chapters 7 and 8 explain that, after 1975, despite Iraqi control over Free Kurdistan and its military superiority, it failed to rule or govern Kurdistan. Instead of offering protection, service, and a better lifestyle, Iraq depopulated a significant part of Iraqi Kurdistan. Second, there was no mutual agreement over the autonomy arrangement between the Kurds and Iraqis. The final war followed the failure of negotiations between the two sides over boundaries and authority of the autonomy. Third, the collapse of the UKQ-I did not result from Iraqi military victory. On the eve of the collapse, the Iraqi military had not yet gained the upper hand.[2] So the military was not the main factor behind the defeat of the UKQ-I. The main reason for the collapse was the shift of Iran's allegiance from the Kurds to Iraq and the termination of Israeli and US patronage. The latter followed the Algeria Agreement which was signed by Iran and Iraq in March 1975. This was clearly admitted by Mustafa Barzani, the leader of the UKQ-I, in his letter to President Carter. He explained that "we were not militarily defeated by our enemy [Iraq].

We were destroyed by our friends [the US, Iran and Israel]."[3] The next sections scrutinise the role of external patronage and support during both the emergence and the fall of the UKQ-I.

The UKQ-I search for outside patronage

The Kurds' three main goals during the period under discussion were (1) to secure the UKQ-I; (2) to expand its authority and control over all Iraqi Kurdistan areas; and (3) the legitimisation of their *de facto* status. These Kurdish aspirations encountered staunch opposition from Iraq and resulted in a constant state of military confrontation. Locating an outside protector became a life-and-death matter for the UKQ-I for two reasons. First, being in a continual state of conflict with Iraq and under a permanent economic blockade, the UKQ-I was in desperate need of arms and financial assistance. Being landlocked and deprived of friendly neighbours, the viability and survival of the UKQ-I rested on finding at least one reliable external patron at any given time. Second, in the absence of Iraqi and international recognition of the UKQ-I, the only option to compensate for the Kurdish quasi-state's lack of legitimacy was to find an external source of patronage. The UKQ-I had established clandestine relationships with several regional states and superpowers from 1961 to 1975. UKQ-I relations with some countries may be considered as client-patron relationships. The most significant support, however, was from the USSR from 1961 to 1972, Israel from 1966 to 1975, the US from 1972 to 1975, and most importantly Iran from 1966 to 1975.

The Soviet Union as patron

Initially, Free Kurdistan had good relations with the Soviet Union. From 1961 to 1972 the UKQ-I received limited but continuous financial, diplomatic, and military support from the Soviet Union. The Soviets provided around one-half to 1 million USD per year of financial support to Free Kurdistan.[4] Though symbolic, Soviet aid significantly impacted Kurdish morale and enabled them to begin their rebellion in 1961.[5] Soviet support also served as a buffer from an Iraqi, Turkish, Iranian, and Syrian joint attack.[6] In 1963 when these countries planned a joint military campaign against Free Kurdistan, the diplomatic intervention of the Soviet Union prevented these countries from launching a joint military action, code named 'Operation Tiger'.[7] Thus, the USSR financially assisted in the establishment of UKQ-I and for many years assumed the role of its protector. In this regard, USSR-Kurdish relations may be considered as that of client-patron.

Kurdish-Israeli relations

Several factors encouraged the UKQ-I to search for other external support. The first was the unreliability and limited nature of Soviet support. The second was Iraq's goal to unify with Syria and Egypt. In 1963, the Iraqi government was in direct negotiations with Syria and Egypt over the union of these three states and the establishment of the tripartite federal United Arab State. The third reason was the direct participation of Syria in the Iraqi-Kurdish war of 1963 against the Kurds. To balance this new power arrangement, the Kurds sought additional and/or alternative external support. The other reason was to balance the pro-Soviet leftists and the pro-American right wing of the KDP. The result, however, was more strength for the latter wing of the KDP. Following the division of the KDP in 1964, the party was dominated by the militant/conservative wing of the KDP that was more willing to seek protection from the American camp rather than from the Soviets. Among those countries that were willing to support the Kurds was Israel. By 1965 Israel became one of the Kurds' main supporters – albeit secretly – and this clandestine support continued until 1975.[8]

Unlike the USSR, Israel intended to involve itself directly into the Kurdish-Iraq conflict. Israel provided intelligence, arms, and finances to Free Kurdistan. With the help of Israel in 1963, the UKQ-I opened a radio station operated by Israeli technicians. This station remained in Free Kurdistan until 1975. Israeli intelligence and military professionals settled in Kurdistan and were directly involved in training the Kurdish army. They also provided the Kurds with heavy artillery.[9] The most symbolic participation of Israel, however, was its role in the establishment of the Kurdish intelligence service, the *Parastin*.[10] Thus, up to this point, Israeli-Kurdish relations could be typed as a patron-client relationship.

The American model of support

Another important player in the region that supported the Kurds was the US. Initially the US was reluctant to establish relations with the Kurds and the Kurds' repeated calls for bilateral relations were rejected. However, in 1972, the US showed interest in supporting UKQ-I.[11] Between 1972 and 1975 the US offered limited aid, mostly in terms of financial support, that amounted to only $16 million.[12] This symbolic support changed the nature of outside patronage towards the UKQ-I in many ways. To understand how American support affected the UKQ-I, it is necessary to look at its effect on the Iranian regime and how that influence reshaped Iranian-Kurdish relations. As will be seen in the next section, Iran was the largest external source of financial, military, and political support for the UKQ-I. But the Kurds were suspicious of Iran's true motivations. Barzani, the leader of UKQ-I, believed that the US had complete control over the Shah and would not allow him to betray the Kurds.[13] The US approach to the Kurds encouraged the Kurds to trust the Shah and facilitated their dependency on Iran. The US was perceived by the Kurds not only as a protector from the Iraqi state, but trustworthy enough to keep Free Kurdistan from being used by Iran as a bargaining chip in any future Iranian-Iraqi conflict. To this end, the US-Kurdish relationship may be considered as that of patron-client.

Iran as patron

In many ways Iranian aid to the Kurds may be categorised as the most practical and 'real'. The first distinction of Iranian-Kurdish relations was that Iran shared a border several hundred kilometres long with Free Kurdistan. Most of the border was controlled by the Kurds and was consequently free from control of the central government of Iraq. Unlike the cases of USSR, Israeli, and US aid to the Kurds, the geographic reality between Iran and Free Kurdistan facilitated direct Iranian cooperation with the Kurds without third-party interference or mediation. Iran felt free to participate and interfere in Kurdish-Iraqi fighting. In the fifth Iraqi-Kurdish war in 1974, Iran provided more effective assistance to the UKQ-I by remilitarising the Iranian Kurds.[14] During the fourth and fifth phases of war, Iranian soldiers were dispatched to Kurdistan to fight with the peshmerga against the government of Iraq.[15] These soldiers were supplied with heavy artillery including 175 mm field guns.[16] Iran also served as an indispensable protective backup to Free Kurdistan.[17]

The second distinction of Iranian patronage to UKQ-I was Iran's ability and willingness to provide a safe haven for the Kurds. The Kurds were allowed to cross borders and move freely between Iran and Free Kurdistan. During prolonged wars on Kurdistan tens of thousands of Kurdish families found shelter in Iran.[18] The third distinction of Iranian support was that Iran served as a gateway to the world for the Kurds. The Shah attempted to find American support for the Kurds. Because of its open and direct relations with the Kurds, Iran served as a third-party mediator with those states wishing to have covert relations with the Kurds. Iran also facilitated the flow of other foreign aid and acted as conduit for arms shipped to the Kurds.[19]

The fourth distinction of Iranian patronage was that, for all intents and purposes, Iran was the only state that established semi-formal relations with Free Kurdistan. The USSR, Israeli, and US relations were unofficial, secret, and indirect, as well as arranged through their respective intelligence agencies. Although the Iranian Savak intelligence played a major role, Iranian-Kurdish relations were established by Iranian and Kurdish top officials. UKQ-I and Iranian semi-formal relations go back to 1962 when Free Kurdistan first established its representative in Iran.[20] By January 1966, an agreement was reached between the two parties and signed by the Iranian prime minister and Barzani. By 1974 UKQ-I representation was, in all but name, a Kurdish embassy in Tehran.[21] The unofficial 'embassy' was headed by Shafiq Qazzaz and supported by 30 staff members.

The most important distinction of Iranian patronage for Free Kurdistan was the size and quality of aid. Iran supplied the Kurds with arms, finances, and logistical support. During the earlier Iraqi-Kurdish wars, Iranian aid played a secondary role; but by 1966, Iran supplied 20 per cent or more of UKQ-I requirements.[22] The Shah's military aid to the UKQ-I was another important symbol of Iranian patronage. In January 1975 Iran began infiltrating Iraq with "two regiments of uniformed troops. Firing 130-mm field guns and ground-to-air Hawk missiles, these units engaged in daily duels with Iraqi forces." Iran also "shelled Iraqi positions from emplacements inside Iran [with] 175-mm guns".[23] With sophisticated and heavy weapons and long artillery, the Iranian army increased UKQ-I resistance in the face of a full-stage Iraqi attack.[24] Thus, Iran played an indispensable role as external patron of the UKQ-I. In sum, during the period of 1961 to 1975, UKQ-I received different forms of patronage from two superpowers, the USSR and US, as well as two important regional states, Iran and Israel. These patron relationships compensated Free Kurdistan for the lack of recognition by the international community. They also provided enough finances, logistics, and weaponry to enable it to survive for 14 years.

Negative patronage as the Kurds' Achilles' heel

This section answers the question as to whether any or all of the four cases of patronages to the Kurds (i.e. USSR, Israel, the US, and Iran) may be considered as 'negative'. Each case is scrutinised in light of the three criteria that determine negative patronage (NPC) as well as their respective roles in the collapse of UKQ-I. As laid out in Chapter 1, external patronage is negative if it fulfils three negative patronage criteria (NPC): (1) the populations of the patron and client states do not share the same ethnic or cultural identity (NPC-I); (2) the patron state is not motivated by the interests, rights, and/or identity of the client state; and (3) the patron state does not seek the client's independence and is not willing to recognise the independent state.

The negative patronage case of the Soviet Union

The USSR assumed the role of protector of the UKQ-I from 1961 to 1972 and provided financial and political support to the Kurds. Soviet support to the Kurds may be considered as a form of negative patronage for several reasons. First, the two sides did not share the same ethnic or cultural background; therefore, Soviet's patronage satisfies NPC-I. Second, the Soviets were not motivated to support the Kurds due to Kurdish political and national rights. The relationship was primarily related to the nature of Soviet-Iraqi relations and Iraqi-Western relations. When Qasim's relations with the Soviets deteriorated in 1961, the Soviets were inclined to support the Kurdish revolt. Similarly when the first Ba'athist regime turned against the ICP in 1963, the Soviets transformed their support from clandestine financial assistance to openly advocating for the Kurdish cause within the UN structure.[25] However, immediately after the removal of the Ba'athists from power in November 1963, the Soviets retreated from their advocacy role for Kurdish rights.[26]

In 1972 Soviet support ceased with the signing of the Iraqi-Soviet Friendship Agreement. In fact, the USSR shifted its support and backed Iraq against the Kurds. Politically the Soviets wooed Iraq into the socialist and progressive camp.[27] Being part of the socialist camp meant that Iraq would be supported and protected not only by the Soviets, but by the socialist bloc. Moreover, Soviet support helped Iraq to successfully nationalise its petroleum companies.[28] In addition to the financial, political, logistical, and military support that the USSR was giving to Iraq, the former directly participated in the war against the Kurds.[29] This contributed to a change in the balance of power against the Kurds. Consequently, from 1972 onward the military, political, and financial status of Iraq was strengthened. This changed the future balance of power in the region against the Kurds. The extent of this balance of power change was so substantial that, without significant foreign assistance, the Kurds could no longer protect their *de facto* rule and challenge the government of Iraq.[30] Thus, the USSR's patronage was conditioned on and depended on its relations with Baghdad. It was motivated by Soviet rather than Kurdish interests and thereby satisfies NPC-II. Third, USSR support was not based on the former's belief in the Kurdish right of independence or autonomy; it was directed at the US-Soviet confrontation context. It did not support the idea of an independent Kurdish state. Thus, the third criterion of negative patronage was met. Soviet support to the UKQ satisfied NPC-III. Soviet support of the UKQ-I satisfied the three criteria of negative patronage.

The Israeli case of negative patronage

Israel extended significant financial, intelligence, and military aid to the Kurds throughout the time period under discussion. Yet, it is one more case of negative patronage. First, like the Soviets, the Israelis did not share the same ethnic or cultural identity with the Kurds. Therefore, Israel's patronage satisfies NPC-I. Second, Israel's aid was not motivated by an altruistic wish to see Kurdish victory over Iraq or a strong autonomous Kurdish region, let alone an independent Kurdish state. Israel viewed the continuation of the Iraqi-Kurdish conflict as a method to immobilise Iraqi military capabilities.[31] Israel's policy for the Kurds was designed to contain Iraq's potential threat by keeping Iraq occupied with the Kurdish conflict. For 14 years, between 1961 and 1975, almost three-quarters of the Iraqi army and almost its entire air force were engaged in fighting in Kurdistan. Thus, the Iraqi-Kurdish war continually prevented Iraq from providing sizeable military support to the Arab-Israel wars. The Iraqi role in the 1967 and October 1973 Arab-Israeli wars illustrate this point. During the Arab-Israel war of 1967, the Kurds mounted a large-scale attack on the Iraqi army and this limited Iraq's ability to play an active role against Israel.[32]

During the October 1973 war, the Kurds and Baghdad were in negotiations over the implementation of the March Manifesto. Despite that, only one Iraqi division participated in the war.[33] This is because Iraq perceived the real threat to its integrity to be from the Kurds. In other words, the Kurdish threat to Iraq prevented Iraq from redirecting its troops to the west against Israel. Israel's interest in Kurdish affairs may be understood within the context of the Arab-Israel conflict and, to a lesser degree, the Cold War. Israeli support was unofficial, covert, and limited. It was directed and organised by Iran and routed through Iran.[34] Finally, Israeli assistance ended with the withdrawal of Iranian support to the Kurds directly after the Algeria Agreement of 1975.[35] Therefore, the Israeli patronage satisfies NPC-II.

Israeli support also satisfies NPC-III, as Israel did not support the establishment of an independent Kurdish state. The unresolved Kurdish-Iraqi conflict proved to be to Israel's advantage – not necessarily an independent Kurdistan. To keep the Iraqis off balance permanently, Israel followed a no-win policy in its actions with the Kurds. Israeli aid to the Kurds was not enough to guarantee Kurdish victory. Hence, Israel's support to the Kurds was another example of negative patronage that would not secure the survivability or development of the Kurds' *de facto* rule.

The negative patronage of the US

From 1972 onward, the US replaced the USSR in providing financial and political support to Free Kurdistan. Indeed, US financial support totalling $16 million within a three-year period exceeded the total support that the USSR provided to Free Kurdistan. Similar to the Israeli and the USSR patronages, US support was another example of negative patronage. First, the US Kurdish policy was not based on a common ethnic or cultural identity; neither was it based on ideological grounds or sympathy with the Kurdish issue. Therefore, the US patronage meets NPC-I. Second, two factors encouraged the US to support the Kurds, though neither were directly related to the latter's struggle for self-rule. One factor was that US support was a reaction to growing Soviet influence. In this context, the US sought to employ the UKQ-I to further its interests and strategic gains in the region. Using the Kurds as a chip in the ongoing Cold War between the US and the USSR would weaken the latter's ally, Iraq.[36]

US aid for the Kurds was in response to the Shah's request. Until 1972 the US had refused to establish any form of bilateral relationship with, or to provide any support for, the Kurds. This time, however, American involvement was designed to confront USSR influence and to appease Iran.[37] US cooperation remained informal, indirect, and covert. Instead of delivering aid directly to the Kurds, the process was managed by the CIA through its proxy, the Shah of Iran.[38] By doing so, the US had the final say in Kurdish affairs to the Shah of Iran. It was Iran, rather than the US or Israel, that emerged as a real patron of the Kurds. The US Kurdish policy was more a Machiavellian game that had nothing to do with the rights and interests of the Kurds. The US and Iran had secretly agreed that their support for the Kurds would cease if Iraq agreed to settle its border conflict with Iran based on the latter's conditions.[39] When Iran settled its border disputes with Iraq and terminated its support, the US also withdrew its support of the Iraqi Kurds. Barzani's statement after the collapse of Free Kurdistan strikingly illustrated the extent of US involvement in Kurdish strategic mistakes and tragedies. He stated that "without American promises, we would never have become trapped and involved to such an extent."[40] In its patronage, the US was not motivated by Kurdish rights and interests. Therefore, it meets the conditions of NPC-II. Third, the US had no intention of promoting Kurdish independence, and it did not give sincere and full support to the Kurds or to the Kurdish cause. In fact, the US' goal was to put pressure on Iraq, rather than to find a solution to the Kurdish issue. It was not intended to assist in the creation of an independent Kurdistan or to dismember the country.[41] Hence, the case of US patronage falls short of achieving or recognising an independent Kurdistan. Accordingly, the US patronage satisfies all three criteria of negative patronage.

The superpower's negative patronage altered the Kurds' destiny in many ways and gave the Kurds a false sense of security. In fact, the Kurds made strategic mistakes that they may not have otherwise made without US influence. The leaders of UKQ-I did not trust the Shah and were less inclined to depend on Iran as an external patron. Expressing his mistrust of the Shah in 1966, Mustafa Barzani, the leader of the UKQ-I, reportedly said that Iraq "wants to eliminate us today but Iran wants to annihilate us after ten years".[42] The Kurds perceived US commitment as sufficient guarantee that Iran would no longer use them as a chip in future border disputes with Iraq.[43] Accordingly, the Kurds relied more on the Shah of Iran, whom they did not trust. Feeling more secure in their international relations, the Kurds became overconfident in their ability to defeat Iraq in a future conflict. They were further misled when the Americans encouraged them to reject the Iraqi autonomous offer and revolt against Baghdad.[44] Within this context the Kurds rejected the Iraqi version of autonomy in 1974 and this led to a renewal of Iraqi-Kurdish fighting. By doing so, Barzani staked the survival of the UKQ-I on support promised by the US and Iran. However, with the withdrawal of Iranian support of the UKQ-I, the US terminated its support of the Kurds.

Iran as patron: from primary supporter to anti-Kurdish coalition

The size of Iran's aid exceeded the total of all foreign aid provided by other foreign powers. Iran's military supply, however, was just enough to help the Kurds resist Iraqi attacks and protect their grip on Free Kurdistan.[45] With Iran's help, nonetheless, the Kurds demonstrated their ability to embrace a full-scale conventional war along a 450-kilometre-long arc in 1974. By early 1975, the war was about to become a disaster for Iraq and Iran was about to accomplish its strategic gains through the Kurdish operation. The Iraqi army and its economy were brought to the verge of collapse. In the final months of war Iran was positioned to topple the Ba'ath regime and dismember Iraq.[46] Had Iran increased its assistance to the Kurds during the fifth war, Iraq might have been defeated.

However, instead of helping the Kurds' defeat its traditional enemy, Iran did just the opposite. Tehran helped the collapse of the UKQ-I, and thereby saved Iraq from potential defeat. In March 1975, Iran signed the Algiers Agreement with Iraq to demolish the UKQ-I. Iran immediately shifted its support from the Kurds to Iraq through an alliance. Iran not only cut its financial and military aid to the UKQ-I, but it forced the Kurds to terminate the war and surrender to Iraq. The Iranians "threatened to join the Iraqis in a combined attack on the Kurds if the latter refused to accept the terms of the Agreement".[47] This shifting of Iran's alliance resulted in the total and immediate collapse of UKQ-I. The dramatic shift from Iran's longstanding support (1966–1975) to its anti-Kurdish stance reveals the nature of the Kurds' foreign patronage over the years.

Several factors contributed to the negative nature of Iran's patronage to the Kurds. The main factor was the transnational character of the Kurdish conflict. Iraqi Kurdistan is a landlocked region and all the countries surrounding Kurdistan, including Iran, have struggled with the Kurdish problem for decades. Like Iraq, Iran had a sizable Kurdish minority, almost twice that of Iraq's. The Kurds of Iran are concentrated in a region adjacent to Iraqi Kurdistan. Iran was worried that any future Kurdish victory in Iraq might have spill-over effects on its own Kurdish population.[48] This was evident in the fact that historically Iran entered into anti-Kurdish pacts with Turkey and Iraq, such as the Saadabad Pact in 1937 and the Baghdad Pact of 1955. Like its counterparts, Iran joined these pacts for the purpose of suppressing the Kurdish movements in the region.[49]

Believing that the Kurds' *de facto* self-rule would undermine Iran's integrity, Iran initially did not hide its fear of the Kurds' grip over a large portion of Iraqi Kurdistan territory in 1961.[50] Thus, Iran vehemently opposed any Kurdish progress in Iraq, especially the establishment of a *de jure* autonomous Kurdish region or an independent state. As the collapse of the government of Iraq could encourage such a result, the Shah's ultimate goal was neither to dismember Iraq nor to topple the Ba'ath regime. Iran's Kurdish policy was neither a matter of principle nor a gesture of abandoning its Kurdish concerns. This required Iran to follow a no-win policy in its Kurdish dealings. The question as to why Iran did not give the Kurds enough support to ensure their success may be understood and answered in this context.

The question that remains is that if Iran was not interested in Kurdish rights and self-rule in Iraqi Kurdistan, why did it offer its support to the UKQ-I? Both Iranian support and its temporary abandonment of its concerns for the UKQ-I was based on several strategic calculations and considerations. The first reason for the Iranian-Kurdish policy was to confront a stronger and riskier nationalism, namely pan-Arabism. In addition to the Kurdish minority, Iran also has a sizeable Arab minority concentrated in the southwest of the country adjacent to southern Iraq. The Iranian-Kurdish rapprochement happened at the time that pan-Arabism was becoming Iraq's official/state ideology in the post-1958 coup. All post-monarch constitutions stressed that Iraq was part of the Arab nation and consequently pushed for the unification of the entire Arab world.

After the first Ba'athist regime of 1963, unification with Arab countries was constitutionalised. According to the Iraqi Interim Constitutions of 1958, 1964, and 1968, the government of Iraq was obligated to work for the unification of other Arab states. However, from the pan-Arab perspective (especially the Ba'athists), Iranian Khuzestan was a part of the Arab nation.[51] The ascendency of anti-Iranian-oriented pan-Arabism in the 1960s as the state ideology would also mean that Iraq, as a traditional enemy of Iran, could potentially make trouble among the Arab minority in the Khuzestan province. Thus, Iran was forced to choose one of two unwanted nationalisms: Arab or Kurdish. Several factors encouraged Iran to cooperate with *Kurdayeti*. First, pan-Arabism was endowed with a state structure and the growing *Kurdayeti* lacked such status. Moreover, the rising Arab nationalism and its ascent to power threatened Iran in other ways. A unified Arab world would challenge the role of the Iranian monarchy as policeman of the Persian Gulf. Pan-Arabism dictated a harder attitude towards Iran than *Kurdayeti* did. It also inherently possessed an antipathetic position towards ambitions in the region. Thus, compared to pan-Arabism, *Kurdayeti* was more conciliatory and weak. Imposing its conditions on the Kurds, the Shah felt confident enough to support the UKQ-I without risking the rise of a similar entity in Iran. Therefore, any temporary alliance and limited support to the Kurds would not threaten Iranian interests.

The second reason behind the Shah's alliance with the Kurds was the Iranian prolonged border dispute with Iraq. In the 1960s and early 1970s border disputes between the two countries escalated. The dispute was over the question of whose right it was to have full access to the Shatt al-Arab.[52] By prolonging the Iraq-Kurdish war through support for the Kurds, Iran contributed in further exhausting Baghdad's strength. Draining the Iraqi budget could be accomplished by pinning down its army in Kurdistan. This was evident in that on many occasions Iraq informed the Kurds that it would *make* territorial concessions to Iran if Iran abandoned the Kurds.[53] Playing the Kurdish card proved to be worth it for Iran. Using the UKQ-I as a bargaining chip, Iran achieved its goal in 1975. Iraq made the most concessions and paid a high territorial price in the Algiers Agreement in return for Iran's withdrawal of its support for the Kurds.

Countering rising Soviet influence in the Persian Gulf was another important factor that accelerated Iranian support for the Kurds. Iran's aim to offset Iraq's strength resulted from its alignment with the USSR. Iraq signed the Treaty of Friendship and Cooperation in 1972. This Iraq-Soviet alignment had two undesirable consequences for Iran. First, Iraq acted as a Soviet client in the Middle East. Iraq also ceded the USSR some naval base docking privileges at the Iraqi port of Umm Qasr.[54] The USSR gained access to the Iraqi oil supply as well as a base in the Persian Gulf. Hence, while Iran emphatically did not want a Soviet presence in the Gulf, it found itself surrounded by Russians on two fronts: Iraq and Afghanistan.[55] Thus, the Soviet influence in the Persian Gulf directly challenged Iran. Iran sought the continuation of the Iraqi-Kurdish war as a method of preventing the strengthening of Soviet-backed Iraq and to balance its military capability. It also reduced Soviet influence in the region.

Another reason that contributed to the Iranian policy to support the Kurds was Turkish animosity to the Kurdish issue in Iraq. Turkey was an ally of the US and was threatened by the expansion of communist influence in the region. As in the case of Iran, the Soviet-Iraqi rapprochement was perceived by Turkey to threaten their interests. The entire Kurdish region inside Iraq on the Iraqi-Turkey frontier was part of the UKQ and was ruled by the Kurds.[56] Hence, like Iran, Turkey had potential interest and ability to use the Kurdish card to counter the ever-growing Soviet influence in the region. However, the fear of *Kurdayeti* spilling over into Turkish Kurdistan took second place to the threat of communism. Therefore, Turkey was not willing to support the Kurds. By contrast, the Turks imposed a rigid blockade against the UKQ-I.[57] Turkey's animosity to Free Kurdistan also pushed the Kurds to further rely on Iran. This increased Iran's ability to control the Kurds and therefore to contain the possibility of *Kurdayeti*'s spilling over to its own Kurdish community. Within the context of the Cold War and the complexity of Middle Eastern politics, Iran emerged as an indispensable patron to the survival of the UKQ. Thus, for the Kurds to counterbalance the superiority of the Soviet-backed Iraqi army, Iranian patronage had greater significance than ever before.[58]

In contrast to previous phases of war with Iraq, during the fifth war on Kurdistan, the Kurds became heavily dependent on Iranian logistics as well as financial and military support. The prolongation of the war against Iraq generated unprecedented demands for Iranian support. The Kurds' dependency became an instrument by which Tehran could control them. The Kurdish reliance on Iran increased

112 *The case of negative patronage*

to such an extent that they were obliged to accept Iranian terms and conditions.[59] Now Iran was in a more confident position to assert its terms and conditions. The Iraqi Kurds avoided cooperating with the Iranian Kurds, thus curtailing their influence on them.[60] The Kurds also accepted Iran's role as an intermediary for any foreign assistance. This unmanageable political reality drove the Kurds into a state of total dependence on Iranian and American good will, thus signalling the beginning of the end for Free Kurdistan.

In sum, the primary weakness of the UKQ-I lay in the quality of patronage it attracted. All foreign patrons had their own agendas in mind; thus their goals were inconsistent with those of the Kurds. None of the four states that provided support or assistance to the Kurds satisfied the three criteria of positive patronage. These countries' patronages generally ended when their conflict with Iraq ceased. What made this patronage so unreliable and negative was that the patron states often turned their support to Iraq and away from the Kurds, as in the cases of the USSR in 1972 and Iran in 1975. As will be explained, Iran practically joined Iraq in fighting the Kurdish peshmerga between 1975 and 1978. Thus, the lack of positive patronage remained the Kurds' Achilles' heel and the main reason for the collapse of the UKQ-I in 1975.

Notes

1 Kolstø (2006: 735).
2 KDP-PC 1979: 102; Farouk-Sluglett and Sluglett 2001: 168; Barzani 2002: 13.
3 Cited in Randal 1997: 181.
4 Barzani 2002: 375.
5 *Ibid.*: 22–23; Sinjari, A. (2006), *Al-Qadhiya al-Kurdiye wa al-hizb al-Ba'ah al-Arabi al-Ishtraki fi al-Iraq (The Kurdish Problem and the Arab Socialist Ba'ath Party in Iraq)*, Duhok, Iraq: Haji Hashim Press: 52.
6 Hussain, S. (1986), "Notes on the Kurdish Struggle," *Race & Class* 27(3): 90–94; 91.
7 *Ibid.*
8 Seale, P. (1988), *Asad of Syria: The Struggle for the Middle East*, Berkeley, CA: University of California Press: 243; Neff, D. (1991) "The U.S., Iraq, Israel, and Iran: Backdrop to War," *Journal of Palestine Studies* 20(4): 25; Barzani 2002: 377.
9 Cockburn, A. and L. Cockburn (1991), *Dangerous Liaison: the Inside Story of the US-Israeli Covert Relationship*, New York: Harper Collins Publishers: 82, 153; Nakdimon, S. (1997), *Al-Mosad fi al-Iraq and Dwal al-Jiwar (Mosad in Iraq and Neighbouring Countries)*, Amman: Jordan Dar al-Jalil li-Alnashir: 101; Tucker, M. (2006), *Hell Is Over: Voices of the Kurds After Saddam*, Guilford, CT: Lyons Press: 39; Little, D. (2010), "The United States and the Kurds: A Cold War Story," *Journal of Cold War Studies* 12(4): 71.
10 Abdulghani, J. M. (1984), *Iraq and Iran: The Years of Crisis*, London: Taylor & Francis: 140; Emin 1997b: 113.
11 Barzani 2002: 337.
12 Abdulghani 1984: 144; Barzani 2002: 378.
13 Abdulghani 1984: 140.
14 Tomasek 1976: 221.
15 Pollack 2004: 179; Nuri 2007: 348.
16 Farouk-Sluglett and Sluglett 2001: 170.
17 Israeli, R. (2003), *War, Peace and Terror in the Middle East*, London: Routledge: 86; Polk, W. R. (2005), *Understanding Iraq*, New York: Harper Collins: 155.
18 Barzani 2002: 345.

19 Catudal 1976: 1036; Abdulghani 1984: 140; Cockburn and Cockburn 1991: 82, 153; Tucker 2006: 39; Little 2010: 71.
20 Korn, D. A. (1994), "The Last Years of Mustafa Barzani," *Middle East Quarterly* 1(2); Barzani 2002: 370.
21 Korn 1994.
22 Gunter M. M. (1992), *The Kurds of Iraq: Tragedy and Hope*, New York: St. Martin's Press: 11; McDowall 2004: 320.
23 Catudal 1976: 1038.
24 *Ibid.*: 1031; Abdulghani 1984: 152; Borovali 1987: 34.
25 Naamani 1966: 293.
26 Sinjari 2006: 53.
27 *Ibid.*: 53.
28 *Ibid.*: 53–55.
29 Catudal 1976: 1036.
30 Tomasek 1976: 225.
31 Stavenhagen, R. (1996), *Ethnic Conflicts and the Nation-State: United Nations Research Institute for Social Development*, New York: Palgrave Macmillan: 204.
32 Abdulghani 1984: 145.
33 Kissinger, H. A. (1979), *The White House Years*, New York: Little, Brown and Company: 256.
34 Lambert, P. J. (1997), "The United States and the Kurds: Case Studies in United States Engagement," Masters thesis, Monterey, CA: 39; Bengio 1998a: 33–34.
35 Stavenhagen 1996: 204; Parsi 2006: 506.
36 Gunter 1992: 8; Lambert 1997: 35.
37 Abdulghani 1984: 144; Borovali 1987: 34; Little 2010: 71.
38 Wagner, J. Q. (1992), *Ethnic Conflict: The Case of the Kurds*, Washington, DC: DTIC Document: 23; Korn 1994; Little 2010: 78.
39 Abdulghani 1984: 145; O'Leary, C. A. (2002), "The Kurds of Iraq: Recent History, Future Prospects," *Middle East Review of International Affairs* 6(4): 26.
40 Cited in Ghareeb, E. (1981), *The Kurdish Question in Iraq*, Syracuse, NY: Syracuse University Press: 1981: 159.
41 Abdulghani 1984: 144.
42 KDP-PC 1979: 82.
43 Korn 1994; Farouk-Sluglett and Sluglett 2001: 159.
44 Abdulghani 1984: 139; Gunter 2004: 4.
45 Tomasek 1976: 221–222; Gunter 1992: 10.
46 Karsh 1990: 264; 2008: 6; Karsh, E. and I. Rautsi (1991), *Saddam Hussein: A Political Biography*, New York: Free Press: 81.
47 Farouk-Sluglett and Sluglett 2001: 170.
48 Abdulghani 1984: 140; Izady 2004: 80; "The Kurdish Minority Identity in Iraq," *Nationalism and Minority Identities in Islamic Societies*, Maya Shatzmiller (ed.), Montreal, Quebec, Canada: McGill-Queen's University Press: 267.
49 Abdulghani 1984: 140.
50 KDP-PC 1979: 81.
51 See: ABSP 2007.
52 O'Leary 2002: 26; Little 2010: 71.
53 Emin 1997a: 20; KDP-PC 1997: 50.
54 Tomasek 1976: 225.
55 In early 1970 Afghanistan was considered an ally of the USSR.
56 *The New York Times*, 01/04/1974.
57 Catudal 1976: 1031; Tomasek 1976: 220.
58 Farouk-Sluglett and Sluglett 2001: 164.
59 Nuri 2007: 373–374.
60 KDP-PC 1997: 59.

7 The rise and fall of Kurdish insurgency (1976–1988)

The Kurdish Nationalist Movement experienced three phases of development during the period under review. The first phase began with the resumption of the peshmerga activity in 1976. The second phase started within the circumstances of the Iraq-Iran war. In this period the peshmerga controlled a significant part of rural Kurdistan that was known by the Kurds as Free Kurdistan. The third phase followed the failure of PUK-Iraqi negotiations that was followed by the Iran-PUK agreement and the reconciliation of the Kurdish parties and the establishment of the IKF. During this period, peshmerga controlled almost the entire Kurdish countryside while Iraqi rule dwindled to the main cities, towns, and highways. Iraq adopted different policies towards the Kurds in each phase. Its reaction to the first phase was ruthless and followed the No-Man's Land (NML) policy. During this policy, 1,400 Kurdish villages were destroyed and inhabitants were resettled in collection camps, all within three years (1976–1979). During the second phase, Iraq followed a more conciliatory policy due to its weakened status. The NML process ceased and Iraq introduced a separate army system in Kurdistan. Finally as a gesture of recognition of the *de facto* existence of Kurdish rebellion, Iraq initiated negotiations with the PUK. During the third phase, Iraq resumed its NML policy and violence escalated to unprecedented levels. Finally under the scorched-earth policy and with frequent use of chemical weapons, the Kurdish insurgency collapsed. By the summer of 1988 Iraq recaptured the entire area of Iraqi Kurdistan. Thus, in 1975, Iraq won the war against the Kurds, but it lost the peace.

The first phase: the emergence of the Kurdish insurgency (1976–1979)

This phase directly followed the Kurds' shock after a 14-year period of quasi-state self-rule dramatically came to an end. *Kurdayeti* in its militant form re-emerged, though in an unprecedented weak state, at least since the monarchy. Two main features of this period are the re-emergence of the Kurdish military movement (peshmerga) and the No-Man's Land policy that Iraq imposed on areas previously under control of the UKQ-I.

The re-emergence of the Kurdish military movement (peshmerga)

In June 1976, one year after the collapse of Free Kurdistan, the KDP, the PUK and several other smaller groups separately commenced an armed struggle against Baghdad. Though small and limited in number, among these groups was the PUK, which started its rebellion with only 160 peshmerga. Initially their activities were limited to the rural areas of Kurdistan. Within a year, however, their number was compounded and by 1977 in Erbil province alone the PUK had 200 to 300 peshmerga.[1] In the same year, the peshmerga appeared to be strong enough to establish their headquarters in the rural areas of Kurdistan. By 1978 the number of peshmerga rose to 1,500 and they were dispersed throughout Kurdistan.[2]

At this stage, the peshmerga force was relatively weak and amounted to less than 2 per cent of their strength prior to their defeat in 1975. Despite that, to counter this small group of peshmerga, Iraq deployed 120,000 men. Three-quarters of the Iraqi army were stationed in Kurdistan to fight the peshmerga.[3] In other words, for every single peshmerga soldier, more than 80 Iraqi soldiers were deployed in Kurdistan. The strength of the peshmerga did not come from their numerical strength, as they were a small group. Rather it came from the fact that they were highly mobile and able to attack, on Kurdish territory, the Iraqi armed forces that were a great distance from their headquarters. As early as 1977 the peshmerga were involved in conventional warfare to protect their headquarters from Iraqi invasion.[4] Thus, the emergence of the peshmerga, though small in number and limited in military and political scope, was enough to challenge and handicap Iraqi authority, at least on the border areas.

The Iraqi policy to depopulate Kurdish areas

Within a few years the reality of peshmerga effectiveness could no longer be denied by Iraq. Failing to accept or contain the presence of the peshmerga, Iraq adopted a more radical and ruthless policy in the attempt to uproot its power base. This was known as the No-Man's Land (NML) policy. As outlined in detail in Chapter 9, under the NML policy, within three years (1976–1979) approximately 1,200 to 1,400 villages, or an area of more than 16,000 square kilometres, were depopulated. By the end of the 1980s, however, the size of the depopulated areas would expand by almost threefold. The depopulation policy revealed two contradictory features of Iraq's rule of Kurdistan. First, it showed its undisputed military superiority in that within three years Iraq removed more than one-quarter of all Kurdish villages from the map without significant resistance. Second, the depopulation policy of these agriculturally rich areas revealed the shaky foundation of Iraqi rule in rural Kurdistan and its failure to manage that area. This was evident in that a significant part of the NML areas became part of what the Kurds called 'Liberated Territories of Kurdistan' and were ruled by peshmerga forces.

Though the emergence of the Kurdish military movement may be used to justify the NML policy, it is not the only factor involved in Iraq's ruthless handling of Kurdistan. The NML policy cannot be isolated from the failure of the Iraqi state to administer or manage the region since the creation of modern Iraq. During the monarchy many tribes of this area enjoyed their Traditional Autonomous Entity status. Between 1961 and 1975 it became an integral part and the first Kurdish quasi-state (UKQ-I). Thus, for many decades the inhabitants of these areas had little, if any, experience with direct central authority. Consequently, Iraq lacked a power base, loyalty, and administrative mechanisms and institutions in these areas. Its presence was limited mostly to military barracks. Iraq faced difficulties governing this unfriendly population and uncontrollable region. Therefore, instead of investing its triumph and superiority to govern and integrate the Kurds into the state, Iraq followed the strategy of depopulating the area and resettling its population into controllable collection camps. Thus, despite its military superiority, following the collapse of the UKQ-I in 1975, Iraq failed to adequately govern the region.

The second phase: administrating the peshmerga controlled areas (1979–1985)

The collapse of the Shah of Iran in 1979 and the commencement of the Iraq-Iran war in 1980 were turning points in the Kurdish rebellion against Iraq. The pro-American, conservative, and now anti-Kurdish regime of the Shah was replaced with an anti-American and radical Islamist regime in 1979. The fall of the Shah and the establishment of the Islamic regime brought a fundamental change in the hitherto Middle Eastern status quo. The first fundamental change was the power vacuum and resulting anarchy in Iran, combined with the revolutionary environment. This strengthened the Kurdish movement and the peshmerga's abilities in many ways. The Kurdish Nationalist Movement in Iran revived following the Iranian revolution. Between 1979 and 1982 a significant part of Iranian Kurdistan fell under the rule of Iranian-Kurdish peshmerga forces. This offered the Iraqi Kurds a safe haven, logistical and political support, free movement to Iranian Kurdistan, and access to weaponry. Thus, finding a geostrategic depth on the other side of the border permitted the intensification of guerrilla warfare in Iraqi Kurdistan.

The second fundamental change was that Iraq became an ideal target for the revolutionary Iranian agenda to export the Islamic revolution. Iraq shared a 1,200-kilometre border with Iran. The largest part of southern Iraq was an extension of Iranian culture as both shared the Shia version of Islam. Iraq has the second largest Shia community in the world and the Shia represent 60 per cent of the Iraqi population. Moreover, the Ayatollah's hierarchy and religious institutions of the Iraqi Shias were heavily influenced by Iranian origins. Khomeini spent part of his exile in Iraq and left his fingerprints on Iraqi political life. Iraq probably was among the first countries that Khomeini called to rebel against its rulers. In the first months of its rule, Khomeini appealed to the Shias of Iraq to overthrow the Ba'ath regime. Several Shia parties responded to the Iranian call and escalated their activities.[5] Furthermore, the majority of Shia tombs, shrines, and holy sites are located in Iraq. The historical Arab-Persian rivalries, border conflicts, and ideological battles of Ba'athist pan-Arabism versus Khomeini's Pan-Shi'ism threatened Iraq from its eastern border.

The third fundamental change was that, with the collapse of the Shah's regime, the Algerian Agreement remained only on paper. For several years within the Algerian framework, Iran aided Iraq militarily and logistically to suppress and contain the Kurdish movement.[6] Ironically, on 17 September 1980, Iraq officially renounced the Algerian Agreement of 1975. The animosity between the two sides reached such an extent that a few days later, on 22 September 1980, Saddam launched his offensive against Iran and the two countries committed to one of the longest wars in the twentieth century.

The fourth fundamental change was the Iran-Iraq war that left a significant power vacuum in Kurdistan. The outbreak of the Iraq-Iran war placed heavy burdens on Baghdad that forced it to further relinquish its control of Kurdistan. To control Kurdistan and suppress the peshmerga, Iraq had stationed most of its ten divisions in Kurdistan up to 1979.[7] Following the outbreak of the Iraq-Iran war, however, Iraq withdrew the majority of its forces from rural Kurdistan. Due to its escalating conflict with Iran, Iraqi troops were transferred to the Iranian front and army garrisons were abandoned or reduced. In Sulaimaniya province, for example, only 26,000 troops of 100,000 were left.[8] The peshmerga, however, swiftly moved to fill the security vacuum and control the abandoned areas. Iraq was no longer in a dominant position in Kurdistan and the peshmerga established more bases throughout the Kurdish countryside. Peshmerga forces that belonged to five political parties increased significantly, from 1,500 in 1978 to 9,000 in 1981.[9] Within approximately two years, this figure doubled. The numbers of the PUK peshmerga alone rose to 9,000 in 1983. The KDP peshmerga increased to 10,000 in 1984.[10] Thus, while the Iraqi military declined dramatically in Kurdistan, the peshmerga forces significantly increased in size and capacity. Consequently, most parts of rural Kurdistan eventually turned into liberated territories.

By 1981 the peshmerga had grown strong enough to utilise both guerrilla and conventional tactics of war. The Kurds' ability to conduct a conventional war meant that they had the ability to control and protect the wider Kurdistan region and establish local self-rule through village councils. By early 1982, the Kurds controlled over 10,000 square kilometres of territory along the Iranian and Turkish borders.[11] The area that was controlled by the peshmerga, however, was much larger than this figure. By the beginning of the Iraq-Iran war, the area of the NML exceeded 16,000 square kilometres. A significant part of these areas had become part of Free Kurdistan several years before the outbreak of the Iran-Iraq war.[12] Moreover, peshmerga control extended far beyond the NML to cover the major part of rural Kurdistan. The majority of rural Kurdistan in 1981 was controlled and administered by peshmerga forces that belonged to five Kurdish rebel political parties.

In the PUK controlled areas, the peshmerga divided the rural Kurdistan areas into several local administrative regions. Each region was administered by a *Malband* (centre or local headquarter office) of the PUK. *Malband* represented the local government and constituted several divisions, each dedicated to a different institution including the judiciary, social, health, and military affairs. At lower levels a local administration known as village councils were founded to administer the Kurdish countryside. Each council was comprised of five people who were elected by village residents. These village councils were connected to the division of social affairs of the *Malband*. Each *Malband* opened schools, hospitals, and courts along with other institutions. Dozens of publications (including weekly, monthly, and periodical ones) were issued regularly. Thus, five years after the collapse of the UKQ-I, the Kurds retained Free Kurdistan, though smaller in size.

The third phase: the expansion of the peshmerga controlled areas (1985–1987)

Iraq and the PUK engaged in negotiations in 1983 that lasted until the winter of 1984/1985. Following the collapse of negotiations, Baghdad found its control of Kurdistan eroding once more. The deterioration of Iraqi rule in Kurdistan was evident in that some 2,000 Kurdish villages had integrated into the already 'liberated territories'.[13] The peshmerga imposed control over wider areas of Iraqi Kurdistan. By 1986 the peshmerga exercised effective control over the rural areas. Baghdad's authority had dwindled in the cities, towns, collection camps (*Mujama'at*), and main highways. In 1987 only 186 out of 1,877 villages in Sulaimaniya province remained under Iraqi control. Many of their inhabitants were armed and organised into Civil Defense Forces.[14] The KDP recruited some 20,000 peasants into the Civil Defense Forces; the PUK probably recruited more than this number.[15]

By 1987, the Kurdish parties united under the Iraqi Kurdistan Front (IKF). The new Kurdish Front with its 15,000 to 20,000 peshmerga forces was further consolidated. Taking advantage of Iranian military support, the peshmerga expanded their operations and proved that the Iraqi main oil industry was no longer immune to attack. The same year the peshmerga attacked the Kirkuk oil installations. In the raid the PUK deployed more than 3,000 peshmerga and 150 Iranian commandos participated in attacking the Iraqi oil industry.[16] In 1987, the PUK used 5,000 peshmerga in one military endeavour.[17] Iraqi troops, though temporary, were driven out of many Kurdish towns, such as Halabja in March 1988, Rawanduz, and Atrush.[18] By early 1988 peshmerga activities reached beyond the Kurdish areas as far as Mosul, Tikrit, and the Baquba city outskirts.[19] The Kurds' tactical alliance with Iran posed an unprecedented threat to the Iraqi regime. Thus, for many years Iraq had no authority in rural Kurdistan, a state of affairs that allowed the peshmerga to establish a limited administration in rural areas. By the end of 1988, the Kurdish insurgency dramatically collapsed. Iraq retained control of the entire Iraqi Kurdistan and for the first time since 1976 the entire peshmerga was exiled to Iran. No single base of any Kurdish party was left in Kurdistan. Iraq launched a series of genocidal operations known as *Anfal*. The campaign made use of chemical weapons by which the entire Kurdish population of the liberated territory was killed, vanished, fled to Iran and Turkey, or forcibly resettled in *Mujama'at* collection camps. Thus, another phase of the Kurdish insurgency, that lasted some eight years, ended.

Do the peshmerga controlled areas meet criteria for unrecognised quasi-states?

Between 1980 and 1988 the peshmerga controlled areas (PCA) shared many features of unrecognised quasi-states (UQs). However, scrutinising its status in light of the unrecognised quasi-state criteria (UQC) reveal that the PCA was not developed to the extent necessary to be classified as a quasi-state. The first criterion to scrutinise the status of the PCA is nation-building (UQC-I). The PCA did not successfully engage in nation-building processes, though there was evidence of nation-building in the liberated territory during this period. Topics such as Kurdistani identity; the Kurdish nationhood, Kurdish separate history; distinct Kurdish culture, language, and customs; reviving common memories; and the glorification of Kurdish heroes and martyrs dominated all Kurdish political party discourses. These discourses were re-emphasised daily through several radio stations belonging to Kurdish political parties, as well as tens of weekly, monthly, and periodical publications.[20] Though a limited local administration was installed in Free Kurdistan, the PCA lacked the requisite state institutions to stimulate the nation-building processes. The nation-building processes never became institutionalised nor did they extend to all aspects of nation-building. The parties did, however, celebrate *Nawroz* as a national day; but they did not adopt the Kurdish nationalist flag and the PCA lacked its own constitution. Though the PCA continued to pose a challenge to the Iraqi nation-building project, the nation-building process of Free Kurdistan, during the period in question, were not developed to the level necessary to satisfy the first criterion of UQC-I.

The second criterion to apply to the PCA for determining its quasi-state status is the militarisation of society (UQC-II). The number of peshmerga was relatively high, especially during the third phase (1985–1988) when there were as many as 20,000 to 25,000 peshmerga supported by a similar number of Kurdish civil defenders. Thus, around 40,000 fighters for a population of one million in the PCA was a relatively high ratio of fighters per resident. Though the PCA was to a large extent a militarised society, it failed to satisfy the militarisation criterion of unrecognised quasi-states (UQC-II) for two reasons. First, the peshmerga and its civil defenders lacked a common command. In fact, they were militias divided into several rival factions that were not united or organised into one institution. Moreover, there was no obligation for civil defenders to join the fighting. Second, the PCA failed to bring a majority of Kurdish fighters into the peshmerga ranks. In UKQ-I (1961–1975), the majority of Kurds were organised into the peshmerga armed forces. The pro-Iraqi militias (*Jash*) represented only a small minority. During this period, however, the peshmerga forces were a small minority, about 20,000 to 25,000 compared to 150,000 to 250,000 pro-Iraqi militiamen who were organised under the semi-autonomous *Jash* militia brigades.

The third criterion to apply to determining quasi-state status is the weak parent state criterion (UQC-III). The PCA fails to meet this criterion. During the Iraq-Iran war (1980–1988), Iraq weakened to an extent that it lost control over a majority of rural Kurdistani citizens. One piece of evidence of the weakness of Iraq as a parent state was its willingness to negotiate with the Kurds over the ceasefire and autonomous arrangement. As explained in Chapter 9, since the collapse of the UKQ-I in 1975, Iraq unilaterally implemented its autonomous law and established an autonomous administration in three Kurdish provinces. By 1983, however, Iraq was in a real dilemma. It was weakened by Iran's repeated offensive manoeuvres, and it lost control over the major part of rural Kurdistan. The existence of the peshmerga and its rule over rural Kurdistan became a *de facto* reality that Baghdad had to deal with. In this set of circumstances, Iraq was forced to initiate talks with the peshmerga. By the end of 1983, Baghdad offered to negotiate with the PUK for the purpose of expanding the autonomy of the Kurdistan region. Based on promises to expand Kurdish autonomy, the PUK, then the largest Kurdish political party, entered direct negotiations with Baghdad. In return, the Kurds were required to sign a ceasefire agreement and to assist Iraq against Iran. A ceasefire agreement between Iraq and the PUK was declared in December 1983.

Iraq initially consented to develop autonomy in favour of the Kurds. According to Emin, negotiations focused on four main issues: (1) authorities of the central government and the autonomous administration in Kurdistan, (2) the border of this autonomous region, (3) the normalisation of the situation in Kurdistan including termination of the Arabisation and NML policies, and (4) the Kurds' role in the central government.[21] Though the negotiations ended in the winter of 1984/1985 without any tangible consequences for either side, they may be considered as a turning point in Kurdish-Iraqi relations. First, considering the dramatic and total collapse of Free Kurdistan in 1975, such recognition was psychologically important for Kurdish nationalists. The Kurdish call for autonomy, other nationalist demands, recognition of the PUK, and the peshmerga as representatives of the Kurds were the bases for negotiations.

Second, the ceasefire and negotiations provided a better environment for the Kurds and permitted the PUK direct contact with the population of cities and towns under Iraqi control.[22] During the negotiations the peshmerga was allowed to enter cities and towns under Iraqi control. Having direct contact with the Kurds in areas under Iraqi control helped the peshmerga find new recruits for its ranks. In less than two years of negotiations, the number of peshmerga increased threefold to fourfold. Prior to the negotiations, the PUK peshmerga in the province of Erbil numbered around 700. By the end of the ceasefire, they numbered around 2,700.[23] During the negotiations, Iraq lifted its embargo on the liberated territories. This put the peshmerga in a better financial position. Third, while Iraq was prevented from entering the liberated territories, the peshmerga extended their political activities into the cities and towns with their arms. During negotiations, Baghdad ceded part of its sovereignty to the peshmerga in areas under Iraqi control.

Other evidence of Iraqi weakness was the temporary failure of the NML policy. As explained in Chapter 9, Iraq followed the NML policy in 1976. Within a few years, hundreds of Kurdish villages were depopulated and hundreds of thousands of Kurdish villagers were resettled in concentration camps (*Mujama'at*). The peshmerga, however, imposed its control over a significant part of rural Kurdistan, including the areas that were depopulated under Iraq's NML policy. Negotiations between the PUK and Baghdad resulted in the temporary cessation of the NML.[24] The Kurds' ability to establish and protect the rural areas, coupled with Iraq's involvement in the devastating war with Iran, resulted in the creation of a new balance of power against Baghdad. Iraq gradually lost control of Kurdistan to the Kurds and faced a staunch counteroffensive from Iran. These harsh circumstances forced Iraq to neutralise the Kurds through suspension of the NML operations and compromise the return of deported villagers to their farms. To placate the Kurds, Iraq initially permitted thousands of exiled Kurds in southern Iraq to return to Kurdistan.[25] The ceasefire, combined with peshmerga control of the liberated territories, encouraged civilians to move back into the depopulated areas. Thousands of Kurds in *Mujama'at* escaped and rebuilt their destroyed villages that were now protected by the peshmerga. Thus, they became part of the liberated territory. The previously depopulated NML became home to thousands of inhabitants of cities and towns that escaped different forms of oppression by the Iraqi security forces. Among others that resided in liberated territories were draft lodgers, army deserters, political members of various factions, and families and relatives of the peshmerga.[26] Free Kurdistan also became the sanctuary for non-Kurdish opposition groups. Thus, from 1980 until the beginning of 1985 when Iraq-PUK collapsed, the NML policy foundered and Kurdistan witnessed a reversal of this process. A disorganised repopulation process eventually replaced the systematic depopulation process as the Kurds returned to their homes.

The Kurdish insurgency also played a role in the collapse of the conscription system in Iraq due to the failure of Iraq to govern Kurdistan. The Ba'ath regime paid a great deal of attention to the recruitment of the Kurds to the army for several reasons. First, Iraq viewed the army as a method of integrating the Kurds into Iraq. Second, the process of recruitment into the Iraqi army became a key factor in the war effort against Iran. Third, conscription was an important method of preventing young Kurds from joining the peshmerga forces. Recruiting Kurds into the Iraqi army also helped to control them. However, against Iraq's wishes and intentions, the conscription and recruitment mechanisms were counterproductive. Iraq soon faced strong opposition to the draft in Kurdistan and the Kurds deserted from the army in droves.

Several factors contributed to the massive acts of desertion and draft dodging by the Kurds. For example, the lack of Kurdish loyalty to Iraq, their non-identification as Iraqis, and lack of Iraqi nationalism was expressed by desertion and draft dodging. As explained in previous chapters, neither during nor following the monarchy was the Iraqi government influence strong enough in Kurdistan to impose conscription laws on the Kurds. Desertion from the army became part of the political culture and reality for both the Kurds and the Iraqi regime. Furthermore, the negative image of the army in Kurdistan due to its longstanding onslaught against *Kurdayeti* dissuaded the Kurds from joining the Iraqi army. Since 1961, the Iraqi army had directly waged war against the Kurds, causing tens of thousands of casualties among Kurdish civilians. This negative image was further exacerbated by the army's role in destroying the rural Kurdistan areas and turning a large portion of it into No-Man's Land. Finally, and most importantly, the dwindling of Iraqi authority in Kurdistan and the expansion of peshmerga rule provided a safe haven to large numbers of Kurdish draft dodgers and army deserters. By the beginning of 1983 the number of Kurdish deserters was just under 50,000.[27] While avoiding a bloody war, the Kurds deserted from the army and provided additional support and manpower to the Kurdish insurgency. Failing to recruit Kurds into the army, Baghdad was compelled to introduce a separate army system in Kurdistan. Initially Iraq offered an amnesty to Kurdish deserters and granted permission for them to be stationed in Kurdistan instead of in the south. These concessions, however, did not encourage the Kurds to join the army. The opposition to the draft remained strong and Iraq was obliged to exempt the Kurds from obligatory service, making their participation voluntary.[28] Thus, those who were willing to serve in the army were exempted from deployment to the Iranian front and in the dreaded area of southern Iraq.

Allowing Kurdish servicemen to serve in Kurdistan and turning soldiering into a voluntary enterprise had ramifications for Kurdish integration into Iraq and for the state's sovereignty. It meant that there were two systems of army service in Iraq: a voluntary recruitment effort in Kurdistan and conscription in other parts. A separate army service in Kurdistan also meant the granting of significant concessions to the Kurds and recognition of their separate status. Though such recognition of separate status for Kurdistan was a tactical step, and it had not been legalised, the practical result was that the Kurds gained increased autonomy. These policies became *de facto* law until the collapse of the Kurdish insurgency in 1988. Furthermore, exempting the Kurds from conscripted service meant the collapse of that system in Kurdistan and the failure of this device for integrating the Kurds into the Iraqi state. The two different army systems further sharpened ethnic differentiation between the Kurds and Arabs. This is because ethnic Arabs, whose majority of young males were recruited to fight in the Iraq-Iran war and who suffered high numbers of casualties, were not granted such a privilege. Finally, the collapse of the Iraqi conscription system in Kurdistan further isolated the regime as its authority dwindled in Kurdistan.

The voluntary service in the army and the exemption of the Kurds from deployment to the Iranian front did not encourage the Kurds to join the army. Despite these significant concessions, desertions in Kurdistan continued non-stop.[29] By the mid-1980s, the conscription system in Kurdistan had totally collapsed. Iraq then revived the *Jash* system to recruit the Kurds into the irregular army under the command of local leaders. The *Jash* system became an alternative to the army system (both conscription and voluntary). Registering as a *Jash* was considered equivalent to military service even though Kurdish recruits did not have to serve under Iraqi officers. Thus, Iraq lost much of its power base, sovereignty, and legitimacy in Kurdistan. The weakness inherent in Iraq, however, was more related to the Iraq-Iran context. Iraq founded one of the largest armies in the region: probably one million strong.[30] The use of this army against the Kurds was a matter of time and depended on the state of conflict with Iran. Thus, once the pressure of Iran eased and the war headed towards its end, Iraq launched a large part of its army against Kurdistan. With the use of chemical weapons (CW), Iraq recaptured the entire liberated territory in six months. While warring with the anti-Western regime of Iran, Iraq enjoyed significant outside support from Western countries and the conservative oil-rich Gulf countries. This regional and international support assisted Baghdad's violation of international human rights standards and international laws and norms without international punishment, pressure, or retribution. Within this liberal environment Iraq used CW and inflicted mass killing on the Kurds. With no checks and balances on its actions, Iraq could ensure Kurdish defeat. Indeed, the destruction of Kurdistan was directly related to the support that Iraq received from the international community, especially from the US.

In many ways, the US and the international community facilitated Iraq's use of CWs against the Kurds. First, their roles in facilitating Iraq's use of CW was evident in the US policy of directly or indirectly supplying conventional weapons to Iraq. It is believed that Iraq imported part of its CW from the US. More than one-quarter of US exports of dual use technology items between 1985 and 1990 was sent to Iraq.[31] This technology was used in the development of biological weapons and CW. Moreover, Iraq used these US-supplied chemicals that were made for warfare purposes, dual technology, and US-made helicopters to attack the Kurds.[32] Second, the US' and international community's role in facilitating Iraq's use of CW was evident in their toleration of Iraq's use of chemicals against Kurdish civilians. As early as 1983, the CIA knew about Iraq's possession and use of chemicals. The memorandum from Jonathan Howe (hereafter called the *Memorandum*), written by CIA officials, confirmed that Iraq "ha[d] built up large reserves of chemicals for further use". The *Memorandum* also confirmed the "available information on Iraqi use of [CW]". The *Memorandum* further explained that "in July and August 1983, the Iraqis reportedly used a chemical agent with lethal results against Iranian forces invading Iraq at Haj Umran and more recently against Kurdish insurgents."[33]

Third, the US' and international community's role in Iraq's ability to use CW against the Kurds was evident in the fact that the US misled the international community regarding Iraq's use of CW. The US attempted to diffuse Iraqi responsibility by claiming that, not only Iraq but also Iran was to blame for the CW attack against the Kurds.[34] The UN also failed to protect the Kurds from Iraqi CW aggressions. Though the UN condemned the use of CW in the war, the condemnation did not spell out the perpetrator.[35] The UN also followed the US in camouflaging the issue of the Iraq-Iran war and refusing to single out Iraq as the perpetrator. Thus, Baghdad had implicit permission to continue the use of the CW attacks on Kurdistan due to the toleration and advocacy on the part of the US and international community. International tolerance was perceived by the Iraqis as a historical opportunity to bring to a head its longstanding effort to end the Kurdish insurgency through the deployment of CW and mass killings. Chapter 9 further highlights the role of international support in Iraq's recapture of the liberated territories. It was the role of CW that changed the balance of power against the Kurds. In sum, from 1980 to 1988, Iraq was too weak to end the survival mechanisms of the Kurdish insurgency. The war in Kurdistan, or the existence of the Kurdish insurgency, was not the major factor accounting for the inherent weakness of

Iraq. It was more a consequence of its war with Iran, rather than the comparative strength of the Kurds. The end of the Iran-Iraq war that was blessed by the international community, coupled with the use of CW, allowed Iraq to recapture the entire Free Kurdistan region. For reasons other than Kurdish factor, the weakness of Iraq disqualified it from meeting the parent state criteria (UQC-III).

The fourth criterion to apply to the PCA to determine its quasi-state criteria is external patronage (UQC-III). The most important, and probably the only, patronage to the Kurds in the period in question was Iran's. The KDP, one of the largest Kurdish parties, had established strong relations with the new rulers of Iran since the Iranian revolution of 1979. The party established its headquarters in Iranian Kurdistan. In 1982, the KDP assisted Iran in its fight against the Iranian Kurds. However, until 1983 the KDP was reluctant to help Iran open the northern front in its war against Iraq. As explained in next section, the Turks intervened militarily into Iraqi Kurdistan. The territory that had been attacked by the Turks was controlled by the KDP. To counterbalance Turkish support for Iraq, the KDP joined Iran for the first time in 1983 and opened another front in Kurdistan. The KDP supported Iran's offensive inside Kurdistan. The KDP's decision was motivated as a reaction against Turkish intervention.

Not all the Kurdish parties followed the KDP. The PUK, for example, refused to cooperate with Iran, but it also vowed to fight any Iranian incursion. The PUK even supported the Iranian Kurds in their fight against Iran. The collapse of its negotiations and the resumption of fighting with Iraq in early 1985 encouraged the PUK to seek Iranian support. By the end of 1986, the PUK and the Iranian top officials signed an agreement of cooperation against Iraq.[36] PUK-Iranian relations were more formal and seemed more like government-state relations than a proxy party of a rival country with a regional state. In October 1986, the PUK and Iran concluded an accord of economic, political, and military cooperation against Baghdad. The most significant aspect of this accord was that Iran promised to break the embargo imposed by Iraq on Free Kurdistan.[37] Following the agreement, Iran opened its hospitals for Kurdish casualties and allowed the PUK to establish headquarters on its territory. The agreement also emphasised the two sides fighting against Saddam until he was toppled. They also agreed that neither side was allowed to negotiate unilaterally with Baghdad. PUK-Iranian relations also incurred the exchange of diplomatic offices. In 1986, Iran opened its office in Free Kurdistan under PUK control and the PUK opened its office in Iran.[38] The importance of this move was that Iran was the only country to open a 'diplomatic' office in Free Kurdistan.

The Kurdish-Iranian cooperation resulted in additional pressure on Iraq and eased Iraqi pressure on Iran on the southern front. One immediate consequence of this agreement was that by 1986 the Kurds helped Iran open a new front in Kurdistan. Facing a new and stronger military challenge in Kurdistan, Iraq withdrew significant portions of its troops from the southern front. According to Emin, 20 Iraqi brigades were redeployed in Kurdistan. Another important consequence of the Iranian-Kurdish alliance was the reunification of Kurdish internal ranks.[39] With the mediation of Iran, the two main Kurdish groups, the KDP and the PUK, which were involved in a bloody internal war, reconciled in Iran. These forces agreed to joint action against Iraq and established bases in their respective territories. Furthermore, in 1987 Iranian mediation efforts helped the establishment of the Iraqi Kurdistan Front. Consequently, for the first time major Kurdish parties joined together to form a Kurdistan front for use as an umbrella for all Kurdish factions. Iran also helped the Kurds to reach the outside world, thus breaking their long-term isolation. Iran, for example, had a significant role in broadcasting the Halabja tragedy of chemical bombardment that resulted in 10,000 to 15,000 civilian casualties. In addition to treating the victims of chemical bombardment, Iran allowed foreign media to cross the border and cover the tragedy. Thus, support that Iran offered to the Kurds during this period corresponded, to an extent, to the UQC-IV.

Iran's patronage was another form of negative patronage. Its support was more tactical and motivated by Iran's own aims than designed to help the Kurds. The no-win policy mostly depended on its war with Iraq. Following the ceasefire with Iraq, Iran halted its support, but allowed the Kurdish parties to take refuge in Iran following the collapse of the Kurdish insurgency in 1988. Therefore, while Iranian patronage satisfied the fourth criterion of the unrecognised quasi-state (UQC-IV) to some extent, the PCA failed to satisfy other criteria, resulting in a failed case for the unrecognised quasi-state.

Despite exhibiting the characteristics of unrecognised quasi-states, the PCA may not be classified as an unrecognised quasi-state during the period under review. Neither the nation-building process nor the militarisation of Kurdish society was developed to the extent to satisfy the first two criteria of the UQC. Though Iraq's weakness facilitated the emergence of the PCA, the weakness was temporary and related more to the Iraq-Iran war than to the strength of the Kurdish Nationalist Movement. With the end of the Iraq-Iran war, and with the use of CW and genocidal campaigns, Iraq recaptured the entire Free Kurdistan area. Iran's limited patronage of the Kurds did not fully meet the criteria of external patronage. Hence, for eight years the Kurds ruled a significant part of Iraqi Kurdistan, but the PCA cannot be classified as an unrecognised quasi-state.

Kurdish insurgency and the devolution of the Iraqi state into a quasi-state

This section examines how the Kurdish insurgency reshaped Iraqi-Kurdish policy and contributed to the devolution of the status of Iraq from a state into a recognised quasi-state (RQ). To tackle the question of whether Iraq fulfilled the qualifications of a recognised quasi-state state (RQ), Iraq's status is scrutinised in light of the recognised quasi-state criteria (RQC). The four criteria of the RQ is only applied to Iraq vis-à-vis the PCA.

The first criterion for a recognised quasi-state is the state's violation of the rule of law and its threat to some of its citizens (RQC-I). As explained in previous sections, to eliminate the Kurdish insurgency, and later to contain it, Iraq implemented the NML policy. Facing more difficulties in halting the expansion of the PCA, which started to incorporate most parts of rural Kurdistan under peshmerga control, Iraq increased its violation of its own laws and international laws. By 1987, harsher measures were followed and the NML policy escalated into the 'Land of the Enemy' policy. Under the NML policy, the Iraqi military was authorised to shoot anyone found in the rural areas of Kurdistan. A more grievous violation of laws and an even greater threat to the Kurdish population was the use of CW and the *Anfal* genocidal campaign. It is estimated that during the *Anfal* campaign tens of thousands of Kurdish civilians were killed or disappeared. The use of CW against civilians was not only against Iraqi rules and laws, it was also against international laws and norms. Thus, one direct consequence of Iraq's treatment of the Kurdish insurgency was the multiple violations of the rule of law and the lethal threat to the majority of the Kurdish population. The extent of the violation of Iraqi and international laws as well as the threat posed to its own population was so grievous that Iraq unquestioningly satisfied the first criterion of RQC-I.

The second criterion for determining a recognised quasi-state is the state's loss of control over Kurdistan (RQC-II). As explained previously, during the period in question, Iraq lost its control over a significant part of the border areas of Kurdistan. By the mid-1980s, Iraqi authority in Kurdistan had dwindled dramatically and only the cities, towns, *Mujama'at*, and main highways remained under its control. Peshmerga activities reached beyond the Kurdish areas, as far as the mixed areas of Mosul and Kirkuk. Thus the extent of Iraqi loss of control in Kurdistan satisfied the second criterion of the unrecognised quasi-state (RQC-II).

The third and fourth criteria are the parent state's search for external support (RQC-III) and the presence of foreign troops on its land (RQC-IV). The Kurdish insurgency's influence on Iraq's status and sovereignty was highlighted in Baghdad's search for external military support. To halt the further deterioration of its rule in Kurdistan, Iraq appealed to the Turks for military involvement against the Kurds. To continue its war with Iran and with the Kurds, Iraq desperately needed to increase its oil export. Baghdad, however, failed to reach an agreement with its Arab neighbours to export oil through their territories. The pipeline through Turkey remained the only operational outlet for Iraqi oil. Therefore, Iraq signed an agreement with the Turks to expand the capacity of the existing pipeline by 25–40 per cent.[40]

Though the Iraqi-Turkish agreement seemed like an economic agreement between two sovereign states, it had several political implications for Iraq that undermined its sovereignty. First, the continuation of Iraq's war with Iran and against the Kurds mostly depended on its oil output. Turkey, however, remained the only route for Iraq to export its oil and this increased Baghdad's strategic dependence on Turkey. As will be explained, this dependency reshaped Iraqi-Kurdish relations in many ways. Second, the pipeline crossed Kurdistan, where Iraqi rule was either weakened or disappeared. The Iraqi-Turkish border region was mostly controlled by the KDP. Iraq was too weak to protect its pipelines and the border region by itself. Baghdad, therefore, appealed to Turkey for military support against the Kurds and to protect the pipeline. On 15 October 1984, the two states signed an agreement that allowed the military from either side to pursue the peshmerga 5 kilometres into the territory of the other.[41]

Apparently, Turkish-Iraqi cooperation entailed joint action against both the Turkish and Iraqi Kurds. However, it was an unbalanced agreement that pointed up the superiority and patronage of the Turks to Iraq. Taking into consideration Iraq's weakness and inability to operate inside its Kurdish territory, let alone inside Turkish territory, it was more an Iraqi call to Turkey to help Baghdad combat Iraqi Kurds than a mutual penetration into each other's territories. This allowed the Turks to make incursions into Kurdistan at will. Turkey's upper hand and ability to interfere into Iraq's internal affairs was also evidenced in several other instances. Iraq authorised Turkish operations against Kurdish dissidents inside Iraq long before the October agreement. In 1978, Turkey entered Iraqi air space and territory, as well as used its airpower and ground forces to kill around 300 peshmerga. In this operation, the ICP and KDP bases were destroyed.[42]

In 1981, three years before the formal agreement, the Turks committed another main offensive against the Kurds inside Iraq.[43] The Turkish army carried out another hot pursuit inside Iraq in May 1983 that continued until June 1983 and resulted in the killing and capturing of hundreds of the KDP and ICP peshmerga.[44] The reality of Turkish incursions exceeded the limits of the agreement. Turkey forces went far beyond the five kilometres that was ratified in the Turkish-Iraqi agreement. As explained by Wright:

> The Turkish military leaders seek to exploit Iraq's military weakness and the ongoing guerrilla war with the Kurds. They would like to occupy a much deeper strip of territory than the one Turkish and Iraqi officials have already agreed to treat as a zone of 'hot pursuit' for operations against the Kurds.[45]

In fact, under the pretext of protecting the pipeline, the Turks penetrated 20 kilometres into Kurdistan. Furthermore, on many occasions following the agreement, Turkish operations inside Iraq were extended to 30 kilometres.[46] The Turks were also authorised to use its air forces to strike Kurdish targets deep inside Kurdistan.[47] Whether Iraq unofficially permitted or failed to prevent the Turks' penetration of 20 to 30 kilometres, instead of 5, Turkey violated Iraq's sovereignty. The Turkish violation of Iraqi sovereignty was not limited to military intervention. Turkey also interfered in Iraqi internal affairs, especially with those polices relating to the Kurdish issue. This was evident in the role that Turkey played in the failure of Iraqi-PUK negotiations in 1984. On the day that the PUK delegation was in Baghdad to sign the final agreement, Saddam refused to sign under the Turkish pressure at the last moment. The Turks threatened Iraq that any agreement with the Kurds would lead to closer ties to Iraqi oil and transportation of commodities routed to the West.[48] Accordingly, the Turkish role was more of a patron to the client, Iraq, rather than a mutual relationship between two sovereign countries. Thus, the Iraqi appeal to Turkish support to challenge the Kurds satisfies the third criterion of recognised quasi-states (RQC-III). The third criterion related to a state that seeks external support to face an internal threat.

Another related development in the period of question is the presence of Iranian troops in Free Kurdistan outside the control of Iraq and outside its permission. Tens, if not hundreds, of Iranian commandos existed in Free Kurdistan, albeit in cooperation with the peshmerga. From 1987 until the collapse of the Kurdish insurgency in the summer of 1988, Iranian helicopters were practically in daily contact with PUK headquarters. Moreover, while involved in the war against Iraq, Iran opened its diplomatic office in Free Kurdistan with full agreement of the PUK.[49] The presence of the Turkish and Iranian troops on Iraqi soil without Baghdad's permission satisfies the fourth criterion of recognised quasi-states (RQC-IV), relating to the presence of foreign troops on state land without permission.

In sum, therefore, Iraq satisfied the conditions of UQC-I during this period. Second, Iraq not only lost control over the rural parts of Kurdistan, but it also failed to impose its sovereignty in areas that remained under its control. The conscription system collapsed and Iraq introduced the *Jash* system in Kurdistan. The loss of control over a part of a state's own territory fulfils the conditions of UQC-II. Iraq appealed for external support from Turkey to confront the Kurdish threat. The extent of Turkey's involvement in the Kurdish-Iraqi conflict satisfied the conditions of UQC-III. The fourth criterion (RQC-IV), related to the presence of foreign troops against a state's wishes, applied to Iraq during this period. Both Turkish and Iranian troops, as two foreign armed forces, existed on Iraqi soil at various time periods without Iraq's official permission. In other words, during this period Iraq satisfied all criteria of a recognised quasi-state and therefore may be classified as a recognised quasi-state. Its quasi-state status reshaped Iraqi behaviour towards the Kurds significantly. In fact, failing to integrate the Kurds into the Iraqi state after 1975 despite its military superiority, losing control over significant parts of Kurdistan, and failing to govern Kurdistan all contribute to Iraq's recognition as a quasi-state. The extreme use of violence in its attempt to destroy Iraqi Kurdistan was the main feature of that period. The next chapter deals with the policies used by Iraq to rule Kurdistan from 1975 to 1991.

Notes

1 Rebaz (1993), *Qendil Beghday Hejand (Qandil Convulsed Baghdad)*, Erbil, Iraq: Zanko Publishing: 67–71.
2 Emin, N. M. (1997a), *Le Kenari Danubewe bo Khri Nawzeng: Diwi Nawewey Rwdawekani Kurdistani Eraq (From the Danaube Shore to the Nawzeng Valley: Political Events in Iraqi Kurdistan from 1975 to 1978)*, Berlin: Postfach: 188.
3 Whitley, A. (1980), "The Kurds: Pressures and Prospects," *The Round Table* 70(279): 245–257.
4 Rebaz 1993: 67; Emin 1997b: 284.
5 Al-Samarrayi, W. (1997), *Hittam al-Bawaba al-Sharqiya (Wreckage of the Eastern Gate), Kuwait City*, Kuwait: Dar al-Qabas lil-Sahafa wal-Nashir: 42.
6 Rebaz 1993: 136–138; Emin 1997a: 188; Al-Samarrayi 1997: 50.
7 Emin 1997a: 145.
8 Komalla 1982a: 60.
9 Bruinessen 1986: 27; Emin 1997a: 188.

The rise and fall of Kurdish insurgency   129

10 Bengio, O. (1984–1985), "Iraq," *Middle East Contemporary Survey; (CD-ROM Version), vol. I–XVIII*, O Bengio (ed.), Tel Aviv, Israel, The Moshe Dayan Center for Middle Eastern and African Studies, Israel: Tel Aviv University: 460–483; 472–481.
11 Bulloch, J. and H. Morris (1992), *No Friends But the Mountains: The Tragic History of the Kurds*, Oxford: Oxford University Press: 152.
12 Bruinessen 1992: 39.
13 HRW, Human Rights Watch (1993), *Genocide in Iraq: The Anfal Campaign Against the Kurds*, available at < https://www.hrw.org/reports/1993/iraqanfal> (accessed 15-04-2017): 48.
14 *HRW* 1993: 7, 48.
15 Bengio 1984–1985: 473; Borovali 1987: 39; Emin 1999: 118.
16 Emin 1999: 11.
17 *Ibid.*: 125.
18 Dunn, M. C. (1995). "The Kurdish Question: Is There an Answer? A Historical Overview," *Middle East Policy* 4(1–2); McDowall 2004: 352.
19 Emin 1999: 123.
20 E.g. see KDP-PC 1979; Komalla 1981, 1982a, 1982b, 1983, 1987; *Rebazi Nwe* 1982; *Peshang KPDP* 1982; *Khabat* 1988.
21 Emin (1999: 11).
22 PUK 1985: 5.
23 *Ibid.*: 75.
24 *Ibid.*: 81–82.
25 U.S. Senate (1988), "Chemical Weapons Use in Kurdistan Iraq's Final Offensive," *Committee on Foreign Relations*, Washington, DC: 10.
26 PUK 1985: 5, 82; Bruinessen 1992: 42–43; *HRW* 1993: 23.
27 McDowall 2004: 348.
28 Bengio, O. (1987), Iraq," *Middle East Contemporary Survey; (CD-ROM Version), vol. I–XVIII*, O. Bengio (ed.), The Moshe Dayan Center for Middle Eastern and African Studies, Israel: Tel Aviv University, 2000: 441.
29 Bengio, O. (1982–1983), "Iraq," *Middle East Contemporary Survey; (CD-ROM Version), vol. I–XVIII*, O. Bengio (ed.), The Moshe Dayan Center for Middle Eastern and African Studies, Israel: Tel Aviv University, 2000: 560–591: 575.
30 Pelletiere, S. C. and D. Johnson (1991), *Lessons Learned: The Iran-Iraq War*, Washington, DC: DTIC Document: 65; Karsh 2002: 20.
31 Smith, R. J. (1992) "Dozens of U.S. Items Used in Iraq Arms," *The Washington Post*.
32 Zilinskas, R. A. (1997). "Iraq's Biological Weapons," *JAMA: the journal of the American Medical Association* 278(5): 419; Borer 2003: 51; 2006: 256.
33 Memorandum from Jonathan Howe to Secretary of State Eagleburger (1983), "Iraqi Use of Chemical Weapons," Document no. 25, available at <www2.gwu.edu/-nsarchiv/NSAEBB/NSAEBB82/iraq25.pdf>, (accessed 18/01/2011).
34 Hiltermann, J. R. (2004), "Outsiders as Enablers: Consequences and Lessons from International Silence on Iraq's Use of Chemical Weapons during the Iran-Iraq War," *Iran, Iraq, and the Legacies of War*, Potter, L. G. and G. G. Sick (eds.), London: Palgrave Macmillan: 124–126, 157, 172, 181, 200.
35 Hiltermann 2004: 157.
36 Emin 1999: 105.
37 *HRW* 1993: 49; Emin 1999: 113.
38 Emin 1999: 105.
39 *Ibid.*: 141.
40 Bengio1982–1983: 577.
41 Bengio1984–1985: 471.
42 McDowall 2004: 347.
43 Randal 1997: 88.
44 Bengio 1982–1983: 576.

45 Wright 1985: 850.
46 Bengio 1984–1985: 471.
47 Polk 2005: 134.
48 *The Economist* 27/04/1991; Emin 1999: 81; Mina 2012: 102.
49 Emin 1999: 105–114.

8 Iraq's failure to govern Kurdistan (1975–1991)

After the collapse of the UKQ-I in 1975, Iraq implemented a limited and symbolic form of autonomy to three Kurdish provinces. Behind the façade of the autonomy, however, Iraq governed Kurdistan with four different modus operandi and adopted a different policy for each. The Iraqi policy that applied to each zone was determined by three factors: first, the degree of a given zone's affiliation with the UKQ-I and the post 1975 Kurdish insurgency; second, the vulnerability of each zone to control by any future attempt of Kurdish self-rule; and third, the degree to which the region was accessible and manageable by the central government.

The Autonomous Region of Kurdistan

In March 1974, one year prior to the collapse of UKQ-I, the Revolutionary Command Council of Iraq (RCCI) ratified the new Law of Autonomy.[1] This law was a clear retreat from the Autonomy Accord agreement signed on 11 March 1970 between Iraq and leaders of Free Kurdistan. Objecting to the authority and border of ARK, Kurdish leaders rejected the law. A full-scale war broke out in 1974 resulting in the collapse of UKQ-I in March 1975 following the Algeria Agreement between Iran and Iraq. For Iraq the collapse of UKQ-I meant the settlement of the Kurdish question unilaterally and on its own terms. Iraq unilaterally implemented the Law of Autonomy in 1975 and founded an autonomous administration in Kurdistan. A legislative council (parliament) and an executive council (government) were established as governing organs for the autonomous Kurdistan region. Erbil became the capitol and administrative centre for the Autonomous Region.[2] As a gesture to the political and cultural importance of Erbil, the city was named as the summer or second capitol of Iraq. Members of the legislative executive assemblies were comprised of people from the region, many of whom were not members of the Ba'ath Party.[3] Top positions, such as the Executive and Legislative Council chairman, were allocated equally between the Ba'athist Kurds and members of Kurdish parties founded by Baghdad. By 1980, additional members of the Legislative Council were elected by the population of the Autonomous Region. The first election was held in September 1980 and was followed by another in August 1983.[4] The Legislative Council had the power to ratify the laws of the Autonomous Region, the revival of local traditions, and the ratification of detailed projects.[5]

Furthermore, the Autonomous Region was favoured with financial and economic development projects intended to rebuild the war-devastated Kurdistan.[6] Even during the Iraq-Iran war, Baghdad continued building the infrastructure including schools, hospitals, roads, and drinking water and electric facilities.[7] The revival of the Kurdish language and local traditions were other responsibilities that were granted to the Legislative Council. Article 2 of the Law of Autonomy ratified that "the Kurdish language shall be, beside the Arabic language, the official language" and "the language of education in the region".[8] Instead of being a compulsory language of instruction from the first grade, Arabic became compulsory only from the fourth grade. In 1982 textbooks were translated into Kurdish and millions of copies were distributed throughout the Kurdish schools. The Kurdish cultural and publishing house was reactivated.[9] Though subject to harsh censorship, the Kurdish language and press flourished in an unprecedented manner.[10] Thus, for the first time in their history, the Kurds of Iraq were entitled to and enjoyed a *de jure* autonomy' sponsored by the central government. These legal, political, cultural, and socio-economic rights granted the Kurds were unprecedented compared to what former Iraq regimes and surrounding countries offered them.

This newfound autonomy, however, suffered from many fundamental weaknesses. The first weakness of the ARK was that the leaders of UKQ-I in 1974 questioned its legitimacy. It lacked mutual consensus between the Kurds and Iraq. Moreover, the law was unilaterally imposed by Baghdad at a time when the Kurds suffered a historical defeat. In the absence of UKQ-I, the Kurds were in their weakest position since the creation of the Iraqi state. They had little, if any, say in the nature of such autonomy. Therefore, the unilaterally imposed autonomy lacked the legitimacy of recognition by the majority of the Kurdish population and was rejected by most Kurdish political parties. The second weakness of the ARK was that the real power over the internal affairs of the ARK was held in Baghdad. The Legislative and Executive Councils of the Autonomous Region were powerless institutions that remained under strict supervision and control. The Law of Autonomy granted Baghdad the real power over the internal affairs of the Autonomous Region. Article 14 of the Law of Autonomy confined the authority of the local administration to education, work and housing, agriculture, the interior, transportation, culture, and religious affairs. Internal affairs were limited merely to police, civil defence, and civil servants. Even this department was "attached to" and its senior personnel were "appointed and transferred by" the "directorates general in the Ministry of Interior".[11] Baghdad retained the right to appoint the head of the Executive Council and to dissolve the Legislative Council.[12] The legality of the resolutions of the Autonomy's bodies subjected the agreement to the central government, and if Baghdad decided a resolution was illegal, it "shall be deemed as null and void".[13]

Until 1978 the members of the Legislative Council were appointed by the RCCI.[14] They were required to swear to the principles of the Ba'ath.[15] Even the

Ba'athist-style election process held in 1980 and 1983 did not change RCC control over the membership in the LC, and only those Kurds proven and supported by the Ba'ath Party were elected as members of the Assembly.[16] The responsibility for coordinating the affairs of the Autonomous Region was assigned to a minister of state appointed by and accountable to the president of Iraq. The minister was also "entitled to attend all the meetings of these bodies".[17] Thus, in addition of being under military siege, ultimate political decisions of the Autonomous Region were made by Baghdad and the 'autonomy' was stripped of any real power to self-rule. The Kurds retained the language of education in the region; some cultural institutions were established and Kurdish cultural practices were permitted. The best description of the Ba'athist style of autonomy was a cultural form of autonomy, rather than actual self-rule.

The third weakness of the ARK was that the Iraqi armed forces enjoyed unquestioned rule in Kurdistan. Article 16 of the Law of Autonomy stipulated that "save Jurisdictions exercised by the Autonomy bodies [. . .] exercising of power [. . .] shall be maintained by the Central bodies".[18] Accordingly, the military and intelligence affairs departments of Kurdistan, and therefore border control and Iraqi relations with the Kurdish movement, were maintained by Baghdad. Post-war Kurdistan, however, was a militarised society. Until 1980 more than 120,000 Iraqi armed forces were stationed in the Kurdistan region. Baghdad exploited its exclusive right to manage security affairs in the ARK and used it to destroy and depopulate the rural region along the Iranian and Turkish borders.

The fourth weakness of the ARK was the unreliable and precarious nature of Baghdad policies as applied to Kurdistan. The extent of implementation of the Law of Autonomy depended on the Ba'ath status in the region. Recognition of Kurdish identity was an example that reflected the weakness and strength of the Kurdish Nationalist Movement. Following the defeat of the Kurds in 1975, the identity of the Autonomous Region of Kurdistan was blurred by the official description of the Autonomous Region without even an oblique reference to the Kurds.[19] Education was another inconsistent institution under Iraq's Kurdish policy. Bengio notes:

> Schools in the areas of Kirkuk, Khanaqin, Mosul and Duhok stopped teaching in Kurdish; the Kurdish section in the College of Arts (in Baghdad) was closed in 1981 and the Kurdish Union of Men of Letters was reportedly harassed. The University of Sulaimani was [closed].[20]

In November 1977, the RCCI decreed that, apart from the study of the Arabic language, 40 per cent of all other subjects should be taught in Arabic.[21]

The fifth weakness of the ARK, as explained in the next section, was that the Ba'athist style of autonomy excluded significant parts of Iraqi Kurdistan. In reality, this limited autonomy comprised only a small part of Iraqi Kurdistan. Kirkuk and other disputed Kurdish areas that comprised over 40 per cent of the traditional Iraqi Kurdistan region were excluded.[22] The majority of rural Kurdistan that was officially part of the ARK was depopulated and displaced, and thus eliminated from the map. Therefore, rural Kurdistan was practically excluded from the ARK.

The Autonomous Region suffered many fundamental weaknesses that did not satisfy the majority of the Kurdish population. Consequently, as explained in the previous chapter, the Kurds rebelled against Iraqi rule in Kurdistan. By 1980, the Kurds founded their *de facto* self-rule in a wider area of Iraqi Kurdistan. To contain the rebellion, Iraq followed the policy that can be described as the annihilation of Iraqi Kurdistan.

Iraqi policy: from Kurdish integration to the annihilation of Iraqi Kurdistan

Behind the façade of the Ba'athist style of autonomy, four different laws and policies were implemented in four different areas of Kurdistan. The first zone consisted of the main cities and districts of Erbil, Sulaimaniya, and Duhok, which had limited and symbolic autonomy granted. The second zone, consisting of small towns and collective camps (*Mujama'at*), were granted *de facto* indirect rule. The third zone was excluded from the Autonomous Region altogether and de-Kurdified, as its inhabitants were relocated beyond this zone. The fourth zone was totally depopulated and its inhabitants were resettled in controlled collection camps in areas belonging to the Autonomous Region. Before studying each zone in detail, it is relevant to illustrate the link between the collapsed UKQ-I and the Iraqi policy vis-à-vis each zone. Three criteria are followed in such a categorisation scheme: first, each zone's relation to the UKQ-I; second, each zone's vulnerability to the control of any future Kurdish *de facto* self-rule; third, the extent of each zone's access to Iraqi armed forces and to what extent they were governable by Baghdad.

The first zone: controllable cities and towns and the nominal autonomy policy

The first zone was the proper Autonomous Region that was comprised of the three provincial centres of Erbil, Sulaimaniya, and Duhok as well as the controllable districts and sub-districts belonging to these provinces. The provision of nominal autonomy was calculated based on the distinguishing features of this zone. First, this zone traditionally remained outside the control of the UKQ-I and the Kurdish insurgency. Second, for many decades the Iraqi armed forces maintained control of this zone and therefore it was less likely to fall into the hands of the peshmerga. Finally, this zone was on a plain and connected to the others by highways. Therefore, for the most part it was managed by a combination of apparent autonomy (a degree of cultural and educational rights) and heavy military presence. The size of the area of what was supposed to be an autonomous region, however, decreased significantly by the 1980s, as many districts and sub-districts were depopulated. This limited autonomy was put forth by Iraq as a façade to hide the actual policies of forcing resettlement in collection camps, de-Kurdifying and depopulating the rest of Iraqi Kurdistan.

The second zone: less controllable towns and cities and the policy of indirect rule

The second zone was located just outside the main city centres of the ARK, on the main highways. It was composed of more isolated smaller towns and newly created *Mujama'at*. From 1976 until 1989, about 4,000 villages or 90 per cent of the Kurdish countryside were destroyed.[23] The population was displaced and forcibly resettled in 110 *Mujama'ats*.[24] Though the majority of inhabitants were displaced villagers, these *Mujama'ats* were quasi-urban settlements located on the main highways in army-controlled areas.[25] Due to the absence of censuses, the population of *Mujama'ats* remained unknown. However, by 1977 some 51 per cent of Kurdish society was considered to be rural.[26] The majority of villagers (90 per cent) and many inhabitants of the towns on the border were resettled in *Mujama'ats*. Hence, one could estimate that over one-third of the Kurdish population was forced to live in these camps.

Iraq adopted separate policies by which to administer this region based on the three criteria mentioned previously. First, many of these towns were previously located within the rule of the UKQ-I and the majority of the population of *Mujama'at* came from rural areas ruled by the UKQ-I. Therefore, compared to the population of the first zone, inhabitants of this region were influenced more by UKQ-I and had less experience with the direct and centralised rule of Baghdad. Second, being geographically an extension of rural Kurdistan, and having a long history of self-rule, this zone was more vulnerable than the first zone to the control of the peshmerga founded in rural Kurdistan. In fact, many towns and *Mujama'ats* of this zone were temporarily controlled by peshmerga in the second half of the 1980s.[27] This zone could have potentially been integrated into the liberated territory. Third, the zone's accessibility and controllability by the government of Iraq gave Iraq a difficult time. Being located between rural areas and main towns, the region was accessible by Iraqi troops or the peshmerga. Therefore, Iraq applied a different set of policies in this region.

The *Mujama'ats* were originally designed to put villagers under the army's complete control and they were to be governed by Baghdad. To guarantee the settlements' total dependence on state handouts and thereby create dependency and loyalty to the state, *Mujama'at* populations were completely cut off from their villages and farms.[28] As HRW explains:

> They were to be deprived of political rights and employment opportunities until *Amn* certified their loyalty to the regime. They were to sign written pledges that they would remain in the *mujama'at* to which they had been assigned – on pain of death.[29]

Thus, in the absence of alternatives for employment and by being controlled by the Iraqi armed forces, the *Mujama'ats* were subject to strict and highly centralised rule. Iraq's policy was to invest in the dependency of the inhabitants of *Mujama'at* at the state level and thereby create loyalty to it.

From 1980 onward with the emergence of the PCA, Iraq's policy for governing this zone was changed from strict direct rule to a *de facto* indirect rule by creating loyalty through middlemen. To govern this region and prevent it from falling into the hands of the peshmerga, Iraq ruled indirectly by depending on local patronage tribal forces.[30] The middlemen were strengthened through tribally based claims to authority through the monopolisation of the distribution of government food supplies to the settlements.[31] Aiming to create new opportunities for clienteles, Iraq reinforced the power of *aghas*. In the absence of alternative employment opportunities, this policy reinforced ordinary settlements' dependency on their chiefs that provided employment and served as mediator with the government.

Another method to prevent the fall of these areas under the control of peshmerga was to reintroduce the *Jash* system, officially known as National Defence Battalions (NDP). This system was based on a policy of indirect rule and quasi-tribal organisation methods. The *aghas* and their tribes were recruited into irregular cavalry regiments and received generous rewards from the state.[32] Each Kurdish tribe was organised into one battalion or more, and in principle, each battalion constituted some 1,000 irregular troops. Thus, by the second half of the 1980s, Iraq had incorporated between 150,000 to 250,000 *Jash* into 250 battalions.[33] The tribal chieftains were appointed as commanders of their respective units and granted the title of *mustashar* (consultant). The *Jash* were "dealt with collectively; all arms, money and commands were communicated through [*mustashar*]".[34]

This *Jash* system was similar to that of the Traditional Autonomous Entities (TAE) that the *aghas* and tribes enjoyed during the monarchy. Similar to the monarchy era, by maintaining arms the security of their tribes, and local affairs, the *mustashars* were allowed a measure of autonomy. However, once created, supported, and organised by the state, the *Jash* system was less indigenous than the TAE. In fact, it was Baghdad that mainly contributed to their strength.[35] In other words, TAE patronage was a bottom-up system while the *Jash* patronage was imposed from above. The *Jash* tended to resemble more of a militia force directed by the state than a pure tribal organisation. Its duty was better described by HRW as:

> The duties of the rank-and-file *Jash* were broadly akin to those of similar militias in other parts of the world. Poorly equipped with light weapons, they maintained road blocks, patrolled the countryside, did advance scouting work for the regular army, searched villages for army deserters and draft dodgers, and handed over suspected peshmerga to the authorities.[36]

For several reasons, however, the *Jash* system was another failed Iraqi policy that added little to the Kurds' loyalty to the state. First, a signed *Jash* ID protected young Kurds from military service. Therefore, the motivation of many Kurds who accepted recruitment into the *Jash* was to avoid army duty. Not all who registered as *Jash* really participated in active duty. In practice, only a fraction of 150,000 to 250,000 nominal *Jash* genuinely bore arms.[37] Second, by introducing the *Jash* system, Iraq in practice ratified a separate system for Kurdistan, which meant the existence of two parallel military systems in Iraq.

Third, the *Jash* was not always an option and tribal leaders often faced threats from the Ba'ath regime when they refused to cooperate in forming *Jash* units.[38] In fact, their loyalty was often dubious, as many joined the *Jash* in agreement with the peshmerga. McDowall explains that:

> Many of these *Jash* signed up only half-heartedly because neither the KDP nor the PUK had the administrative capacity to absorb such large numbers of new recruits. As a result, while indirectly on the Iraqi state payroll, many of them gave information to the Kurdish resistance.[39]

Moreover, the undecided loyalty of the *mustashars* was well known and well documented by Iraqi intelligence services.[40] Fourth, by allowing *Jash* to serve in Kurdistan, Baghdad allowed them to be part of their homeland and participate in collective activities with their countrymen. Thus, though this zone was officially located within the ARK, Iraq installed a separate system which was founded on the tribally based indirect rule. Iraqi policy to govern this zone was affected by the zone's relation to the UKQ-I and its vulnerability to control of peshmerga founded in the 1980s. To prevent this zone from integrating into the PCA, Baghdad ceded a degree of sovereignty to the inhabitants of this zone.

The third zone: the disputed areas and the de-Kurdification policy

The areas that were considered to be 'disputed' formed a broad arc that ran from Syria to the Iranian border. This zone included parts of Mosul province (i.e. Sinjar, Tal Afar, Makhmour, Shekhan), Kirkuk province and Tuz, and parts of Dyala province (Khanaqin and Mandali).[41] The size of this zone was estimated to be around 35,000 to 40,000 square kilometres of about 75,000 to 80,000 square kilometres of traditional homeland claimed by the Iraqi Kurds.[42] Iraq's Kurdish policy in this zone was unique and shaped by the zone's relation to the UKQ-I. First, this zone was oil rich and geopolitically strategically located in the plain area that was excluded from the Law of Autonomy. With the exception of the rural areas of Kirkuk, this zone traditionally remained outside the UKQ-I. In other words, Iraq traditionally maintained its rule in most parts of this region. Based on the criterion of this zone's relation to the UKQ-I during 1961 to 1975 and the PCA (1980–1988), this zone was distinctly different from the first and second zones and treated as such. Second, except for the rural area of the Kirkuk environs that traditionally was controlled by the peshmerga, the location on the plain with the Arab community and exposure to the Arabisation policy made the region less vulnerable to peshmerga control. Third, the zone's response to the third criterion was another distinguishing feature of this region. For Iraq this zone was one of the most accessible and manageable regions, administratively speaking.

The ownership and identity of these areas, whether Kurdistani or Iraqi, were the central issues of concern in Kurdish and Iraqi politics. Determining the identity of the disputed areas was one of the main topics of failed negotiations between the Kurds and Iraqis since 1961. Successive Iraqi regimes rejected the claim of

Kurdistani identity of these areas. Consequently, its destiny was postponed in the March Manifesto of 1970 between leaders of the UKQ-I and Baghdad. The March Manifesto specified that the destiny of these areas would be determined on the basis of a census to be held in the areas of dispute. A city or town with a clear Kurdish majority would be part of the Autonomous Region; otherwise it would be governed by Baghdad. Masud Barzani, member of the political bureau of the KDP, explained in 1974 that the Kurds refused to accept the Autonomous Law that determined the borders of the Autonomous Region mainly because the law excluded these areas.[43] Consequently, intense fighting ensued between the government and the Kurds, resulting in the collapse of the first Kurdish quasi-state. It was also a main reason for the fall of Kurdish-Iraqi negotiations between Baghdad and the Kurds in 1985 and 1991. Throughout the last century, the fate of these areas was a flashpoint of contention and the main reason for all Kurdish-Iraqi confrontations since 1961. Thus, the Iraqi policy vis-à-vis this zone was strongly reshaped by the UKQ-I and Kurds' claim to it.

To prevent this region's falling into the hands of the Kurds in any future arrangement, Iraq followed different forms of the de-Kurdification policy. The first form was the change of the region's demography through the construction of Arab settlements. This form of Arabisation began with the discovery of oil in the region in 1927. During the monarchy, 28,000 Arabs had been settled in the Hawija district of Kirkuk and 700 settlements were built for 80,000 settlers in the Kurdish districts of Mosul.[44] During the period in question, the Arabisation process was intensified. For instance, in the province of Kirkuk alone 20,000 houses were built for Arab settlers.[45] If an average Arab family consisted of approximately five members, the total Arab settlers between 1976 and 1991 in Kirkuk province could be estimated at around 100,000. During the same period, a similar number of Arabs were probably settled in other districts of this zone.

The second form of de-Kurdification was the expulsion of the Kurds from this area. Following the collapse of the UKQ-I in 1975, Baghdad expelled the Kurds from this zone. All districts and sub-districts were exposed to the policy of expulsion. Within six years, from 1984 to 1990, about 120,000 Kurds were deported from Kirkuk.[46] The third form of de-Kurdification was the policy of depopulation and destruction of Kurdish villages. By 1991, 779 Kurdish villages in Kirkuk province and 195 of 196 Kurdish villages in the Makhmour district of Erbil were destroyed or given to Arab settlers.[47] The inhabitants of this region were forcibly resettled in areas outside this zone, mostly in the three provinces of ARK. The total number of Kurdish families that were deported from cities and villages of this zone since the creation of the Iraqi state is estimated to be around 200,000.[48] Kurdish families have an average of five members. Therefore the total deported Kurds of this zone is as high as one million.

The fourth form of de-Kurdification was the forced assimilation through the 'nationality correction' policy. In 1977 the general census showed that non-Muslim Kurdish religious groups inhabited this area. The Yezidis, Kakays, and Christians were forcibly registered as Arabs. The change of ethnicity was imposed on many, but not all, Muslim Kurdish tribes. The Shabak, Gargar, Salayi, Gezh,

Palani, Sheikh-Bzeni, and Kikan were also forcibly registered as Arabs.[49] Thus within the de-Kurdification policy, tens of thousands of the Kurds were forcibly Arabised.

The fifth form of de-Kurdification was the remapping of the disputed areas through slicing and detaching sections of Kurdish-inhabited districts and administratively attaching them to other provinces. This policy was first implemented in 1969 in the Kurdish districts in Mosul province. The RCC decrees #211 and #1066 detached three out of six Kurdish districts from Mosul and attached them to the new Kurdish province of Duhok.[50] The RCC decrees #608 and #41 that were issued in 1976 redrew the boundaries of Kirkuk in irregular and dramatic ways. Apart from the central districts of Kirkuk and the Arab-settled district of Hawija, four out of six districts were detached from Kirkuk. The Chamchamal and Kelar districts were attached to Sulaimaniya, while Kifri and Duz were attached to the Arab provinces of Diyala and Salahaddin, respectively.[51] The Kurdish districts of Diyala were subjected to a similar policy. Mandaly was dissolved and reduced to a sub-district and attached to Baladruz.

The sixth form of de-Kurdification involved the stripping of Faili/Shia Kurds of their Iraqi citizenship and the right of Iraqi residency, as well as deporting them to Iran. During the period in question some 100,000 to 150,000 Faili-Kurds were stripped of their citizenship and exiled to Iran.[52] It is noteworthy to mention that in 1970 some 40,000 Faili-Kurds were stripped of their citizenship and exiled to Iran.[53] Faili-Kurds once comprised 10 per cent of the total Kurdish population in Iraq. Many of them resided in the southern part of the disputed areas, such as Khanaqin and Mandaly districts in Diyala province. Accordingly, the Faili-Kurds constituted 10–20 per cent of the total population of the disputed areas. They dominated Iraqi trade and controlled the largest part of the Baghdad market.[54] There were several immediate consequences of such a policy: first, the ethnic and economic weight of the Kurds in disputed areas was diluted; second, Kurdish influence and involvement in Iraqi trade radically declined; third, the RCCI decree #1566 issued on 9 October 1980 authorised the Iraqi state to confiscate all deportees' properties, small and large.[55] Their properties were given to the Arabs, mostly Sunni, as an incentive to settle in the disputed areas.[56] Thus, the expulsion of the Faili-Kurds resulted in a significant alteration of the ethnic demography of this zone.

The final and probably more belligerent and systematic form of de-Kurdification was the physical liquidation of the bulk of the Kurds in the rural areas of the Kirkuk environs. Within this campaign thousands of Kurdish families in this zone were eliminated. In 1988, Kurdistan was exposed to eight stages of a genocidal operation known as *Anfal*. In the *Anfal* operation, which lasted six months, between 50,000 and 200,000 Kurdish civilians were killed. Three out of eight stages of *Anfal* (namely *Anfal* II, III, and IV) targeted the rural areas of the Kirkuk environs. Part of the areas that were subjected to *Anfal* II, III, and IV officially belonged to the Sulaimaniya and Erbil provinces. For three reasons, however, they cannot be separated from the Garmiyan (Kirkuk environ) region of the disputed areas. First, a significant part of the area that was originally part of Kirkuk province, and subject to *Anfal* III and the de-Kurdification policy, was originally part of the Kirkuk region. But with the policy of remapping, the disputed areas were detached from Kirkuk province. The Kurds rejected the remapping policy and insisted that these areas be included and its population have the right to vote in any future referendum on the residency of Kirkuk province.[57] Second, these areas bordered the disputed areas and culturally, economically, and geopolitically were an extension of the Kirkuk environs. Third, the majority of disappearances from *Anfal* II were those who fled only to be captured in the villages located within the Kirkuk environs.[58]

By scrutinising the pattern of disappeared (killed) persons of all stages of *Anfal*, it is clear that Iraqi behaviour in *Anfal* II, III, and IV was affected by the de-Kurdification policy. Iraq dealt with civilians differently in this zone compared to the rest of the areas faced with *Anfal*. Apart from *Anfal* II, *Anfal* III, and *Anfal* IV, the lives of the people were spared to some extent.[59] Only in these three stages of *Anfal* were women and children treated like the men and exposed to mass killing.[60] In the other five stages of *Anfal* (I, V, VI, VII, and VIII), the total number of disappearances was estimated to be only in the thousands.[61] Therefore the overwhelming majority of the victims were from *Anfal* II, III, and IV. According to some calculations, 13 per cent of all *Anfal* victims were from *Anfal* II, 65 per cent from *Anfal* III, and 10 per cent from *Anfal* IV.[62] The total victims of *Anfal* in this zone may be estimated at up to 88 per cent of the population. If the total number of disappeared Kurds in all *Anfal* campaigns is estimated at 100,000, then 88,000 of them were from the Kirkuk environs. Thus the Iraqi genocidal operation in this region was designed to carry out the de-Kurdification policy of this zone. Within the de-Kurdification policy of the third zone (DA), hundreds of thousands of Arabs were settled in this region. A half million Kurds were affected by the de-Kurdification policy. Being stripped of citizenship and deported to Iran, being forcibly displaced and resettled in areas outside this zone, and being killed during *Anfal* operations were all part of the de-Kurdification process. The rest of the Kurds in this zone faced different forms of forced assimilation or discrimination.

The fourth zone: rural Kurdistan and the depopulation policy

This zone was a mountainous region located in the north, extending to the northeast of Iraqi Kurdistan on the border of Turkey and Iran. The zone covers most of the mountainous and rural areas of Kurdistan. As explained previously, Iraq used three criteria to formulate and implement its policies towards different zones of Kurdistan. The three criteria clarify that this zone was distinguished from the others. First, this zone traditionally remained outside of Iraqi control and represented a stronghold and strategic depth in the UKQ-I. Second, this zone was the most vulnerable to falling into the peshmerga's hands. Less than one year after the collapse of the UKQ-I in 1976, the peshmerga controlled some parts of this area. Third, this zone was mostly mountainous and therefore less accessible. It was less likely to be governable by Iraq, causing Iraq to follow the depopulation policy. The monarchy failed to rule the Kurdish countryside directly. This allowed the tribes a modicum of autonomy in their internal affairs. Between 1961 and 1975, this area became part of Free Kurdistan and remained outside of Iraqi control. Since the creation of Iraq, Baghdad failed to impose its authority on and administer this region directly. Following the collapse of the Kurdish quasi-state (UKQ-I) in 1975, the Iraqi army entered this region for the first time since 1961. Despite its triumph and the deployment of tens of thousands of security forces in the region, Baghdad failed to govern this region. Instead of reinstating its authority and establishing its institutions in the region, Iraq started the process of what HRW called "physically redrawing the map of Northern Iraq".[63] In this redrawing process, vast areas of the former Free Kurdistan was turned into an NML. The process started in 1976 with depopulating a 5–10-kilometre strip and expanding it to as much as 70 kilometres deep by the late 1980s. It ended with the destruction of almost the entire rural area of Kurdistan. The NML policy may be divided into two phases.

The first phase of the NML policy occurred between 1975 and 1979. The systematic depopulation of rural Iraqi Kurdistan was imposed at a time when the Kurds were defeated and Iraq enjoyed full control of Kurdistan. According to HRW, the process of NML in Kurdistan meant "removing rebellious Kurds from their ancestral lands and resettling them in new areas under strict military control of the Baghdad authorities".[64] On 21 August 1976, Vice President of Iraq Saddam Hussein revealed the Iraqi plan in a booklet: to turn a 20-kilometre deep strip of land running from Iran to the Syrian frontier into an NML.[65] Following the declaration of the plan in a booklet, Baghdad began to clear a strip of land 5 kilometres deep and 800 kilometres long along the borders of Iran and Turkey. This was to be expanded to 20 kilometres deep by 1979. In this process, some 1,200 to 1,400 villages disappeared from the map and 500,000 inhabitants of these areas were forcibly relocated.[66] Thus, by 1979 an area larger than 16,000 square kilometres, roughly the size of Lebanon and Palestine combined, was depopulated.[67] These depopulated areas turned into a 'strip of death' and anyone found entering this region was imprisoned and/or executed.[68] Considering that the size of the KRI was 40,643 square kilometres,[69] roughly equal to that of the three provinces of the Autonomous Region of Kurdistan (ARK), one can say that in this phase of NML policy, 40 per cent of the ARK was depopulated.

This phase of systematic destruction began with a military operation led by tanks and helicopters bent on besieging villages. The region was to be depopulated and then the operation turned towards abducting its inhabitants. After the attack, the entire population was arrested and, along with their cows and sheep, stuffed into army vehicles. They were to be resettled in the *Mujama'ats* or collection camps. In addition to the destruction of these villages, Iraq cut down fruit trees and filled water wells with concrete. Agricultural areas, livestock, and drinking water installations were all burned or destroyed.[70] Thus, the Iraqi policy took the form of a scorched-earth policy. By 1980, this phase of the NML was terminated for three reasons: first, the Iran-Iraq war that started in 1980 required a significant part of the Iraqi armed forces that was serving in Kurdistan.[71] Iraq did not have enough forces in Kurdistan to continue the NML policy. Second, by 1980 the peshmerga were strong enough to resist the Iraqi NML policy. Third, involved in negotiations with the PUK between 1983 and 1985, Baghdad followed a more conciliatory approach and suspended its scorched-earth policy.

The second phase of the NML policy started in 1985 and continued until the late 1980s. By the beginning of 1985, negotiations between the PUK and Baghdad broke down and another period of armed conflict and NML policy commenced. There were several main differences between this phase and the previous phase of the NML process. First, Iraq dealt with this zone as the land of the enemy rather than as Iraqi land. The fighting between the two sides was unprecedented in that Iraq did not exempt any Kurdish villages and it indiscriminately attacked civilians and the peshmerga in the 'liberated territory'.[72] The population of this zone not only faced forced resettlement by the Iraqi forces but also mass killing by means of a wide range of chemical weapons. Second, Iraq also used more sophisticated and prohibited weapons, including CW, in its war with Kurdistan. Third, the depopulation process also extended to many towns, villages, and *Mujama'ats* that were either controlled directly by government forces or indirectly by *Jash*.[73]

The unique trait of this phase is that at the end of it Iraq committed more systematic *Anfal* operations that lasted six months (February to August 1988). The *Anfal* operations took place in eight stages and their destruction impacted most parts of the rural Kurdistan area. Each *Anfal* stage started with widespread and indiscriminate use of chemical weapons against civilians and peshmerga in the targeted region. The next step was the systematic destruction of entire villages, including their infrastructures, farms, and rivers. Each stage terminated with detentions and the disappearance of masses of villagers.[74] The first chemical attack began in April 1987, several months before the commencement of the *Anfal* operation, and the final attack ended in early September 1988.[75] Within this period, 250 Kurdish villages, towns, and agricultural areas were attacked by CW.[76]

In eight stages of *Anfal*, tens of thousands of civilians were killed or vanished without trace. A fortunate 160,000 managed to escape to Turkey and Iran.[77] Other survivors of *Anfal*, estimated at around 500,000 elders, children, and women, were resettled in a dozen newly opened *Mujama'ats*.[78] Hence, in eight stages of *Anfal* operations, between 500,000 to one million villagers were killed, detained, displaced, or forced to flee to Iran and Turkey. Or they resettled in one of the *Mujama'ats*.[79] In these two phases of the NML, 90 per cent or 4,500 out of 5,000 Kurdish villages and 80 to 85 per cent of the infrastructure in Iraqi Kurdistan were destroyed.[80] Thus, a significant part of Kurdistan was no longer considered a part of the country of Iraq. Kurdistan was dealt with as the land of the enemy and its population was treated as an official enemy of state. For all intents and purposes, a significant part of the Kurds in Iraq were 'de-Iraqified'.

A study of Iraqi behaviour during this period reveals the nature of the de-Iraqification process of the inhabitants of this zone. Initially the region was declared to be a prohibited area and its population was marginalised.[81] Then, the region was excluded from a nationwide census taken on 17 October 1987. The entire subpopulation, that consequently failed to participate in the census, was eventually stripped of its Iraqi citizenship. The next step was the indiscriminate criminalisation of the subpopulation. Based on the applicable decree, all that failed to participate in the census not only were no longer regarded as part of the citizenry of the state, but they were also considered saboteurs who deserved the death penalty.[82] Therefore, a shoot-on-sight policy was implemented.[83] Another step was to re-label the peshmerga controlled areas as the land of the enemy and its inhabitants as active enemies of the state of Iraq. The most unconscionable and outrageous decision was that Free Kurdistan was to be *Anfal*ised, which meant to be physically liquidated along with its inhabitants. This was to be done by any means possible regardless of international laws, institutional rules, morals, regulations, repercussions, or public opinion. Thus, by considering Free Kurdistan as the land of the enemy, stripping its population of national citizenship, criminalising its inhabitants, and committing the genocidal *Anfal* operations against it, a significant part of Kurdish society was labelled as enemy of state. Its members excluded legitimate citizens of Iraq.

The depopulation policy after the collapse of the Kurdish insurgency

The second phase of the depopulation policy ended with the collapse of the Kurdish insurgency in the summer of 1988. During the last stage of *Anfal*, Iran and Iraq declared a ceasefire and the war between the two countries ended. The end of the war and the collapse of the Kurdish resistance did not end the depopulation policy, however. Iraq implemented a new phase of the NML policy. The main targets of this phase were the cities and towns of the second zone that had been under Iraqi control since 1975 and bordered the fourth zone. In December 1988, "[Iraq] announced its intention to create 22 new towns, each to accommodate 10,000–15,000 resettled Kurds".[84] In the summer of 1989 the town of Qaladiza, a town of 70,000, and its environs was systematically bulldozed and dynamited.[85] This resulted in 200,000 Kurds being resettled to the more accessible and controllable plains of southern Erbil and Sulaimaniya. The district of Ranya and its environs were listed to be depopulated and destroyed.[86] Thus, by 1991 more than two-thirds of Iraqi Kurdistan was depopulated.[87] Many Kurds saw this as a first step to wipe the entire Iraqi Kurdistan area off the map and displace the Kurds to southern (Arab) Iraq. The process only ceased with the Iraqi invasion of Kuwait in 1990. Whether pro-government *Jash* militiamen, ordinary civilians, peshmerga families, former residents of Free Kurdistan, residents of cities or *Mujama'at*, all of Kurdish society faced the same destiny. They found themselves as the spoils of war rather than as citizens of Iraq.[88] These measures only served to further alienate the Kurds from Iraq, increase the bases of their victimisation complex, and increase their desperate search for a way to escape from Iraq.

The Kurds respond to the de-Iraqification policy: the uprising of 1991

These ruthless measures became a powerful motivator for Kurdish expressions of collective grievances, shared unity, and integrated destiny. The whole scenario provoked a fundamental transformation within Kurdish society that showed itself in unprecedented Kurdish collective and group behaviour. All Kurdish factions that were in rebellion against Iraq united under the IKF. Though established earlier, the IKF acted as the overarching umbrella for all their grievances only during the *Anfal* operation. Another indicator of unity was the reconciliation process that evolved within Kurdish society. To achieve such reconciliation, the IKF issued general amnesty to all *Jash* prior to the uprising of 1991.[89] The third indication of the Kurds' collective behaviour was the defection of the hitherto pro-Baghdad *Jash*. During the uprising of 1991 the *Jash* had collectively defected, joined the peshmerga, and rebelled against the government. Only a few *Jash* leaders opted to remain loyal to Saddam.[90] The *Jash*'s decision to rebel and join the peshmerga resulted in the expansion of the Kurdish armed forces from 15,000 to well over 100,000 men in the space of a few days.[91] Thus the collective social behaviour of the Kurds who survived the *Anfal* onslaught resulted in a new era of Kurdish and Iraqi politics.

Several examples shed light on the significant transformation that took place with the balance of power between the Kurds and Baghdad after the de-Iraqification policy; and these weighed in favour of the former. First, in March 1991 Kurds from all cities in Iraqi Kurdistan rose up against Iraq. For the first time in modern Iraqi-Kurdish history, all cities including Sulaimaniya, Erbil, Dohuk, and Kirkuk were controlled by peshmerga forces. Second, for the first time in any Kurdish-Iraqi conflict, the *Jash* played a central role and the peshmerga a secondary role in the Kurdish struggle. In fact, the peshmerga merely threw their weight behind the uprising, which was dominated by ordinary *Jash*, and followed them onto the streets.[92] Without *Jash* support, it would have been impossible for the IKF to seize control of most of Iraqi Kurdistan. Hence, the uprising of 1991 was a direct consequence of the Kurds' collective experience with policies of depopulation, forced resettlement, *Anfal*, and de-Iraqification.

Another important indicator of the Kurds' collective behaviour, and therefore a consequence of the de-Iraqification policy, was the Kurdish mass exodus in April 1991. After the defeat of the uprising, over two million people took refuge in Turkey and Iran or on their borders.[93] Masud Barzani, the Kurdish leader, estimated the number of Kurdish refugees at around three million.[94] In 1992, the Kurdish population of the three Kurdish provinces was estimated to be at just over three million.[95] Accordingly, over two-thirds of the Kurdish population in Iraq participated in the mass exodus. According to the UN assessment, more than 20,000 Iraqi Kurds died during this exodus and in the border camps.[96] The Kurdish mass exodus was "one of the largest and fastest exoduses of refugees in history".[97] Thus, the collective defection of the *Jash*, the popular uprising, and the exodus together functioned as an unofficial referendum of the Kurds' rejection of their status as 'Iraqis'. Baghdad's adoption of ruthless polices, highlighted earlier in this chapter, along with Iraq's failure to responsibly govern Kurdistan, elicited these collective behaviours.

Notes

1. For the full text of the Law of Autonomy see: RI-MI, Republic of Iraq, Ministry of Information (1977), *Law of Autonomy*, Third edition, Baghdad, Iraq: Al-Hurriya Printing House.
2. RI-MI 1977, Article 1-e.
3. Bengio 1986: 382; Farouk-Sluglett and Sluglett 2001: 175.
4. Bengio1986: 410.
5. RI-MI 1977, Article 12: 18–19.
6. Senate 1988: 10; Bruinessen 1986: 19; Izady 2004: 80.
7. Bengio1981–1982: 599.
8. RI-MI 1977.
9. Bengio1982–1983: 574–575.
10. Dunn 1995: 73.
11. RI-MI 1977, Article 17-a, -c.
12. *Ibid.*, Articles 13, 20.
13. *Ibid.*, Articles 19-a, -b, -c, -e.
14. Bengio and Dann 1977–1978: 521.
15. Bengio1979–1980: 512.
16. Bengio1986: 382.
17. RI-MI 1977, Article 18-c.
18. RI-MI 1977.
19. Bengio and Dann 1976–1977: 410.
20. Bengio 1981–1982: 597.
21. Bengio and Dann 1977–1978: 521.
22. Barzani 2003a: 7; Mina 2012: 138.
23. Gunter 1994: 148; Romano 2004: 159.
24. *Coalition for Justice in Iraq* 2000; *IFDH* 2003: 7.
25. Mina 2012: 186.
26. Marr 1985: 285.
27. Dunn 1995; McDowall 2004: 352.
28. Leezenberg 2006: 9.
29. *HRW* 1993: 19.
30. Leezenberg 2006: 10.
31. Graham-Brown 1999: 217; Bruinessen 2002: 172; McDowall 2004: 357; Leezenberg 2006: 10.
32. Bruinessen 1992: 40; Leezenberg 2006: 9.
33. Al-Khafaji 1992: 19; Graham-Brown 1999: 217; McDowall 2004: 46.
34. Bruinessen 2002.
35. Leezenberg 2006: 10.
36. *HRW* 1993: 47.
37. *Ibid.*: 46.
38. *Ibid.*: 45.
39. McDowall 2004: 356.
40. Leezenberg 2006: 10.
41. *Draft Constitution of the Kurdistan Region 2009.*
42. O'Leary 2002: 17; Gull 2007: 41; Mina 2012: 219, 251.
43. Barzani 2002: 296–297.
44. Talabany, N. (2001), *Arabisation of the Kirkuk Region*, Uppsala, Sweden: Kurdistan Studies Press: 25; Makhmwri, G. (2010), *Bisaraha: Hiwarat Hawla al-Qadhiya al-Kurdiya (Frank Dialogues About Kurdish Issues)*, Erbil, Iraq: Minara Press: 30.
45. Talabany, N. (2004), "Iraq's Policy of Ethnic Cleansing: Onslaught to Change National/Demographic Characteristics of the Kirkuk Region," 58–62; Kirmanj, S. (2010), "The

Construction of the Iraqi State and the Question of National Identity," Ph.D thesis, University of South Australia: Makhmwri 2010: 60–61; Mina 2012: 246–250.
46 Makhmwri 2010: 49.
47 Talabany 2004: 72; Makhmwri 2010: 50.
48 Aziz 2011: 75.
49 Kirmanj 2010: 170; Mina 2012: 247–249.
50 *Al-Waqaii' al-Iraqiya* 03/06/1969.
51 *Al-Waqai' al-Iraqiya* 15/12/1975; 29/02/1976.
52 *HRW* 1993 XIV, 17; Mina 2012: 128–130; Gull 2007: 34.
53 Freedman, R. O. (2002), *The Middle East Enters the Twenty-First Century*, Gainesville, FL: University Press of Florida: 33; *HRW* 1991.
54 Al-Barak 1984: 151–152; Fawcett, J. and V. Tanner (2002), *The Internally Displaced People of Iraq, Brookings Institution-SAIS Project on Internal Displacement*, Washington, DC: Brookings Institution-SAIS Project on Internal Displacement: 15.
55 *Al-Waqai' al-Iraqiya* 16/07/1980.
56 Fawcett and Tanner 2002: 15.
57 After the invasion, the Kurds insisted on the re-adjustment of the Kirkuk border and the inclusion of the population of detached districts in a referendum over the destiny of Kirkuk. This claim was included in Article 58 of the Transitional Administrative Law (TAL) and restated in Article 140 of the Iraqi constitution.
58 Hiltermann, J. R. (2008),"The 1988 *Anfal* Campaign," *Online Encyclopedia of Mass Violence*, available at <www.massviolence.org/IMG/article_PDF/The-1988-Anfal-Campaign-in-Iraqi-Kurdistan.pdf>, (accessed 12/11/2012): 6–7; Kirmanj 2010: 178.
59 *HRW* 1993: 49; ICG 2004: 10; Kirmanj 2010: 174–178.
60 Hiltermann 2008: 6–7.
61 *Ibid.*: 7.
62 Kirmanj 2010: 177.
63 *HRW* 1993: 35.
64 *Ibid.*
65 Hussein, S. (1977), *Khandaq Wahid aw Khandaqan: (One Trench or Two Trenches)*, Baghdad, Iraq: Dar Altorh for Press and Publishing.
66 Farouk-Sluglett et al 1984: 24; Olson, R. (1992), "The Kurdish Question in the Aftermath of the Gulf War: Geopolitical and Geostrategic Changes in the Middle East," *Third World Quarterly* 13(3): 475–499: 476; *HRW* 1993: 37; Graham-Brown 1999: 214; Farouk-Sluglett and Sluglett 2001: 188.
67 Komalla *1983*: 25; Hussain 1986: 92.
68 O'Leary 2002: 26.
69 KRG, Kurdistan Regional Government (2010), "The Kurdistan Region in Brief," Available at, <www.krg.org/articles/detail.asp?lngnr=12&smap=03010300&rnr=140&anr=23911>, (accessed 10/12/2011).
70 Emin 1997a: 261–263.
71 *HRW* 1993: 39.
72 Emin 1999: 88.
73 *HRW* 1993: 15, 48; Rubin, M. (2003), "Are Kurds a Pariah Minority?" *Social Research: An International Quarterly* 70(1): 295–330: 302; Gull 2007: 57.
74 *HRW* 1993: 12; Cordesman 2000: 222; Hiltermann 2004: 153; 2008: 7.
75 *HRW* 1993: 51.
76 Rubin 2003: 13–15.
77 Cowell, A. (1988), "A Defeat for the Kurds: Iraqi Drive Tied to Gulf Truce Compounds Guerrillas' Disunity and Setbacks in Turkey," *New York Times Book Review*; McDowall, D. and M. Short (1996), *The Kurds*, Minority Rights Group: 27; Farouk-Sluglett and Sluglett 2001: 269.
78 Global IDP Database 2003.

79 Stages II, III, and IV of the *Anfal* operation were levelled against the rural areas of Kurdistan that were considered to be part of the Kirkuk environs. The majority of the killings and disappearances of these three stages of *Anfal* (third zone) were consistent with the central government's de-Kurdification policy. The overwhelming majority of resettled and displaced populations, however, were residents of the fourth zone. The areas subject to *Anfal* and the fourth zone shared two significant characteristics: they were considered to be uncontrollable areas of rural Kurdistan and both areas were part of the 'liberated territories' that were mostly ruled by Free Kurdistan. The population was influenced by and supported the peshmerga.
80 Gunter 1994: 148; Berwari 2003; Romano 2004: 159.
81 *HRW* 1993: 10; Totten, S. and W. S. Parsons (2009), *Century of Genocide: Critical Essays and Eyewitness Accounts*, London: Taylor & Francis: 386.
82 *HRW* 1993: 10; Totten and Parsons 2009: 386.
83 Totten and Parsons 2009: 386.
84 McDowall 2004: 360.
85 *HRW* 1993: 333; McDowall 2004: 360.
86 McDowall 2004: 360.
87 Gull 2007: 57.
88 Emin 1999: 153.
89 McDowall 2004: 372; Aziz 2011: 82.
90 Baram, A. (1997), "Neo-Tribalism in Iraq: Saddam Hussein's Tribal Policies 1991–96," *International Journal of Middle East Studies* 29(1): 7; McDowall 2004: 371.
91 McDowall 2004: 372.
92 Litvak, M. (1991–1992), "Iraq," *Middle East Contemporary Survey*; *(CD-ROM Version), vol. I–XVIII*, O. Bengio (ed.), The Moshe Dayan Center for Middle Eastern and African Studies, Israel: Tel Aviv University, 2000: 425; McDowall 2004: 372.
93 Malanczuk, Peter (1991), "The Kurdish Crisis and Allied Intervention in the Aftermath of the Second Gulf War," *European Journal of International Law* 2: 118; Graham-Brown1999: 23.
94 Malanczuk 1991: 118.
95 "A De Facto Kurdish State in Northern Iraq," *Third World Quarterly* 14(2): 315.
96 Ofteringer, R. and R. Bäcker (1994), "A Republic of Statelessness: Three Years of Humanitarian Intervention in Iraqi Kurdistan," *Middle East Report* (187/188): 40–45; Hooglund 1991: 3.
97 Clarry, S. (2007), "Iraqi Kurdistan: The Humanitarian Program," *Kurdish Identity: Human Rights and Political Status*, Charles G. MacDonald and Carole S. O'Leary (eds.), Gainesville, FL: University Press of Florida: 149.

9 The second unrecognised Kurdish quasi-state (1992–2003)

The Iraqi failure to govern Kurdistan and its Kurdish policies in the 1980s resulted in the annihilation of Kurdistan and the de-Iraqification of a significant part of Kurdish society. This profoundly impacted the Kurds' ability to accept integration into the Iraqi state. These policies fundamentally transformed Kurdish society. For most Kurds, the main question was how to escape from Iraq – not how to join in and integrate with the oppressor. The second Gulf War offered the Kurds a golden opportunity. The 150,000 pro-Iraqi *Jash* militiamen collectively defected and joined the IKF. Within two weeks, all of Iraqi Kurdistan was 'liberated'. The exodus, which most Kurds were forced to participate in to survive, was the unofficial Kurdish referendum of their rejection of the state of Iraq. The Kurdish uprising of 1991 uprooted Iraqi rule in Kurdistan and it never recovered. The Kurdistan region eventually turned into a second unrecognised quasi-state (UKQ-II). The uprising and the UKQ-II directly resulted from the Iraqi policies of annihilation and de-Iraqification of the Kurds. The annihilation of Iraqi Kurdistan was a logical extension of Iraq's failure to adequately govern the region. The main reason behind the Iraqi failure was the legacy of the UKQ-I and its deep impact on Iraqi-Kurdish relations and the emergence of the Kurdish insurgency after 1976. In sum, each phase of Kurdish self-rule logically followed the circumstances of the former phase. This chapter examines the second phase of Kurdish self-rule, namely the UKQ-II that was established following the uprising of 1991

The establishment of the Kurdistan Regional Government

Iraq successfully suppressed the Kurdish uprising of 1991 but failed to recapture the entire Kurdistan territory. Despite their defeat, the Iraqi Kurdistan Front (IKF) maintained its hold on a broad strip of land along the Iranian and Turkish border, including several towns, such as Halabja, Qala Diza, Raniya, and Rawandiz.[1] Within a month or so, the IKF managed to re-organise and recruit tens of thousands of defected pro-government Kurdish tribal militia (popularly known as *Jash*) into its ranks, as well as penetrate into other cities and towns that were recaptured by the Iraqi army. By June the Iraqi army found it impossible to deny the peshmerga presence in Kurdish cities. One month later fighting between the peshmerga and Iraqi troops broke out in the main cities and towns. This led to the withdrawal of Iraqi forces while the peshmerga took control of Kurdish cities. Consequently, Iraqi troops remained encamped on the outskirts, and were mostly surrounded and often protected by the peshmerga.[2] Losing its power base and failing to find any support among the Kurds, the central government failed to maintain its authority in the region. By autumn of 1991, Iraq was compelled to withdraw its army and administrative personnel from Kurdistan.

Following the withdrawal of Iraq, the IKF moved swiftly to fill the vacuum in the region. To achieve internal legitimacy, the IKF planned elections for 19 May 1992. The Kurdistan National Assembly (KNA) and the Kurdistan Regional Government (KRG) were thereby established. On 4 October 1992, the KNA unilaterally declared its federal region within the state of Iraq.[3] Whatever title the Kurds chose for their entity, the KRI was independent from Baghdad and acted as an independent state in all but name. Whether the KRI may be considered as another (second) phase of an unrecognised quasi-state may be determined by the four criteria that pertain to the unrecognised quasi-state (UQC) status.

The weak parent state criterion (UQC-III)

The emergence and survival of the Kurdish *de facto* state after 1991 has often been attributed to the American-led alliance's interference into the Iraqi state after the second Gulf War. Little attention has been given to the change in the balance of power between the Kurds and Iraq in favour of the former. As will be explained, external patronage played a crucial role in the case of the KRI's quasi-state aspirations. The weakness of Iraq, however, is an important element in the emergence and survivability of the KRI and its ability to function as an independent quasi-state.

The first major weakness of the Iraqi state was the turmoil within the Iraqi-Arab communities (Shia and Sunni Arab) following the defeat of Iraq from the second Gulf War. Iraqi society was mired in political chaos and economic hardship due to engagement in the second Gulf War and its subsequent loss of control of the Shia region. This state of affairs showed itself in the rebellion of nine Shia provinces against Baghdad in 1991. This Shia uprising was clearly a sectarian, anti-Ba'ath, and anti-Sunni rebellion. The uprising's main slogan was "no custodian, only Ali; we want a Shi'a commander."[4] The main goal of the uprising was to establish Shia rule in Iraq. Therefore, no Sunni governorates participated in the uprising. The Ba'ath regime reacted ruthlessly. Under the slogan of "no Shias after today," the regime spared no blood in squelching the uprising.[5] Although the Shia uprising was crushed, it changed the balance of power between the Kurds and Baghdad significantly. Unlike the Kurdish uprisings and rebellions, the Shia uprising threatened not only Ba'ath rules, but also Sunni domination in Iraq. In contrast to the Kurdish rebellions and uprisings that never managed to reach Baghdad, the Shia uprising reached the suburbs of Baghdad. Since Baghdad is the capitol and symbol of national rule, whoever controls Baghdad rules the country. The uprising caused unprecedented cleavage among Sunni and Shia Arabs. For the first time since the creation of Iraq, Baghdad had to confront two rival regions simultaneously: an emerging Shia region in the south and the Kurdistan region in the north. Hence, Baghdad had to turn the attention of part, if not most, of its forces from Kurdistan to the south. This further weakened the Iraqi regime in Kurdistan and changed the balance of power in that area in favour of the Kurds.

The second major Iraqi weakness in this period was the loss of international support. Following the Iraqi invasion of Kuwait, Iraq lost much external and internal support and a comprehensive international sanction was imposed on the country by the UN. Iraqi sovereignty was violated and its status as an independent state was undermined by external military interventions. Moreover, Iraqi sovereignty was restricted by tens of Security Council Resolutions (SCR). For instance, within four months alone, from 2 August to 31 December 1990, the UNSC ratified 12 resolutions against Iraq. Passing SCR660 paved the way for international intervention by "condemn[ing] the Iraqi invasion of Kuwait and demand[ing] Iraq's immediate and unconditional withdrawal".[6] The second resolution, SCR661, imposed comprehensive sanctions on Iraq and authorised member states to use force to expel it from Kuwait.[7] Twelve other SCR were issued against Iraq in 1991.

Another important resolution that reshaped Iraqi-Kurdish relations was SCR688. As will be explained in detail, SCR688 did not portray the Iraqi-Kurdish conflict as an internal matter of a sovereign state. Rather, it threatened Iraq from any future attack on Kurdistan. The resolution demanded that Iraq end its repression against the Kurds; it allowed for subsequent humanitarian intervention on the part of the UN; and it led to the establishment of the Safe Haven and the NFZ. Another relevant resolution is SCR687 (3 April 1991) which stated that "the statements by Iraq threatening to use weapons in violation of its obligations under the Geneva Protocol" and "grave consequences would follow any further use by Iraq of such weapons". The resolution also recalled that Iraq has subscribed to the 'Declaration adopted by all States participating in the Conference of States Parties to the 1925 Geneva Protocol and Other Interested States', held in Paris from 7 to 11 January 1989, establishing the objective of universal elimination of chemical and biological weapons. The resolution called Iraq to adhere to Chapter VII of the UN Charter, conscious of the need to take the following measures acting under Chapter VII of the Charter. Moreover, Iraq was obliged to reaffirm unconditionally its obligations under the 'Geneva Protocol for the Prohibition of the Use in War of Asphyxiating, Poisonous or Other Gases, and of Bacteriological Methods of Warfare', signed at Geneva on 17 June 1925. Though SCR687 addressed the Iraqi violation of international laws in the context of the invasion of Kuwait, it was indirectly applied to the Kurds.

Preventing Iraq from purchasing, developing, and using chemical weapons (CW) changed the balance of power between the Kurds and Baghdad significantly. By preventing Iraq access to acquire and use CW, Iraq was unable to threaten the Kurds. Since 1987, the use of CW had changed the balance of power against the Kurds and was the main factor for the Kurds' defeat on two occasions. One incident was in 1988 when CW caused the termination of the Kurdish insurgency. It was a factor that has resulted in the collapse of the Kurdish uprising of 1991. Rumours about Iraq's intention to use CW played a significant role in the collapse of the uprising.[8] Furthermore, holding Iraq to Article VII of the UN Charter and preventing Iraq from having access to weaponry further diminished Iraq's military ability. Portraying Iraq as a threat to international peace and regional security brought the country into direct conflict with the international community throughout the 1990s.

Finally, sanctions on Iraq limited its ability to finance the development of its military machinery or to fund military operations against the Kurds. The combination of Iraq's defeat in the second Gulf War, international sanctions, obligations, and restrictions imposed on Iraq by UN resolutions resulted in dramatic limitations on Iraq's military forays. Following the Iraqi defeat in the second Gulf War (1990–1991), its army was reduced by two-thirds.[9] In contrast to this dramatic decline of Iraq's military capabilities, the Kurdish uprising of 1991 increased the number of Kurdish peshmerga from 15,000 to well over 100,000 men.[10] Despite ongoing internal fighting between Kurdish parties during 1994 to 1998, the KRI was sufficiently strong to keep the Iraqi state at bay after 1991. Thus, after the 1990s a significant swing in the balance of power favouring the Kurds transpired. From 1991 onward, Baghdad was so weak that it failed to recapture Kurdistan. Accordingly, the Kurdistan region during 1991 to 2003 satisfied the weak parent state criterion of unrecognised quasi-states (UQC-III).

The militarisation criterion

An important characteristic of a quasi-state is the militarisation of society as a method to aid its survivability and legitimate itself internally by providing security to its population. On the eve of the Kurdish uprising of 1991, Kurdistan was a militarised region. Despite Iraqi involvement in the war against the Allies, and despite its high demand for manpower, Iraq devoted two of its eight military corps to Kurdistan. Masud Barzani, the president of KRI, explained that during the uprising two Iraqi army corps (the First and the Fifth) surrendered to the Kurdish rebels.[11] Prior to the Gulf War, the Iraqi army numbered around one million. Therefore, the number of Iraqi troops that surrendered to the Kurds may be estimated at around 100,000 to 150,000. This facilitated access to arms for tens of thousands of civilians. Moreover, the majority of *Jash* rebelled against Baghdad. As the number of *Jash* was estimated at around 150,000 to 250,000, the number of *Jash* that joined the Kurdistan Front may be estimated at around 150,000. Furthermore, the IKF already had 15,000 peshmerga soldiers. Thus, following the uprising, over 100,000 fighters were in Kurdistan. Following its establishment in 1992, the KRG attempted to organise these forces and established an armed force of about 80,000 peshmerga and 20,000 police.[12] Thus, after the 1991 uprising, Kurdistan became one of the most militarised societies in the region. Therefore, the Kurdistan region during the period in question satisfies the militarisation criterion (UQC-II).

The symbolic nation-building criterion

Since the establishment of the KRG in 1992, the Kurdistan region has paid significant attention to the nation-building process. This process included use of the

Kurdish national flag for public and official offices, anthem and holidays, its own currency, museums, educational system, publishing, broadcasting in the Kurdish language, and many other processes that symbolise nationhood. One of the most important symbols of nation-building is the use of a national flag. Legislation no. 14 of the Kurdistan National Assembly (KNA) in 1999 ratified the Kurdistan national flag that "reflected the feats and glories, the history and struggle and aspirations of its people".[13] Article 6 ordered the Iraqi flag to fly alongside the Kurdistani flag on occasions where required, and only after the recognition of the Kurdish right of federalism. In other words, the flying of the Iraqi flag was occasional, optional, and conditional. The importance of the flag for the Kurdistan region relates to two interconnected issues. First, according to the legislation, the Kurdistani flag "reflects the pride and dignity of his people and symbolises the home of that people". The legislation also emphasises that "the flag is the same flag that Qadhi Mohammad, the president of the Republic of Mahabad, handed to Mustafa Barzani." Prior to the execution of the former by the Iranian regime in 1947, Barzani "maintained and defended [it] for the sake of its glory with all [. . .] dedication and devotion".[14] Flying the same Kurdish flag of the Republic of Kurdistan founded by Qazi Mohammad in 1947 was:

> [An] acknowledgement of this historic march and this sincerity, dedication and appreciation, and to fulfil the dream of our people and in response to its desire, and in compliance with his will, but for the embodiment of the Legislative and legal framework for this flag, which is for the first time in the history of the Kurds and Kurdistan, has initiated this law.[15]

Thus, the Kurdish flag is the symbol the Kurdish struggle in the last century, through which the Kurdish *de facto* state was established.

Second, the Kurdistani flag was more than merely a symbol of a federal region within a federal state. It was a declaration that the Kurds were a separate nation with its own history that went beyond the borders of the Iraqi state. Glorifying the Kurdish flag as a symbol of a separate Kurdish nation (rather than a minority within Iraq) was further highlighted in the description and interpretation of its colours. According to the legislation, the flag's red colour symbolised "the martyrs of the Kurdish liberation movement". Its white colour symbolised "peace and freedom, democracy and tolerance desired by the people of Kurdistan".[16] The Kurdish flag represented and continues to represent for the Kurds one of the most important symbols of the nation-building process and the crafting of a separate identity for Kurdistan.

Another important symbol of the nation-building process in Kurdistan was the Kurdish national anthem, known in Kurdish as *Ey Reqib*. It was first created and adopted as the Kurdish national anthem outside Iraqi Kurdistan by the short-lived Kurdish Republic of Mahabad in Iranian Kurdistan in 1946.[17] The KRG official website described *Ey Reqib* as a part of "Kurdish nation's culture with a glorious status in the Kurdish liberation movement of Kurdistan and in the hearts of its people. It is a mirror of the thoughts and the conscience of all segments and strata of the Kurdistani nation."[18] Moreover, *Ey Reqib* emphasises that "we [Kurds] are the children of the Medes and Cyaxares [first king of Medes]. Both our faith and religion are our homeland." Hence, similar to the sun of Zoroastrianism represented in the Kurdish flag, by tracing Kurds to Medes and Zagrossian civilisations, *Ey Reqib* abnegated any Kurdish relations to Iraq.

Another important symbol of the nation-building process is the Kurdish national day *Nawroz*. In 1997, the KNA in its Legislation no. 2 promulgated *Nawroz* as the Kurdish national holiday. Similar to the dominant theme that is reflected in *Ey Reqib*, *Nawroz* is another pre-Islamic myth. It represents the myth of the Kurds' victory over tyranny in 700 BC.[19] It also represents both the Kurdish New Year and calendar. Thus, the goal behind the Kurdish national flag, anthem, and national day was to sustain pre-Islamic myths, create a common mentality, and construct an overarching identity for the Kurdish nation.

The process of reviving the Kurdish language and reshaping or rebuilding Kurdish identity is another important step towards nation-building. During the period in question (1991–2003), the KRG focused on the Kurdification or de-Arabisation of Kurdish society. All stages of education, media, communication, and street signs were Kurdified. Moreover, functional nation-building processes were manifested in the Kurdistani civil society and media, such as 40 Kurdistani-based political parties and 120 civil society institutions belonging to different ethnic, religious, and political backgrounds. Furthermore, 30 TV and radio broadcast stations, as well as 167 newspapers and magazines mostly based on the Kurdish language and underlined by nationalist themes, were founded.[20]

As a result of 12 years of Kurdish education in KRI schools and universities, and the dominance of the Kurdish language in the public sphere, a new generation had emerged that could not speak Arabic. Since 1991, the KRI engaged in a relatively successful nation-building process and the development of a common national identity in Kurdistan. Thus, nation-building in the KRI satisfied the first symbolic nation-building criterion (UQC-I).

The external patronage criterion

After 1991, the UN, the American-led coalition (Allies), and the INGOs replaced Iran as external patrons of the Kurds. The Allies' patronage was more official and significant than that of previous patronages offered the Kurds during the UKQ-I and the Kurdish insurgency between 1976 and 1988. SCR688 and SCR986 allowed the Allies and INGOs to intervene on behalf of the Kurds. Based on the nature, form, and chronology of support, international patronage may be categorised into five phases: SCR688, the Safe Haven, the NFZ, SCR986, and the Oil-for-Food Program (OFFP).

Security Council Resolution 688

SCR688 (5 April 1991) was the international response to the refugee crisis following the Kurdish exodus. It legitimised clear acts of interference in Iraqi internal affairs, thus violating Iraq's sovereignty. The resolution condemned the repression of the Iraqi civilian population in Kurdish populated areas and demanded the immediate end of repression. There are five implications of the resolution. The first implication was the internationalising of the Kurdish issue in Iraq. SCR688 perceived Iraq's repression of the Kurds as a threat to "international peace and security in the region".[21] Consequently, the Kurdish cause was elevated from a purely internal affair to an international incident. The second implication of SCR688 was the legalisation of international intervention into what was heretofore considered as an 'Iraqi internal affair'. The resolution ordered that:

> Iraq [had to] allow immediate access [to] international humanitarian organisations to [aid] all those in need of assistance in all parts of Iraq and to make available all necessary facilities for their operations [. . .] in particular [with regard to] the Kurdish population, suffering from the repression in all its forms inflicted by the Iraqi authorities [. . .]; [it] appeal[ed] to all Member States and to all humanitarian organisations to contribute to these humanitarian relief efforts.[22]

Thus, the resolution gave the UN and INGOs the legal power to intervene in the internal affairs of Iraq in favour of the Kurds.

The third implication of SCR688 was the compromise of Iraq's sovereignty by authorising the INGOs to help the Kurds, and by forcing Iraq to accept the establishment of the INGOs in Kurdistan. The fourth implication is that the Security Council laid the grounds for the UN-sponsored patronage of the Kurds. The resolution authorised the UN control of two matters that would normally fall within the exclusive domain of a sovereign nation: the protection of Iraqi citizens (Kurds), and the delivery of goods and services to them. The fifth and most important implication of SCR688 was that it offered a framework for international organisations and Allies to simultaneously assume the role of patron to the Kurds and to usurp a measure of Iraq's sovereignty. This was clearly evident in three cases of international intervention, namely the establishment of INGOs in Kurdistan, imposing the Safe Haven, and the creation of the NFZ by US-led Allies. Hence, SCR688 authorised programs of international intervention in an unprecedented manner and authorised the Security Council to enforce measures of particular concern to the Kurds to aid them in a time of crisis.

International non-governmental organisations

Responding to SCR688, tens of INGOs became involved in humanitarian activities in Kurdistan. From 1991 on, the Kurdistan region was open to aid agencies, human rights workers, and journalists. By 1994, 50 INGOs were established in the Kurdistan region.[23] These INGOs delivered financial help, goods and other humanitarian aid, and support for the Kurds. From 1991 to 1996, the Kurdistan region received over $1 billion in humanitarian assistance that sustained 1.25 million Kurds.[24] This financial assistance mitigated the economic hardship resulting from the double embargo on the region: one international that was imposed on the entire state of Iraq and the other imposed on Kurdistan by the central government. Within the harsh environment of post-1991 sanctions, INGO involvement had many implications that went beyond humanitarian and financial assistance. First, the INGOs provided an important source of revenue that aided political stability. Their work within the SCR688 context meant that the KRI enjoyed the symbolic blessing of the UN. The Kurds found a channel via the INGOs to share their plight with the international community. This was important because the Kurds historically were among the most politically and geographically isolated people in the region. Furthermore, the INGOs proved to offer the first big step on the road to engagement with the outside world. The INGOs that became active in Kurdistan belonged to and were directed by a dozen donor nations. Though informal, indirect, and at the level of humanitarianism, their involvement in Kurdish affairs brought Kurdish civil servants directly into contact with the UN and NGO organisations. Thus, a humanitarian relationship was established between donor nations and the Kurdish administration.

Moreover, the INGOs reinforced the separatist and independent status of the Kurdistan region. By focusing on the Kurdistan region while ignoring other parts of Iraq, they unintentionally reinforced the ethnic division between the Kurds and Arabs and therefore further alienated the Kurdistan region from Iraq. Finally, a latent consequence of INGO activity in Kurdistan was the provision of a form of protection to the Kurds. Offices and staff members of 50 INGOs were scattered in different parts of the Kurdistan region. These multi-national INGOs assumed a role akin to a human shield that discouraged Iraq from attacking the region. An attack from the Iraqi military would have harmed INGO members and result in more drastic interference from those nations represented to protect their citizens. In other words, the INGOs offered the Kurds a level of protection that the central government would have to think twice about violating. Hence, the INGOs' assumed role of patronage to the KRI provided protection, stability, financial support, and political support while strengthening the independent status of Kurdistan.

The establishment of a Safe Haven

An important form of patronage granted by the Allies was the establishment of the Safe Haven in April 1991 in Iraqi Kurdistan close to the Turkish border. The Safe Haven was established for Kurdish refugees by a US-led military operation that was code named 'Operation Provide Comfort' (OPC). It consisted of a 10,000-square-kilometre strip of land that was patrolled by more than 13,000 soldiers from 11 countries including the US and the UK.[25] The main tasks of the OPC and the establishment of the Safe Haven were to halt the further influx of refugees to Turkey and to prepare for the return of refugees who had already crossed the Turkish border. The OPC also provided humanitarian aid and security.[26] Thus, the OPC prevented Iraq from committing further acts of atrocity upon Kurdish refugees.

The Safe Haven presented a turning point in the nature of patronage that would be provided to the Kurds in the future. The Allies' patronage evolved from the mere condemnation of Iraq to direct military intervention for the first time. Consequently, the operation involved direct invasion of parts of Iraq. The operation undermined Iraq's status as a 'sovereign state'. Moreover, it was the first time in history that the UN intervened in the internal affairs of a sovereign state in support of a non-sovereign region or people. SCR688 provided the legal framework for the establishment of the Safe Haven. This means that there was consensus within the international community to protect the Kurds. Furthermore, unlike the INGOs, the Allies engaged directly by military means. This was regarded as a departure from historic Kurdish-client patron relationships. Since 1961, most patronages were hidden, usually operated at the security level, and were dominated by a regional country such as Iran. With the establishment of the Safe Haven, however, 11 countries including three members of the Security Council, (the US, the UK, and France) provided overt military protection. The Safe Haven was an important form of external patronage that encouraged Iraq to withdraw its troops and the KRI to establish itself. By the autumn of 1991, Baghdad had withdrawn its army and administration from three provinces of Iraqi Kurdistan, provinces that eventually turned into the Kurdistan Regional Government. Thus, the Safe Haven was one of the most significant and influential types of external patronage granted to the Kurds. It adjusted power relations between the KRI and Baghdad as well as permanently reoriented and reshaped Kurdish-Iraqi relations.

The No-Fly Zone

In April 1991, the No-Fly Zone (NFZ) was put in place by the Allies to protect the Kurds from any future Iraqi air assaults. This NFZ continued until the collapse of the Ba'ath regime in 2003. Under the NFZ, Iraqi aircraft were forbidden to fly inside the Kurdistan region north of the 36th parallel. Thus, Iraq was prevented from launching major attacks on the Kurdistan region in order to bring it back into the Iraqi fold. Both in scope and duration, the NFZ was more comprehensive than the Safe Haven. Unlike the Safe Haven, under the NFZ the Allied troops were not actually on the ground of Iraqi Kurdistan. The region, however, was protected by Allied air forces that patrolled the region's air space. Similar to the Safe Haven, the NFZ was founded under the banner of humanitarian intervention and within the framework of SCR688. The role of the NFZ was crucial to the survival of the KRG. In fact, many believe that the Kurdish semi-independent state was enforced and guarded by it.[27] In other words, the establishment and survival of the Kurdish quasi-state (1991–2003) may be attributed to the goodwill of the Allies and their commitment to protect the zone.

The role of the Allies was not limited to merely patrolling the Kurdish air space and physical protection of the KRG; it also dominated Kurdish internal politics. The Allies involved themselves in the establishment of the Iraqi opposition bases in the Kurdistan region. Moreover, the Allies played a crucial role in the reconciliation of Kurdish rival factions. In 1998, for example, the two rival Kurdish leaders were invited to Washington, DC and top American officials including the secretary of state mediated a peace process between them.[28] The resulting Washington Agreement ended the Kurdish civil war. Thus, the establishment of the NFZ was another significant phase of the patron-client relation between the superpowers and the Kurds. Within the NFZ mechanism, US-led Allies provided different forms of protection and political support to the Kurds. For the first time in history, the international community and superpowers demonstrated their long-standing commitment to protect the Kurds from the perceived and actual acts of aggression by Baghdad.

The Oil-for-Food Program

The Oil-for-Food Program (OFFP) was authorised by Security Council Resolution 986 (SCR986) in 1995. The OFFP was a temporary measure to provide for the humanitarian needs of the Iraqi people. It authorised the import of petroleum and petroleum products originating in Iraq to produce a sum not exceeding a total of 1 billion USD every 90 days. These funds were used to finance the export to Iraq of medicine, health supplies, foodstuffs, and materials and supplies for essential civilian needs.[29] The program began functioning late in 1996 and ended in 2006 following the US invasion of Iraq.

Scrutinising the nature and size of funds provided to the Kurdistan region and the way they had been administered demonstrates how the UN assumed the role of external patron to the Kurds. The first important and probably an unintentional consequence of the OFFP was the further alienation of Iraq from Kurdistan. Though OFFP funds originated from the sale of Iraqi oil, it was the UN's obligation to monitor the sale of petroleum and petroleum products to be exported by Iraq.[30] UN agencies assumed the role of external funding to the Kurdistan region at the expense of Iraqi sovereignty. Therefore, the OFFP was perceived by the Kurds to be more of a UN program than an Iraqi one. The second important consequence of the OFFP was the recognition and consolidation of the status quo of Kurdistan as a *de facto* self-rule region. The resolution emphasised the equitable distribution of humanitarian relief to all segments of the Iraqi population throughout the country. To achieve an equitable distribution Article 8-b of SCR986 authorised the Security Council to provide between 130 million and 150 million USD every 90 days to the Kurdistan region. The sale of oil for 90 days totalled 1 billion USD. Thirteen to 15 per cent of this revenue had been allocated to the Kurdish region. SCR986 justified a separate budget for the Kurds due to the exceptional circumstances prevailing in the three Kurdish governorates.[31] In the first year of the OFFP, the Kurdistan region had received 520 to 600 million USD.

Moreover, the government of Iraq was not allowed to administer the OFFP program in Kurdistan as it did in other parts of Iraq. SCR986 made clear that OFFP funds should be provided to the UN Inter-Agency Humanitarian Program operating in the Kurdistan region. Thus the UN followed two programs in Iraq: one administered by Baghdad, the other in Kurdistan that was administered by the UN, with the UN acting as trustee for the OFFP money. UN agencies acted on behalf of the central government in Kurdistan to supply, transport, and distribute the funds. This arrangement enabled the KRG to directly cooperate with 12 UN agencies in the region instead of Baghdad. Nine of these agencies were involved directly in the management of the OFFP in Kurdistan.[32] Thus, though the OFFP fund was from Iraq's oil wealth and had to come through Baghdad, it was authorised, monitored, and, in the case of Kurdistan, administered by the UN. The program strengthened the independent and separate status of the Kurdish *de facto* state. The UN distributed and therefore assumed a degree of Iraq's sovereignty while acting as patron of the Kurdish quasi-state.

The third important consequence of the OFFP was the provision of a degree of economic independence for the KRI. Dedicating $520 to $600 million annually to Kurdistan was a significant step towards the latter's economic revival and survivability. The significance of such financial aid was evident in that the KRI budget for 1994 was less than 25 million USD.[33] Hence, the OFFP program by 1997 multiplied the economy of the region by 20 times what it had been in 1994. In February 1998, SCR986 was replaced by SCR1153. Under the new resolution, funds that the KRI received nearly tripled. This is because SCR1153 increased total Iraqi oil sales from $1 billion per 90-day period to more than $2.5 billion.[34] The funds allocated for the Kurdistan region nearly tripled from 130–150 million USD every three months to 340–390 million USD for the same period. Based on these figures, between 1996 and 2003, a total of 8 to 9 billion USD from the OFFP was allocated to the Kurdistan region. This figure was eight times higher than the total value of humanitarian aid, or 1 billion USD that the KRI received from INGOs from 1991 to 1996.

The significance of the OFFP funds in consolidating economic independence for the KRI may be understood within the economic context of the KRG, which inherited the wholesale devastation of Kurdistani villages and its agricultural infrastructure. Combined with the high rate of unemployment and social deprivation resulting from the double embargo, the Kurdistan region had suffered extreme hardship. The majority of the population in the region relied on UN handouts for basic needs. The OFFP was one of the most important components in the Kurdistan region's prosperity. It can be credited for rehabilitating Kurdistan and improving the health and education sectors in Kurdistan. The OFFP also decreased KRI dependence on neighbouring countries and therefore reduced its vulnerability. Thus, the OFFP helped to keep the Kurdish quasi-state alive.

The fourth important consequence of the OFFP was its latent function in assisting the Kurdistan region to find a source of protection. With 12 UN agencies scattered throughout the Kurdistan region and nine of them involved in the administration of the OFFP, any aggression from Baghdad would potentially threaten the security of these agencies. Therefore, the presence of these UN agencies played a role similar to that of INGOs in the first half of the 1990s by providing moral support to the Kurds. The fifth unintentional consequence of the OFFP program was its contribution to the stability of Kurdistan. The OFFP revenue reduced the imbalance of funds available to the KDP and the PUK administrations. It was no coincidence that the internal Kurdish war between the PUK and the KDP terminated in 1997, the year of the implementation of the OFFP. In addition, the final peace process between the two rival Kurdish factions was followed by the availability of sufficient funds due to the implementation of SCR1153. In sum, by comparing figures due to SCR688, the INGOs, the Safe Haven, the NFZ, SCR986, and the OFFP program, it is clear that the KRI was physically, financially, and politically protected. The UN and US-led Allies' support to the Kurds was so important that it can truly be considered as a patron-client relationship that satisfies the fourth criterion, namely the external patronage criterion (UQC-IV).

The KRI (1991–2003) as a second unrecognised Kurdish quasi-state

The KRI thus met all qualifications necessary to classify it as an unrecognised quasi-state during the period under review. The KRI exercised symbolic nation-building enterprises (UQC-I); Kurdish society had been militarised (UQC-II); Iraq as a parent state was too weak to recapture the region (UQC-III); and finally the KRI was protected by external patrons (UQC-IV). Satisfying all criteria of unrecognised quasi-state status, this *de facto* state may be classified as an unrecognised Kurdish quasi-state (UKQ). This UKQ was the second Kurdish quasi-state in the history of Iraqi Kurdistan. The first existed between 1961 and 1975. Therefore, this phase of Kurdish self-rule shall be called the second unrecognised Kurdish quasi-state (UKQ-II).

The case of negative patronage

The UN and the Allies contributed to the emergence, survival, and consolidation of the UKQ-II. However, the aims and scopes of this external patronage were insufficient to help the Kurds move towards independent statehood. Failing to evolve into a *de jure* independent state, the UKQ-II rejoined Iraq following the US occupation in 2003. One of the main reasons behind the Kurds' decision to rejoin Iraq was their lack of a reliable, permanent, and positive patron. In Chapter 2, three criteria were introduced to distinguish negative patronage from positive patronage. The patronage is considered negative if it satisfied the three negative patronage criteria (NPC). First, the patron and client states do not share the same ethnic or cultural identity (NPC-I). Second, the patron state is not motivated by the interests, rights, or identity of the client state (NPC-II). Third, the patron state is not willing to recognise the client's independence (NPC-III). There was no Kurdish state in the world and none of the members of the US-led Allies who provided patronage to the UKQ-II had shared any ethno-cultural identity with the Kurds. Therefore, the patronage provided during this period satisfied the conditions of NPC-I. Therefore, this section only scrutinises the nature of the patronage provided to the Kurds based on NPC-II and NPC-III.

Security Council Resolution 688

As explained previously, SCR688 laid the legal framework for INGO activities in Kurdistan: the Safe Haven and the NFZ. A close look at the resolution reveals that the Kurdish cause was not the main concern for these international actions. First, the purpose of the resolution was to eliminate the impact of the April 1991 Kurdish exodus on international and regional peace and security (especially Turkey's). SCR688 described the Kurdish exodus as "a massive flow of refugees towards and across international frontiers and to cross-border incursions". SCR688 emphasised that the consequences the Kurdish exodus "threaten international peace and security in the region". To prevent such a threat, SCR688 demanded that Iraq "remove the threat to international peace and security in the region [and to] immediately end this repression". Hence, international and regional peace and security, rather than the protection of Kurdish self-rule, was the main purpose for SCR688. The resolution, therefore, satisfies the first criterion (NPC-II) of the negative patron-client relationship.

Second, SCR688 emphasised the Security Council's "duties and responsibilities under the Charter of the United Nations for the maintenance of international peace and security". SCR688 recalled Article 2, paragraph 7 of the UN Charter that stipulated two obligations. One obligation was the condition of limited UN intervention, both in scope and duration. The Article emphasised that "nothing contained in the present Charter shall authorise the United Nations to intervene in matters which are essentially within the domestic jurisdiction of any state or shall require the Members to submit such matters to settlement under the present Charter."[35] Based on the Charter, UN intervention within the scope of SCR688 could not go beyond humanitarian aid and only for a short period. Moreover, the resolution portrayed the Kurdish exodus as a threat to international peace and regional security. In other words, the resolution was adopted when the Kurdish problem posed a threat to regional peace and the world order. Whenever the Kurdish problem ceased to pose such international ramifications, the resolution would hypothetically lose its power and effect, become an internal Iraqi affair, and be dealt with as such. This is the way it had been traditionally dealt with at least until 1991. Consequently, the Allies and the international community did not come up with any political solutions to the Kurdish problem, nor was it intended to once the Kurdish problem ceased to threaten other nations.

Another obligation was the commitment of the world body to the territorial integrity of Iraq. This was clearly reflected in SCR688, which reaffirmed "the commitment of all Member States to the sovereignty, territorial integrity and political independence of Iraq". Such commitment was at the expense of the Kurds' right to self-determination and evidence that the international body while offering a degree of protection to the Kurds stood against the establishment of a Kurdish state in Iraq. The resolution, therefore, fulfilled the requirements of NPC-III. Though the implementation of SCR688 provided a form of external support and patronage to the Kurds, it was just another form of negative patronage.

The Safe Haven

The Safe Haven was another form of negative patronage. It was established with the same logic that underlined the passage of SCR688, namely, to remove the refugees' threat to international peace and security in the region. The Safe Haven was established on the Iraqi border with Turkey and within an area that covered one-eighth of Iraqi Kurdistan. It was obvious that no safe haven was created for those Kurdish refugees who fled to Iran, nor was one created for those Kurds who failed to leave the cities and towns recaptured by the Iraqi military. Since only 500,000 refugees headed to the Turkish border, the Safe Haven was offered for a small proportion, or about 15 per cent, of the Kurds. Some three million Kurds, including over 1.5 million refugees who headed to the Iranian border, were left without protection of any sort.[36] Only those refugees who threatened the stability of Turkey were offered safe haven. This is clear evidence that the motivation behind the Safe Haven was to protect Turkey and Europe from the influx of Kurdish refugees.

Iran was in conflict with Western countries, whereas Turkey was an American ally, a member of NATO, and considered to be the refugees' gateway to Europe. By implication, the main goal behind the Safe Haven was to protect Turkey from any refugee crisis caused by the influx of the Kurds. In other words, the Allies' priority and main concern behind the creation of the Safe Haven was to protect Turkey, rather than to establish Kurdish self-rule. Thus, the Safe Haven resolution fulfilled the requirements of NPC-II. The mechanisms and principles of the Safe Haven also did not offer any form of recognition to Kurdish self-rule. Therefore, the Safe Haven also fulfilled the requirements of NPC-III. It was another form of negative patronage.

The No-Fly Zone

The No-Fly Zone (NFZ) was another arrangement in which the Kurdish cause was not the primary concern behind the Allies' actions. First, if the Safe Haven had been established to entice the Kurds to return to their homes, the NFZ was established to prevent any future refugee crises. Similar to the Safe Haven, the NFZ covered most areas adjacent to the Turkish border. Other parts of Iraqi Kurdistan were excluded from the NFZ protection. Second, the NFZ caused further fragmentation and disintegration of Iraqi Kurdistan. Under the NFZ, Kurdistan was divided into four zones. The first zone was an area that mostly bordered Turkey, was covered by the NFZ, and was located within the KRG administration. The second zone was covered by the NFZ, but excluded from KRI rule. The third zone was administered by the KRG, but not covered by the NFZ. The fourth zone was a Kurdish area that was neither covered by the NFZ nor administrated by the KRG. Thus, the NFZ left out over two-thirds of Iraqi Kurdistan, which was either not protected by the Allies or not included in the KRI.

Third, the Kurds were not protected from ground aggression committed by Iraq and neighbouring countries. Throughout the 1990s, the Allies had not obligated themselves to keep the Turkish, Iranian, and even Iraqi ground troops from the NFZ. During the 1990s, Turkey managed 50 military incursions into the Kurdistan region.[37] In some of these military incursions, more than 50,000 troops participated.[38] Turkey had not been restrained by the Allies from attacking Kurdistan during this time. The US usually demonstrated its 'understanding' of these incursions by offering logistical and intelligence assistance to the Turks.[39] Iran is another country that threatened the security of the Kurdistan region, either through military attacks or other violations. In July 1996, for example, 3,000 Iranian commandos attacked Koysenjaq, hundreds of kilometres beyond its border in the Iraqi Kurdistan region.[40] Similarly, on 31 August 1996, at the invitation of the KDP, Iraq invaded Erbil with 30,000 troops and 400 tanks.[41] Though the Iraqi attack was coordinated with and in support of the KDP, it was a clear violation and threat to the Kurdistan region's security. Considering the Kurdistan region as an integral part of Iraq, the Allies did not prevent the economic embargo to which the zone had been subjected. Thus, the NFZ offered no protection from Iraq, Turkey, and Iran. Nor did it offer protection from all the other forms of violence to which the zone had been subjected.

Fourth, the region was used as a base by the Allies to contain the threat of Iraq to its neighbours. Following the second Gulf War, Kurdistan was the US' only window into Iraq's internal politics. The NFZ also used by the US as a base to interfere in Iraq's internal politics and to maintain pressure on Baghdad. This was evident in that the region was used to support Iraqi opposition parties. The US, for example, funded Arab deserters who fled to Kurdistan and put pressure on the Kurds to allow the Iraqi National Congress (INC) to establish bases in Kurdistan in late 1992.[42] The NFZ was also a useful tool designed to provide a buffer between Iraq and Turkey.

Fifth, the NFZ offered an important early warning of any perceived Iraqi aggression against Kuwait and to prevent the spread of weapons of mass destruction (WMD). The US' goal was highlighted by Tommy Franks of the US Central Command, who stated that the NFZ was designed to establish a continued troop presence to show the US' commitment to forcing Saddam to comply with sanctions and WMD inspections and to ensuring that Iraq remain sufficiently clear of sophisticated surface-to-air missile systems.[43] The NFZ was exploited by the Allies as a key component of their containment policy against Baghdad, and even as a potential base to overthrow the Iraqi regime.

In sum, none of the goals and interests that motivated the Allies in their NFZ arrangement put the Kurdish cause and interests as the primary concern. Therefore the NFZ operation satisfies the criteria for NPC-II. Within the NFZ, the UN and Allies provided no legal or formal status to Kurdish self-rule, and they denied any kind of political recognition of the KRI. This state of non-recognition left Kurdistan under constant threat from Iraq and other neighbouring states. It thus fulfils the negative patronage requirements of NPC-III. Hence, through the NFZ, the Kurds were provided another form of negative patronage.

Security Council Resolution 986 and the Oil-for-Food Program (OFFP)

The Kurds enjoyed benefits, prosperity, and special treatment from SCR986 and the OFFP. However, they offer more examples of the greater powers' negative patronage of the Kurdistan region. Several pieces of evidence demonstrate that the OFFP was designed to assure the territorial integrity of Iraq, rather than to provide long-term provisions for the survival of the Kurdish quasi-state. First, as mentioned, throughout the period in question, international sanctions were placed on the Kurdistan region as part of the UN sanction against Iraq to contain Saddam's regime. Despite the Kurdistan region being outside of Iraq's control, the UN refused to lift sanctions on the Kurdistan region, justifying that such a move would encourage the secessionist aspirations of the region.[44] Second, as explained previously, the UN took full charge of the OFFP in Kurdistan, while leaving Iraq to administer the program for the rest of Iraq. The UN, however, excluded the KRG from decision-making or implementation processes. This meant that the overall (OFFP) program in Kurdistan remained in the control of UN-Baghdad and not the KRG.

There are two implications of the OFFP. First, by denying the KRG from participation in the decision-making process of OFFP projects, the UN undermined the internal sovereignty of the UKQ-II and limited its self-sufficiency. Second, by depriving the KRG from decision-making while offering Iraq such rights, the OFFP practically proved its dedication to the one-Iraq policy. Hence, the manner in which the OFFP was handled was clear evidence that the UN was more interested in the unity of Iraq than the Kurds' and KRG's interests. Therefore, the OFFP satisfies the negative patronage criteria of NPC-II. Moreover, the scope of the OFFP did not offer support and recognition to an independent Kurdish state. Therefore, the OFFP satisfies the criteria of NPC-III, making the OFFP another form of negative patronage.

In sum, none of the UN and Allied programs (namely, SCR688, the INGOs, the Safe Haven, the NFZ, and the OFFP) was motivated by sympathy for the Kurdish plight, and certainly not with concerns involving Kurdish ethnicity and identity. The independent state of Kurdistan simply was not supported. Such a hypothetical state posed a threat to the status quo and would promote instability in the region, so it was thought. These programs were designed to promote 'one-Iraq' while protecting the interests and stability of the regional governments, particularly Turkey. The UN and Allies provided a degree of patronage to the UKQ-II that aided its survival. At the same time, however, they denied the UKQ-II recognition and prevented it from attaining independence. Hence, the UN's and Allies' patronage can be considered as negative.

Iraq between 1991 and 2003: a recognised quasi-state

During the period under investigation, Iraq satisfied all criteria of the recognised quasi-state (RQC). The first criterion was a state that violated, instead of imposed, the rule of law and threatened some of its citizens (RQC-I). Three examples demonstrate how Iraq violated its own laws and threatened the Kurdish population. The first was the indiscriminate bombardment against civilians during the uprising of 1991 that led to the mass exodus that resulted in the death of 20,000 civilians.[45] The second was the deportation of Kurds from areas outside of the disputed areas. It is estimated that, during 1991 to 2003, as part of the Arabisation and de-Kurdification processes in the disputed areas, over 120,000 Kurds were deported. Their properties and farms were confiscated by the government and given to Arabs who had been imported from southern Iraq and resettled to these areas.[46] This process was a clear violation of Article 19-a of the Interim Constitution of Iraq (1990) that was enacted during this period. The article promulgated the principle that "citizens are equal before the law, without discrimination because of sex, blood, language, social origin, or religion." The third example of the violation of Iraqi rules and laws that threatened the population was the internal embargo that was imposed by Iraq on the Kurdistan region from 1991 to 2003. Thus, the extent of Iraq's violation of its own laws and rules, as well as the Iraqi threat to the Kurds, based on their ethnic background, satisfy the criterion of RQC-I.

Iraq also satisfied the second criterion (RQC-II). Since 1991, Iraq had lost control over three governorates of Kurdistan, known officially as the Kurdistan region. The third criterion (RQC-III) is the condition in which a state seeks external patronage from a stronger state because it is incapable of confronting and conquering its separatist region. Iraq apparently did not seek external support to challenge UKQ-II because it was too weak. Unlike the UKQ-I, where Iraq perpetrated five major wars on the Kurdistan region between 1991 and 2003 in hopes of recapturing it, there was not one single such attempt. Another reason behind Iraq's reluctance to seek outside support was its isolation, both regionally and internationally. Hence, though Iraq did not seek outside support, this criterion is still compatible with Iraq's circumstance. The fact is that Iraq was weak and isolated; it was not strong nor was it integrated with regional and international powers. It simply lacked superior strength.

The final criterion of the recognised quasi-state (RQC-IV) is a state that suffers the violation of its sovereignty from external powers. Iraq's sovereignty was violated in many areas by the UN and the Allies. First, SCR688 legitimised the international community's interference in Iraq's internal affairs and the subsequent establishment of INGOs in the Kurdistan region. This state of affairs clearly compromised Iraq's sovereignty. Second, the creation of the Safe Haven, the expulsion of Iraqi forces from the areas, and the deployment of thousands of Allied troops were other violations of Iraq's sovereignty. Third, the creation of the NFZ, the control of the Iraqi air space by the Allied air forces, and the prevention of Iraq from flying over a significant part of the Kurdistan region were other significant violations of Iraq's sovereignty. In the period in question, Iraq faced another Safe Haven in the southern region, south of the 32nd parallel. Fifth, Iraq was subjugated to comprehensive international sanctions. Hence, Iraq satisfied all RQC and therefore was clearly a recognised quasi-state during the period in question. The existence of two quasi-states, the UKQ-II and the Iraqi RQ, side-by-side within the same internationally recognised country, means that Iraq was a country of two quasi-states.

Notes

1 Malanczuk 1991: 128.
2 Graham-Brown 1999: 39; McDowall 2004: 378.

3 KNA, Kurdistan National Assembly (1992), "Briyari Rageyandni Fidraly" (The Decision of Declaration of Federalism), available at <http://perleman.org/files/articles/080108073542.pdf>, (accessed 03/06/2014).
4 Al-Salihi, N. (2000), *Al-Zilzal: Matha hadatha fi al-Iraq ba'da al-insihab min al-Kuwait (The Earthquake: What Happened in Iraq after the Withdrawal from Kuwait)*, Suleymaniya, Kurdistan Region: Khak Press: 318; Jabar, Faleh A. (2003), *The Shi'ite Movement in Iraq*, London: Saqi Books: 230.
5 Makiya, K. (1994), *Cruelty and Silence: War, Tyranny, Uprising, and the Arab World*, London: W. W. Norton & Company: 97; al-Salihi 2000: 321.
6 Security Council Resolution, "United Nations," SCR660 02/08/1990, available at <www.casi.org.uk/info/undocs/gopher/s90/14>, (accessed 27/09/2014).
7 Security Council Resolution, "United Nations," SCR661 06–08–1990, available at <www.casi.org.uk/info/undocs/gopher/s90/15>, (accessed 27/09/2014).
8 Adelman 1992: 4–38.
9 Graham-Brown 1999: 193.
10 McDowall 2004: 372–380.
11 Fayad, M. (2008), "A Talk with Kurdish President Massoud Barzani," Interview by Ma'ad Fayad, Asharq Al-Awsat, available at <www.asharq-e.com/news.asp?id=13920>, (accessed 29/04/2015); Russia Today (2010), "As Long as Iraq Abides by the Constitution, we're Iraqis," Interview with Masud Barzani, available at <http://rt.com/politics/kurdistan-iraq-barzani-election/>, (accessed 18/06/2012).
12 McDowall 2004: 372–380.
13 KNA, Kurdistan National Assembly (1999), Qanun 'Alam Eqlim Kurdistan al-Iraq Raqam 14 li-Sinna 1999 (Law of the flag of the Kurdistan Region of Iraq, resolution no 14 of the year 1999), Al-Waqai' al-Iraqiya (Iraqi Official Gazzeta).
14 *Ibid.*
15 *Ibid.*
16 *Ibid.*
17 Aydin 2005: 35, 69.
18 KRG, Kurdistan Regional Government (1997), "Ala u Srwdi Nishtimani" (The Flag and National Anthem), available at <www.krg.org/articles/detail.asp?lngnr=13&smap=03010100&rnr=168&anr=16877>, (accessed 12/07/2014).
19 KNA, Kurdistan National Assembly (1997a), "Qarar raqam 2 li-Sinna 1997 (Resolution No. 2 for the year 1997)," *Al-Waqai' al-Iraqiya* (Iraqi Official Gazzeta).
20 Berwari, N. (2003), "Women in Iraq, Future Prospects," Paper delivered at Winning the Peace: Women's Role in Post-Conflict Iraq conference, Washington, DC, April.
21 SCR688, The Security Council Resolution (1991), "The United Nations Security Council," 05/04/1991, available at <www.casi.org.uk/info/undocs/gopher/s91/5>, (accessed 27/09/2014).
22 *Ibid.*
23 Natali 2010: 31.
24 Graham-Brown, S. (1995), "Intervention, Sovereignty and Responsibility," *Middle East Report* (193): 7; Natali 2010: 30.
25 Malanczuk 1991: 121; Graham-Brown 1995: 34; O'Leary 2002: 17–29: 18.
26 Graham-Brown 1995: 4; 1999: 120; Ahmed, M. A. M. (2007), "Laying the Foundation of a Kurdistani State in Iraq: 1991–2006," *The Evolution of Kurdish Nationalism*, M. A. M. Ahmed and M. Gunter (eds.), Costa Mesa, CA: Mazda Publication: 150.
27 For example see: Graham-Brown 1999: 110; Stansfield, G. R. V. (2003), "The Kurdish Dilemma: The Golden era Threatened," *Iraq at the Crossroads: State in the Shadow of Regime Change*, Toby Dodge and Steven Simon (eds.), London and Oxford: Adelphi Papers: 131–148: 131; Barkey, H. J. and E. Laipson (2005), "Iraqi Kurds and Iraq's Future," *Middle East Policy* 12(4): 67; Freij, H. Y. (2007), "The Iraqi State, the Opposition, and the Road to Reconciliation," *Kurdish Identity: Human Rights and Political Status*, Charles G. MacDonald and Carole S. O'Leary (eds.), Gainesville, FL: University Press of Florida: 131.

28 Leezenberg, M. M. (2002) "Urbanization, Privatization, and Patronage: The Political Economy of Iraqi Kurdistan," *Iraq's Economic Predicament*, K. A. Mahdi (ed.), Lebanon: Ithaca Press: 21; Ackerman, Spencer (2006), "Good Actors – The Kurds' Cunning Plan," *New Republic* 235(4): 1–10.
29 SCR986, Security Council Resolution 986 (1995), "The United Nations Security Council," 14/04/1995, available at <www.casi.org.uk/info/undocs/scres/1995/9510988e.htm>, (accessed 27/09/2014).
30 *Ibid.*
31 *Ibid.*
32 O'Leary 2002: 20.
33 KNA, Kurdistan National Assembly (1994), "Qarar Raqam 4 li-Sinna 1994," (Resolution No. 4 of the Year 1994), *Al-Waqai' al-Iraqiya* (Iraqi Official Gazzeta).
34 SCR1153, Security Council Resolution 1153 (1998), "The United Nations Security Council," 20/02/1998, available at <www.casi.org.uk/info/undocs/scres/1998/sres1153.htm>, (accessed 27/09/2014)
35 The Charter of the United Nations 1945.
36 Malanczuk 1991: 121; Izady 2004: 85.
37 Bengio, O. (1998a), *Saddam's Word: Political Discourse in Iraq*, Oxford: Oxford University Press: 310.
38 Graham-Brown 1999: 114; Lawrence 2008: 88.
39 Bengio, O. (1998b), "Iraq," *Middle East Contemporary Survey; (CD-ROM Version), vol. I–XVIII*, O. Bengio (ed.), The Moshe Dayan Center for Middle Eastern and African Studies, Israel: Tel Aviv University, 2000: 286–315: 302.
40 Tahiri, H. (2007), *The Structure of Kurdish Society and the Struggle for a Kurdish State*, Costa Mesa, CA: Mazda Publisher: 27.
41 Graham-Brown 1999: 232.
42 *Ibid.*: 116.
43 Phillip Gibbons (2002), "U.S. No-Fly Zones in Iraq: To What End? The Washington Institute for Near East Policy Policywatch," no. 632.
44 Graham-Brown 1999: 72.
45 Hooglund, E. (1991), "The Other Face of War," *Middle East Report* (171): 3–12.
Memorandum from Jonathan Howe to Secretary of State Eagleburger. (1983), "Iraqi Use of Chemical Weapons," Document no. 25, available at <www2.gwu.edu/-nsarchiv/NSAEBB/NSAEBB82/iraq25.pdf>, (accessed 18/01/2014): 3; Ofteringer and Bäcker (1994):40–45: 40–45.
46 HRW, Human Rights Watch (2003), "Iraq: Forcible Expulsion of Ethnic Minorities," *HRW* 15(3): 2.

10 The third unrecognised Kurdish quasi-state after the 2003 invasion

Following the US invasion, KRI officials (such as Jalal Talabani, Masud Barzani, and Barham Salih) declared their voluntary reunion with Iraq and seemed satisfied with the federalism arrangement. Federalism apparently became the dominant theme in Kurdish official party media and the Kurds actively participated in the reconstruction of the Iraqi state. Article 117 of the Iraqi constitution recognised the legitimacy of the KRG in a federal Iraq. Existing legislation and decrees promulgated by the KRI Parliament were formally recognised in Article 141 of Iraq's permanent constitution, which also favoured the KRI with revenues (Articles 106 and 121). The new Iraqi state was rebuilt on the basis of consensus, parliamentary power-sharing, and federalism. Articles 110, 111, 112, 113, 114, and 115 ratified the authority of both the KRI government and the central government. In addition to the power-sharing arrangement in some fields of authority by Baghdad and Erbil, pertinent exclusive rights were allocated to each side with the central government apportioning a degree of its sovereignty to the KRI. In post-invasion Iraq, the KRI had generally portrayed itself as a *de jure* federal region within Iraq.[1] Many scholars on the Kurdish issue have argued that since 2003, the KRI has compromised its independent status by becoming an integral part of a federal Iraq.[2] Based on this argument one might argue that Iraq was transformed from a unitary state into a federal one, and the Kurdish quasi-state was terminated by rejoining Iraq.

Termination of UKQ-II or a new phase of the Kurdish quasi-state?

From the Kurdish perspective, reunification was interpreted to mean that they would not compromise their *de facto* independence. After the invasion of Iraq, Kurdish leaders insisted that they would not accept less than their existing situation. The Kurdish version of 'reunification' was clearly reflected in the Iraqi constitution. Article 117 stipulated that "this Constitution, upon coming into force, shall recognise the region of Kurdistan, along with its existing authorities, as a federal region." Article 121 authorised that "the regional government shall be responsible for all the administrative requirements of the region." The article also emphasised that "the regional powers shall have the right to exercise executive, legislative, and judicial powers in accordance with this Constitution." Article 141 stipulated that "legislation enacted in the region of Kurdistan since 1992 shall remain in force, and decisions issued by the government of the region of Kurdistan, including court decisions and contracts, shall be considered valid." The KRI parliament, armed forces, the Kurdistan region's *de facto* border with Iraq, rules and legislation, treaties, and external relations all remained intact. Reunification did not diminish KRI status or its internal sovereignty. In addition to attaining legal status, the KRI reserved and further consolidated its *de facto* rule in the Kurdistan region. The KRI's legal status during post-invasion Iraq provided new opportunities for the Iraqi Kurds to nation-build. The second Kurdish quasi-state (UKQ-II) suffered many weaknesses. To guide the analysis of the KRI's status during post-invasion Iraq, the four criteria that determine quasi-state status will be applied.

The first criterion (UQC-I): nation-building

Chapter 9 focused on the nation- and state-building processes significant to the second Kurdish quasi-state (KUQ-II) during 1991 to 2003. Though the nation-building process was unsuccessful and therefore unable to transform the KRI into a recognised independent state, they progressed sufficiently to prevent the evolution of the Kurdistan region into post-invasion Iraq, despite its official reunification with Iraq. Instead of integrating into the Iraqi state, the Kurds used the legal status that they had acquired after the invasion to accomplish the mission that began in 1991. In fact, after the invasion the KRI engaged wholeheartedly in comprehensive nation-building.

Emphasising a common external enemy is a useful tactic for the nation-building process and a powerful motivator for national unification. Ironically, despite the Kurds' representatives in Baghdad and the formal recognition of the KRI by Iraq, the latter was portrayed in the Kurdish media and in official discourse as a 'common external enemy'. For example, KRI President Masud Barzani emphasised that "our fear is the mentality [of Iraqi rulers] that still believe in using planes, artillery and tanks to solve problems."[3] He regards the Iraqi army "as an extension of the dictatorial Ba'athist army that destroyed Kurdistan and destroyed Iraq".[4] In 2009, Speaker of the Kurdish Parliament Kamal Kirkuki called Shia Prime Minister of Iraq Nuri Maliki a "second Saddam".[5]

Rewriting history is another task of the nation-building process. A fourth-grade textbook entitled *Social Education* provides an example of the extent of rewriting history in the Kurdistan region. On the cover page are seven photos representing 'Kurdistani' civilisation from the dawn of time to the present day. One photo of the Shanadari Cave, where the remains of the Neanderthal were found, represents the pre-historic era. Other photos show two old castles believed to have been built several thousand years BC. Other photos show the Kurdish tragedies under Iraqi rule including the chemical bombardment of Halabja in 1988 and the Kurdish exodus of 1991. The last two photos show the progress that the Kurdistan region made after 1991 under self-rule. Finally, as a symbol of Kurdistan's internal sovereignty, the KRG emblem was printed at the top. However, there is no symbol or photo on the cover page to indicate that the Kurdistan region is part of Iraq. Another example that demonstrates the rewriting of history appears in a grade 12 history textbook. Its cover shows two photos of the map of greater Kurdistan and the emblem of the KRG Council of Ministry. Again, no symbol or photo of Iraq appears on the cover of the textbook.[6] This avoidance of association with Iraq can be found on all textbooks printed after 2003 in the Kurdistan region. Thus, textbooks present a prime example of the nation-building process and the development of a common national identity – to the exclusion of Iraq.

Courses in KRI universities offer other examples of rewriting history. Of 34 subjects, for example, offered in the history department of the University of Sulaimani, only two related to Iraq. One is dedicated to Iraqi history and the other to the history of Iraq and Iran. 'The history of modern Iraq', for third-year history students, demonstrates how Iraq's history was rewritten from the Kurdish perspective. Three of six references used for this course are Kurdish, one was European, and two were from Iraqi-Arab historians.[7] The two Arab historians whose works were used in the university program are known for their critical analyses of Iraqi history and society. One of the historians' work (Ali al-Wardi's) emphasises the failure of the nation-building process and undermines the status of the Iraqi people as a nation.[8]

Establishing national universities was another post-invasion area of nation-building for the Kurdistan region. In 1991, there was only one university, the University of Salahaddin. By 2012, however, there were ten universities established in different areas of the Kurdistan region. Establishing new universities reflected a clear departure from the Iraqi education system because Baghdad had no say in the Kurdish educational system and university policies in the Kurdistan region. Funding, devising programs, writing textbooks, and the choice of language to study was solely the responsibility of the Kurdistan region's education officials. Kurdistan enjoyed self-sufficiency in terms of establishing ten universities. Students from the Kurdistan region did not enter Iraqi universities and vice versa. Opening universities that were limited to students from the Kurdistan region created feelings of solidarity and provided a common identity in terms of educational purpose. Courses and programs offered within Kurdistan region universities were mostly Kurdified. Another importance of the universities was their role in the nation-building process. They promoted the study of the Kurdish language and culture, as well as educated generations that could not speak or write Arabic. Thus, universities were an important area of nation-building. The importance of universities also lies in the fact that they represent the intellectual and the official face of society.

The official website of the University of Sulaimani shows the extent of the nation-building process in Kurdistan. First, it shows the Kurdification of the educational system in the Kurdistan region. As the figure indicates, the signboard was written only in Kurdish and English. The absence of Arabic was blatant in the official websites of the Kurdistan region universities.[9] Five of seven major universities in the Kurdistan region use Kurdish as their main language next to English on their official websites. Only two of them use the Arabic language, next to Kurdish and English, on their official websites: the University of Raparin and the University of Duhok. Ironically, the University of Duhok does not offer courses in the Arabic language and there are no Arabic departments as there are English and Kurdish departments. Second, symbols, placards, and banners appearing on the entrance of the university exemplify how the common national identity developed among the people of the Kurdistan region. The university displayed Kurdistan region emblems, thus demonstrating how the nation-building process took place in the KRI. A nation's flag is a predominant symbol of nation-building. Since the 1990s, the KRI has officially adopted its own national (Kurdistani) flag, national day (*Nawroz*), and national emblem. Article 11 of the Draft Constitution of the Kurdistan Region re-emphasised and constitutionalised these important symbols of post-invasion Iraq. The Iraqi flag was mostly replaced by the Kurdistani flag and draped throughout the Kurdistan region. There are a few exceptions, such as Parliament and the Council of Ministers, where the Iraqi and Kurdistani flags hang side-by-side. In lower institutions, however, the Iraqi flag was rarely flown; for example, the Kurdistani flag without the Iraqi flag was flown in the Kurdistani armed forces and at public events. Another important nation-building enterprise is the construction of war memorials. Throughout Kurdistan the names of Kurdish heroes and martyrs are put on the streets, stadia, and buildings in the suburbs. At the entrance of the University of Sulaimani, for example, one can find a statue of a student leader who was executed by Iraq in the late 1970s. Thus, the extent of the Kurdistan region's nation-building processes meets the first criterion by which to classify the separatist KRI as a quasi-state (UQC-I).

The second criterion (UQC-II): the militarisation of Kurdish society

Chapter 9 pointed out that between 1991 and 2003 the Kurdistan region was a militarised society. However, the trend towards militarisation increased during post-invasion Iraq for several reasons. One reason was that Iraq recognised the KRI's right to maintain its own armed forces, including police and regional guards or peshmerga. Following the US invasion and the collapse of Iraq's armed forces, the peshmerga was the only organised armed forces in post-invasion Iraq. Baghdad not only failed to abandon these forces or integrate them into the Iraqi armed forces, but succeeding Iraqi rulers gave legal recognition to these *de facto* forces. Article 54(A) of the Law of Administration for the State of Iraq for the Transitional Period stipulated that "the Kurdistan Regional Government shall retain regional control over police forces and internal security."[10] Article 121 of the Iraqi constitution ratified in 2005 recognised the KRI right to establish and organise internal security forces "such as police, security forces, and guards of the region". Thus the government of Iraq recognised the legality of the peshmerga. The Coalition Provisional Authority (CPA) tacitly recognised the status of the peshmerga. Order no. 2 of the CPA formally abolished the Iraqi army and its defence system.[11] Contrary to their deal with the Iraqi armed forces, the peshmerga forces remained intact. The peshmerga, by contrast, was credited as part of the Coalition forces. As ex-Speaker of Kurdistan Parliament Jawhar N. Salim explained, in the first year of invasion the KRI armed forces (including the peshmerga, police, *Asayish*, and intelligence services) numbered around 100,000 troops.[12]

Another reason was that the KRI focused on the institutionalisation and constitutionalisation of the peshmerga. The Kurdistan region's parliament issued laws and regulations to institutionalise and legalise the peshmerga forces. Law no. 19, for example, stipulates that the peshmerga "protects and guards the Kurdistan region and defends it and ensures its national interests and nationalism". Another mission of the peshmerga was the "protection of the political entity of the region and the system of democratic rule and to defend its constitutional institutions".[13] The law stipulated that the peshmerga was an independent army that was administered by the Ministry of Peshmerga. Unlike the Iraqi army for which the Iraqi prime minister was commander in chief, the Kurdistan region armed forces were under the command of the president of the KRI. Furthermore, the Kurdish armed forces were unified in post-invasion Iraq, whereas previously they lacked a unified body and command due to the Kurdish civil war in the 1990s and the division of the KRI into two (KDP and PUK) rival administrations. Recognition of the Kurdish armed forces by the Iraq constitution gave the KRI the financial resources and power to maintain and develop their armed forces. The Iraqi revenue sharing law increased the status of the KRI at the expense of the political parties' status because now the KRI replaced the PUK and KDP in administering the peshmerga. Hence, the new environment helped the KRI to reunify the peshmerga and other armed forces. A unified Ministry of Peshmerga and Ministry of Interior were established in 1992, thereby replacing those previously set up by the KDP and the PUK in their respective regions.

Moreover the peshmerga forces had access to the Kurdish areas outside the KRI and this provided thousands of new recruits. The Kurds participated in the coalition-led invasion against Iraq. The US ground forces' participation in the northern front was mostly symbolic and the peshmerga worked with them to defeat the Iraqi military there. The peshmerga advanced into Kurdish cities, towns, and villages that were previously outside KRI rule and under Iraq's rule. Within a few days, they 'occupied' Kirkuk city. The disputed areas, where the Kurds were a majority of the population, covered 40,000 square kilometres, almost the same size of the Kurdistan region. The area had a population of two million, about one-half of the KRI population. Thus, peshmerga access to these areas added a logistical depth, a new source of manpower, and additional areas of influence to peshmerga forces.

Furthermore, the peshmerga had access to the weaponry of the defeated Iraqi army in post-invasion Iraq. The peshmerga directly and openly participated in the battle against Iraq at the request and support of the Allies. In fact, the peshmerga were the only significant force inside Iraq to participate in war against Saddam's regime during the invasion of Iraq. The unprecedented opportunity to access the defeated army's weaponry gave the peshmerga hundreds, if not thousands, of the collapsed Iraqi army's tanks and artillery.[14] Thus, the seizure of large amounts of sophisticated Iraqi weaponry further facilitated the militarisation process and enhanced the peshmerga's military capability. The Coalition Authorities provided logistical support and training to the peshmerga. In the first years of occupation, Iraq had no viable military forces of its own. The US occupation faced staunch resistance by many Iraqi militia groups. The peshmerga emerged as ideal 'native' or indigenous forces to confront the insurgents. Not only the Americans but also the new rulers of Iraq appealed to the peshmerga to impose order in Baghdad and many other Iraqi cities. This encouraged the US to provide logistical support and training to the peshmerga.[15]

In addition, while the Kurds initially participated in rebuilding the Iraqi army, the Iraqi government failed to recruit ordinary Kurds into the Iraqi armed forces. Masud Barzani, the president of the KRI, emphasised that the Kurds were one of the founders of the new Iraqi state and the first three brigades of Iraq's army in post-invasion Iraq were founded by peshmerga.[16] Despite that, as the Kurdistan Regional Presidency (KRP) explains, the Kurds' participation and proportion in the army was 4 per cent and, of 407 officers in the Defence Directorate, only two of them were Kurdish.[17] As the Kurdish percentage of the overall Iraqi population was estimated at 17–20 per cent, they were practically absent in the sensitive security institutions in Baghdad. This was despite the fact that a significant proportion of the Kurds lived outside the KRI under direct Iraqi rule. Probably more than one-third of the total Kurdish population in Iraq lived either in disputed areas or other mixed areas such as Baghdad, Mosul, and Dyala. This meant that the population of these areas had little desire to participate in the Iraqi army or the Iraqi rulers did not want them in the national army. The situation provided the KRI an ideal opportunity to monopolise the recruitment of the Kurds inside and outside the KRI.

Finally, having the revenue sharing program with Baghdad, the KRI was able to promote its own defence system. Some 24 per cent of the total KRI budget in 2011 was dedicated to the armed forces.[18] The total KRI budget for that year was estimated at around 11 billion USD.[19] Thus, 2.5 billion USD was dedicated to the armed forces. This caused a dramatic increase in the number of peshmerga recruits. In February 2011, Jaf'ar Mustafa, the minister of peshmerga, announced that the KRI had 200,000 peshmerga.[20] Since the population of the Kurdistan region was estimated at around four million, this meant that there was a peshmerga soldier for every 20 inhabitants. Thus, the Kurdistan region during post-invasion Iraq may be considered as one of the most militarised societies in the region. During post-invasion Iraq, the peshmerga and Kurdish armed forces was consolidated into a capable fighting force by regional standards. The process of militarisation in Kurdistan satisfied the second criterion (UQC-II) for classifying a separatist region as an unrecognised quasi-state (UQ).

The third criterion (UQC-III): Iraq as a weak parent state

When the US invaded Iraq, the country lost both internal and external sovereignty. The post-invasion Iraq period may easily be considered as the weakest Iraqi era since the founding of the Iraqi state. For the first time since the 1920s the Kurds dealt with an occupied and disarmed Iraq. After the invasion, Iraq experienced wholesale collapse. The country was left in chaos as the Shia and Sunni conflicts that were deeply rooted in Islamic history intensified. Shia and Sunni radicals carried out ethnic cleansing campaigns against each other based on identity alone. Furthermore, the new Iraqi rulers failed to regain or re-impose their authority or to redeploy the Iraqi army in Kurdistan. Article 65 of the Draft Constitution of the Kurdistan region issued in 2009 stipulated that the Iraqi army was not allowed access to Kurdistan without the Kurdistan Parliament's permission. During the years of invasion, the US did not establish military bases in the Kurdistan region and only Kurdish armed forces were operating to control Kurdistan. This state of affairs created an unprecedented imbalance of power. Hence, Iraq may be considered as a weak parent state that qualifies the KRI to have satisfied the third criterion for unrecognised quasi-states (UQC-III).

The fourth criterion (UQC-IV): external patronage

During post-invasion Iraq, the Kurdistan region received significant external patronage, particularly from the US. As part of the patron-client relationship that was established after 1991, the US followed a separate policy during post-invasion Iraq in the Kurdistan region. For example, the KRI was exempted from occupation; the US did not establish bases in Kurdistan and the KRI; and its institutions and armed forces remained intact. The US used the peshmerga as part of its northern front in return for financial assistance, weapons, and military training for the Kurds. Moreover, the US offered Kurdistan protection from any Turkish, Iranian, or even Iraqi invasions. In 2007, Turkey threatened the KRI with military operations in the Kurdistan region and they even crossed the border into Kurdistan. Under pressure from the US, however, Turkey terminated its military operation. Similarly, in 2008, during the standoff between the KRI and Baghdad, the US military immediately interfered. Kurdish leaders were provided moral and diplomatic support as well. The president of the KRI was welcomed to Washington, DC as head of state. The US extent of support and patronage to the Kurds therefore satisfied the fourth criterion of the unrecognised quasi-state (UQC-IV).

Kurdish strategy to find positive patronage during and after the invasion

Negative patronage had been the Kurds' Achilles' heel during the phases of the first and second unrecognised Kurdish quasi-states. Though negative patronage provided the Kurds enough support to survive, the support was insufficient to guarantee development into a recognised quasi-state. No state provided sufficient support to the Kurds to satisfy the criteria of positive patronage. The Kurds' key strategy during post-invasion Iraq focused on finding alternatives to negative patronage. Such a strategy must be built on at least three considerations: the need to create a self-reliant economy; the creation of long-term interests for potential patron states through a policy of support in exchange for oil; and the transformation of the KRI from the periphery to an emerging regional oil power.

Iraq since 2003: a recognised quasi-state

This section scrutinises whether post-invasion Iraq fulfils the four RQC to qualify as recognised quasi-state. The first criterion for qualifying as an RQ is a state that violates the rule of law and threatens some of its citizens (RQC-I). A brief examination of the role of the Iraqi army and police in perpetrating internal violence between the Shia and Sunni communities in post-invasion Iraq explains how Iraq's armed forces have violated Iraqi laws and rules and posed a serious threat to the Sunni Arab population. With 700,000 troops at its disposal, Iraq was one of the most militarised societies in the region. This number was twice as large as the Iraqi army under Saddam's rule prior to the US invasion. The makeup of the Iraqi army does not reflect the ethnic mosaic of Iraq as not all Iraqi communities were included. First, the Iraqi army was dominated by the Shia. The Kurds are practically non-existent in the Iraqi army and the army was not allowed to enter the Kurdistan region. The Iraqi army was not a national army from the Kurdish leaders' perspective. A strong Iraqi army with sophisticated aircraft was viewed as a danger to the Kurds. The Kurds' refusal to accept the legitimacy of the Shia-dominated Iraqi military after 2008 was demonstrated by the stalemate over control of the disputed territories that was currently in place between the KRI peshmerga and the Iraqi army. Second, taking advantage of their domination, the Shia used the police and armed forces as a façade to organise anti-Sunni death squads. These camouflaged death squads united under the Shia police force kidnapped, imprisoned, tortured, and killed Sunnis in mixed areas. One result of killing and displacing hundreds of thousands of Sunnis was that many mixed areas were cleansed of Sunnis altogether. Kurdish officials in post-invasion Iraq constantly complained of Iraqi army involvement in the ethnic cleansing and displacement of Kurds in mixed or disputed areas of Diyala province under Iraq's control. The Iraqi army was accused by both the Kurds and the Sunnis of being victims of killings and displacement of thousands of Sunnis in Baghdad and Kurds in Diyala province.

Rejecting the legitimacy of the Shia-dominated state, and to protect the Sunnis from Shia 'oppression', many Sunnis departed from their traditionally centrist status and called for a type of self-rule. After the withdrawal of US troops, provincial councils of three Sunni provinces (Tikrit, Diyala, and al-Anbar) voted to establish a federal region in their respective provinces. Tariq Al-Hashimi, the ousted vice president of Iraq, for example, called for the establishment of a Sunni region akin to the KRI that included the Sunni provinces of Salahaddin, Diyala, al-Anbar, and Mosul.[21] Usama al-Nujaifi, speaker of the Iraqi parliament, was another Sunni leader who overtly called for a Sunni region. He justified his call to protect Sunnis from Shia exploitation.[22] Thus, the Shia-dominant government of Iraq posed a threat to a significant part of the Iraqi population. Therefore, post-invasion Iraq satisfies the first criterion of the recognised quasi-state (RQC-I).

The second criterion used to classify a state as a recognised quasi-state is a state that loses its monopoly on the legitimate use of force in a territory of the country (RQC-II). As explained in previous sections, during post-invasion Iraq, the central government failed to impose its authority on the Kurdistan region and the result was the absence of Iraqi administrative mechanisms, institutions, or armed forces in the Kurdistan region. Since 2003, the Kurdistan region has been heading towards further independence from Baghdad. The Iraqi armed forces are not allowed to enter the Kurdistan region and the KRG developed economic and political relations with the outside world. The UKQ-III was acting as an independent state in all but name. Therefore, Iraq satisfies the criteria of RQC-II. Implementing the third and fourth recognised quasi-state criteria shows that Iraq satisfies both criteria. The third criterion is a state that fails to confront the separatist region on its own and seeks external patronage from a stronger state to challenge the separatist region (RQC-III).

The fourth criterion is a state that suffers violation of its sovereignty from external powers (RQC-IV). Though the occupation of US troops on Iraqi soil was the result of the Iraqi-Kurdish conflict, the US troops acted as protectors of Iraq's integrity and unity in post-invasion Iraq. Moreover, the invasion of Iraq reshaped Iraq's status as well as the Kurdish-Iraqi conflict. For the first time since 1932, the Kurds had to deal with an Iraq that was occupied. At least until 2005 the Kurds had to deal more with occupiers than with Iraqi rulers.

The occupation may be divided onto two phases: (i) the civilian, and (ii) the military occupations. The two bodies were created by Security Council Resolution 1483 (SCR1483) which recognised the CPA as an occupier with limited and temporary sovereignty. In the first year of the war and occupation, the US ruled Iraq through the CPA and the Coalition Task Force (CTF). The CPA represented the civilian wing of the occupier's authority. The CTF, however, represented the military wing of the occupation. To administer Iraq, the US authority established a civil administration known as the CPA. SCR1483 provided the legal framework for this authority in Iraq. The first regulation of the CPA began with "Pursuant to my [Paul Bremer] authority as Administrator of the Coalition Provisional Authority (CPA), relevant U.N. Security Council resolutions, including Resolution 1483 (2003), and the laws and usages of war".[23] Then the regulation promulgated that "the CPA shall exercise powers of government temporarily in order to provide for the effective administration of Iraq during the period of transitional administration." It also emphasised that "the CPA is vested with all executive, legislative and judicial authority necessary to achieve its objectives."[24] Thus, the CPA was vested with the right to act on behalf of the sovereign state of Iraq. In addition to administering the country, the CPA exercised all legislative and judicial authority in Iraq.

Being the absolute ruler of Iraq, the CPA attempted to transform its entire system of governance. This transformation included the deconstruction and reconstruction of the Iraqi state. The CPA's first order targeted the ruling Ba'ath Party by ratifying the de-Ba'athification of Iraqi society. The order eliminated the party's structures and removed its leadership from positions of authority and responsibility in Iraqi society.[25] CPA Order no. 2 dissolved the entire Iraqi defence system as well as the parliament.[26] The combination of the de-Ba'athification of Iraq and the dissolution of the defence system and legislative bodies resulted in the deconstruction of the entire system of governance and the termination of 80 years of Sunni rule. More than half a dozen new ministries were created by the CPA.[27] Many symbols of Iraqi sovereignty and national identity were replaced by new ones including the dinar banknotes,[28] penal code,[29] the Council of Judges,[30] tax law,[31] Central Bank Law,[32] Traffic Code,[33] the Electoral Law,[34] and finally a new Political Parties and Entities Law.[35] Thus, the CPA role in deconstructing and reconstructing the Iraqi system was no less significant than the role of the British in Iraq during the mandate period in the 1920s. In this regard, if the monarchy in Iraq was a 'British Iraq', then post-invasion Iraq may easily be called the 'American Iraq'.

If the CPA role was to reshape the entire system of governance in Iraq, then the role of the Coalition Task Force (CTF) was to implement and maintain such change. The CPA vested authority in the CTF similar to that of a sovereign state's armies with the job to maintain Iraq's territorial integrity and security.[36] The CTF possessed a dual mission: that of providing security and assuming the role of civilian authority in many parts of Iraq. The CTF was authorised to fill the gap created as a result of the collapse of civilian authority throughout the Arab part of Iraq. In other words, the CTF filled the power vacuum by imposing order and stability and mediating between the conflicted ethno-sectarian communities of Iraq. By carrying the major share of the stability and reconstruction missions, the CTF possessed a role akin to that of a military authority. On 28 June 2004, the CPA civilian administration was dissolved and the authority was transferred to the Iraqi Interim Government.[37] The CTF, however, did not hand over its authority to the Iraqis. The occupation was continued and only non-security-related sovereignty was transferred to the Iraqis.

As an occupying power, the US military was authorised by SCR1546 "to take all necessary measures to contribute to the maintenance of security and stability in Iraq".[38] The US mandate was extended each year by UNSC resolutions, such as SCR1637 (11 November 2005), SCR1723 (28 November 2006), SCR1790 (18 December 2007), and SCR1859 (22 December 2008). The CTF mission continued until the end of 2010 when the ISF replaced it to provide security to population centres. Some 140,000 US troops maintained final authority on most security-related issues until the end of 2010. Although the US role from 2004 to 2011 was supposedly limited to security issues, it actually involved political, economic, judicial, and governance affairs, making it the real authority in Iraq. In fact, Iraq was united in name only – not because of the ability of the Iraqi state to maintain unity, but because more than 140,000 US-led coalition troops enforced the goal. The US-led coalition possessed a dual mission: to occupy Iraq and to maintain the country's integrity. Thus Iraq fulfilled both RQC-III and RQC-IV during this period. It was an occupied country (RQC-IV) and its integrity was protected and defended by US military forces (RQC-III).

By the end of 2011, the US withdrew its military from Iraq and terminated its occupation of the country. The withdrawal of US forces was based on the

Status of Forces Agreement (SOFA) signed at the end of 2008 by the two countries. Implementing SOFA, the US completed the withdrawal of its troops on 18 December 2011. SOFA was followed by the Strategic Framework Agreement (SFA), which established long-term strategic relations. SOFA, SFA, and the US withdrawal, taken together, did not necessarily mean that Iraq regained full sovereignty. Finding itself lacking internal legitimacy and struggling to maintain its integrity following the US military withdrawal caused Iraq to appeal to the US as a patron.

Scrutinising the US-Iraq strategic agreements of this period reveals that the two states played the roles of patron and client. SOFA begins with a genuine desire of Iraq and the US "to establish a long-term relationship of cooperation and friendship".[39] This 'long-term relationship', however, was not a mutual relationship between two sovereign states. The US was acting like a patron and Iraq as its client. Article 27 concluded that the US and Iraq "agree to continue close cooperation in strengthening and maintaining military and security institutions and democratic political institutions in Iraq". Thus, the main goal behind SOFA was to maintain Iraqi civilian and military institutions. Hence, maintaining these institutions did not remain the exclusive mission of Iraq as a 'sovereign' state; rather, with external (i.e. the US) support, Iraq could fulfil this mission. To achieve this goal, SOFA authorised the US to interfere through military or any other measure to prevent internal or external threats to Iraq's unity and sovereignty. In this regard, SOFA promulgated that:

> In the event of any external or internal threat or aggression against Iraq that would violate its sovereignty, political independence, or territorial integrity, waters, air space, its democratic system or its elected institutions, and upon request by the Government of Iraq [. . .] the United States shall take appropriate measures, including diplomatic, economic, or military measures, or any other measure, to deter such a threat.

Though intervention required the 'request of central government', the US could take "diplomatic, economic, or military measures" against any threat to Iraqi integrity and sovereignty.

The SFA covered areas that were not addressed by SOFA. The patron-client relationship between the US and Iraq was more clearly identified in the SFA. Article 5 of the SFA "reaffirm[ed] that such a long relationship in economic, diplomatic, cultural and security fields [would] contribute to the strengthening and development of democracy in Iraq". It also confirmed US support for Iraq's institutions and "in so doing, enhance Iraq's capability to protect these institutions against all internal and external threats".[40] The US was required to support Iraq's regional and international status. External support of the US according to the SFA covered all aspects of governance in Iraq including economic and energy (section V) and health and the environment (section VI).

US patronage also extended to Iraq's internal affairs by demanding that the US support political reconciliation between Iraqi ethno-sectarian groups.

As in any patron-client relationship of any quasi-state, the US-Iraq relationship was based on providing external support to protect Iraq's integrity. SOFA and SFA are evidence that after the withdrawal of US armed forces, Iraq still needed external patronage from a stronger state to maintain its integrity. It was also required to cede some of its sovereignty to a foreign state. Therefore, despite regaining its sovereignty, Iraq still satisfied all criteria of the recognised quasi-state.

How two quasi-states in one country hindered Kurdish integration into Iraq

As analysed, post-invasion Iraq satisfied all four criteria necessary to qualify as a recognised quasi-state. The KRI in post-invasion Iraq was considered as the third and the most developed phase of the Kurdish quasi-state. Post-invasion Iraq was a country of two quasi-states: one an unrecognised Kurdish quasi-state (UKQ) and the other a recognised Iraqi quasi-state. Thus, Iraq has the experience of being a country of two quasi-states for several decades: from 1961 to 1975, and from 1991 to the present. The existence of the two quasi-states side-by-side means that there are two state-building and nation-building processes going on simultaneously, one Kurdistani and the other Iraqi. This state of affairs by definition had deprived Iraq from exercising sovereignty in the Kurdistan region. Therefore, Kurdish integration into Iraq was unlikely.

When only one quasi-state exists within a country, the issue of integration of all segments of society and the improvement of the system of governance is more likely than in the case of two quasi-states within a country. In the case of one quasi-state there is only one nation- and state-building process going on, though such a process may be challenged by a portion of that state's inhabitants. In the case of two quasi-states, however, there are two necessarily oppositional state- and nation-building projects going on. Two different (and usually oppositional) identities and loyalties make each state- and nation-building project counterproductive to the success of the other. Moreover, in such dual quasi-states, two rival forces seek to monopolise the exercise of violence. There are two separate systems of army recruitment, two armed forces defending their respective territories, and two entities pushing their respective legitimacies on the other. There is also a *de facto* boundary that separates the two states in which the institutions of the RQ are absent in the areas of the UQ.

The monarchy of Iraq, for example, satisfied most criteria of the quasi-state including the institutions of the armed forces, schools, and administrative units that existed in Kurdistan, particularly in the main cities and towns. But during the era of UKQ-I (1961–1975), UKQ-II (1991–2003), and UKQ-III (after 2003), Iraqi institutions were expelled from Kurdistan and the Kurdish administration, institutions and armed forces replaced them. In a country of one unrecognised quasi-state, the process of integrating the inhabitants of different territories and ethnic/national backgrounds is more likely than in a country with two quasi-states.

Notes

1. See *The Draft of the Constitution of the Kurdistan Region* 2009.
2. Brancati 2004: 11–12; Galbraith 2006: 169; Gunter 2008: 20–22; Natali 2010: 110.
3. Cited in "Massoud Barzani: Flying the Kurdish flag," *Aljazira TV*, 29/07/2012, available at <www.aljazeera.com/programmes/talktojazeera/2012/07/2012726121141649305.html>, (accessed 30/07/2017).
4. Barzani, M. (2008), "Kurdistan Is a Model for Iraq: Our Path to a Secular, Federal Democracy is Inspired by the U.S.," *The Wall Street Journal*, available at <http://online.wsj.com/article/SB122645258001119425.html>, (accessed 02/11/2009).
5. Asharqalawsat 17/01/2009.
6. KRG-ME 2008.
7. University of Sulaimani (2012a), "Mezhwi Nwe u Hawcherkh" (The Modern and Contemporary History), available at <www.univsul.org/K_D_WaneDireje.aspx?Besh=65&Jimare=944>, (accessed 09/07/2012).
8. E.g. Al-Wardi, A. (1994), *Mantiq Ibn al-Khaldun (The logic of Ibn al-Khaldun)*, London: Kufaan.
9. The University of Sulaimani Official Website, available at <www.univsul.org>, (accessed 27/11/2013).
10. The law was also called *Iraqi Transitional Administrative Law* (TAL); it was Iraq's provisional constitution following the US invasion in 2003.
11. CPA, Coalition Provisional Authority, (2003), Order 2, available at <www.iraqcoalition.org/regulations/20030823_CPAORD_2_Dissolution_of_Entities_with_Annex_A.pdf>, (accessed 07/08/2014).
12. Salim 2008: 74.
13. Waqai' Kurdistan 15/08/2007.
14. According to Loney (2011), "About 4,000 Tanks Left by the Former Iraqi Army in the Streets and Cities Disappeared, and Our Investigations Indicate that the Kurds Have Most of them".
15. 'KRP' stands for Kurdistan Regional Presidency, which is headed by KRI President Masud Barzani.
16. Kirishan 2008; Khabat 04/04/2010.
17. KRP (Kurdistan Regional Presidency) (2012a), "Welami Diwani Serokayety Heremi Kurdistan bo Witekani Berez Nwri Malki Legel Kenali (N.R.T) in Roji 13/05/2012" (The Response of the Kurdistan Regional Presidency to the Speech of Nuri Maliki on NRT Channel on 13/05/2012), available at <www.xendan.org/img4/kurdish/barham/88884/maliki24520112wwww.pdf>, (accessed 23/06/2012).
18. Kamaran, R. (2011), "Se Parezgakey Herem Niwey Panze Parezgakey Eraq Hezi Chekdari Heye" (The Armed Forces of the Three Provinces of the Region Are as Much as Half of the Armed Forces of Fifteen Iraqi Provinces), available at <www.chawyxelk.com/Detail.aspx?id=1078&TypeID=1&AutherID=46>, (accessed 29/01/2012).
19. ICG 2012.
20. Spokesman (2011), Jaf'ar Sheikh Mustafa: Jmarey Peshmerga 200,000 u Baghda Deyewet le 70,000 kemtrman Nebet" (Jaf'ar Sheikh Mustafa: The number of Peshmerga is 200,000 and Baghdad claims that we have no more than 70,000), Ministry of Peshmerga, available at <www.witebej.com/K_WitarDireje.aspx?Cor=Chawpekewtin&Jimare=25>, (accessed 23/12/2012).
21. Al-Hamdani, H. (2012), "Eqlim Tariq al-Hashimi" (The Region of Tariq al-Hashimi), *Asharq al-awsat*, 29/04/2012, London.
22. Al-Buratha (2011), "Na'ib 'an al-'Araqiya yu'ayid Tasrihat al-Nujaifi wa yad'u ila Iqama al-Mantiqa al-Gharbiya lil-Hifadh 'Ala Abna' al-Sunna aw Istifa'a Kamil Hiququhum" (A Member of Parliament from the al-Iraqiya Bloc supports al-Nujaifi statements and calls for the establishment of the Western region to protect and grant full rights to the Sunnis), available at <www.burathanews.com/news_article_128977.html>, (accessed 14/01/2012).

180 *The third unrecognised Kurdish quasi-state*

23 CPA Coalition Provisional Authority (2003), "Regulation 1," available at <www.iraqcoalition.org/regulations/20030516_CPAREG_1_The_Coalition_Provisional_Authority_.pdf>, (accessed 07/08/2011).
24 *Ibid.*
25 CPA, Coalition Provisional Authority (2003), "Order no. 96," available at <www.iraqcoalition.org/regulations/20040615_CPAORD_96_The_Electoral_Law.pdf>, (accessed 11/08/2011).
26 CPA, Coalition Provisional Authority (2003), "Order no. 2," available at <www.iraqcoalition.org/regulations/20030823_CPAORD_2_Dissolution_of_Entities_with_Annex_A.pdf>, (accessed 07/08/2011).
27 See: CPA, Coalition Provisional Authority (2003), "Order no. 24," available at <www.iraqcoalition.org/regulations/20030824_CPAORD_24_Ministry_of_Science_and_Technology.pdf>, (accessed 07/08/2011); CPA, Coalition Provisional Authority (2003), "Order no. 33," available at <www.iraqcoalition.org/regulations/20030909_CPAORD33.pdf>, (accessed 07/08/2011); Coalition Provisional Authority (2003), "Order no. 44," available at <www.iraqcoalition.org/regulations/20031126_CPAORD44.pdf>, (accessed 07/08/2011); CPA, Coalition Provisional Authority (2003), "Order no. 50," available at <www.iraqcoalition.org/regulations/20040112_CPAORD50_MODM.pdf>, (accessed 07/08/2011); CPA, Coalition Provisional Authority (2003), "Order no. 60," available at <www.iraqcoalition.org/regulations/20040220_CPAORD60.pdf>, (accessed 09/08/2011); CPA, Coalition Provisional Authority (2003), "Order no. 68," available at <www.iraqcoalition.org/regulations/20040405_CPAORD68.pdf>, (accessed 09/08/2011).
28 CPA, Coalition Provisional Authority (2003), "Order no. 43," available at <www.iraqcoalition.org/regulations/20031014_CPAORD_43_New_Iraqi_Dinar_Banknotes.pdf>, (accessed 09/08/2011).
29 CPA, Coalition Provisional Authority (2003), "Order no. 35," available at <www.iraqcoalition.org/regulations/20030921_CPAORD35.pdf>, (accessed 09/08/2011).
30 CPA, Coalition Provisional Authority, (2003), "Order no. 37," available at <www.iraqcoalition.org/regulations/20030919_CPAORD_37_Tax_Strategy_for_2003.pdf>, (accessed 09/08/2011).
31 CPA, Coalition Provisional Authority (2003), "Order no. 56," available at <www.iraq-coalition.org/regulations/20040306_CPAORD_56_Central_Bank_Law_with_Annex.pdf>, (accessed 10/08/2011).
32 CPA, Coalition Provisional Authority (2003), "Order no. 86," available at <www.iraqcoalition.org/regulations/20040520_CPAORD86_Traffic_Code_with_Annex_A.pdf>, (accessed 10/08/2011).
33 CPA, Coalition Provisional Authority (2003), "Order no. 97," available at <www.iraqcoalition.org/regulations/20040615_CPAORD_97_Political_Parties_and_Entities_Law.pdf>, (accessed 10/08/2011).
34 CPA, Coalition Provisional Authority (2003), "Order no. 100," available at <www.iraqcoalition.org/regulations/20040628_CPAORD_100_Transition_of_Laws__Regulations__Orders__and_Directives.pdf>, (accessed 10/08/2011).
35 CPA, Coalition Provisional Authority (2003), "Order no. 1," available at <www.iraqcoalition.org/regulations/20030516_CPAORD_1_De-Ba_athification_of_Iraqi_Society_.pdf>, (accessed 10/08/2011).
36 CPA, Regulation no. 1.
37 CPA, Coalition Provisional Authority (2003), *Achieving the Vision: Taking Forward the CPA Strategic Plan for Iraq*, 18/07/2003.
38 CR15, Security Council Resolution, United Nations, SCR1546 08–06–2004, "The Situation Between Iraq and Kuwait," available at <http://unscr.com/en/resolutions/1546>, (accessed 22/11/2017).

39 SOFA, U.S.–Iraq Status of Forces Agreement (2008), "Agreement Between the United States of America and the Republic of Iraq on the Withdrawal of United States Forces from Iraq and the Organization of Their Activities during Their Temporary Presence in Iraq. US Department of State," available at <www.state.gov/documents/organization/122074.pdf>, (accessed 08/11/2014).
40 SFA, (Strategic Framework Agreement). (2008). "US Department of State," available at <www.state.gov/documents/organization/122076.pdf>, (accessed 08/11/2014).

11 Oil for external patronage and financial independence

This chapter traces the question of how the Kurds' use of oil as a mechanism by which to achieve positive patronage. The third unrecognised Kurdish quasi-state (UKQ-III) enjoyed significant external support – particularly military, diplomatic, and financial – from the US. The quasi-state departed from traditional forms of quasi-statehood founded since 1991. The most significant development was in the patronage issue. The UKQ-III policy focused on finding alternatives to negative patronage that it had received from the external powers. To achieve this goal, the UKQ-III actively invested in its newly discovered oil wealth. UKQ-III policy was formulated as oil for external support and patronage. The UKQ-III provided relatively lucrative oil contracts and a friendly environment for tens of IOCs as it portrayed itself as an emerging regional oil power. Consequently, the UKQ-III headed towards finding positive patronage based on mutual interests and relations. Another important development in post-invasion Iraq was the UKQ-III policy of creating an independent economy, through production and exporting of oil as well as investing its oil product for the Kurdistan region's internal needs. These developments contributed in the transformation of the KRI to a more functional quasi-state. The KRI oil policy, however, backfired, especially following Baghdad's decision to cut the total 17 per cent budget allocated to the Kurdistan region in 2014.

From financial dependency on external patrons to revenue sharing with Baghdad

Traditionally, the lack of a viable and independent economy had been a fundamental weakness of Kurdish quasi-states due to the fact that they posed a financial burden on any potential patron state. The chronic economic dependency, backwardness, isolation, and marginalisation of Kurdish society underlined the failure of previous Kurdish quasi-states. The situation was exacerbated by frequent international and internal embargos on Kurdistan. Consequently, Kurdish society remained under-developed, without integrity, and politically dependent. During the 1990s, the KRI relied on an economy based on smuggling and external aid. This financial dependence was replaced by the Oil-for-Food Program (OFFP) in 1996. Following the invasion of Iraq, however, the KRI shifted its economic base from an economy based on smuggling and external aid to a revenue sharing economy with Baghdad. After 2003, 17 per cent of the total Iraqi national budget was dedicated to the KRI. The net yearly budget allocated to the KRI since 2008 had ranged from 8 to 11 billion USD. In 2008, the KRI received about $8 billion from Baghdad, and in 2012 it received $11 billion of Iraq's $100 billion national budget. This represents 12.39 and 11.67 per cent of the total Iraqi budget for those years, respectively. This revenue sharing source of income constituted approximately 95 per cent of the total KRI budget. Thus, by 2012 the revenue sharing plan resulted in the KRI budget increasing sevenfold, from 1.5 billion USD to 11 billion USD, compared to 2002.

The revenue sharing scheme, however, was probably the main source of the anomalies in the Kurdish situation during post-invasion Iraq. On the one hand, the scheme created sufficient financial resources for the KRI. It decreased the poverty level and social unrest that dominated Kurdistan during the 1990s. Revenue sharing also diminished KRI dependence on neighbouring countries. This reduced foreign intervention in internal Kurdish affairs and allowed the consolidation of the KRI internal authority. On the other hand, revenue sharing constitutes the main bond between the KRI and Iraq due to economic dependency. As the sole financial source of support, the Kurdistan region will most assuredly remain a part of federal Iraq in the short term. In the long term, however, revenue sharing leaves the Kurdistan region weak and dependent. Moreover, revenue sharing maintains the political culture of Kurdistan's 80 years of financial dependence on Baghdad. Relying on Baghdad for finances will prevent the KRI from integrating into the international community in terms of trade and the international economy. A handy budget will, in time, undermine the region's capacity building, long-term development, and internal sovereignty because the KRI will need to compromise its nationalist rights to secure its yearly budget from Baghdad. Having a ready budget had further exacerbated, rather than rehabilitated, the region's devastated agricultural sector. During post-invasion Iraq, few Kurds lived in the villages. Once the bread-basket of Iraq, the Kurdistan region still imports 90 per cent of its food sources from the outside.[1] The Kurdistan region exists in a constant state of uncertainty regarding food security. Finally and most importantly, without an alternative source of support, the KRI will remain vulnerable to blackmail or embargos and blockades. Iraq's role as the sole source of financial support may, in the long term, threaten the very survival of the Kurdish quasi-state.

A KRI key strategic objective during post-invasion Iraq was the development of its own economic base and the achievement of financial independence and self-sufficiency. Transitioning from revenue sharing to an economy based on oil production was their only hopeful strategy. To achieve this goal, the KRI was following a set of policies among which was the creation of a legal framework for exploring, producing, and exporting the region's petroleum; signing oil contracts with international oil companies (IOCs) independently without Iraq's permission; attempting to export oil; using oil for external patronage; creating foundations for an independent economy; laying a strategic framework to become a regional oil power; and finally preparing for integration into the world economy.

The first crucial development on the road to financial independence was the KRI ability to create a legal framework to explore and produce its oil. The KRI had put much weight in their negotiations with new Iraqi rulers to achieve this goal. KRI President Masud Barzani stresses that the Kurdistan region's top priority was to exercise their right to develop the oil on its territory.[2] Moreover, in post-invasion Iraq the Kurdish representatives advocated for the KRI's right to exploit and manage its oil fields. Though they failed to impose their vision on their Arab countrymen, the Iraqi constitution hints at the KRI right to develop its oil sector. Article 111, for example, specifies that "oil and gas are owned by all the people of Iraq in all the regions and governorates". Article 112 stipulates that:

> First: The federal government, with the producing governorates and regional governments shall undertake the management of oil and gas extracted from present fields [. . .] Second: The federal government, with the producing regional and governorate governments, shall together formulate the necessary strategic policies to develop the oil and gas wealth.

Moreover, Article 115 states that:

> All powers not stipulated in the exclusive powers of the federal government belong to the authorities of the regions and governorates that are not organised in a region. With regard to other powers shared between the federal government and the regional government, priority shall be given to the law of the regions and governorates not organised in a region in case of dispute.

These two vague articles have been used by the KRI as a legal framework by which to draft its Oil and Gas Law of the Kurdistan Region in which Article 3 states:

> Paragraph 1: Petroleum in the Region was owned in a manner consistent with Article 111 of the Federal Constitution. The Regional Government shall share Revenue derived from Petroleum with all the people of Iraq, pursuant to Article 112 of the Federal Constitution and this Law.
>
> Paragraph 2: The Regional Government shall oversee and regulate all Petroleum Operations, pursuant to Article 115 of the Federal Constitution and in a manner consistent with Article 112 of the Federal Constitution. The Minister may license Petroleum Operations to third parties to maximise timely returns from the Petroleum resources of the Region.
>
> Paragraph 3: The Regional Government shall oversee and regulate the marketing of the Regional Government's share of the extracted Petroleum from the Delivery Point where that Petroleum has been extracted from Petroleum Operations, and may license the marketing of that share to third parties.[3]

Article 4 of the Oil and Gas Law ratifies the establishment a five-member Regional Council for Energy Affairs. The Regional Council was authorised to "formulate the general principles of petroleum policy, prospect planning and field development. Second: approve Petroleum Contracts; and third: limit production levels in the Region."[4] Similarly, Article 74 of the Draft Constitution of the Kurdistan Region emphasised the KRI's right to:

> Manage, in accordance with the laws of the Kurdistan Region, all exploration, production, management, development, sales, marketing, and export activities, as well as all other operations, required for crude oil and gas fields, including oil and gas that has not been extracted or that has been extracted but not put into commercial production before August 15, 2005.

The combination of the Iraqi and KRI laws and regulations provided the KRI a legal framework by which to explore and produce its oil independently from Iraq. Accordingly, the right of ownership and management of the petroleum in the region was the exclusive right of the KRI and Baghdad had little authority over the Kurdistan region hydrocarbon sector. Thus, one crucial step towards financial independence of the KRI was its insistence on the right to develop its oil fields independently.

The second crucial development on the road to financial independence of the KRI is its oil contracts with international oil companies (IOCs). The KRI succeeded in implementing its carbohydrate law despite Baghdad's staunch objection. The KRI official website, for instance, in 2012 listed 43 contracts with 30 IOCs from 17 countries that are designed to allow for the exploration and production of oil and gas in 43 different locations in the Kurdistan region.[5] By 2013, the number of ICOs increased to 50 companies.[6] Baghdad had frequently voiced its opposition to these oil contracts and most of these companies have been blackmailed by Baghdad. The Exxon Mobile and TOTAL, the two largest oil companies in the world, were the last two examples that signed contracts with the KRI. Despite Baghdad's opposition to Erbil's oil contracts and its frequent emphasis on their illegality, tens of IOCs have signed contracts with the KRI. There are several reasons behind IOCs' involvement in this adventure. First, the KRI had emerged as one of the largest non-explored oil-rich regions in the world. Second, in contrast to the chaos and instability in other parts of Iraq, the KRI had created an environment-friendly and secure region. Third, as explained later, the KRI had awarded the IOCs with lucrative Production Share Contracts (PSCs).

The third crucial development on the road to financial independence of the KRI was its success in exporting its oil. The KRI's decision and actions to export its oil independently through Iraqi pipelines and through tankers was another step towards economic independence. By early 2012, the KRI exported some 200,000 barrels per day (bpd) through Iraqi pipelines.[7] To show further independence from Iraq, the KRI began to find alternative routes for exporting oil. From 2010 onward, the Turkish and KRI governments began to construct a direct Kurdistan-Turkey oil pipeline. The construction was planned to be completed by 2013. In May 2012, the KRG Minister of Natural Resources Ashti Hawrami declared that in the next 12 months, a million-barrel oil pipeline would be constructed to connect to the Ceyhan pipeline.[8]

In 2010, the KRI started negotiations with the Turkish authority to build a gas pipeline from the Kurdistan region to Ceyhan on Turkey's Mediterranean coast and to supply NABACO with Kurdish natural gas. Minister Hawrami highlighted that the region plans for a new gas pipeline to supply Turkey's BOTAS gas grid.[9] These two pipelines would be separate from and bypass the Iraqi export network and remain under KRI control. In May 2014, the KRG completed the first sales of crude oil produced in the Kurdistan region and piped to Ceyhan (Turkish Mediterranean port).[10] In August 2015, KRI exported some 470,000 barrels to the global market.[11] By June 2017, according to Nechirvan Barzani, KRI prime minister, the region's export capacity of 700,000 barrels per day had been reached.[12]

The fourth crucial development on the road to financial independence of the KRI was its ability to create an income from the oil sale. After 2010, the KRI started producing oil at a significant commercial level. Iraqi officials stated that the KRI exported some 68.11 million barrels of oil in 2011.[13] Kurdistan's oil exports through Iraqi pipelines amounted to 175,000 bpd. If the total Iraqi daily export for 2012 was considered to be around 2.6 million bpd, Kurdish oil exports constitute 6.7 per cent of total Iraqi oil sales. Ninety-five per cent of the Iraqi budget comes from oil revenue. Hence, the overall Kurdish contribution was around 6 per cent of the total Iraqi budget. The Iraqi budget for 2012 was approximately $100 billion, of which about $6 billion came from KRI oil sales. In 2012, al-Shahrstani, then the Iraqi deputy prime minister for energy affairs, insisted that the KRI also smuggled part of its oil supply for sale to external markets. He reported that Kurdish oil exports, including those that take place through Iraqi pipelines and smuggling, generated 8.475 billion USD. The proportion of total KRI oil sales to the total Iraqi budget was around 8 per cent if both 'legal' and 'illegal' sales are considered. Additional oil was produced for local consumption and, by 2013, there were 200 refineries.[14]

The KRI aimed to increase its oil production to one million barrels per day by 2016 and there was a steady increase in Kurdish oil production. If the KRI succeeds in producing and exporting such an amount, it could make over 20 billion USD annually at an average price of $75 per barrel. Officially, 17 per cent of the total Iraqi national budget was allocated to the KRI. As part of the budget was dedicated by Baghdad for sovereignty purposes, the net yearly budget allocated to the KRI ranges from 11.6 per cent to 12.4 per cent, or 8–11 billion USD for the last three years. By August 2017, the KRG produced oil wealth that exceeded the amount that it received from the Iraqi revenue sharing arrangement. According to Hawrami, the KRG Minister of Natural Resources, the revenue gained from direct oil sales "is significantly higher than the amount the federal government was able to allocate to the KRG on a monthly basis". However, he admitted that the revenue was "still below Kurdistan's 17 percent share of the federal budget".[15] Thus, UKQ-III was on the way to becoming an economically independent quasi-state. Alternate and independent oil revenues will reduce the region's dependency on Baghdad and other external actors. Iraq eventually lost its main leverage and pressure source which was its economic superiority over the UKQ-III. Similarly, the Kurdistan region lost one of its main ties to Iraq, which was financial dependency. This situation, however, was reversed following Iraq's reclaiming of Kirkuk and other disputed areas in October 2017.

The fifth crucial development was the KRI ability to provide its domestic energy requirements. The Kurdistan region was already producing enough energy to satisfy its domestic needs. Oil production has facilitated the establishment of tens of private and small-sized refineries. Three refineries with a total capacity of 200,000 bpd have been built that provide 80 per cent of the KRI's energy requirements.[16] Satisfying part of its domestic needs has already decreased UKQ-III dependency on Baghdad. Since 2010, the Kurdistan region has only had received 35,000 bpd instead of 130,000 bpd, or 5 per cent instead of 17 per cent of its share of Iraq's refined crude oil. Following the escalation of tension between Baghdad and Erbil in 2012, this figure decreased to less than 15,000 bpd, which was less than 3 per cent of the Kurdistan region's share of national oil. The KRI managed to produce and refine domestic energy needs themselves, making them less susceptible to Baghdad's blackmail. Thus, the UKQ-III was considered to be self-sufficient in terms of energy.

The Kurds' quest for financial independence, however, fell far short from its great imagining. Several factors played a major role in impeding Kurdish financial independence. These include the sharp decline of oil prices in early 2015, as the region's economy depends particularly on these hydrocarbon revenues. Moreover, the corruption and lack of transparency in the oil industry of the Kurdistan region amplified any pre-existing difficulties and oil disputes. War with ISIS was another factor that led to the impediment of the KRI independence. On the border of a 1000-kilometre front with ISIS, the Kurdistan region turned into the forefront in the war against ISIS, which had put a significant economic burden on the region. The huge influx of refugees from Sunni areas of Iraq and many others from Syria into Kurdistan was yet another contributor to the region's difficulties in obtaining financial independence. Since the beginning of 2014, the region has suffered an unprecedented financial crisis, to the extent that the KRG was unable to pay state employees, including peshmerga forces. This, coupled with the internal Kurdish conflict over the issue of the presidency, has resulted in deep division within Kurdish society. Despite these overwhelming pressures, the KRG has not compromised its stance on financial independence from Iraq.

The financial independence of the KRI related to both internal and external sovereignty areas of concern. Obviously, this was a source of central conflict between the two competing entities. Both sides claimed exclusive rights to own, produce, and export oil in the Kurdistan region. Thus, from 2007 onward, another conflict was added to the protracted Iraqi-Kurdish conflict. The KRI started exploring, producing, and exporting the region's petroleum and signing oil contracts with international oil companies (IOCs) independently without Iraq's authorisation. The KRI has intended to emerge as one of the largest non-explored oil-rich regions of the world. Rows over oil show that the conflict has remained one of the country's most pervasive problems since the American invasion of Iraq. It also shows the nature of the Iraqi-Kurdish conflict. Despite the central government's opposition, the KRI has independently produced and exported petroleum from the region. The KRI has signed oil contracts with international oil companies (IOCs) that are involved in multi-billion dollar investment projects.

The Kurdistan region's energy self-sufficiency has reshaped Kurdish-Iraqi relations in several ways. First, oil wealth relieved, to a large extent, Kurdistan's 80 years of financial dependence on Baghdad as the KRI become more self-reliant. Until 2014, one of the main, if not the only, shared or common bond between the two entities was the revenue shared by the two quasi-states. The shared revenue was based on the separate and autonomous entities: 17 per cent of Iraq's total budget was dedicated to Kurdistan. In an attempt to challenge the KRI's financial independence (primarily through the development of its oil sector), Baghdad cut the total 17 per cent budget allocated to the Kurdistan region in 2014. In doing so, what was possibly the last shared bond between the two entities was severed. Second, Baghdad's attempt to blackmail the KRI and cut its oil-share will not cause the social or economic turbulence that Baghdad counts on. Third, the oil sector has strengthened KRI internal sovereignty and political leverage in the country. Thus, if Kurdistan's oil and gas fields evolve as UKQ-III plans call for, oil wealth will likely become the Kurdistan region's ticket to independence.

Oil for external support and positive patronage

Using oil as a bargaining chip for diplomacy, to win political support and even physical protection, was clear from official KRI statements. KRG Prime Minister Nechirvan Barzani states that:

> [e]conomic and commercial activity can often lead to reducing political tensions, [. . . and] as a result of working together [with Turkey] and maintaining strong economic ties, we are able to make major political achievements. [Therefore. . .], cooperation and coordination [with Turkey] across all economic fields in general, but particularly in the energy sector, is a key foundation of the KRG's functioning policies.[17]

Similar statements are made by Mas'ud Barzani, president of the KRI. He explains that countries in which IOCs belong will defend the area if their interests are there. In 2011, the world's largest oil companies, Exxon Mobil and TOTAL, signed a multi-billion-dollar contract with the KRI. Barzani highlighted the role of such a contract in encouraging the US to protect the KRI, stating that "if Exxon Mobil came, it would be equal to 10 American military divisions."[18]

Beyond economic independence, the KRI oil policy was designed to attract external protection. Both the KRI and Turkish officials emphasise the role of oil in reshaping their relations. Nechirvan Barzani stated that, as a result of a "welcoming environment and a generous investment law, Turkey has become a major foreign partner and investor in the Kurdistan Region". He also explains that the KRI's ambition was to build "strategic relationship between Turkey and the

Kurdistan Region".[19] Turkish Minister of Energy Affairs Yeldiz shares this view of KRI officials and, representing Turkey in an energy conference in Erbil, the minister emphasised that Turkey should also be considered as the KRI's gateway to the West. Yeldiz affirmed that

> Turkey's future energy requirement was 48–50 billion cubic metres of gas. [. . .] With the Kurdistan Regional Government and the Iraqi government, we will develop such projects and we will stand by them when they face problems.[20]

Thus, for an energy-hungry Turkey, there was no more relating to the UKQ-III as a pan-Kurdish nationalistic threat to Turkey's integrity. Instead, Turkey was ready to become the KRI's lifeline and positive patron in return for the KRI's oil supply. Similarly, for financial- and diplomatic-hungry Kurdistan, Turkey was no more the 'occupier of a part of greater Kurdistan'. Rather, as the KRG Minister of Natural Resources Hawrami said, Turkey means for the KRI the access route to monetise oil and gas.[21] Accordingly, the KRI was willing to abandon its pan-Kurdish sentiment and supply Turkey with oil and gas in return for protection, financial gains, and diplomatic gains. Turkey was willing to abandon its acrimony towards the KRI and offer its protection to the region in return for satisfaction of its energy requirements.

The KRI hydrocarbon law reflects its policy of oil for outside protection and political achievement. The law awards Production Sharing Contracts (PSCs) instead of technical service contracts as in the case of Iraq and other oil-producing countries. Article 24 of the Oil and Gas Law of the Kurdistan Region stipulates that a Petroleum Contract may be based on a Production Sharing Contract. Article 37 explains that under the PSC model an IOC recovers the costs of exploration and production from the percentages of oil produced and sold in given fields. Thus, the KRI hydrocarbon law was designed to assure the long-term presence and involvement of IOCs in the oil sector in Kurdistan. This was expected to encourage contractee countries to protect the interests of their nationals' companies and accordingly the UKQ-III.

The KRI goal: from periphery to emerging regional oil power

With its huge oil reserve, the UKQ-III ambition was to emerge as a regional oil power. The KRI's minister of natural resources, Ashti Hawrami, announced that the Kurdistan region keeps on hand 45 billion barrels of proven oil reserves.[22] The KRI ambitiously seeks to boost its oil production to two million bpd by 2019. This could bring KRI oil production up to the world's 16th largest oil exporter in the world, on par with Algeria and Angola.[23] This could also mean that in the future an independent Kurdistan could be in the world's ten richest countries in terms of oil reserves. It was also estimated that the region's reserves are at about 100–200 trillion standard cubic feet of natural gas.[24] The KRI's gas reserves surpass some of the leading piped-gas suppliers to the EU, including Norway, Libya, Azerbaijan, the Netherlands, and the UK. This huge oil and gas reserve makes the KRI confident enough to behave like a developed state rather a federal region within a sovereign state. Prime Minister Nechirvan Barzani insists that as a result of this KRI carbohydrate policy the region has been able "to put its fingerprint on the global energy map, and there was no doubt that Kurdistan will have an important role in providing energy to the world".[25] Hence, oil wealth has helped the Kurdistan region catch up with the rest of the world in some respects. Due to its unexplored oil reserves, within a few years the Kurdistan region will move from being one of the most marginalised regions in the world to the heart of the international economy.

In post-invasion Iraq, the Kurdistan region attempted to change its image from a war-devastated marginalised region to a savvy, investment-friendly 'second Dubai'. Based on the Dubai model, the KRI plans to expand the scope of its economy by shifting from a purely oil-based economy to tourism and services. To achieve such a goal, the KRI has adopted a set of policies designed to attract foreign investment. First, instead of being a centre of pan-Kurdism in the region, the KRI has attempted to transform itself into a centre for attracting foreign direct investment. Barham Salih, former prime minister of the KRI, explains what was involved in the multi-billion-dollar investment projects and lucrative commercial activities with neighbouring states.[26] Second, to achieve its dream to be the region's 'second Dubai', the KRI passed a liberal and competitive investment law in 2006 destined to attract foreign investment. Article 3 of the Law of Investment in Kurdistan Region-Iraq promulgates that foreign investors and foreign capital are "dealt with on equal footing with national investors and capital. The foreign investor has the right to own the entire capital of any project that he establishes in the Region under this law."[27] This strategy has already proven successful to some extent. In 2010, for example, foreign firms have invested more than 18 billion USD in various projects. Of this amount 29 per cent has been invested in the industrial sector.[28] The KRI has also attracted 1,200 foreign firms into the Kurdistan region.[29] Being open to the outside world has attracted 400,000 foreign workers to the Kurdistan region. By October 2014, some 3,000 foreign companies "registered to operate in the Kurdistan Region, including: 1329 Turkish companies, 335 Iranian companies, 157 Lebanese companies, 155 Emirati companies, 125 British companies, 117 American companies and 81 German companies".[30] The success of the KRI policy was that during post-invasion Iraq the KRI had increasingly been looking outward towards the regional countries rather than inward to Baghdad.

Up until the KRI independence referendum on 25 September 2017, the KRI's policy of heading towards integration into the world economy seemed to be successful. This was evident in the regional, and to some extent the international, community's willingness to accept the KRI as an emerging member and partner in the regional and world markets. Turkey, a state that has traditionally opposed any Kurdish entities, has become a vital trade partner with the KRI. In fact, the Turks dominate the Kurdish market. In 2014, for example, 1,329 of 3,000 firms

(44 per cent) investing in Kurdistan are Turkish.[31] Turkey was also the major exporter of consumer and luxury goods in the region. The result was that the KRI has become among the top ten trading partners of Turkey. Some reports show that the KRI market was the second largest for Turkish exports.[32] In 2009 alone, the trading volume between the two entities was around 5–6 billion USD.[33] In 2012, the KRI accounted for 70 per cent of the $11 billion dollars of Turkish trade with Iraq.[34] These significant Turkish economic interests in the Kurdistan region have had significant political implications. Turkish business interest in Iraqi Kurdistan was believed to be a key reason that Ankara did not escalate its incursion into the Kurdistan region in 2007. As a gesture of recognition of the KRI, Turkey opened a consulate in the Kurdistan region. Turkish officials, including the Turkish prime minister and foreign ministers, have officially visited the region, and vice versa.

A similar figure was true for KRI trade relations with Iran. In 2011, the amount of trade between Iran and the KRI was estimated at approximately $5 billion. Similar to KRI-Turkey trade, the size of KRI-Iran trade exceeds the quantity of Iran-Iraq trade. The KRI represents 65–70 per cent of total Iranian trade to Iraq.[35] The volume of trade between the two countries was more than $10 billion, out of which 70 per cent was with the KRI. Moreover, there were 355 active Iranian companies in the Kurdistan region.[36] The Kurdistan region has made a remarkable recovery from the chronic state of being on the periphery of regional and international relations and involvement to being at the very centre of regional economics and politics. In sum, the KRI during post-invasion Iraq had as its goal to depart from its historic pattern of attracting negative patronage (mostly since the 1960s). As a result, it was making progress in its attempt to secure positive external patrons. To achieve this goal, the UKQ-III aims to secure diplomatic relations and security in return for trade and oil. There are signs that some countries, including Turkey, are willing to provide a more positive patronage and supportive relationship to the UKQ-III.

The failure of the financial independence policy?

By 2015, the dispute between Baghdad and Erbil took another form. The two sides failed to reach an agreement on ways to export Kurdistan's oil to foreign markets and how to include it in the Iraqi federal budget. Baghdad asked the region to export 400,000 barrels per day through the Iraqi State Oil Marketing Organization (SOMO) and the KRG offered to export 100,000 barrels per day. Baghdad warned that, if Erbil rejected its offer, it would cut the equivalent amount from the region's share in the general budget.[37] Erbil, however, chose to sell its oil independently, and in mid-2015 the KRG started to export its oil to global markets.[38] Baghdad, however, suspended its financial allocations to the KRG.

From 2014 onward, oil prices continued to decrease and by 2017 reached half price compared to the value in 2014 (from over $100 in the spring of 2014 to around $50 in October 2017).[39] The fall of oil prices and the cut of the Iraqi budget, combined with the cost of the fight with ISIS and widespread corruption, resulted in the depletion of the KRG budget. By December 2016, KRG had a monthly operational deficit of over $460 million.[40] The KRG was compelled to follow the policy of spending reductions in its budget. Public sector employees have seen their salaries plunge by three-quarters. These harsh circumstances resulted in the economic crises and rise of poverty, as well as further increased the political stalemate and public discontentment. Opposition parties in KRI linked the KRG failure of the salary payment to the widespread corruption in the oil sector. Oil sales were the main source of income in KRI. Until 25 September 2017, the KRI had exported more than half a million barrels of oil per day. Despite this relatively huge oil sale, the KRG failed to pay public sectors' salaries regularly.

The KRI's decision to produce and export its oil independently without a prior agreement with Baghdad had a profound effect on the KRI's economic and political situation. Oil revenues have facilitated economic independence and therefore decreasing dependence on Baghdad. The KRI, however, faced many challenges due to KRI economic independence policy. The first challenge that KRI faced was the issue of the legality of its oil exports. This has resulted in continuous uncertainty that deters major international companies from investing further in the region. Since 2015, the only major international company that signed a contract with the KRG was the Russian company Rosneft. In February 2017, Rosneft and KRI signed a contract on purchase and sale of crude oil in 2017 to 2019. In June 2017, the two sides signed a series of agreements on widening their cooperation. The June agreements provided for further phased investments of Rosneft in the Kurdistan region.[41] The Rosneft-KRG agreement, however, may be considered as an indication of other Western companies' disappointment with their investments in KRI. Another negative affect of disagreement with Baghdad was that the KRI had to sell its oil at a lower price than the market. The KRG had to give a discount to potential customers to compensate for the legal risks they take on themselves. Thus, selling its oil at a cheaper price in an era in which oil value was the lowest in many years had a profound effect on deepening the KRI's financial crises.

Moreover, because of the unresolved legal dispute between Erbil and Baghdad over who has the rights to export the oil, many countries avoided buying the KRI oil. Thus, the KRI faced another challenge not only in terms of finding a reliable market but also in terms of finding new patron states. As discussed previously, one of the main goals of Kurdish oil policies was to use its oil as a bargaining chip for political support and even physical protection. Failing to find an alternative market, the KRI mostly relied on Israel. Israel became the top buyer of the KRI crude oil and some half of the region's oil was sold to this country in 2017.[42] The KRI oil trade with Israel is a good example to explain how this natural resource reshapes international relations and how it affects the patron-client equation. On one hand, with the exception of Israel, most regional and international communities opposed the KRI referendum. Israel publicly endorsed statehood for the Kurds. In a public statement, released on 12 September 2017, Benjamin Netanyahu, Israeli prime minister, said Israel "supports the legitimate efforts of the Kurdish people to attain a state of its own".[43] On 16 October 2017, some three weeks after the independence referendum, the Iraqi army recaptured Kirkuk and marched towards Erbil.

Israeli officials said Netanyahu was lobbying world powers to prevent further setbacks to KRI.[44]

On the other hand, getting a market for their oil and support for their referendum put the Kurds at odd with the regional states. For example Hasan Nasrullah, the leader of Lebanese Hizbullah, described the referendum as "part of a U.S.-Israeli plot to carve up the region".[45] Similarly Erdoghan, the president of Turkey, accused Israel of backing the Kurds' independence referendum and said "there is no country other than Israel that recognizes [the referendum]."[46] Khamenei, the supreme leader of Iran, is another who shared Nasrullah's and Erdoghan's view on the Kurdish referendum. He said that only "America and Israel benefit from the vote" and accused the two states of planning to create another Israel.[47]

Being geographically landlocked and surrounded by unfriendly neighbours, the KRI failed to diversify the possible outlets for its oil. Independence oil means the KRI's dependency on Turkey to export its oil. Relying on Turkey to export its oil increased the Turks' leverage on KRI significantly. Turkey was in a position to blackmail the KRI if Kurdish leaders opposed the Turkish policies in Iraq and the region. The Turkish policy, however, was built on the basis of the denial of a Kurdish independent state. When Kurds moved towards the independence referendum on 25 September 2017, Turkey raised this card against the Kurds. For example, after the Kurds voted for independence, Erdoghan, the Turkish president, threatened to turn off the taps of the oil pipeline that carries Kurdish crude through Turkish territory to Mediterranean coasts. "We have the [KRI oil] tap [. . .] It will be over when we close the oil taps, all revenues will vanish, and they will not be able to find food when our trucks stop going to northern Iraq."[48] He also threatened the establishment of a regional coalition to prevent the export of KRI oil.[49]

Notes

1 Kwrdistani Nwe (2010). "Herem 90% Khorak le Derewe Dehenet" (The Region imports 90% of its food from outside), available at <www.knwe.org/Direje.aspx?Jimare=3287&Cor=11&Besh=Araste>, (accessed 01/02/2011).
2 Barzani, M. (2008), "Kurdistan Is a Model for Iraq: Our Path to a Secular, Federal Democracy is Inspired by the U.S.," *The Wall Street Journal*, available at <http://online.wsj.com/article/SB122645258001119425.html>, (accessed 02/11/2013).
3 KRP, Kurdistan Regional Presidency (2007), "Oil and Gas Law of the Kurdistan Region, Law No. (22) – 2007," available at <www.krg.org/uploads/documents/Kurdistan%20Oil%20and%20Gas%20Law%20English__2007_09_06_h14m0s42.pdf>, (accessed 09/08/2013).
4 *Ibid.*
5 KRG, Kurdistan Regional Government (2012a) "KRG Ministry of Natural Resources Production Sharing Contracts," available at <http://krg.org/pages/page.asp?lngnr=12&rnr=296&PageNr=1>, (accessed 29/07/2012); KRG, Kurdistan Regional Government (2012b), "Prime Minister Barzani: Kurdistan's energy relations with Turkey to enter a new phase," available at <www.krg.org/articles/detail.asp?rnr=223&lngnr=12&smap=02010100&anr=44020>, (accessed 27/11/2012).
6 "Wazir Altharawat Altabyeit: Tahdidat Baghdad Lilsharikat Alnaftiat Tusi' Lisumeat Aleiraq Fi Alkharij (Minister of Natural Resources: Baghdad's Threats to Oil

Companies Harm Iraq's Reputation Abroad), Kurdistan Regional Government," 07–02–2013, available at <http://cabinet.gov.krd/a/d.aspx?l=14&a=46560>, (accessed 21/03/2015).
7 The Kurdish Globe (2012b), "Hawrami Announces KRG Oil and Gas Strategy," available at <www.kurdishglobe.net/display-article.html?id=1542DF665716C1D274B73E 32DEFE562D>, (accessed 29/09/2012).
8 KRG, Kurdistan Regional Government (2012b), "Prime Minister Barzani: Kurdistan's Energy Relations with Turkey to Enter a New Phase," available at <www.krg.org/articles/detail.asp?rnr=223&lngnr=12&smap=02010100&anr=44020>, (accessed 27/11/2012).
9 Ibid.
10 KRG, Kurdistan Regional Government (2014), "KRG Statement on First Oil Sales through Pipeline Export," 23/05/2014, available at <http://cabinet.gov.krd/a/d.aspx?l=12&a=51589>, (accessed 19/06/2016).
11 Hukumati Haremi Kurdistan Drezha be Hanardekrdni Rastawxoy Nawt Dadat bo Qarabu Krdnaway Kwrthenani Budja (The Kurdistan Regional Government Continue in Exporting its Oil Directly to Compensate the Budget Deficit)," Kurdistan Regional Government, 15/09/2015, available at <http://cabinet.gov.krd/a/d.aspx?s=010000&l=13&a=53677>, (accessed 13/11/2016).
12 "Prime Minister Barzani Discusses Russian Rosneft Agreement," Kurdistan Regional Government, 07/06/2017, available at <http://cabinet.gov.krd/a/d.aspx?s=010000&l=12&a=55681>, (accessed 08/09/2017).
13 Tiron, R. and K. Klimasinska (2012). "No Contract Freeze for 'Committed' Exxon, Kurdish Minister Says," available at <www.bloomberg.com/news/2012-04-02/no-contract-freeze-for-committed-exxon-kurdish-minister-says.html>, (accessed 06/04/2012).
14 ICG, International Crisis Group (2012), "Iraq and the Kurds: The High-Stakes Hydrocarbons Gambit," available at <www.crisisgroup.org/~/media/Files/Middle%20 East%20North%20Africa/Iraq%20Syria%20Lebanon/Iraq/120-iraq-and-the-kurds-the-high-stakes-hydrocarbons-gambit.pdf>, (accessed 12/11/2012).
15 "Ministry of Natural Resources announces producing IOCs payment plan," Kurdistan Regional Government, 04/08/2015, available at <http://cabinet.gov.krd/a/d.aspx?s=040000&l=12&a=53610>, (accessed 09/11/2017).
16 Gunter, M. M. (2011), "Economic Opportunities in Iraqi Kurdistan," *Middle East Policy* 18(2): 102–109: 103.
17 KRG, Kurdistan Regional Government(2012d), "Prime Minister Barzani's Speech at the Erbil Energy Conference," available at <www.krg.org/articles/detail.asp?smap=02 040100&lngnr=12&rnr=268&anr=44037>, (accessed 23/06/2012).
18 Gulf Time (2012), "Iraq Premier Must Not Get F-16s: Kurd President," available at <www.gulf-times.com/site/topics/article.asp?cu_no=2&item_no=501290&version=1 &template_id=37&parent_id=17>, (accessed 25/04/2012).
19 KRG, Kurdistan Regional Government (2012d), "Prime Minister Barzani's Speech at the Erbil Energy Conference," available at <www.krg.org/articles/detail.asp?smap=02 040100&lngnr=12&rnr=268&anr=44037>, (accessed 23/06/2014).
20 KRG 2012b.
21 Ibid.
22 The Kurdish Globe 2012b; Rudaw 06/01/2011.
23 For a list of world's largest oil exporters, see EIA, U.S. Energy Information Administration, (2011), "Top World Oil Producers 2011," available at <http://205.254.135.7/countries/>, (accessed 05/04/2012).
24 Gunter 2011: 103.
25 KRG, Kurdistan Regional Government (2012d), "Prime Minister Barzani's Speech at the Erbil Energy Conference," available at <www.krg.org/articles/detail.asp?smap=02 040100&lngnr=12&rnr=268&anr=44037>, (accessed 03/09/2014).

Oil for external patronage 195

26 Salih, B. (2012), "PUKmedia," available at <www.pukmedia.com/ansat/lmk.pdf>, (accessed 05/04/2012).
27 KRG, Kurdistan Regional Government, (2006), "Law no. (4) of 2006: Law of Investment in Kurdistan Region – Iraq," available at <www.krg.org/uploads/documents/InvestmentLaw_KRGOfficialEng__2006_08_04_h11m20s33.pdf>, (accessed 03/09/2009).
28 Salih 2012.
29 "Le koy ew 1200 Kompaniyay le Kurdistan Kar Deken, 720 yan hi Turkyaye" (Of a Total 1200 Companies Working in Kurdistan 720 are Turkish), *Gulan newspaper*, 22/12/2012.
30 "Foreign Companies Resume Regular Activity in Kurdistan," Kurdistan Regional Government, 02/10/2017, available at <http://cabinet.gov.krd/a/d.aspx?s=010000&l=12&a=52312>, (accessed 01/07/2017).
31 *Ibid*.
32 Ergin, E. (2012). "Iraqi Kurds to Sell Gas Directly to Turkey – Minister," *Reuters*, available at <www.reuters.com/article/2012/07/03/us-turkey-iraq-kurds-gas-idUSBRE8620PR20120703>, (accessed 05/07/2012).
33 Khabat Newspaper, "The Mouthpeace of the Kurdistan Democratic Party," 07/04/2009.
34 KRG 2012b.
35 Zawya (2011), "Iran-KRG Trade to Hit $5b, Zawya," available at <www.zawya.com/story/ZAWYA20110907050008>, (accessed 03/01/2012); The Kurdish Globe 2012b.
36 The Kurdish Globe (2012c), "Iran's Consul in Erbil Describes Trade Relations as Extensive," available at <www.kurdishglobe.net/display-article.html?id=1151D9DFDB21981DCFBEB32B0C6C1831, (accessed 16/05/2012).
37 *Al-Moinitor*, 16/05/2014, Iraqi Kurdistan economy suffers amid budget dispute with Baghdad, available at <www.al-monitor.com/pulse/tr/business/2014/05/iraq-kurdistan-region-budget-dispute-economic-effects.html>, (accessed 05/10/2017).
38 42= "Why Iraqi Kurdistan Is Struggling to Pay Its Bills," *Stratfor Worldview*, 28/01/2016, available at <www.stratfor.com/analysis/why-iraqi-kurdistan-struggling-pay-its-bills>, (accessed 19/12/2016).
39 Daniel R. DePetris (2017), "Did Iraq's Kurds Lose Their Big Bet on Independence?" available at <https://qz.com/1092028/did-iraqs-kurds-lose-their-big-bet-on-independence/>
40 "Deputy Prime Minister: Kurdistan will become independent one day," Kurdistan Regional Government, 12/12/2017, available at <http://cabinet.gov.krd/a/d.aspx?s=010000&l=12&a=55206>, (accessed 18/01/2017).
41 "Rosneft and Iraqi Kurdistan Government Agree to Expand Strategic Cooperation", *Rosneft*, 02/06/2017, available at <www.rosneft.com/press/releases/item/186811/>, (accessed 04/11/2017).
42 "Israel and Iraqi Kurdistan: The Oil Connection," *i24News*, available at <www.i24news.tv/en/news/international/middle-east/157303-171009-israel-and-iraqi-kurdistan-the-oil-connection>, (accessed 24/10/2017).
43 For the full text of Netanyahu's statement see: "Israeli prime minister backs Kurdish independence in Iraq," *The National*, 13/09/2017, available at <www.thenational.ae/world/mena/israeli-prime-minister-backs-kurdish-independence-in-iraq-1.628057>
44 "Netanyahu lobbies world powers to stem Iraqi Kurd setbacks," *Reuters*, 20/10/2017, available at <www.reuters.com/article/us-mideast-crisis-kurds-israel/netanyahu-lobbies-world-powers-to-stem-iraqi-kurd-setbacks-idUSKBN1CP181>, (accessed 29/10/2017).
45 "Hezbollah says Kurdish vote a step toward wider Mideast partition," *Reuters*, 01/10/2017, available at <www.reuters.com/article/us-mideast-crisis-kurds-referendum-hezbollah/hezbollah-says-kurdish-vote-a-step-toward-wider-mideast-partition-idUSKCN1C50RK>, (accessed 02/10/2017).
46 "Erdogan in Iran Again Claims that the Mossad Is in Cahoots with Separatist Kurds," *i24News*, available at <www.i24news.tv/en/news/international/156911-171004-erdogan-visits-iran-as-ties-warm-amid-shared-fears>, (accessed 16/10/2017).

47 "Khamenei Says Iran, Turkey Must Act Against Kurdish Secession: TV," *Reuters*, 05/10/2017, available at <www.reuters.com/article/us-mideast-crisis-iran-turkey/khamenei-says-iran-turkey-must-act-against-kurdish-secession-tv-idUSKBN1C91YW>, (accessed 10/10/2017).
48 Cited in "Kurds Voted: So Is the Middle East Breaking Up?" *New Yorker*, 2709–2017, available at <www.newyorker.com/news/news-desk/kurds-voted-so-is-the-middle-east-breaking-up>, (accessed 22/10/2017).
49 "Turkey to Close Borders, Air Space to KRG: Erdoğan," *Hurriyet Daily News*, 05/10/2017, available at < www.hurriyetdailynews.com/turkey-iran-iraq-to-jointly-decide-on-closing-flow-of-n-iraq-oil-erdogan-120394>, (accessed 07/10/2017).

12 Independence referendum and the case of negative patronage

On Monday, 25 September 2017, the people of the Kurdistan Region of Iraq (KRI) headed to poll stations to cast their votes and decide whether to remain a part of Iraq or establish an independent state. Voters had to answer the question as to whether or not they wanted the Kurdistan region and Kurdistani areas outside the administration of the region to become an independent country. The question was asked in the four languages used in the KRI: Kurdish, Arabic, Turkish, and Assyrian. Voters had to tick 'yes' or 'no'. Some 4,581,255 people were eligible to vote in the referendum and the turnout was high. More than 3.3 million people or 72.16 per cent of voters took part in the ballot. The result showed that Kurds are overwhelmingly in favour of independence. The 'yes' vote won the majority of votes with 92.73 per cent whereas the 'no' vote gained only 7.27 per cent.[1]

The September referendum was the second Kurdish attempt of this kind since the American occupation of Iraq in 2003. The first independence referendum was held on 30 January 2005. The 2005 referendum was informal and conducted by an NGO, the Referendum Movement in Kurdistan (RMK), with about 98 per cent of the two million eligible voters expressing their support for independence. The 2005 referendum, however, was unofficial and was not officially supported by the KRG or Kurdish political parties. In this period, there was a clear difference between the official policies of Kurdish parties and what the Kurdish people really wanted. While Kurdish public opinion was in favour of secession from Iraq, the trend of Kurdish major political parties at that time was to have a federal arrangement with Iraq. Though the KRG and Kurdish leaders did not officially support the 2005 referendum, it captured the imagination of Kurds who longed to have their own state.

Contrary to the 2005 referendum, in 2017 both the KRG officials and Kurdish public opinion were overwhelmingly in favour of secession from Iraq. The September referendum was arranged officially by the KRG and supported by the main Kurdish political parties. The referendum campaign was spearheaded by Masud Barzani, then the *de facto* president of KRI. On 7 June 2017, Barzani held a meeting with Kurdish political parties and confirmed that an independence referendum would be held on 25 September 2017. The meeting also decided on mechanisms and plans to conduct the referendum and negotiate with other Kurdish, Iraqi, and international players. Moreover, the referendum was ratified by the Kurdistan regional Parliament in a session attended by only 65 of its 111 members. However, the referendum was unilateral, as Baghdad did not agree on it. Nevertheless, despite strong opposition from Iraq, neighbouring countries, the US, and international communities, Barzani decided to go ahead with the project.

Internal challenges

Barzani's decision to go ahead with the referendum was also challenged internally. Up until a few days before the referendum, the opposition parties openly expressed their disapproval of the referendum. Internal challenges are evident in that only 65 of its 111 members attended the Parliament session that was held to endorse the independence referendum decision. Two main opposition parties did not attend the session: the Gorran Movement (which held 24 seats in the KRI Parliament) and the Islamic Group (six seats). The disapproval of these two parties, however, did not stem from their belief that Iraqi Kurdistan should stay within Iraq, but rather came from their disagreement with Barzani over KRI internal politics and the governance system. From 2014 onward, the KRI had fallen into deep political and economic crises. Barzani's term should have ended in 2013 and conflict between the two sides began when Barzani's tenure was extended beyond his second term. Barzani rejected the opposition's demand for his resignation following two terms of service as the KRI president and they called for an amendment to the KRI system from a semi-presidency to a parliamentary system.

The dispute over Barzani's presidency reached another level when he again refused to step down in August 2015. He remained in his position as *de facto* president, despite the rejection of this by the main opposition parties. His term was extended for another two years based on a decision by the Kurdistan Consultative Council on 17 August 2016. The Consultative Council as a government body was similar to the High Court in Iraq and other countries. The Council decided that the incumbent, Barzani, could stay in office for a further two years. However, the opposition parties rejected the legitimacy of the Council's decision and called for Barzani to step down. By rejecting Barzani's presidency, they also rejected the legitimacy of his decisions, including the independence referendum. In their official statement, the opposition parties insisted that the referendum for independence would lack legitimacy unless it was confirmed by a decision of the Parliament. They also charged that Barzani would use the referendum to bolster his own legitimacy as president. In October 2015, the speaker of Parliament was barred from entering Erbil and four ministers were removed from the Cabinet.[2] The speaker and ministers were all members of the Gorran Movement, and their barring meant that the Parliament had not convened for almost two years, resulting in a dysfunctional KRI parliament. The Parliament was only opened few days before 25 September 2017 to legitimate the referendum process. Thus, the opposition's disapproval arose within this context of internal political disputes.

Though opposition parties voiced their disagreement with the referendum, they did not hide their aspiration for independence. Initially, they stated that their support for the referendum would be conditional on economic and political reforms, the unconditional activation of the Parliament, and the amendment of the residential law.[3] Although none of their demands were met, on the eve of the referendum, Gorran gave its members a free choice as to whether they wanted to vote for or against independence. On the polling day, Omer Said Ali, the leader of Gorran, stated that he had voted 'yes' as a gesture and guidance for his party's members voting in the referendum. The Islamic Group took a more directly supportive stand and asked its supporters to vote 'yes'. Thus, none of the main political parties adopted a 'no' vote position, despite their dispute with the KRI authority. This does not mean that there were no advocates of 'no'. Opponents of the referendum organised themselves and established a 'No for Now' movement. The movement, however, stayed unpopular, despite its ability to dedicate several television channels for its campaign against the referendum. The unpopularity of the 'No' movement was evident in that none of the well-known Kurdish politicians nor any Kurdish parties joined the movement. In their bid for 'no', organisers of the 'No for Now' movement did not advocate the unity and the integrity of Iraq, nor did they reject the establishment of a Kurdish state. Similar to the opposition parties, their discourse was built on issues such as the poor timing of this referendum, the corruption of KRG officials, and the possibility of dragging the region into a war.[4] The 'No for Now' movement managed to collect only 7.3 per cent for 'no' voting.

Factors behind the Kurds' move towards an independence referendum

The year 2014 can be considered as a turning point in Iraqi-KRI relations that pushed the region towards an independence referendum. In his resignation address on 29 October 2017, Barzani explained that KRI preparations for holding a referendum had begun in July 2014, when he had paid a visit to the Kurdistan Parliament and asked to discuss a resolution to establish a commission for a referendum. On 20 July 2014, the Parliament ratified the resolution for the establishment of an Independent High Elections and Referendum Commission. The referendum, according to Barzani, was postponed because of the rise of ISIS and the KRI fighting against the organisation. In June 2014, Barzani told the BBC he intended to hold a referendum on independence within months.[5] In addition to the long Kurdish aspiration for independence, there are several main factors that had encouraged the KRI, since 2014, to move towards holding an independence referendum.

The failure of consensus in Iraq

The first factor behind the KRI move towards independence was their belief that principles of consensus that the post-2003 Iraq was built on had failed. In terms of the economy, for example, Baghdad and Erbil had agreed on the allocation of 17 per cent of Iraq's budget to KRI, but by 2014 Iraq cut this budget. The previous chapter explained in detail the KRI's attempt to achieve economic independence from Baghdad through the direct sale of oil. However, a dispute over the Kurdish attempt to sell its oil independently resulted in Baghdad's decision to cut the KRI budget. Until 2014, some 17 per cent of Iraq's total budget had been allocated to the KRI. Baghdad's funding cuts sparked a salary crisis in the KRI and hit the Kurdish economy hard. The KRI needed over $700 million monthly to pay more than one million people who were on a government payroll. This funding cut encouraged the KRI to produce more oil and gas independent of the central government. The KRI accelerated its building of a pipeline to Turkey in defiance of Baghdad.[6]

By mid-2014, the KRI disclosed the negative consequences of the budget cut on its economy. For example, the trade rate had fallen by half, banks were bankrupt, there were delays in paying salaries, and there was cessation of projects.[7] In terms of the military, Kurds comprised less than 2 per cent of the Iraqi, much lower than the percentage of the Kurdish population in Iraq. Following the collapse of the Iraqi army in Sunni areas in 2014, all the Kurdish units in the Iraqi army joined the peshmerga forces. The authoritarian leadership of Nuri al-Maliki further alienated the Kurds and Kurdish officials in the Baghdad government, including the deputy prime minister and ministers, who complained frequently that their role in the government was merely symbolic since they were not allowed to participate in any decision-making processes. In his resignation address on 29 October 2017, Masud Barzani clearly highlighted the Kurdish move towards an independence referendum as a result of the failure of the Kurdish-Iraqi partnership policy. He stated that "after the liberation of Iraq in 2003 we did everything possible in pursuit of creating a federal, democratic and pluralistic Iraq [. . .] However, it became clear that the concept of true partnership with Iraq was simply not possible." Viewed in this way, according to Barzani, the Kurds decided "to become good neighbours since we failed to become true partners".[8]

The rise of the Islamic State in Iraq and Syria

The second factor that had encouraged the KRI to prepare for an independence referendum since 2014 was the rise of the Islamic State in Iraq and Syria (ISIS). In June 2014, the Iraqi army collapsed across almost the entire Sunni region of Iraq, including the two main cities of Mosul and Tikrit, as a result of unrelenting ISIS attacks. Following this victory over the Iraqi army, ISIS declared its caliphate in an area straddling Iraq and Syria and said its leader, Abu Bakr al-Baghdadi, was the caliph of Muslims everywhere. The rise of ISIS reframed KRI-Iraqi relations dramatically. It allowed the KRI to successfully consolidate its quasi-statehood status in many ways.

One way that ISIS helped the consolidation of the KRI was that the organisation did not only undermine Iraqi unity, but also the world order and Western interests. ISIS called itself a state rather than an organisation, with the goal of breaking other borders and ending the Sykes-Picot political division in the Middle East, in order to establish its caliphate. This was a direct and real threat to the interests of Western countries and, therefore, they showed their support to the Kurds who were, at least on the northern front, the only force on the ground that was ready to fight ISIS. In fact, having a frontline of more than 1000 kilometres with ISIS, the KRI became the main partner of the Global Coalition against the organisation. This critical role of the KRI armed forces helped the region to consolidate its international status and to emerge as an important ally to Western countries.

Another way that the ISIS situation helped improve the status of the KRI internationally was that ISIS was a non-state actor, as was the KRI. Considering ISIS as a non-state actor allowed Western countries to provide military assistance to KRI. This is because Western countries could claim that they were providing military assistance to KRI to fight non-state actors rather a state. During this period, many Western leaders paid visits to Erbil and emphasised their support for the KRI in fighting against ISIS. François Hollande, the president of France, for instance, paid an official visit to Erbil on 13 September 2014. During the visit, President Hollande emphasised his country's commitment to supporting the KRI in its war against the Islamic State (ISIS). Showing its commitment to protect the Kurds, France started shipping weapons to Erbil. Many other Western countries – including Germany, Italy, the US, the UK, and Canada – followed France in shipping weapons directly to the Kurds. In April 2016, Washington provided $415 million of aid to the KRI to feed and pay its peshmerga forces.[9] In July 2016, the US and the KRI concluded a military agreement. By fighting ISIS, the Kurds' ambition was not only to further strengthen its armed forces with the help of Western countries, but also to redraw the border of the Kurdistan region with Iraq. At this stage, the KRI was confident enough to think about an independence referendum.

The rise of ISIS also helped the strengthening of the KRI in that it resulted in the emergence a new border between the KRI and Iraq. Fighting against ISIS helped redraw the border between KRI and Iraq in favour of the Kurds. The collapse of the Iraqi army resulted in a security vacuum in the disputed areas and brought the peshmerga into direct fighting with ISIS. In its fight against the ISIS, the KRI not only barred the ISIS march towards the Kurdish region but also protected disputed areas from ISIS assault. Between June and August 2014, the peshmerga made important territorial gains and controlled most of the disputed territories, including Kirkuk. This almost doubled the size of the KRI and gave it access to an oil-rich region. The Kurds' victory against ISIS revived the Kurdish leaders' ambition for an independence referendum. This intention was clearly reflected in the KDP's General Congress held in December 2015. During this congress, Barzani asked his party to prepare for an independence referendum.[10]

KRI control over the disputed areas was considered, at least by the Kurds, as a *de facto* solution and an end to the KRI-Iraq border dispute. On 18 February 2015, Masud Barzani, visited peshmerga frontlines in the fight against ISIS in the province of Kirkuk. In a speech to peshmerga commandos, Barzani stated that "they [Iraqis] must know that either we will all die, or Kirkuk will never fall to the enemy ever again." Barzani emphasised that "today's reality has been achieved with precious blood and we will not tolerate any change to these borders."[11] The terms 'enemy' and 'border' used here are clear indications of the tense nature surrounding the Iraqi state and the new border line between Iraq and the Kurdistan region.

The border conflict between Baghdad and Erbil gives the impression of being more of a dispute between two rival neighbouring quasi-states than between two regions within one country. Kirkuk is an indispensable moral and historical symbol for the Kurds. It is also geopolitically and economically important for them, as well as being a key to fulfilling the Kurdish dream of an independent state. Disputed areas were one of the main issues that reshaped Kurdish relations with both Shias and Sunnis in post-invasion Iraq. In the post-invasion period, Kirkuk was essential to the Kurdish decision to return to Iraq, to help rebuild the Iraqi state, and to be involved in negotiations with the different competing groups. The Kurdish strategy was focused on incorporating Kirkuk into Kurdistan. However, the Shiites and Sunnis, for different reasons, were opposed to that claim. If retaining Kirkuk was one of the major justifications for continuing to remain within Iraq, this was not the case any longer because, since 2014, the Kurds have been the unchallenged *de facto* rulers of Kirkuk and other disputed areas.

One more ISIS-related factor that encouraged the Kurds to call for a referendum was that the organisation acted as a buffer zone between the KRI and the rest of Iraq for almost two years. The peshmerga were defending more than 1,000 kilometres along the frontline, from Sinjar on the Syrian border to Khanaqin on the Iranian border, but this time against ISIS not the Iraqi army. Almost all Sunni Arab territory controlled by ISIS separated the KRI from Iraqi controlled territory. The separation of the two sides, Iraq and the KRI, has further isolated the two sides and consolidated KRI independence. Moreover, the humiliated way in which the Iraqi army was defeated at the hands of ISIS militants demonstrated to the Kurds that Iraq no longer can challenge the Kurds' ambition. Kurds being more vocal in calling for independence following the rise of ISIS can be understood in this context. Thus, instead of wanting involvement in rebuilding the Iraqi state, now the Kurds look the other way.

The demise of the Iraqi national army and the rise of popular mobilisation

Another factor that encouraged the Kurds to call for a referendum was the demise of the Iraqi national army and the rise of Popular Mobilisation Units (*Hashd al-Shaabi*). Following the collapse of the Iraqi army in the face of ISIS, it was clear that the defeated Iraqi army was unable to protect Baghdad and the rest of Iraq. A euphoric ISIS revealed the organisation's plan to march towards Baghdad and the Shiite region. However, the Iraqi armed forces had either disintegrated or fled southward and were not in a position to defend Baghdad or the Shiite region. This alarmed the Shiite rulers and leaders of the religious establishment. Iraq's top Shiite cleric, Grand Ayatollah Ali al-Sistani, issued a fatwa on 13 June 2014 urging able-bodied Iraqis to take up arms against Sunni extremists. In response to the fatwa, tens of thousands of Shiite youths joined tens of Shiite militia groups that reorganised under the umbrella of *Hashd al-Shaabi* (from now on *Hashd*). In this way, *Hashd* became a state-sponsored umbrella organisation comprised of tens of militias largely outside of direct government control.

The creation of *Hashd* alarmed the Kurds for several reasons. First, *Hashd* was a Shiite paramilitary militia. The militia's loyalty was to the Shiites rather to all Iraqi ethno-religious groups or the state. The *Hashd* was also known for being dominated by warlords with close links to Iran. The establishment of the militia was not initiated by the Iraqi parliament or the Iraqi government or the defence ministry, but rather came from the Shiite religious leaders and came in the form of a fatwa. People who joined the organisation did so mostly because it was a religious duty. Though *Hashd* was recognised by the Iraqi parliament as a legal body, the Kurds neither had a say in the establishment of the organisation nor in its structure, policies, and ideologies. Moreover, many of the already established Shiite militias that joined *Hashd* did not hide their enmity towards the KRI. The Kurds' concern about the organisation did not come merely from the threats from many *Hashd* leaders. In fact, the Kurds' main concern came from *Hashd* looking like a state within the state. It acted as an alternative to the Iraqi armed forces and, in many cases, *Hashd* was better equipped than the army and had a more central role in the provision of security.

By the end of 2016 and early 2017, *Hashd*, supported by the Iraqi armed forces, successfully regained most of the Sunni areas from ISIS. This affected the Kurdish decision to go ahead with a referendum in two ways. First, the KRI armed forces were no longer on the frontlines, and this alarmed Kurds that they may not remain their key US ally. Therefore, if they did not take this opportunity to establish their own state now, they may have had to postpone this dream for many years. Therefore, the decline of ISIS and the key role of *Hashd* in fighting the organisation further pushed Kurds towards the independence referendum. Second, the Kurds found themselves on the frontlines with another militia, this time *Hashd*. By 25 September 2017, the referendum day, the ISIS buffer zone had been reduced to the Hawija district. The rise of a state-sponsored paramilitary such as *Hashd* has worried many Kurds. This was not only because *Hashd*, as a militia, was less controlled by the state, but also because the Kurds have a negative memory in terms of dealing with state-sponsored militias. State-sponsored paramilitary organisations, such as *al-Haras al-Qawmi* (National Guards) in the 1960s and the *al-Jaysh al-Sha"abi* (the Popular Army) in the 1980s played a crucial role in the mass killings of the Kurds, displacing them and destroying Kurdish villages.

Moreover, being a Shiite paramilitary, many non-nationalist Islamist Kurds adopted a more nationalist discourse compared to their previous stance towards Kurdish nationalism. They changed the balance of power in favour of Barzani the leader of the referendum movement. The Islamic Union of Kurdistan, with its ten out of 111 seats in the Kurdistan Parliament, became a king-maker in the process of referendum. The parliament convened for the first time in two years on 15 September 2017. Without the help of the Islamic Union, the session could not have been held, as the two other opposition parties (Gorran and Komall) refused to attend the session. The session was held to provide parliamentary legitimacy for the referendum process. Komall, who refused to join the Parliament, adopted a more nationalistic stance than the Gorran Movement towards the referendum vote of 25 September. While Gorran gave its members freedom of choice whether or not to participate in the referendum and to vote 'yes' or 'no', the Islamic Group asked its members to participate and to vote 'yes'.

Negative patronage as the KRI's Achilles' heel

On the eve of the referendum day, Barzani emphasised that "the partnership with Baghdad has failed and we will not return to it," and "we will never go back to the failed partnership [with Baghdad]."[12] However, Iraq started its military operation on 16 October 2017; the peshmerga withdrew from Kirkuk and other districts and the US did not oppose the Iraqi military's intervention. Iraq retook Kirkuk in the space of a few hours without significant resistance from the KRI's armed forces. By 20 October 2017, Iraqi militias and army controlled the last Kurdish-held area, Kirkuk province. On 24 October 2017, after losing control over all disputed areas, the KRI officially froze the results of the referendum. This freeze, according to a statement by the KRI, was implemented to avoid "grave and dangerous circumstances" that "Iraq and Kurdistan are faced with". KRI officials also called for an "immediate ceasefire and halt of all military operations in the Kurdistan Region" and to "start an open dialogue between the Kurdistan Regional Government and Iraqi Federal Government on the basis of the Constitution".[13] There are several main questions that require answers, including why instead of consolidating the legitimacy of the KRI's status and boosting the KRI's bargaining power, the referendum backfired spectacularly, and why, instead of paving the way to statehood, the referendum has triggered a humiliating reversal of fortunes for the KRI. The case of negative patronage can help answer these questions.

Understanding the role of the US in the failure of the 25 September referendum shows that negative patronages were the Kurds' Achilles' heel. It helps to understand the importance of external patronage in the rise and demise of quasi-states, including the KRI. As laid out in Chapter 2, external patronage is positive if supporting and consolidating the territorial rights of the client region become the patron state's main priorities. In this case, the patron state does not see independence of its client state as being against its national interests. Therefore, the patron state supports and often recognises the independence of its client state. External patronage, however, is negative if it fulfils three negative patronage criteria (NPC): (1) the populations of the patron and client states do not share the same ethnic or cultural identity (NPC-I); (2) the patron state is not motivated by the interests, rights, and/or identity of the client state (NPC-II); and (3) the patron state does not seek the client's independence and is not willing to recognise the independent state (NPC-III).

The US as the KRI's main and longstanding external patron fulfils all of the previously defined three criteria. First, the US-Kurdish policy was not based on a common ethnic or cultural identity; neither was it based on ideological grounds or sympathy with the Kurdish issue. Therefore, the US patronage meets NPC-I. Second, a major Kurdish priority in post-invasion Iraq has been to secure and consolidate its quasi-state status. In contrast, US policy puts the emphasis on ensuring Iraq's sovereignty and on having a strong central government. The US also prioritised fighting against ISIS, maintaining Iraq's integrity and reducing the Iranian influence in Iraq, rather than facilitating Kurdish independence. Almost all US statements during and after the referendum process emphasised that Americas' priorities were fighting against ISIS and the integrity of Iraq.[14] The rejection of the KRI independence referendum came within the two US priorities outlined earlier. Therefore, the US patronage meets both NPC-II and NPC-III.

According to Masud Barzani, the KRI by acting as the main partner in fighting ISIS did not take advantage of Iraq's weakness against the organisation at the start of the war. Instead, it "prioritized the war on the terrorists". Prioritising the war on ISIS, in fact, was to guarantee the US' patronage and its protection in the future. Historically, the Kurds have not fought outside Kurdish areas. However, they have supported the US-led coalition in its fight in Sunni areas. The Kurdish decision to postpone the referendum until the defeat of ISIS was at the request of the US.[15] According to Masud Barzani, the Kurdish leadership thought that in return for the KRI decision to postpone the referendum and to prioritise fighting against ISIS, the US may respect the will of Kurdish people. Barzani further explains that KRI was "hoping that such action will be remembered [. . . and the KRI's] brave struggle would have been appreciated by the international community".[16] Based on Barzani's statements, one can understand that he viewed the US patronage as positive. In fact, the Kurds' calculation was not baseless. The KRI armed forces have formed a critical part of the US fight against the Islamic State and have become US allies. Cooperation between the KRI and the US has for years provided advantages for US interests in Iraq. Until the liberation of Mosul province, the Nineveh Operations Command was in Makhmour, in the Kurdistan Region of Iraq. This 'partnership' gave the Kurds the impression that the US would protect them if Iraq or neighbouring countries attacked the KRI. Hence, Barzani's criticism of the US and the international community for abandoning the Kurds comes within this context. KRI leaders believed that, even if the US did not recognise their state, it would not allow Iraq and neighbouring countries to launch a military attack on Kurdistan. Barzani and other KRI leaders, therefore, were shocked when they realised that the US chose to remain silent regarding the use of weapons to kill the peshmerga forces by what Barzani described as "certain people who are on America's list of terrorists".[17]

The way that the US dealt with the KRI, before, during, and after the referendum, shows that America's patronage to the KRI is far from being a positive one. The US policy towards the Kurdish independence referendum was developed and implemented in three stages. All three stages reflect the nature of America's negative patronage of the Kurds. The first stage started with the KRI decision to conduct an independence referendum. During this period, on many occasions the US called on the KRI to cancel the referendum and to commit to Iraq unity. For example, on 8 June 2017, one day after the KRI decision to hold a referendum, a State Department spokeswoman expressed her concerns to the authorities in the KRI about "holding a referendum, even a nonbinding resolution".[18] In another statement issued on 20 September 2017, the US reiterated its opposition to the referendum. The statement emphasised that "the United States strongly opposes the

Iraqi Kurdistan Regional Government's referendum on independence, planned for September 25." The State Department also stated that "all of Iraq's neighbours, and virtually the entire international community, also oppose this referendum". The State Department also threatened that "if this referendum is conducted, it is highly unlikely that there will be negotiations with Baghdad, and the above international offer of support for negotiations will be foreclosed."[19] Such a threat meant that the US intended to abandon the KRI to its own fate if it conducted the independence referendum.

One of the areas of concern in the State Department's statement was the oil-rich disputed areas. The State Department warned that "the decision to hold the referendum in disputed areas is especially de-stabilizing," thus demonstrating its concern that the referendum may result in a change of boundaries in favour of the KRI. In this regard, the State Department emphasised that "the status of disputed areas and their boundaries must be resolved through dialogue, in accordance with Iraq's constitution, not by unilateral action or force." Disputed areas were not formally under KRI control but had been under *de facto* control of the KRI armed forces since 2014, when Kirkuk was recaptured from ISIS. KRI control over the disputed areas was achieved with US military support. In order to coordinate with the KRI armed forces and support them in their fight against ISIS, US military personnel were stationed in these areas. US concern about the fate of disputed areas was but a threat to punish the Kurds, if the KRI insisted on conducting the referendum. Hence, this first stage of US policies shows the negative nature of US patronage. The US perceived the independence referendum as being against its interests and priorities in Iraq and the region.

The KRI move towards independence was at the time of the total collapse of the Islamic State. Washington showed only a small interest in the KRI fate once its fighters were no longer needed. Thus, despite the fact that the KRI considered itself and was portrayed by others as the closest ally of the US-led Coalition forces in Iraq, the patronage that the US provided to the Kurds, especially in terms of the move towards independence, was that of negative patronage. This negative patronage was the main weakness underlying the referendum and the way that it was suppressed by Iraq and its neighbouring countries.

The second stage began directly after the referendum and continued until Iraq regained control over the entire disputed areas. On 29 September 2017, four days after the referendum, Secretary of State Rex Tillerson explained in a statement his country's perspective on the referendum. This was a critical moment for both the KRI and Iraqi, as both sides were testing the US' reaction to the first major step taken by Iraq in retaliation against the referendum. Tillerson clearly took the Iraqi side. He emphasised that "the United States does not recognize the Kurdistan Regional Government's unilateral referendum [and] the vote and the results lack legitimacy." Undermining the whole process, he highlighted that the US would "continue to support a united, federal, democratic and prosperous Iraq". He cleared the way for Baghdad to impose its rule on the KRI by urging "Iraqi Kurdish authorities to respect the constitutionally-mandated role of the central government".[20] The significance of this statement is that it was issued only one day after Iraqi lawmakers authorised Prime Minister Haider al-Abadi to send in the army and *Hashd* to Kirkuk and retake the area by force. It also came on the same day Iraq imposed a ban on KRI international flights and Iraqi troops prepared to seize the region's border controls. The Iraqi military units, dominated by *Hashd*, were already massing near the KRI-Iraqi borders and preparing to conduct a major military operation to reclaim the disputed areas.

Moreover, on 29 September 2017, both Turkey and Iran implemented a ban on direct flights from the KRI. On 6 October 2017, Turkey, Iran, and Iraq adopted a posture of coordinated aggressive force. Iraq joined Turkey and Iran in massing solders in an attempt to blockade KRI territory through taking control of the crossings between these neighbouring countries and the KRI.[21] Tillerson's call also served as a green light for Iraq to cooperate with Iran and Turkey in its attempt to control the KRI. Not only the US but also other Western countries were not ready to protect the Kurds. Bernard-Henri Lévy, one of Barzani's advisers for the independence referendum and who was in Eerbil at the time, recalls that "on the evening of Sept. 26 [2017. . . .] I watch and listen as Prime Minister Nechirvan Barzani makes calls to some Western capitals, where no one seems to be answering the phone."[22] The deafening silence from the international community not only emboldened Iraq, but also Iran and Turkey. Thus, the US gave a virtual green light to Baghdad and Tehran by declaring both the referendum and its result illegitimate and by calling on the Kurds to respect the constitutionally mandated role of the central government.

The *Hashd* and Iraqi armies advanced towards Kirkuk on 16 October 2017. The US did nothing to prevent the *Hashd* and the Iraqi army attack on disputed areas using American supplied sophisticated weapons. The US response to the Iraqi military attack also shows that its policy was built on the protection of the unity of Iraq at all costs. This means that the US was opposed to any Kurdish attempt towards gaining independence. The Iraqi military operations were one-sided as the KRI forces largely avoided fighting and withdrew without resistance. Prior to the Iraqi attack, Kurdish field commanders revealed that the US had warned them that coalition aircraft would attack any side, Iraqi or KRI, that initiated fighting against the other side. However, this warning seems to have been directed solely to the KRI forces. There are several clues that support this argument. First, the Iraqi armed forces started their operation without any reaction from the US. Second, the State Department statement issued on 16 October 2017 clearly sided with Iraq. The statement called on "all parties to coordinate military activities and restore calm". Calling for coordination and staying calm instead of calling for a cessation of Iraqi military operations means a call for the Kurds to not resist these operations. The statement emphasised that "we support the peaceful exercise of joint administration." It means that the US supported the reimposition of the central authority within disputed areas. Third, the statement clarified that "we are working [. . .] to reduce tensions, avoid further clashes, and encourage dialogue." A call to avoid clashes at a time when Iraqi armed forces were advancing towards disputed areas means the Kurds should not prevent the Iraqi armed forces from entering these areas.

By 20 October 2017, Iraq had reclaimed the entire Kirkuk province. Within a week, the peshmerga withdrew from all disputed areas from Khanaqin on the border of Iran, in the far southeast, to Shangal on the border of Syria, in the far northwest. During this period, the US still remained silent. The US did not use its leverage on Baghdad to stop its military operations in disputed areas, and even attempted to create an environment to help the KRI and Iraqi sides coordinate. The US president, Donald Trump, for example, said that "they're clashing, but we're not taking sides." In fact, "not taking sides" can be interpreted as we are not objecting to or interfering with the Iraqi government operations and that is in fact what happened on the ground. American troops were in the area but took no role in preventing the conflict. Thus, it was clear that the US was ready to sacrifice the KRI to protect Iraq's integrity. The US was also ready to permit the *Hashd* and Iraqi armies to use advanced US military equipment and was even ready to accept the role of the Iranian Revolutionary Guards in attacking KRI forces. In an interview published on 7 November 2017, Barzani said that the Iraqi military operation to control Kirkuk was led by the Iranians with the knowledge and approval of the US.[23] Thus, the US effectively took the side of Baghdad and, therefore, it clearly showed the negative nature of its patronage to the Kurds.

It seems that the Kurds moved towards independence based on their belief that the US would act as their patron and protector.

Counting on the US' commitment to protect the KRI and prevent the outbreak of an Iraqi-KRI conflict, the Kurds did not take the Iraqi threat to send in troops to the disputed areas seriously. There is some evidence that shows Barzani did not expect an Iraqi military operation against the Kurds. On 15 October 2017, one day before the Iraqi attack, top leaders from the two main political parties, the KDP and PUK, met to discuss the Iraqi threat of an attack on the disputed areas. Those who attended the meeting revealed that Masud Barzani emphasised that Iraq would not attack peshmerga forces and that there would only be some provocation. Barzani thought that there would be some measures taken such as border closures or economic sanctions, but not a military offensive. A similar view was re-emphasised by Barzani himself. In an interview with the NRP, he stated that "We were expecting some kind of reaction, but we had not calculated on a military attack."[24] The collapse of peshmerga forces and their defeat in disputed areas was largely due to these mistaken calculations that Baghdad would not attack Kurdistan.

It seems that the Kurds were not prepared for such a war. The question is why an Iraqi military offensive was ruled out. The answer is simple: there were US-led Coalition forces on the ground that had been coordinating and cooperating with the KRI armed forces since 2003, and this cooperation reached to another level following the rise of ISIS. Moreover, Kurds were widely known for being the US' closest allies in Iraq. It seems that Kurds believed that the US would interfere in the case of any Iraqi military attack on Kurdish positions. In other words, Kurds took the US' patronage as being guaranteed. If the Kurds had not considered the US as their patron and protector, they either would not have conducted the referendum in the first place or they would have been better prepared to resist any possible Iraqi attack. However, the KRI found that the US' patronage was both a limited and negative patronage.

The US supported the Iraqi side to control the entire disputed areas and to reduce the territorial, economic, and military power of the KRI in favour of Iraq. Therefore, the US' patronage of the Kurds was a negative one, and this is one of the main weaknesses of the Kurds' position in the post-referendum period. The KRI leaders discovered that the US' patronage was a limited one and that the Kurds would not be protected if they went beyond American lines. Therefore, the Kurds were in state of shock and disappointment when they found that the US had abandoned them and supported Baghdad. This state of shock and disappointment can be clearly read in Kurdish political statements, issued after the Iraqi attack on Kurdistan. For example, as a way to describe their desperate situation, Kurdish leaders recalled the popular Kurdish proverb, "Kurds have no friends but the mountains." This proverb was used during the Iraqi *Anfal* campaign in 1988 to condemn the international silence towards the Iraqi genocide campaign against the Kurds. Among many other leaders who used this proverb were Masud Barzani, the KRI president, and Kosrat Rasul, the KRI deputy president and leader of the PUK.

In his resignation speech, delivered on 29 October 2017, Barzani stated that he thought that the Kurds' struggle against ISIS "would have been appreciated by the international community [but] they once again showed the world that the people of Kurdistan have no friends but the mountains". In a statement issued on 18 October 2017, two days after the Iraqi military operation on Kirkuk, Kosrat Rasul repeated his disappointment with the US-led Coalitions' "abandonment" of the Kurds. He stated that Kurds have been in the frontline of coalition fighting against ISIS. Kurds thought the US and international community would reward them for their fight by listening to the Kurds' concerns and show respect to the will of the Kurds expressed in the independence referendum. However, against Kurds' expectations, the Coalition forces (i.e. the US) and the international community have facilitated multilateral military operations against the KRI. They left the Kurds to their own fate in the wake of the Iraqi militia and the army's military offensive. Rasul concluded that, once more, the silence of international communities showed that Kurds have no friends but the mountains.[25] Understanding the real nature of the US' patronage following the Iraqi military operations, Barzani suggested that the KRI will need to reassess its relationship with the US.[26]

The third stage of the US' policy commenced after Iraqi forces gained control over the entire disputed area. Having successfully pushed back Kurdish armed forces to their pre-2003 positions, and facing neither significant military resistance from the KRI armed forces nor diplomatic pressure from the US and international communities, Iraqi officials took the opportunity to reinstall their authority over the entire KRI. They did not hide their wish to control the whole Kurdistan region. The dominant public rhetoric in Baghdad was to occupy the KRI and to reinstate the central authority.

In their official statements, Shiite leaders avoided the use of terms such as 'Kurdistan' or 'Kurdistan region', and instead used the terms 'north' or 'northern

Iraq', the same language that was used by Iraqi officials in the 1970 to 1980s. For example, in the Iraqi 2018 Budget Bill, prepared by the Iraqi Ministry of Finance, the Kurdistan region as 'an entity' was ignored and the term "Kurdistan Region-Iraq" was replaced with "the Governorates of Northern Iraq," and "Kurdistan Regional Government" with "Government of the Governorates".[27] Moreover, instead of allocating 17 per cent of the budget to the Kurdistan region, as was the norm in previous years, it allocated a separate budget to each of the cities of Erbil, Sulaimaniya, and Duhok. In other words, Baghdad showed that it wants to deal directly with the Kurdish provinces rather than the officially recognised KRI.

Within less than a month, the Kurds had lost many of the gains they had enjoyed since 2003. Kurds lost their control over the entire disputed areas. Until 2014 there had been a *de facto* joint administration with Baghdad in these areas, with the Kurds having the majority of the control in almost all areas. From 2014 onward, with the absence of a central authority, these disputed areas were administrated and protected by the Kurds. The KRI also lost control over oil revenue that came from these areas, which represented over 50 per cent of the total KRI revenue. Moreover, the KRI, to a large extent, lost its control over international airports, independent economy, natural resources, and exporting oil directly from within the Kurdistan region. Iraqi troops even retook, or attempted to retake, borders with Iran, Turkey, and Syria that the Kurds have controlled since the 1990s. Iraq appears to be heading towards eliminating the Kurdish quasi-state and even terminating the federal status of the KRI.

Baghdad also declared the end of the disputed status of Kirkuk and other areas described by the Constitution as disputed areas. Iraq imposed a new *de facto* status and pre-2003 borders as the new border line. The Kurdish flag was removed, Kurdish political parties' offices were closed, Kurdish security elements were banned in disputed areas, and some 168,000 Kurds were displaced.[28] In fact, the total withdrawal of the KRI and abandoning the entire disputed areas to the *Hashd*, within three days, resulted in the semi-collapse of the KRI defence system. This humiliating defeat of the KRI, combined with the Shiites' euphoria, the cooperation of Turkey and Iran with Iraq, the silence of the US and international community, and the polarisation of Kurdish society led the KRI to the verge of collapse. These harsh circumstances pushed KRI leaders to issue a statement on 24 October 2017 and declare the freezing of the referendum results. According to the statement, the freeze was to avoid "grave and dangerous circumstances" that the KRI faced. KRI officials also called for an "immediate ceasefire and halt to all military operations in the Kurdistan Region" and for the "start [of] an open dialogue between the Kurdistan Regional Government and Iraqi Federal Government on the basis of the Constitution".[29] This move, however, did not stop the Shiite leaders from attempting to impose Baghdad's authority on the KRI and their conditions on defeated Kurdish leaders.

Baghdad's attempt to re-control the entire KRI militarily and to put a limitation on and, if possible, to eliminate the KRI's status seems to be beyond the US goal in Iraq. On 20 October, when the *Hashd* militia and the Iraqi army headed towards Erbil province, KRI forces started fighting back and stopped the Iraqi armed forces around the town of Altun Kupri, only 50 kilometres south of Erbil. At this stage, and for the first time, the US State Department declared its concern about "violent clashes" and urged "the central government to calm the situation by limiting federal forces' movements in disputed areas to only those coordinated with the Kurdistan Regional Government". As a gesture of its awareness of the intention of some Iraqi politicians to restore central authority over the entire KRI, the State Department emphasised the US' commitment "to the Kurdistan Regional Government as an integral component of the country". The statement declared that "we will continue working with officials from the central and regional governments to reduce tensions, avoid further clashes, and encourage dialogue." The US' call to avoid further clashes was more a call to the Iraqi forces to reduce their military operations. The State Department also stated that "the reassertion of federal authority over disputed areas in no way changes their status – they remain disputed until their status is resolved in accordance with the Iraqi Constitution."[30] Though the US' call may help Kurds to ask for the implementation of Article 140, as part of any negotiation package with the central government, it came too late. The defeated KRI chances of success would be very weak. This is because when the government of Iraq was at its weakest, it did not implement Article 140 of the constitution and at the time of this writing, when it is at its strongest, there are very few reasons to encourage Baghdad to implement this Article.

It seems that the Kurds are ready to accept the current reality and to deal with Baghdad based on their experience with the US' patronage. There are many indications that show that, by understanding the negative nature of the US' patronage, the KRI did not want to challenge Baghdad. The first indication is that the KRI dissolved the Kurdistan presidency institution. On 29 October 2017, the KRI Parliament approved the dissolution of the presidential institution and the distribution of presidential powers to the prime minister, the Council of Ministers, the presidential body of the Parliament, and the president of the Judicial Council. Though "as part of the Bill, the Diwan of the presidency will continue in its duties,"[31] the dissolving of the presidential institution is nothing but a response to accumulated Iraqi pressure to eliminate the sovereignty of the KRI. The second indication is that the KRI has agreed to hand over oil and border revenues if Baghdad allocates 17 per cent of the budget share.[32] These measures taken by the KRI that have ceded Baghdad more sovereignty seem to be measures accepted by the US.

The US officials, who showed no enthusiasm towards diplomatic communications with Erbil, re-established connections with Kurdish officials following the dissolution of the presidential institution and the resignation of Masud Barzani. For example, in a phone call with Prime Minister Nechirvan Barzani on 3 November 2017, Tillerson "expressed his concerns over recent tensions between Erbil and Baghdad". He also "voiced his support to the constitutional rights of the Kurdistan Region in Iraq".[33] Support for the KRI's constitutional rights means that the US is ready to accept and support the KRI entity in its new status, a weak entity that can be kept under control in a way that poses no threat to Iraqi unity and US interests in the region.

Thus, American patronage of the Kurds was limited and conditional upon the KRI's commitment to the integrity of Iraq, as well as upon taking the US' priorities, such as fighting against ISIS, as its own priorities. However, once KRI moved beyond the US' wish to safeguard Iraqi unity, and once the fight against ISIS was no longer needed, the KRI forfeited the support of the US and permitted the Iraqi attack on the KRI. However, it seems that the US does not want to see the total fall of the KRI; nor does it want the KRI to be strong enough to threaten the integrity of Iraq, as happened following the rise of ISIS in 2014.

Notes

1 "92.73% 'Yes' for Independence: Preliminary Official Results," *Rudaw*, 27/09/2017, available at <www.rudaw.net/english/kurdistan/270920174>, (accessed 30/09/2017).
2 "Political Crisis Escalates in Iraq's Kurdistan Region," *Reuters*, 12/10/2017, available at <www.reuters.com/article/us-iraq-kurds/political-crisis-escalates-in-iraqs-kurdistan-region-idUSKCN0S60HX20151012>, (accessed 13/10/2017).
3 For the full text of the statement issued from Gorran's General Council in Kurdish see: "Gorran Daway Dwakhsti Enjamdani Refrandom Dekat (Gorran Asks for Postponing the Referendum), *NRT*, available at <www.nrttv.com/Details.aspx?Jimare=81194>, (accessed 08/11/2017).
4 For more information about the 'No for Now' movement's perspective on the independence referendum see an interview in Kurdish with Shaswar Abdul-Wahid, the leader of the movement: Shaswar Abdul-Wahid in NRTTV *Tawtwe* Show, *NRTTV*, 17/09/2017, available at <www.youtube.com/watch?v=0KJeNK6gww8>, (accessed 07/11/2017).
5 "Iraq Kurdistan Independence Referendum Planned," *BBC News*, 01/07/2014.
6 "Baghdad Money Squeeze Tests Limits of Iraqi Kurdistan's Autonomy," *Reuters*, 18/03/2017, available at < https://uk.reuters.com/article/kurds-iraq/baghdad-money-squeeze-tests-limits-of-iraqi-kurdistans-autonomy-idUKL6N0MC03S20140317>, (accessed 10/10/2017).
7 "Iraqi Kurdistan Economy Suffers Amid Budget Dispute with Baghdad," *Al-Mointor*, 16/05/2014, available at <www.al-monitor.com/pulse/tr/business/2014/05/iraq-kurdistan-region-budget-dispute-economic-effects.html>, (accessed 05/10/2017).
8 "President Barzani Meets with Kurdistan Region's Political Parties to Set the Date for the Referendum," *Kurdistan regional Presidency*, 07/06/2017, available at <http://presidency.krd/english/articledisplay.aspx?id=/99h3Oipowc=>, (accessed 12/09/2017).
9 De Luce, D. (2016), "ISIS Is Using Chemical Weapons Against the Kurds: Why Won't the U.S. Help?" available at <http://foreignpolicy.com/2016/04/22/isis-is-using-chemical-weapons-against-the-kurds-why-wont-the-u-s-help/>, (accessed 09/09/2017).
10 "Barzani Asks KDP Leadership to Prepare for Conducting Referendum," *Kurdistan24*, 26/01/2016.
11 "Barzani: Kirkuk Is Kurdistan; It Won't Fall to Enemy Ever Again," *Rudaw*, 18/02/2015, available at <www.rudaw.net/mobile/english/kurdistan/18022015?ctl00_phMainContainer_phMain_ControlComments1_gvCommentsChangePage=4_5>, (accessed 16/12/2016).
12 "Barzani: Kirkuk Is Kurdistan; It Won't Fall to Enemy Ever Again," *Rudaw*, 18/02/2015, available at <www.rudaw.net/mobile/english/kurdistan/18022015?ctl00_phMainContainer_phMain_ControlComments1_gvCommentsChangePage=4_5>, (accessed 16/12/2016).
13 "Statement from Kurdistan Regional Government," Kurdistan Regional Government, 24/10/2017, available at <http://cabinet.gov.krd/a/d.aspx?s=040000&l=12&a=55938>, (accessed 25/10/2017).
14 For example see: Press Statement by Heather Nauert, *Department Press Briefing*, 08/06/2017, available at <www.state.gov/r/pa/prs/dpb/2017/06/271653.htm>, (accessed 09/09/2017); Press Statement by Heather Nauert, Iraqi Kurdistan Regional Government's Planned Referendum, *Department Spokesperson*, 20/09/2017, available

at <www.state.gov/r/pa/prs/ps/2017/09/274324.htm>, (accessed 01/10/2017); Press Statement by Rex W. Tillerson, Iraqi Kurdistan Regional Government's Referendum, 29–09–2017, available at <www.state.gov/secretary/remarks/2017/09/274522.htm>, (accessed 02/10/2017).
15 "President Barzani Addresses the People of Kurdistan," *Kurdistan Region Presidency*, 29/09/2017, available at <www.presidency.krd/english/articledisplay.aspx?id=/99h3Oipowc=>, (accessed 03/10/2017).
16 *Ibid.*
17 *Ibid.*
18 Press Statement by Heather Nauert, 08/06/2017.
19 Press Statement by Heather Nauert, 20/09/2017.
20 Press Statement by Rex W. Tillerson, 29/2017.
21 "Tillerson Says Kurdish Independence Referendum Is Illegitimate," *The Washington Post*, 29/09/2017, available at <www.washingtonpost.com/world/middle_east/iraq-bans-flights-to-kurdish-region-as-rift-grows-over-independence-bid/2017/09/29/860e326e-a532-11e7-b573-8ec86cdfe1ed_story.html?utm_term=.113767c2ac41>, (accessed 30/09/2017).
22 Lévy, B. H. (2017), "Who Betrayed the Kurdish People?" *Tablet Magazine*, available at <www.tabletmag.com/jewish-news-and-politics/247574/who-betrayed-the-kurdish-people>, (accessed 12/11/2017).
23 "War in Iraq: Masoud Barzani, Ex-Kurdish Leader, Says U.S. Knew in Advance About Iraqi Assault on Kirkuk," *Newsweek*, 07/11/2017, available at <www.newsweek.com/iraq-kurds-isis-betrayal-america-barzani-iran-independence-kirkuk-704480>, (accessed 08/11/2017).
24 Cited in Arraf, J. (2017), "After Iraqi Kurdish Independence Vote Backfires, 'I Do Not Regret It,' Says Barzani, *NPR*, available at <www.npr.org/sections/parallels/2017/11/07/562514981/after-iraqi-kurdish-independence-vote-backfires-i-do-not-regret-it-says-barzani>, (accessed 08/11/2017).
25 For the full text of Rasul's statement in Kurdish see: "Kosrat Rasul Issued a Statement on Kirkuk," *Livin*, 18/10/2017, available at <www.lvinpress.com/n/dreja.aspx?=hewa1&jmare=59741&Jor=1>, (accessed 05/10/2017).
26 Cited in Arraf (2017).
27 "KRG Council of Ministers' Follow Up Statement on 2018 Draft Federal Budget Bill," *Kurdistan Regional Government*, 05/11/2017, available at <http://cabinet.gov.krd/a/d.aspx?s=040000&l=12&a=55989>, (accessed 07/11/2017).
28 "More than 168, 000 People Displaced from Kirkuk and Other Areas," *Kurdistan Regional Government*, 25/10/2017, available at <http://cabinet.gov.krd/a/d.aspx?s=040000&l=12&a=55943>, (accessed 05/11/2017).
29 "Statement from Kurdistan Regional Government," 25/10/2017, available at <http://cabinet.gov.krd/a/d.aspx?s=040000&l=12&a=55938>, (accessed 04/10/2017).
30 "Press Statement by Heather Nauert, Department Spokesperson," 20/10–2017, available at <www.state.gov/r/pa/prs/ps/2017/10/274980.htm>, (accessed 01/11/2017).
31 "Kurdistan Parliament in Session to Address Region's Presidency, Hear Statement from Barzani," *Rudaw*, 29/10/2017, available at <www.rudaw.net/mobile/english/kurdistan/291020175?ctl00_phMainContainer_phMain_ControlComments1_gvCommentsChangePage=2_5>, (accessed 30/10/2017).
32 "KRG to Handover Oil, Border Revenues if Baghdad Sends 17 Percent Budget Share: Barzani," *Kurdistan24*, 06/11/2017, available at <www.kurdistan24.net/en/news/73611554-853d-4b14-a355-ad724284b275>, (accessed 08/11/2017).
33 "Barzani and Tillerson Discuss Tensions Between the Kurdistan Region and Iraq," Kurdistan Regional Government, 03/11/2017, available at <http://cabinet.gov.krd/a/d.aspx?s=010000&l=12&a=55982>, (accessed 05/11/2017).

References

"92.73% 'Yes' for Independence: Preliminary Official Results," *Rudaw*, 27/09/2017, available at <www.rudaw.net/english/kurdistan/270920174>, (accessed 30/09/2017).

Abdulghani, J. M. (1984), *Iraq and Iran: The Years of Crisis*, London: Taylor & Francis.

Abdulla, N. (2008), "I Do Not See Iraqi Kurdistan Becoming Independent in the Near Future, US Professor Says," Interview with Natali, The Hawler Tribune, (accessed 24/9/2008).

Abdullah, A. M. (2007), *Ey Reqib Lenewan Jestey Zman w Jestey Neteweda (Ey Reqib between body Language and the Nation's Body)*, Sulaimaniya, Iraq: Khaney Chap w Blawkrdnewey Wezareti Roshinbiri.

Abdullazada, S. (2012), "Kurd la Sa'adiya w Jalawla Shari Man u Neman Dakan" (The Kurds' war in Sa'adiya and Jalawla is one of life and death), available at <http://rudaw.net/kurdish/index.php/news/16745.html>, (accessed 01/12/2015).

ABSP, Arab Ba'ath Socialist Party (1983), *Al-Taqrir al-Markazi lil-Mu'tamar al-Qutri al-Tasi', Huzayran 1982 (Central Report of the Ninth Regional Congress, June 1982), Baghdad*, Iraq: al-Dar al-Arabiya.

——— (2007), "Dastur Hizb al-Ba'ath al-Arabi al-Ishtraki (The Constitution of the Arab Ba'ath Socialist Party)," *Shabaka al-Basrah*, available at <www.albasrah.net/ar_articles_2007/0307/dstor-b3th_070307.htm>, (accessed 09/8/2016).

Abu-Bakr, A. O. (2005), *Kurd u Kurdistan le Komalla Wtareki Mezhwiyda (Kurds and Kurdistan in some historical articles)*, Erbil, Iraq: Mukiryani.

Ackerman, S. (2006), "Good Actors – The Kurds' Cunning Plan," *New Republic* 235(4): 1–10.

Adelman, H. (1992), "Humanitarian Intervention: The Case of the Kurds," *International Journal of Refugee Law* 4: 4.

Aflaq, M. (1987), *Fi Sabil al-Ba'ath* (On the Way to Resurrection), Vol. 5, Baghdad: Maktab al-Thaqafah wal-Ilam al-Qawmi.

Agnew, J., Thomas W. Gillespie, Jorge Gonzalez and Brian Min (2008), "Baghdad Nights: Evaluating the US Military 'Surge' Using Nighttime Light Signatures," *Environment and Planning* 40: 2285–2295.

Ahmed, A. M. (2008), *Mamosta Ali Abdul-Aziz Temenek Xizmet le Bizavi Islamida (Islamic Scholar Abdul-Aziz and an age of Islamic movement)*, Publisher unknown.

Ahmed, K. (2006), *Al-Masira: Safahat min Nidhal Karim Ahmed (The Journey: Pages in Karim Ahmed's Struggle)*, Erbil, Iraq: Matba'at Shahab.

Ahmed, M. A. M. (2007), "Laying the Foundation of a Kurdistani State in Iraq: 1991–2006," *The Evolution of Kurdish Nationalism*, M. Gunter and M. A. Ahmed (eds.), Costa Mesa, CA: Mazda Publisher.

AKnews, 27/09/2012; 17/11/2011, "Demo in Diyala to Denounce Federal Region in Iraq," available at <www.aknews.com/en/aknews/4/273026/>, (accessed 27/11/2012).

Akrawi (2007), "Kurd u Dawlati Serbekho Bepey Belganame Newdawlatoyakan" *(Kurds and the Independent State Based on International Documents), Erbil*, Iraq: Mukiryani.

Al-Ahram Newspaper, 23/11/2011, Cairo.

Al-Barak, F. (1984), *Al-Madaris al-Yahudiya wa al-Iraniya fi al-Iraq (The Jewish and Iranian schools in Iraq), Baghdad*, Iraq: Dar al-Rasheed.

—— (1989), *Mustafa al-Barzani: al-Istura wa al-Haqiqa (Mustafa Barzani: The Myth and the Reality), Baghdad*, Iraq: Dar al-Sh'un al-Thaqafiya al-'Amma.

Al-Barzani, A. H. (2002), *A-Haraka Alqawmiye al-teharruriya al-Kurdiye (The Kurdish Nationalist Liberation Movement), Erbil*, Iraq: Dar al-Spirez li Taba'a wal-Nashir.

Al-Bayati, A. (2005), *Sheikh Mahmud al-Hafid wa al-Nifuz al-Britani fi Kurdistan al-Iraq hatta 'am 1925 (Sheikh Mahmud al-Hafid and British influence in Iraqi Kurdistan up to 1925)*, London, UK: Dar al-Hikma.

Al-Botani, A. F. A. Y. (2001), *Watha'q 'an al-Haraka al-Qawmiya al-Kurdiya al-Taharruriya: Mulahadhat Tarikhiya wa Dirasat Awaliya (Documents on the Kurdish nationalist liberation movement: Historical observations and Primary Studies), Erbil*, Iraq: Dazgay Mukiryani.

—— (2007), *Mawqif al-Ahzab al-Siyasya al-Iraqiya mn al-Qadhiya al-Kurdiya (The position of Iraqi political parties on the Kurdish issue), Duhok*, Iraq: Markaz al-Dirasat al-Kurdiya w Hifdh al-Wethaeq.

Al-Buratha (2011), "Na'ib 'an al-'Araqiya yu'ayid Tasrihat al-Nujaifi wa yad'u ila Iqama al-Mantiqa al-Gharbiya lil-Hifadh 'Ala Abna' al-Sunna aw Istifa'a Kamil Hiququhum" (A Member of Parliament from the al-Iraqiya Bloc supports al-Nujaifi statements and calls for the establishment of the Western region to protect and grant full rights to the Sunnis), available at <www.burathanews.com/news_article_128977.html>, (accessed 14/1/2012).

Alexander, A. and S. Assaf (2005), "Iraq: The Rise of the Resistance," *The Rise of Socialism*, available at <www.isj.org.uk/index.php4?id=52>, (accessed 5/2/2010).

Al-Fil, M. R. (1965), *Al-Akrad fi Nadhar al-'Ilm (The Kurds in the eyes of science)*, Najaf, Iraq: Maktaba al-Adab.

Al-Fukaiki, H. (1993), *Awkar al-Hazima: Tajrubati fi Hizb al-Ba'th al-Iraqi (The den of defeat: My experience in the Iraqi Ba'th Party)*, London: Riad El-Rayyes.

Al-Ghamrawi, A. S. (1967), *Qisat al-Akrad fi Shimal al-Iraq (The Story of the Kurds in the North of Iraq)*, Cairo, Egypt: Dār al-Nahḍah.

Al-Hamdani, H. (2012), "Eqlim Tariq al-Hashimi" (The Region of Tariq al-Hashimi), *Asharq al-awsat*, 29/4/2012, London.

Al-Hassani, A. R. (1988), *Tarikh al-Wizarat al-Iraqia (The history of Iraqi cabinets)*, Baghdad, Iraq: Dar al-Sh'un al-Thaqafiya al-Amma.

Al-Hayat newspaper, 16/3/1970, London.

Al-Husri, S. (1967), *Mudhakarati fi al-Iraq 1921–1927 (My memoir in Iraq 1921–1927)*, Beirut: Dar al-Tali'a.

Al-Husri, S. (1985), *Abhath Mukhtare fi al-Qawmiya al-Arabiya (Selected essays on Arab nationalism)*, Beirut: Dar al-Mustaqbal al-Araby.

Ali, N. (2005), "Haremi Kurdistan Razi bwe ke Peshmega Bibete Gardi Harem" (The Kurdistan Region agrees that the peshmerga will become a regional guard), *Kurdistani News*, 26/5/2005.

Ali, O. (2003), *Dirasat fi al-Hereke al-Taharruriye al-kurdiye al-Ma'asre 1833–1946 (A Study of the Contemporary Kurdish Liberation Movement), Erbil*, Iraq: al-Tafsir.

Al-Iraq Newspaper, 18/03/1993.

Al-Jabouri, N. A. and S. Jensen (2010), "The Iraqi and AQI Roles in the Sunni Awakening," *Prism* 2: 3–18.

Al-Jamhuriya Newspaper 13/2/1966, Bagdad.

——— 13/9/1983, Baghdad.

Al-Janabi, M. (2004), *Al-Iraq wa Mu'asarat al-Mustaqbal (Iraq and Future Convoying)*, Damascus: Dar al-Mada.

Al-Khafaji, I. (1992), "State Terror and the Degradation of politics in Iraq," *Middle East Report* 176: 15–21.

Allawi, A. (2007), *The occupation of Iraq: Winning the War, Losing the Peace*, New Haven, CT: Yale University Press.

Al-Qaeda Newspaper, 16/3/1944, Baghdad.

Al-Salihi, N. (2000), *Al-Zilzal: Matha hadatha fi al-Iraq ba'da al-insihab min al-Kuwait (The Earthquake: What Happened in Iraq After the Withdrawal from Kuwait)*, Suleymantya, Iraq: Khak Press.

Al-Samarrayi, W. (1997), *Hittam al-Bawaba al-Sharqiya (Wreckage of the Eastern Gate)*. Kuwait City, Kuwait: Dar al-Qabas lil-Sahafa wal-Nashir.

Al-Taghalubi, N. (1967), "Israel 'ala hdud al-Iraq" (Israel on the Border of Iraq), *Al-Hawadith Magazine*, 639.

Al-Thawra Newspaper, 17/2/1961, Baghdad.

——— 23/2/1979 Baghdad.

Al-Waqai' al-Iraqiya (The Official Gazette of Iraq), 30/8/1958, Baghdad.

——— 3/6/1969, Baghdad.

——— 5/12/1975, Baghdad.

——— 29/2/1976, Baghdad.

——— 9/2/1976, Baghdad.

——— 16/7/1980, Baghdad.

——— 12/12/1988, Baghdad.

——— 17/9/2001, Baghdad,

Al-Wardi, A. (1994), *Mantiq Ibn al-Khaldun (The logic of Ibn al-Khaldun)*, London: Kufaan.

Al-Watan al-Arabi Newspaper (1989a), "Hathihi al-'ashaer al-Kurdiya aslihn Arabiyun (The origin of these Kurdish Tribes is Arab)," (Part 1), 648, 14/7/1989.

——— (1989b), "Hathihi al-'Ashaer al-Kurdiya Aslihn Arabiyun" (The origin of these Kurdish Tribes is Arab), *Al-Watan al-Arabi*, (Part 2), 649, 21/7/1989.

Anderson, B. (1991), *Imagined Communities: Reflections on the Origin and Spread of Nationalism*, New York: Palgrave Macmillan.

Anderson, L. and G. Stansfield (2005), *The Future of Iraq: Dictatorship, Democracy, or Division?* New York: Palgrave Macmillan.

Andres, R. (2006), "The Afghan Model in Northern Iraq," *The Journal of Strategic Studies* 29(3): 395–422.

Andrews, D. (1982), *The Lost Peoples of the Middle East: Documents of the Struggle for Survival and Independence of the Kurds, Assyrians, and Other Minority Races in the Middle East*, Salisbury, NC: Documentary Publications.

Arraf, J. (2017), "After Iraqi Kurdish Independence Vote Backfires, 'I Do Not Regret It,' Says Barzani," *NPR*, available at <www.npr.org/sections/parallels/2017/11/07/562514981/after-iraqi-kurdish-independence-vote-backfires-i-do-not-regret-it-says-barzani>, (accessed 08/11/2017).

Asharq al-Awsat Newspaper, 17/2/2009, London.

Awene Newspaper (2012), available at <www.awene.com>, (accessed 03/11/2016).

Aydin, D. (2005), "Mobilizing the Kurds in Turkey: Newroz as a Myth," Masters Thesis, Middle East Technical University.

Ayoob, M. (1995), *The Third World Security Predicament: State Making, Regional Conflict, and the International System*, Boulder, CO: Lynne Rienner Publishers.

Azadi (19552a), "The Mouthpiece of the Kurdish Branch of the ICP", no. 3.

——— (19552b), "The Mouthpiece of the Kurdish Branch of the ICP", no. 4.

——— (1956), "The Mouthpiece of the Kurdish Branch of the ICP", no. 1.

Aziz, M. A. (2011), *The Kurds of Iraq: Ethnonationalism and National Identity in Iraqi Kurdistan*, London, UK: IB Tauris.

Aziz, S. (2010), "Kurdistan, Democracy and the Future of the Muslim World," *Iraq, Democracy and the Future of the Muslim World*, A. John and L. Esposito (eds.), London: Routledge, pp. 50–65.

Baghdad Newspaper, 24/8/1960, Baghdad.

——— 23/8/1960, Baghdad.

——— 20/8/1960, Baghdad.

"Baghdad Money Squeeze Tests Limits of Iraqi Kurdistan's Autonomy," *Reuters*, 18/03/2017, available at <https://uk.reuters.com/article/kurds-iraq/baghdad-money-squeeze-tests-limits-of-iraqi-kurdistans-autonomy-idUKL6N0MC03S20140317>, (accessed 10/10/2017).

Baker, P. H. (2004), *Iraq as a Failed State: A Six-Month Progress Report*, Washington, DC: The Fund for Peace.

Bakhash, S. (2004), "The Troubled Relationship: Iran and Iraq, 1930–1980," *Iran, Iraq and the Legacies of War*, Lawrence G. Potter and Gary G. Sick (eds.), New York: Palgrave MacMillan.

Baram, A. (1997), "Neo-Tribalism in Iraq: Saddam Hussein's Tribal Policies 1991–96," *International Journal of Middle East Studies* 29(1): 1–31.

Barkey, H. J. and E. Laipson (2005), "Iraqi Kurds and Iraq's Future," *Middle East Policy*, 12(4): 66–76.

"Barzani: Kirkuk Is Kurdistan: It Won't Fall to Enemy Ever Again," *Rudaw*, 18/02/2015, available at <www.rudaw.net/mobile/english/kurdistan/18022015?ctl00_phMainContainer_phMain_ControlComments1_gvCommentsChangePage=4_5>, (accessed 16/12/2016).

"Barzani: Kirkuk Is Kurdistan: It Won't Fall to Enemy Ever Again," *Rudaw*, 18/02/2015, available at <www.rudaw.net/mobile/english/kurdistan/18022015?ctl00_phMainContainer_phMain_ControlComments1_gvCommentsChangePage=4_5>, (accessed 16/12/2016).

Barzani, A. (2011), *Al-Haraka al-Taharruriya al-Kurdiya: Wa Sira'a Qwa al-Aqlimiya we al-Dawliya (The Kurdish Liberation Movement and the Regional and International Conflict)*, Geneva, Switzerland: Dar al-Nashir Haqaiq al-Mashriq.

"Barzani Asks KDP Leadership to Prepare for Conducting Referendum," *Kurdistan24*, 26/01/2016.

Barzani, M. (2002), *Barzani wal-Haraka al-Taharruriya al-Kurdiya (Barzani and the Kurdish Liberation Movement)*, Erbil, Iraq: Aras Publications.

——— (2003a), "Iraqi Kurdish Claim for Federalism," *KRG website*, available at <http://old.krg.org/docs/mb-federalism-kurdistan-dec03.asp>, (accessed 05/09/2016).

——— (2003b), *Mustafa Barzani and the Kurdish Liberation Movement*, New York: Palgrave Macmillan.

——— (2004), *Barzani we al-Haraka al-Taharruriya al-Kurdiya (Barzani and the Kurdish Liberation Movement)*, Erbil, Iraq: Aras Publications.

——— (2005), "A Kurdish Vision of Iraq," *The Washington Post*, available at <www.washingtonpost.com/wpdyn/content/article/2005/10/25/AR2005102501390.html>, (accessed 03/04/2015).

―――― (2008), "Kurdistan Is a Model for Iraq: Our Path to a Secular, Federal Democracy Is Inspired by the U.S.," *The Wall Street Journal*, available at <http://online.wsj.com/article/SB122645258001119425.html>, (accessed 02/11/2016).

―――― (2012), "Mehalle Tiroristan Binkeyek le Kurdistán Dabnen yan Teyda Seqamgirbn" (It is impossible for terrorists to establish a base in Kurdistan or operate from it), Khabat, 3436: 3.

―――― (2012), "Massoud Barzani: Flying the Kurdish flag," *Aljazira TV*, available at <www.aljazeera.com/programmes/talktojazeera/2012/07/2012726121141649305.html>, (accessed 30/7/2012).

Barzani, N. (2007), "Perspective of Nechirvan Barzani, Prime Minister, Kurdistan Regional Government," *Kurdish Identity: Human Rights and Political Status*, C. G. MacDonald and Carole S. O'Leary (eds.), Gainesville, Florida: University Press of Florida.

―――― (2010), "Eme Em Hukumete be hi Khoman Dezanin" (We Consider this Government as Ours), *Khabat*, 3447.

"Barzani and Tillerson Discuss Tensions Between the Kurdistan Region and Iraq," *Kurdistan Regional Government*, 03/11/2017, available at <http://cabinet.gov.krd/a/d.aspx?s=010000&l=12&a=55982>, (accessed 05/11/2017).

Bashkin, O. (2008), *The Other Iraq: Pluralism and Culture in Hashemite Iraq*, Stanford, CA: Stanford University Press.

Batatu, H. (1992), *Al-Iraq, the Second Book*. Afif al-Razaz (trans.), Beirut, Lebanon: al-Hizb al-Shiuii.

―――― (2004), *The Old Social Classes and the Revolutionary Movements of Iraq*, London: Saqi Books.

Beaumont, P. (2005), "Revealed: Grim World of New Iraqi Torture Camps," *The Guardian*, available at <www.guardian.co.uk/world/2005/jul/03/iraq.peterbeaumont>, (accessed 06/07/2014).

Beck, P. J. (1981), "A Tedious and Perilous Controversy: Britain and the Settlement of the Mosul Dispute, 1918–1926," *Middle Eastern Studies* 17(2): 256–276.

Bekas, F (2005), *Diwani Bekas (Divan of Bekas)*, O. Ashna (ed.), Erbil, Iraq: Aras Publishers.

Benard, A. (2004), "Lessons from Iraq and Bosnia on the Theory and Practice of No-fly Zones," *Journal of Strategic Studies* 27(3): 454–478.

Bengio, O. (1979–1980), "Iraq," *Middle East Contemporary Survey; (CD-ROM Version), vol. I-XVIII*, O. Bengio (ed.), The Moshe Dayan Center for Middle Eastern and African Studies, Tel Aviv University, Tel Aviv, Israel, 2000, pp. 501–534.

―――― (1981–1982), "Iraq," *Middle East Contemporary Survey; (CD-ROM Version), vol. I-XVIII*, O. Bengio (ed.), The Moshe Dayan Center for Middle Eastern and African Studies, Tel Aviv University, Tel Aviv, Israel, 2000, pp. 582–628.

―――― (1982–1983), "Iraq," *Middle East Contemporary Survey; (CD-ROM Version), vol. I-XVIII*, O. Bengio (ed.), The Moshe Dayan Center for Middle Eastern and African Studies, Tel Aviv University, Tel Aviv, Israel, 2000, pp. 560–591.

―――― (1983–1984), "Iraq," *Middle East Contemporary Survey; (CD-ROM Version), vol. I-XVIII*, O. Bengio (ed.), The Moshe Dayan Center for Middle Eastern and African Studies, Tel Aviv University, Tel Aviv, Israel, 2000, pp. 465–493.

―――― (1984–1985), "Iraq," *Middle East Contemporary Survey; (CD-ROM Version), vol, I-XVIII*, O. Bengio (ed.), The Moshe Dayan Center for Middle Eastern and African Studies, Tel Aviv University, Tel Aviv, Israel, 2000, pp. 460–483.

―――― (1984–1985), "Iraq," *Middle East Contemporary Survey; (CD-ROM Version), vol. I-XVIII*, O. Bengio (ed.), The Moshe Dayan Center for Middle Eastern and African Studies, Tel Aviv University, Tel Aviv, Israel, 2000, pp. 460–483.

────── (1986), "Iraq," *Middle East Contemporary Survey; (CD-ROM Version), vol. I-XVIII*, O Bengio, (ed.), The Moshe Dayan Center for Middle Eastern and African Studies, Tel Aviv University, Tel Aviv, Israel, 2000, pp. 361–392.

────── (1987), "Iraq," *Middle East Contemporary Survey; (CD-ROM Version), vol. I–XVIII*, O Bengio (ed.), The Moshe Dayan Center for Middle Eastern and African Studies. Tel Aviv University, Tel Aviv, Israel, 2000, pp. 423–456.

────── (1998a), *Saddam's Word: Political Discourse in Iraq*, Oxford: Oxford University Press.

────── (1998b), "Iraq," *Middle East Contemporary Survey; (CD-ROM Version), vol. I-XVIII*, O Bengio (ed.), The Moshe Dayan Center for Middle Eastern and African Studies, Tel Aviv University, Tel Aviv, Israel, 2000, pp. 286–315.

────── (2006), "Autonomy in Kurdistan in Historical Perspective," *The Future of Kurdistan in Iraq*, B. O'Leary, J. McGarry and Salih, K. (eds.), Philadelphia, PA: University of Pennsylvania Press, pp. 173–185.

────── (2012), "Turkey: A midwife for a Kurdish state?" *The Jerusalem Post*, available at <www.jpost.com/Opinion/Op-EdContributors/Article.aspx?id=273632>, (accessed 09/12/2015).

Bengio, O. and Dann, U. (1976–1977), "Iraq," *Middle East Contemporary Survey; (CD-ROM Version), vol. I-XVIII*. O. Bengio (ed.), The Moshe Dayan Center for Middle Eastern and African Studies, Tel Aviv University, Tel Aviv, Israel, 2000, pp. 403–520.

────── (1977–1978), "Iraq," *Middle East Contemporary Survey; (CD-ROM Version), vol. I-XVIII*, O. Bengio. (ed.), The Moshe Dayan Center for Middle Eastern and African Studies, Tel Aviv University, Tel Aviv, Israel, 2000, pp. 513–532.

Bensahel, N., O. Oliker, O. Oliker, K. Crane, Jr. R. Richard and H. S. Gregg (2008), *After Saddam: Prewar Planning and the Occupation of Iraq*, Santa Monica, CA: Rand Corporation,

Bernard, A. (2004), "Lessons from Iraq and Bosnia on the Theory and Practice of No-fly Zones," *Journal of Strategic Studies* 27(3): 454–478.

Bernhardsson, M. T. (2006), *Reclaiming a Plundered Past: Archaeology and Nation Building in Modern Iraq*, Austin, TX: University of Texas Press.

Berwari, N. (2003), "Women in Iraq, Future Prospects," Paper delivered at Winning the Peace: Women's Role in Post-Conflict Iraq conference, Washington, DC, April.

Biddle, S., M. E. O'Hanlon and K. M. Pollack (2008), "How to Leave a Stable Iraq-Building on Progress," *Foreign Affairs* 87: 40–58.

Bilgin, P. and A. D. Morton (2004), "From 'Rogue' to 'Failed' States? The Fallacy of Short-Termism," *Politics* 24(3): 169–180.

Bill, J. A. (1969), "The Military and Modernization in the Middle East," *Comparative Politics* 2(1): 41–62.

Bitlisi, S. (1860), *Sharafname*, Petersburg: Dar al-Taba'a Ekadimiyah Impratoriya.

Blanc, H. (1959), "Iraqi Arabic Studies," *The Middle East Journal* 13(4): 449–453.

Blanchard, C. M. (2010), *Iraq: Oil and Gas Sector, Revenue Sharing, and U.S. Policy*, Washington, DC: Congressional Research Service.

Bnkey Zhin. (2012), "Nawrozi Rojaneki Rabrdu" (Nawroz of the Old Days), Suleymaniya, Iraq.

Bois, T. (1966), *The Kurds*, M. W. M. Welland (trans.), Beirut: Khayats.

Borer, D. A. (2003), "Inverse Engagement: Lessons from US-Iraq Relations, 1982–1990," *Parameters* 33(2): 51–65.

────── (2006), "Problems of Economic Statecraft: Rethinking Engagement," *US Army War College: Guide to National Security Policy and Strategy*, Second edition, Washington, DC.: DIANE Publishing

Borovali, A. F. (1987), "Kurdish Insurgencies, the Gulf War, and Turkey's Changing Role," *Journal of Conflict Studies* 7(4): 29–45.

Bozarslan, H. (1996), "Kurds: States, Marginality and Security," *Margins of Insecurity: Minority and International Security, Nolutshungu*, C. Sam (ed.), New York: University of Rochester Press.

Brancati, D. (2004), "Can federalism stabilize Iraq?" *Washington Quarterly* 27(2): 5–21.

——— (2006), "Decentralization: Fuelling the Fire or Dampening the Flames of Ethnic Conflict and Secessionism?" *Decentralization and Ethnic Conflict International Conference* 60(3): 651–685.

Brinkerhoff, D. W. and J. B. Mayfield (2005), "Democratic Governance in Iraq? Progress and Peril in Reforming State-Society Relations," *Public Administration and Development* 25(1): 59–73.

Brooks, R. E. (2005), "Failed States, or the State as Failure?" *The University of Chicago Law Review* 72(4): 1159–1196.

Bruinessen, M. V. (1986), "The Kurds Between Iran and Iraq," *MERIP Middle East Report* 141: 14–27.

——— (1992), *Agha, Sheikh, and State: The Social and Political Structures of Kurdistan*, London: Zed books.

——— (1999), *The Kurds and Islam, Islamic Area Studies Project*, Tokyo, Japan: [publisher unknown].

——— (2002), "Kurds, states and tribes," *Tribes and power: nationalism and ethnicity in the Middle East*, Faleh A. Jabar & H. Dawod (eds.), London: Saqi Books, pp. 165–183.

Bulloch, J. and H. Morris (1992), *No Friends But the Mountains: The Tragic History of the Kurds*, Oxford: Oxford University Press.

Burns, J. F. (2002), "Kurds Must Endure Iraq's 'Nationality Correction," *The New York Times*, available at <www.nytimes.com/2002/08/11/world/kurds-must-endure-iraq-s-nationality-correction.html>, (accessed 08/09/2016).

Çakar, E. (2002), "According to the Qanunname of Sultan Suleyman I: The Administrative Divisions of the Ottoman Empire In 1522," *F.U. Sosyal Bilimler Dergisi* 12(1).

Call, C. T. (2008), "The Fallacy of the 'Failed State," *Third World Quarterly*, 29(8).

Catudal, H. M. (1976), "The War in Kurdistan: End of a Nationalist Struggle?" *International Relations* 5(3): 1024–1044.

CHAK, Center of Halabja Against Anfalisation and Genocide of the Kurds (2007), "Anfal: The Iraqi State's Genocide Against the Kurds," available at <www.chak.be/anfal.The%20Iraqi%20States%20Genocide%20against%20the%20Kurds.2007.pdf>, (accessed 12/07/2015).

The Charter of the United Nations (1945), "United Nations," available at <www.un.org/en/documents/charter/chapter1.shtml >, (accessed 07/01/2015).

Chiyawk, M. (2001), *Ma'sat Barzan al-Mazlumeh (The Tragedy Oppressed Barzan), Second edition, Erbil*, Iraq: Aras Publishers.

Chorev, M. (2007), "Iraqi Kurdistan: The Internal Dynamics and Statecraft of a Semistate," *Al Nakhlah*.

Chung, C. (2012), "The Peshmerga: Capabilities, Challenges and the Future of Kurdistan's Guardians," *Rudaw Newspaper*, available at <www.rudaw.net/english/kurds/4844.html>, (accessed 25/11/2015).

CIA, Central Intelligence Agency (2011), "The Worlds Fact Book," available at <www.cia.gov/library/publications/the-world-factbook/rankorder/2173rank.html>, (accessed 05/04/2015).

Clarry, S. (2007), "Iraqi Kurdistan: the Humanitarian Program," *Kurdish Identity: Human Rights and Political Status*, Charles G. MacDonald and Carole S. O'Leary (eds.), Gainesville, Florida: University Press of Florida.

Coalition for Justice in Iraq (2000), "Ten Years Since the Invasion, Just Another Day in a Lifetime of Brutality," *Kurdish Media*, available at <www.kurdmedia.com/article.aspx?id=7753>, (accessed 24/08/2015).

Cockburn, A. and L. Cockburn (1991), *Dangerous Liaison: The Inside Story of the US-Israeli Covert Relationship*, New York: HarperCollins Publishers.

Cockburn, P. (2009), "Arab-Kurd Tensions Rise as US Pulls Out," *New Zealand Herald*, available at <www.nzherald.co.nz/world/news/article.cfm?c_id=2&objectid=10590097>, (accessed 02/03/2015).

Constitution of the Kurdistan Toiler Party, The (2011), *Kurdistan Toilers Party*, Publisher unknown.

Cordesman, A. H. (2000) "The Gulf and Transition-US Policy Ten Years After the Gulf-Policy Issues on the Periphery," available at <www.csis.org30:2000>, (accessed 23/09/2016).

Corum, J. S. (2000), "The Myth of Air Control: Reassessing the History," *DTIC Document: 61–76*, available at <www.dtic.mil.proxy.library.adelaide.edu.au/cgi-bin/GetTRDoc?AD=ADA522125>, (accessed 01/12/2011).

Cottam, M. L. and R. W. Cottam (2001), *Nationalism & Politics: The political behavior of nation states*, Boulder, CO: Lynne Rienner Publishers.

Cowell, A. (1988), "A Defeat for the Kurds: Iraqi Drive Tied to Gulf Truce Compounds Guerrillas' Disunity and Setbacks in Turkey," *New York Times Book Review*.

CPA, Coalition Provisional Authority (2003a), "Regulation no. 1," available at <www.iraqcoalition.org/regulations/20030516_CPAREG_1_The_Coalition_Provisional_Authority_.pdf>, (accessed 07/08/2015).

—— (2003b), "Order no. 24," available at <www.iraqcoalition.org/regulations/20030824_CPAORD_24_Ministry_of_Science_and_Technology.pdf>, (accessed 07/08/2015).

—— (2003c), "Regulation no. 6," available at <www.iraqcoalition.org/regulations/20030713_CPAREG_6_Governing_Council_of_Iraq_.pdf>, (accessed 08/08/2016).

—— (2003e), "Order no. 2," available at <www.iraqcoalition.org/regulations/20030823_CPAORD_2_Dissolution_of_Entities_with_Annex_A.pdf>, (accessed 07/08/2015).

—— (2003f), "Regulation no. 9," available at <www.iraqcoalition.org/regulations/20040609_CPAREG_9_Governing_Council_s_Dissolution.pdf>, (accessed 10/08/2015).

—— (2003h), "Order no. 33," available at <www.iraqcoalition.org/regulations/20030909_CPAORD33.pdf>, (accessed 07/08/2015).

—— (2003i), "Order no. 44," available at <www.iraqcoalition.org/regulations/20031126_CPAORD44.pdf>, (accessed 07/08/2015).

—— (2003j), "Order no. 50," available at <www.iraqcoalition.org/regulations/20040112_CPAORD50_MODM.pdf>, (accessed 07/08/2015).

—— (2003k), "Order no. 60," available at <www.iraqcoalition.org/regulations/20040220_CPAORD60.pdf>, (accessed 09/08/2015).

—— (2003l), "Order no. 68," available at <www.iraqcoalition.org/regulations/20040405_CPAORD68.pdf>, (accessed 07/08/2015).

—— (2003m), "Order no. 43," available at <www.iraqcoalition.org/regulations/20031014_CPAORD_43_New_Iraqi_Dinar_Banknotes.pdf>, (accessed 9/8/2011).

—— (2003n), "Order no. 35," available at <www.iraqcoalition.org/regulations/20030921_CPAORD35.pdf>, (accessed on 09/08/2015).

―――― (2003o), "Order no. 37," available at <www.iraqcoalition.org/regulations/20030919_CPAORD_37_Tax_Strategy_for_2003.pdf>, (accessed 09/08/2015).
―――― (2003p), "Order no. 56," available at <www.iraqcoalition.org/regulations/20040306_CPAORD_56_Central_Bank_Law_with_Annex.pdf>, (accessed 10/08/2015).
―――― (2003q), "Order no. 86," available at <www.iraqcoalition.org/regulations/20040520_CPAORD86_Traffic_Code_with_Annex_A.pdf>, (accessed 10/08/2015).
―――― (2003r), "Order no. 97," available at <www.iraqcoalition.org/regulations/20040615_CPAORD_97_Political_Parties_and_Entities_Law.pdf>, (accessed 10/08/2015).
―――― (2003s), "Order no. 1," available at <www.iraqcoalition.org/regulations/20030516_CPAORD_1_De-Ba_athification_of_Iraqi_Society_.pdf>, (accessed 10/08/2015).
―――― (2003t), "Order no. 96," available at <www.iraqcoalition.org/regulations/20040615_CPAORD_96_The_Electoral_Law.pdf>, (accessed 11/08/2015).
―――― (2003u), "Order no. 100," available at <www.iraqcoalition.org/regulations/20040628_CPAORD_100_Transition_of_Laws__Regulations__Orders__and_Directives.pdf>, (accessed 10/8/2011).
―――― (2003v), "Achieving the Vision: Taking Forward the CPA Strategic Plan for Iraq," 18 July 2003, available at <www.iraqcoalition.org/regulations/20040615_CPAORD_96_The_Electoral_Law.pdf>, (accessed 11/08/2015).
―――― (2003w), "Regulation no. 10," available at <www.iraqcoalition.org/regulations/20040609_CPAREG_10_Members_of_Designated_Iraqi_Interim_Government_with_Annex_A.pdf>, (accessed 10/08/2015).
―――― (2003x), "Regulation no. 7," available at <www.iraqcoalition.org/regulations/20030610_CPAORD_7_Penal_Code.pdf>, (accessed 10/08/2015).
Cuthell, D. (2004), "A Kemalist Gambit: A View of the Political Negotiations in the Determination of the Turkish-Iraqi Border," *The Creation of Iraq, 1914–1922*, Reeva Spector Simon and Eleanor H. Tejirian (eds.), New York: Columbia Press.
Dann, U. (1986), "The Iraqi-Iranian War," *Middle East Contemporary Survey Middle East Contemporary Survey; (CD-ROM Version), vol. I–XVIII*, O Bengio, (ed.), The Moshe Dayan Center for Middle Eastern and African Studies, Tel Aviv University, Tel Aviv, Israel, 2000, pp. 157–162.
Davis, E. (2004), " Democracy's Prospects in Iraq," *American Diplomacy* 9(3).
―――― (2005), *Memories of State: Politics, History, and Collective Identity in Modern Iraq*, Los Angeles, CA: University of California Press.
Dawisha, A. (2005), "The Prospects for Democracy in Iraq: Challenges and Opportunities," *Third World Quarterly* 26(4–5): 723–737.
Dawisha, A and K. Dawisha (2003), "How to build a democratic Iraq," *Council on Foreign Affairs* 82(3): 36–50.
De Luce, D (2016), "ISIS Is Using Chemical Weapons Against the Kurds: Why Won't the U.S. Help?" available at <http://foreignpolicy.com/2016/04/22/isis-is-using-chemical-weapons-against-the-kurds-why-wont-the-u-s-help/>, (accessed 09/09/2017).
Devigne, J. (2011), " 'Iraqoncilable' Differences? The Political Nature of the Peshmerga," NIMEP Insights, 48–64, available at <www.tuftsgloballeadership.org/files/resources/nimep/v5/NIMEP_Insights_2011_48-64.pdf>, (accessed 29/01/2015).
Dizeyi, M. (2001), *"Ahdath A'aserteha" (Events that I Witnessed), Erbil*, Iraq: Dar Aras lil-Taba'a wal-Nashir.
Dodge, T. (2006), "Iraq: the Contradictions of Exogenous State-Building in Historical Perspective," *Third World Quarterly* 27(1): 187–200.
Draft Constitution of Kurdistan Region (2009), "Kurdistan Parliament – Iraq," available at <www.perleman.org/default.aspx?page=Constitution&c=Constitution-Kurdistan>, (accessed 09/07/2015).

Dueck, C. (2006), "Strategies for Managing Rogue States," *Orbis* 50(2).
Dunn, M. C. (1995), "The Kurdish Question: Is There an Answer? A Historical Overview," *Middle East Policy* 4(1–2): 72–86.
Economist (1991), "They Deserve a Break." 366(8317): 12.
Edmonds, C. J. (1928), "Two More Ancient Monuments in Southern Kurdistan," *The Geographical Journal* 72(2): 162–163.
——— (1931), "Third Note on Rock Monuments in Southern Kurdistan," *The Geographical Journal* 77(4): 350–355.
——— (1957), "The Kurds of Iraq," *Middle East Journal* 11(1): 52–62.
——— (1959), "The Kurds and the Revolution in Iraq," *Middle East Journal* 13(1): 1–10.
EIA, (U.S. Energy Information Administration), (2011), "Top World Oil Producers 2011," available at <http://205.254.135.7/countries/>, (accessed 05/04/2015).
Eland, I. and D. Lee (2001), "The Rogue State Doctrine and National Missile Defense," *Foreign Policy Briefing* 2.
Elliot, M. (1996), *Independent Iraq: British Influence from 1941–1958*, London: IB Tauris.
Elphinston, W. G. (1946), "The Kurdish Question," *International Affairs* 22(1): 91–103.
Emin, N. M. (1997a), *Le Kenari Danubewe bo Khri Nawzeng: Diwi Nawewey Rwdawekani Kurdistani Eraq (From the Danaube Shore to the Nawzeng Valley: Political events in Iraqi Kurdistan from 1975 to 1978)*, Berlin: Postfach.
——— (1997b), *Penjekan Yektri Deshkenin: Diwi Nawewey Rwdawekani Kurdistani Iraq le Newan 1979–1983 (Fingers that crush each other: Political Events in Iraqi Kurdistan from 1979–1983)*, Berlin: Postfach.
——— (1999), *Khwlanewe le Naw Bazneda: Diwi Nawewey Rwdawekani Kurdistani Iraq 1984–1988 (Going around in circles: the inside story of events in Iraqi Kurdistan 1984–1988)*, Berlin: Malbwndi Awedani Kurdistan.
——— (2000), *'Asr al-Qalam wa al-Muraja'at 1928–1931 (The age of pen and petitions 1928–1931)*, Suleymaniya, Iraq: Khak Press.
——— (2004), *Chand Laparayak la Mezhwi Rojnamawani Kurdi (Some Pages in the History of Kurdish Journalism)*, Publisher unknown.
Encyclopedia Britannica (2012), "Tanzimat", *Encyclopedia Britannica*, available at <www.britannica.com/EBchecked/topic/582884/Tanzimat>, (accessed 03/06/2015).
Entessar, N. (1984), "The Kurds in Post-Revolutionary Iran and Iraq," *Third World Quarterly* 6(4): 911–933.
Ergin, E. (2012), "Iraqi Kurds to Sell Gas Directly to Turkey – Minister," *Reuters*, available at <www.reuters.com/article/2012/07/03/us-turkey-iraq-kurds-gas-idUSBRE8620PR20120703>, (accessed 05/07/2015).
Eskander, S. (2000), "Britain's Policy in Southern Kurdistan: The Formation and the Termination of the First Kurdish Government, 1918–1919," *British Journal of Middle Eastern Studies* 27(2): 139–163.
Farouk-Sluglett, M. and P. Sluglett (2001), *Iraq Since 1958: From Revolution to Dictatorship*, London: IB Tauris.
Farouk-Sluglett, M., P. Sluglett and Joe Stork (1984), "Impact of the War on Iraq," *MERIP Reports* 125/126: 22–30.
Fatih, M. (2012), *Hizb u Rek-khrawe Syasiya Eraqiyekan 1910–2010 (Iraqi political parties and organisations: 1910–2010), Sulaimaniya*, Iraq: Akadimiay Wishiyari Pegeyandni Kadiran.
Fawcett, J. and V. Tanner (2002), *The Internally Displaced People of Iraq*, Washington, DC: Brookings Institution-SAIS Project on Internal Displacement.
Fawzi, A. (1961), *Qasim wa Akrad aw Khanajir we jibal (Qasm and Kurds or Daggers and Mountains)*, Cairo: D.N.

References

Fayad, M. (2006), "Iraqi President Jalal Talabani Talks to Asharq Al-Awsat, Asharq Alawsat," available at <www.asharqalawsat.com/english/news.asp?section=3&id=4972>, (accessed 17/09/2015).

────── (2008), "A Talk with Kurdish President Massoud Barzani," Interview by Ma'ad Fayad, Asharq Al-Awsat, available at <www.asharq-e.com/news.asp?id=13920>, (accessed 29/04/2015).

Ferguson, N. (2003), "The Empire Slinks Back," *New York Times Magazine*, 27/04/2003, available at <www.nytimes.com/2003/04/27/magazine/27EMPIRE.html?pagewanted=all>, (accessed 09/07/2015).

Fieldhouse, D. K. (2002), "Introduction: The Background, Iraq 1918–1944," *Kurds Arabs and Britain*, D. K. Fieldhouse (ed.), London: IB Tauris, pp. 1–58.

Floyd, C. (2007), "Assassinations, Terrorist Strikes and Ethnic Cleansing: Bush's Shadow War in Iraq," *Truth Out.org*, available at <www.alternet.org/story/48016/assassinations,_terrorist_strikes_and_ethnic_cleansing%3A_bush's_shadow_war_in_iraq>, (accessed 12/11/2009).

Foster, B. R. (2003), "Missing in Action: The Iraq Resume and the Human Past," *The Iraq War and Its Consequences: Thoughts of Nobel Peace Laureates and Eminent Scholars*, I. Abrams and G. Wang (eds.), Singapore: World Scientific Publishing, pp. 295–314.

Franzen, J. (2011), *Red Star Over Iraq: Iraqi communism Before Saddam*, London: C. Hurst & Co.

Freedman, R. O. (2002), *The Middle East Enters the Twenty-First Century*, Gainesville, FL: University Press of Florida.

Freij, H. Y. (1993), "Kurdish Nationalism," *The Muslim World* 83(3–4): 324–328.

────── (2007), "The Iraqi State, the Opposition, and the Road to Reconciliation," *Kurdish Identity: Human Rights and Political Status*, Charles G. MacDonald and Carole S. O'Leary (eds.), Gainesville, FL: University Press of Florida.

Fuccaro, N. (1997), "Ethnicity, State Formation, and Conscription in Postcolonial Iraq: The Case of the Yazidi Kurds of Jabal Sinjar," *International Journal of Middle East Studies* 29(04): 559–580.

Fukuyama, F. (2005), "Stateness First," *Journal of Democracy* 16(1): 84–88.

Fuller, M. (2005), "Crying Wolf: Media Disinformation and Death Squads in Occupied Iraq," *Global Research*, available at <http://globalresearch.ca/index.php?context=va&aid=1230>, (accessed 14/02/2015).

Fund for Peace (2011), "Country Analysis Indicators and Their Measures," available at <www.fundforpeace.org/global/library/cr-10-97-ca-conflictassessmentindicators-1105c.pdf>, (accessed 20/01/2015).

────── (2011), "The Failed States Index 2006," available at <www.fundforpeace.org/global/?q=fsi-grid2006>, (accessed 22/10/2015).

────── (2011), "The Failed States Index 2009," available at <www.fundforpeace.org/global/?q=fsi-grid2009>, (accessed 20/10/2015).

────── (2011), "The Failed States Index 2010," available at <www.fundforpeace.org/global/?q=fsi-grid2010>, (accessed 22/10/2015).

Galbraith, P. W. (2006), "Kurdistan in a Federal Iraq," *The Future of Kurdistan in Iraq*, B. O'Leary, J. McGarry and K. Salih (eds.), Philadelphia, PA: University of Pennsylvania Press, pp. 268–281.

Gérard, C. (1993), "Introduction," *A People Without a Country: The Kurds and Kurdistan*, G. Chaliand (ed.), Michael Pallis (trans.), London: Zed Press, pp. 1–10.

Ghareeb, E. (1981), *The Kurdish Question in Iraq*, Syracuse, NY: Syracuse University Press.

Global IDP Database (2003), "Profile of internal displacement: Iraq Compilation of the information available in the Global IDP," Database of the Norwegian Refugee Council, available at <www.unhcr.org/refworld/pdfid/3ae6a62b4.pdf>, (accessed 12/11/2016).

"Gorran Daway Dwakhsti Enjamdani Refrandom Dekat (Gorran Asks for Postponing the Referendum)," *NRT*, available at <www.nrttv.com/Details.aspx?Jimare=81194>, (accessed 08/11/2017).

Graham-Brown, S. (1995), "Intervention, Sovereignty and Responsibility," *Middle East Report* 193: 2–32.

─── (1999), *Sanctioning Saddam: The Politics of Intervention in Iraq*, London: IB Tauris.

Guibernau, M. (1999), *Nations Without States: Political Communities in a Global Age*, Cambridge: Polity Press.

Gulan newspaper (2012), "Le koy ew 1200 Kompaniyay le Kurdistan Kar Deken, 720 yan hi Turkyaye" (Of a total 1200 companies working in Kurdistan 720 are Turkish), 22/12/2012.

GulfTime (2012), "Iraq Premier Must Not Get F-16s: Kurd President," available at <www.gulf-times.com/site/topics/article.asp?cu_no=2&item_no=501290&version=1&template_id=37&parent_id=17>, (accessed 25/04/2015).

Gull, M. O. (2007), *Jenosidy Geli Kurd (The Genocide of the Kurdish People)*, Erbil, Iraq: Aras Publisher.

Gunter, M. M. (1992), *The Kurds of Iraq: Tragedy and Hope*, New York: St. Martin's Press.

─── (1993), "A de facto Kurdish State in Northern Iraq," *Third World Quarterly* 14(2): 295–319.

─── (1994), "A Trip to Free Kurdistan," *Political Science and Politics* 27(1): 146–148.

─── (1996), "The KDP-PUK Conflict in Northern Iraq," *The Middle East Journal* 224–241.

─── (2003), "Kurdish Future in a Post-Saddam Iraq," *Journal of Muslim Minority Affairs* 23(1): 9–23.

─── (2004), "The Kurdish Question in Perspective," *World Affairs* 166(4): 197–205.

─── (2005), "The Kurdish Minority Identity in Iraq," *Nationalism and Minority Identities in Islamic Societies*, Maya Shatzmiller (ed.), Montreal, Quebec, Canada: McGill-Queen's University Press, pp. 261–282.

─── (2007), *Re-Evaluation of Kurdish question Identity Conflicts: Can Violence Be Regulated?* New Bruniswick: Transaction Publisher.

─── (2008), *The Kurds Ascending: The Evolving Solution to the Kurdish Problem in Iraq and Turkey*, New York: Palgrave Macmillan.

─── (2011), "Economic Opportunities in Iraqi Kurdistan," *Middle East Policy* 18(2): 102–109.

Gurr, T. R. (2000), *Peoples Versus States: Minorities at Risk in the New Century*, Washington, DC: United States Institute for Peace Press.

Gurr, T. R. and B. Harff (2004), *Ethnic Conflict in World Politics*, Boulder, CO: Westview Press.

Habib, M. (2011), "Nass al-Muqabala Ejraha Mawqi' al-Niqash Ma'a al-Ustath Tariq al-Hashimi" (Transcript of Interview Conducted by al-Niqash professor Rariq al-Hashimi), available at <http://alhashimi.org/newsdetail.asp?sno=2929>, (accessed 02/09/2015).

Hafidh, H. J. (2012), "Iraq Says Kurdish Oil Exports to Turkey Are Illegal," *The Wall Street Journal*, available at <http://online.wsj.com/article/SB10001424052702303343404577517090563153240.html?mod=googlenews_wsj>, (accessed 01/02/2016).

Hanauer, L, J. Martini and O. Al-Shahery (2011), *Managing Arab-Kurd Tensions in Northern Iraq After the Withdrawal of US Troops*, Washington, DC: DTIC Document.

Hassanpour, A. (1994), "The Kurdish Experience," *Middle East Report* 189: 2–7, 23.

Hassanpour, A. and S. Mojab (2005), "Kurdish Diaspora," *Encyclopedia of Diasporas: Immigrant and Refugee Cultures Around the World*, M. Ember, R. E. Carol and Ian Skoggard (eds.), New York: Springer Publisher.

Hawkari Newspaper, 18/8/1988; 28/4/1988; 24/3/1988.

——— 27/12/2012.

Hawlati (2011), "Khopishandanekan le Roji Nawroz le Seray Azadi," (The Rallies on Nawroz Day in Saray Azadi), available at <www.hawlati.co/wp-content/uploads/2012/06/sara__.jpg>, (accessed 08/09/2015).

Heuvelen, B. V. (2012), "Exxon Out of 4th Bid Round," available at <www.iraqoilreport.com/business/companies/exxon-out-of-4th-bid-round-7826/>, (accessed 25/04/2015).

Hilmi, R. (2003), *Yadasht (Memoir), Third edition, Sulaimaniya*, Iraq: Dezgay Chap w Pakhshi Sardam.

Hiltermann, J. R. (2004), "Outsiders as Enablers: Consequences and Lessons from International Silence on Iraq's Use of Chemical Weapons during the Iran-Iraq War," *Iran, Iraq, and the Legacies of War*, L. G. Potter and G. G. Sick (eds.), London: Palgrave Macmillan, pp. 151–167.

——— (2008), "The 1988 Anfal Campaign," *Online Encyclopedia of Mass Violence*, available at <www.massviolence.org/IMG/article_PDF/The-1988-anfal-Campaign-in-Iraqi-Kurdistan.pdf>, (accessed 12/11/2015).

Hiro, D. (1989), *The Longest War: The Iran-Iraq Military Conflict*, London: Routledge.

Hmeidi, J. A. (1976), *Al-Tattawrat al-Syasiya fi al-Iraq 1941–1952 (The Political Developments in Iraq: 1941–1952)*, Najaf, Iraq: Matba'a al-Nu'man.

Hooglund, E. (1991), "The Other Face of War," *Middle East Report* (171): 3–12.

Hoyt, P. D. (2000), "'Rogue States' and International Relations Theory," *Journal of Conflict Studies* 20(2).

Human Rights Watch (1993), "Genocide in Iraq: The Anfal Campaign Against the Kurds," available at <www.hrw.org/reports/1993/iraqanfal>, (accessed 01/06/2016).

——— (1995), *Iraq's Crime of Genocide: The Anfal Campaign against the Kurds*. New Haven, CT: Yale University Press.

——— (2003), "Iraq: Forcible Expulsion of Ethnic Minorities," *HRW* 15(3).

——— (2003), "Iraq and Iraqi Kurdistan," available at <www.hrw.org/reports/pdfs/worldreports/2k2/iraq.pdf>, (accessed 26/12/2015).

Hussain, S. (1986), "Notes on the Kurdish Struggle," *Race & Class* 27(3): 90–94.

Hussein, A. (1998), *Al-Jabha al-Arabiya al-Iraniya Dhid al-Hilf Al-Amriki al-Sahyoni (The Arabic and Iranian Front Against the American and Zionist Allaince)*, Cairo: Al-markaz al-Arabi al-Islami lil-Dirasat.

Hussein, F. (1977), *Mushkilet al-Mosul (The Mosul Problem)*, Baghdad: Matba'at Eshbiliya.

Hussein, S. (1977), *Khandaq Wahid aw Khandaqan: (One Trench or Two Trenches) Baghdad*, Iraq: Dar Altorh for Press and Publishing.

ICP, Iraqi Communist Party (1956), "Taqrir al-Lijneh al-Merkaziyeh lil-Hizb al-Shiyu'i al-Iraqi allathi Sadaqa 'aleyhi Alkonfrans al-Thani fi Aylul 1956" (The Report of the Central Committee of the Iraqi Communist Party), Ratified by the Second Conference in September 1956.

——— (1959), *Qadhiyatuna al-Wataniya: Bi Qalam al-Rafiq al-Khalid Fahid (Our National Cause: Written by the Immortal Comrad Fahad)*, Baghdad: Matba'a al-Najwm.

——— (1973), *Wethaeq al-Hizb al-Shui'i al_Iraqi : Majmu'a wethaeq Bernamjye (Document of the Iraqi Communist Party: Collection of Program Documents)*, Baghdad: Manshurat al-Thaqafa al-Jadida.

––––––– (1997), "Al-Mu'tamar al-Watani al-Sadis: 26–29 Tammuz 1997," (The Sixth National Congress: July 26–29, 1997), available at <www.iraqicp.com/images/stories/librery/The%206%20National%20Congress.pdf>, (accessed 27/09/2015).
IFDH, International Federation for Human Rights) (2003), "Iraq: Continuous and Silent Ethnic Cleansing: Displaced Persons in Iraqi Kurdistan and Iraqi Refugees in Iran," available at <www.fidh.org/IMG/pdf/iq350a.pdf>, (accessed 12/03/2015).
Ihsan, M. (2000), *Kurdistan wa Dawamat al-Harb (Kurdistan and the Spiral of War)*, Erbil, Iraq: Dar Aras.
IKF, Iraqi Kurdistan Front (1988), *Mithaq wa al-Nidham al-dakhili li-Jabha al-Kurdistaniya (The Charter and Program of Iraqi Kurdistan Front)*, Publisher unknown.
Interim Constitution of Iraq (1990), "International Constitutional Law," available at <www.servat.unibe.ch/law/icl/iz01000_.html#A001>, (accessed 22/05/2015).
International Crisis Group (2004), "Iraq's Kurds: Toward an Historic Compromise?" available at <www.crisisgroup.org/~/media/Files/Middle%20East%20North%20Africa/Iraq%20Syria%20Lebanon/Iraq/Iraqs%20Kurds%20Toward%20an%20Historic%20Compromise.pdf>, (accessed 12/03/2015).
––––––– (2007), "Iraq and the Kurds: Resolving the Kirkuk Crisis," available at <www.crisisgroup.org/home/index.cfm?id=4782>, (accessed 29/01/2015).
––––––– (2012), "Iraq and the Kurds: The High-Stakes Hydrocarbons Gambit," available at <www.crisisgroup.org/~/media/Files/Middle%20East%20North%20Africa/Iraq%20Syria%20Lebanon/Iraq/120-iraq-and-the-kurds-the-high-stakes-hydrocarbons-gambit.pdf>, (accessed 12/11/2016).
Iraqi Constitution (2005), "United Nations Assistance Mission for Iraq," available at <www.uniraq.org/documents/iraqi_constitution.pdf>, (accessed 09/06/2015).
"Iraq Kurdistan Independence Referendum Planned," *BBC News*, 01/07/2014.
Iraqi Interim Constitution (1958), "Iraqi National Congress," available at <http://inciraq.com/Arabic/Classifieds/Iraqi%20Temp%20Constitution%201958.htm>, (accessed 22/05/2016).
Iraqi Interim Constitution (1964), "Iraqi National Congress," available at <http://inciraq.com/Arabic/Classifieds/Iraqi%20Temp%20Constitution%201964.htm>, (accessed 22/05/2015).
Iraqi Interim Constitution (1968), "Iraqi National Congress," available at <http://inciraq.com/Arabic/Classifieds/Iraqi%20Temp%20Constitution%201968.htm>, (accessed 22/05/2015).
"Iraqi Kurdistan Economy Suffers Amid Budget Dispute with Baghdad," *Al-Mointor*, 16/05/2014, available at <www.al-monitor.com/pulse/tr/business/2014/05/iraq-kurdistan-region-budget-dispute-economic-effects.html>, (accessed 05/10/2017).
Israeli, R. (2003), *War, Peace and Terror in the Middle East*, London: Routledge.
Istiqlal Newspaper, 18/2/1931, no. 1359, Baghdad.
Izady, M. R. (2004), "Between Iraq and a Hard Place: The Kurdish Predicament," *Iran, Iraq, and the Legacies of War*, Lawrence G. Potter and Gary G. Sick (eds.), New York: Palgrave Macmillan, pp. 71–99.
Jabar, F. A. (2003), *The Shi'ite Movement in Iraq*, London: Saqi Books.
Jackson, R. H. (1993), *Quasi-States: Sovereignty, International Relations and the Third World*, Cambridge: Cambridge University Press.
Jaf, A. M. B. (2011), "Dete gwem" (Comes to My Ear), *Pasok*, available at <www.pasok.eu/pdf%5CAhmad_Muxtar_Jaf.pdf>, (accessed 01/07/2016).
Jalal, I. (1984), *Komallay Renjderani Kurdistan bo Kurdistaniye (The Reason for the Kurdistani-ness of the Kurdistan Toilers League)*, Second edition, Kurdistan: Chapkhaney Shehid Ibrahim Ezzo.
Jam, K. (2007), "Talabani Calls for US Military Base in Kurdistan," *The Kurdish Globe* 115: 7.

——— (2012), "Foreign Workers and Tourists Benefit from Kurdish Growth, But Key Deficiencies Remain," *The Kurdish Globe* 354: 7.

Jawad, S. N. (1979), *The Kurdish problem in Iraq, The Integration of Modern Iraq*, A. Kelidar (ed.), New York: St. Martin's Press.

——— (1990), *Al-Iraq wal-Masa'ala al-Kurdiya (Iraq and the Kurdish Question)*, London: Dar al-Laam.

Jwaideh, W. (2006), *The Kurdish National Movement: Its Origins and Development*, Syracuse, NY: Syracuse University Press.

Kamaran, R. (2011), "Se Parezgakey Herem Niwey Panze Parezgakey Eraq Hezi Chekdari Heye" (The Armed Forces of the Three Provinces of the Region Are as Much as Half of the Armed Forces of Fifteen Iraqi Provinces), available at <www.chawyxelk.com/Detail.aspx?id=1078&TypeID=1&AutherID=46>, (accessed 29/01/2016).

Karsh, E. (1990), "Geopolitical Determinism: The Origins of the Iran-Iraq War," *Middle East Journal* 44(2): 256–268.

——— (2002), *The Iran-Iraq War, 1980–1988*, Oxford: Osprey Publishing.

——— (2008), *The Iran-Iraq War*, New York: The Rosen Publishing Group.

Karsh, E. and I. Rautsi (1991), *Saddam Hussein: A Political Biography*, New York: The Free Press.

Katzman, K. (1998), *Iraq's Opposition Movements*, Congressional Research Service, Library of Congress, Washington, DC.

Katzman, K. (2012), "Iraq: Politics, Governance, and Human Rights," Congressional Research Service, 13/7/2012, available at <www.fas.org/sgp/crs/mideast/RS21968.pdf>

KDP, Kurdistan Democratic Party (1979), *Tariq al-Haraka al-Taharruriye al-Kurdiye: Taqim Thawra Aylul wa barnamj al-Jadid lil-Hizb al-dimuqrati al-Kurdistani (The Path of the Kurdish Liberation Movement: The Evaluation of the September Revolution and a New Political Program of the Kurdistan Democratic Party)*, Publisher unknown.

——— (1993), *Program u Payrewi Nawxoy Parti Democrati Kurdistan (The Constitution of the Kurdistan Democratic Party), Erbil*, Iraq: Chapkhaney Xebat.

——— (2004), "Al-Mnhaj wal-Nidham al-Dakhili" (The Platform and Internal System), available at <www.kdp6.com>, (accessed 04/01/2017).

——— (2010), "Constitution & Bylaws," available at <www.kdp.se/kdpprogram.pdf >, (accessed 18/04/2016).

——— (2011), "Kurdistan Women Union" (KWU), available at <www.kdp.se/?do=women (accessed 08/09/2015).

KDP-PC, The Kurdistan Democratic Party-The Preparatory Committee (1997), *Taqim al-Thawra al-Kurdiye wa Inhiyaruha: Al-Drws wal-Ibre al-Mustakhlasa Minha (The Evaluation of the Kurdish Revolution and Its Collapse: Lessons Derived from It)*, Second edition, Publisher unknown.

Kelidar, A. (1992), "The Wars of Saddam Hussein," *Middle Eastern Studies* 28(4): 778–798.

Khabat (1959), "The Mouthpeace of the Kurdistan Democratic Party," 14/09/1959, Baghdad.

——— (1959), "The Mouthpeace of the Kurdistan Democratic Party," 31/08/1959, Baghdad.

——— (1960), "The Mouthpeace of the Kurdistan Democratic Party," 07/12/1960, Baghdad.

——— (1960), "The Mouthpeace of the Kurdistan Democratic Party," 21/10/1960, Baghdad.

——— (1960), "The Mouthpeace of the Kurdistan Democratic Party," 13/10/1960, Baghdad.

——— (1960), "The Mouthpeace of the Kurdistan Democratic Party," 09/10/1960, Baghdad.

——— (2009), "The Mouthpeace of the Kurdistan Democratic Party," 05/08/2009, Erbil.

——— (2010), "The Mouthpeace of the Kurdistan Democratic Party," 11/06/2010, Erbil.

——— (2010), "The Mouthpeace of the Kurdistan Democratic Party," 04/04/2010, Erbil.

Khabati Kurdistan Newspaper (1957), "Kurds and Arabs," 3.
Khadduri, M. (2000), "Nuri Al-Sa'id's Disenchantment with Britain in His Last Years," *The Middle East Journal* [Volume, number?]: 83–96.
Khalil, L. (2009), *Stability in Iraqi Kurdistan: Reality or Mirage?* Washington, DC: Brookings Institution.
Khani, A. (1968), *Mem u Zin (Mem and Zin)*, Third edition, Hewler, Iraq: Chapkhaney Mukriyani.
Kinnane, D. (1964), *The Kurds and Kurdistan*, Oxford: Oxford University Press.
Kirişçi, K. and G. Winrow (1997), *The Kurdish Question and Turkey: An Example of a Trans-State Ethnic Conflict*, London: Frank Cass & Co. Ltd.
Kirishan, M. (2008), "Masud Barzani: Nwqat al-Khilaf Ma'a al-Hkume al-Merkeziya" (Ma'sud Barzani: Points of disagreement with the central government), Al-Jazeera (Arabic), interview by Mohammad Kirishan, available at <www.aljazeera.net/NR/exeres/14863230-9624-4FE9-9656-EEB47FD9114B.htm>, (accessed 23/09/2016).
Kirmanj, S. (2010), "The Construction of the Iraqi State and the Question of National Identity," Ph.D thesis, University of South Australia.
Kissinger, H. A. (1979), *The White House Years*, New York: Little, Brown and Company.
Klare, M. (1996), *Rogue States and Nuclear Outlaws: America's Search for a New Foreign Policy*, New York: Hill and Wang.
KNA, Kurdistan National Assembly (1992), "Briyari rageyandni fidraly" (The decision of declaration of federalism), available at <http://perleman.org/files/articles/080108073542.pdf>, (accessed 03/06/2017).
―――― (1993), "Qarar Raqam 4 li-Sinna 1994 (Resolution no. 4 of the Year 1994)," *Al-Waqai' al-Iraqiya* (Iraqi Official Gazzeta).
―――― (1994), "Qarar Raqam 4 li-Sinna 1994" (Resolution no. 4 of the Year 1994), *Al-Waqai' al-Iraqiya* (Iraqi Official Gazzeta).
―――― (1997a), "Qarar raqam 2 li-Sinna 1997 (Resolution no. 2 for the year 1997)," *Al-Waqai' al-Iraqiya* (Iraqi Official Gazzeta).
―――― (1997b), "Qarar raqam 3 li-Sinna 1997 (Resolution no. 3 for the year 1997)," *Al-Waqai' al-Iraqiya* (Iraqi Official Gazzeta).
―――― (1999), "Qanun 'Alam Eqlim Kurdistan al-Iraq Raqam 14 li-Sinna 1999 (Law of the flag of the Kurdistan Region of Iraq, resolution no 14 of the year 1999)," *Al-Waqai' al-Iraqiya* (Iraqi Official Gazzeta).
KNCNA, Kurdish National Congress of North America (2010), "The Map of Greater Kurdistan," available at <www.kurdishnationalcongress.org/docs/map.html>, (accessed 10/11/2016).
Kolstø, P. (2006), "The Sustainability and Future of Unrecognized Quasi-States," *Journal of Peace Research* 43(6): 723–740.
Komalla Magazine, "Organi Komallay Ranjderani Kurdistan," (The Review of the Kurdistan Toilers League) (1987), 3(6); (1982a), 2(2); (1982b), 2(3); (1981), 1(9).
Komalla, Komallay Renjderani Kurdistan (1983), "Eraqcheti dagirker u borzhwazi Kurdistan" (The Iraqism of the occupation and Kurdistan's bourgeoisie), Blawkrawekani Komallay Renjderan.
Korn, D. A. (1994), "The Last Years of Mustafa Barzani," *Middle East Quarterly* 1(2).
Kosrat (1985), "Keshey Kurd le Eraqda" (The Kurdish Question in iraq), *Kurdayeti* 3(1): 38–64.
"Kosrat Rasul Issued a Statement on Kirkuk," *Livin*, 18/10/2017, available at <www.lvinpress.com/n/dreja.aspx?=hewal&jmare=59741&Jor=1>, (accessed 05/10/2017).
Koyi, H. Q. (2004), *Diwani Haji Qadri Koyi (Divan of Haji Qadri Koyi)*, Stockholm: Nefel.

Kreyenbroek, P. G. and S. Sperl (1992), *The Kurds: A Contemporary Review*, London: Routledge.

"KRG Council of Ministers' Follow Up Statement on 2018 Draft Federal Budget Bill, Kurdistan Regional Government", 05/11/2017, available at <http://cabinet.gov.krd/a/d.aspx?s=040000&l=12&a=55989>, (accessed 07/11/2017).

KRG, Kurdistan Regional Government (1997), "Ala u Srwdi Nishtimani" (The Flag and National Anthem), available at <www.krg.org/articles/detail.asp?lngnr=13&smap=0301 0100&rnr=168&anr=16877>, (accessed 12/07/2015).

――― (2006), "Law no. (4) of 2006: Law of Investment in Kurdistan Region – Iraq," available at <www.krg.org/uploads/documents/InvestmentLaw_KRGOfficialEng_2006_08_04_h11m20s33.pdf>, (accessed 03/09/2016).

――― (2006), "Statement by Prime Minister Nechirvan Barzani on Non-Implementation of the Iraqi Constitution," available at <www.krg.org/a/print.aspx?l=12&smap=010000&a=13950>, (accessed 25/08/2015).

――― (2007), "Mezhwi Koni Kurdistan" (The Ancient History of Kurdistan), available at <www.krg.org/articles/detail.asp?lngnr=13&smap=03010600&rnr=173&anr=22043>, (accessed 12/07/2015).

――― (2008), "Full Text of KRG's Response to Iraqi Prime Minister's Accusations," available at <www.krg.org/articles/print.asp?anr=26811&lngnr=12&rnr=223>, (accessed 20/10/2015).

――― (2010), "The Kurdistan Region in Brief," available at <www.krg.org/articles/detail.asp?lngnr=12&smap=03010300&rnr=140&anr=23911>, (accessed 12/12/2016).

――― (2012a) "KRG Ministry of Natural Resources Production Sharing Contracts," available at <http://krg.org/pages/page.asp?lngnr=12&rnr=296&PageNr=1>, (accessed 29/07/2015).

――― (2012b), "Prime Minister Barzani: Kurdistan's energy relations with Turkey to Enter a New Phase," available at <www.krg.org/articles/detail.asp?rnr=223&lngnr=12&smap=02010100&anr=44020>, (accessed 27/11/2015).

――― (2012c), "Nechirvan Barzani: Demanewet Baghdad leser Bnemay Hawbeshi w Sheraketda Mamele Legel Heremi Kurdistanda Bikat" (Nechivan Barzani: We want a Baghdad deal with the Kurdistan Region based on powersharing), available at <www.krg.org/articles/detail.asp?rnr=26&lngnr=13&smap=01010200&anr=44068>, (accessed 23/04//2015).

――― (2012d), "Prime Minister Barzani's Speech at the Erbil Energy Conference," available at <www.krg.org/articles/detail.asp?smap=02040100&lngnr=12&rnr=268&anr=44037>, (accessed 23/06/2017).

"KRG to Handover Oil, Border Revenues if Baghdad Sends 17 Percent Budget Share: Barzani," *Kurdistan24*, 06/11/2017, available at <www.kurdistan24.net/en/news/73611554-853d-4b14-a355-ad724284b275>, (accessed 08/11/2017).

KRG-ME Kurdistan Regional Government – Ministry of Education (2004), "Babaten Komallayati Pola Penje Saratayi" (Societal Topics for the Grade Five Primary School), Erbil, Iraq.

――― (2008), *Mezhwi Nwe w Hawcharkh Poli Dwazdahami Amadayi Wejayi (New and Modern History for Grade Twelve High School – Humanities)*, Beirut, Lebanon: Al-Mustaqbal Press.

――― (2016), "KRG-MR, Kurdistan Regional Government-Minister of Education (2016)," Social Subjects for Year Four Elementary Schools.

KRP, Kurdistan Regional Presidency (2007), "Oil and Gas Law of the Kurdistan Region, Law no. (22) – 2007," available at <www.krg.org/uploads/documents/Kurdistan%20

Oil%20and%20Gas%20Law%20English__2007_09_06_h14m0s42.pdf>, (accessed 09/08/2015).

—— (2012a), "Welami Diwani Serokayety Heremi Kurdistan bo Witekani Berez Nwri Malki Legel Kenali (N.R.T) in Roji 13/5/2012" (The Response of the Kurdistan Regional Presidency to the Speech of Nuri Maliki on NRT Channel on 13/5/2012), available at <www.xendan.org/img4/kurdish/barham/88884/maliki24520112wwww.pdf>, (accessed 23/06/2015).

—— (2012b), "Seroki Heremi Kurdistan Sardani Peshmergay Kurdistani le Parezgay Kerkuk Kird" (The President of Kurdistan Region Visited the Kurdistan Peshmerga in Kirkuk), available at <www.krp.org/kurdish/articledisplay.aspx?id=63SGNH4CSRw=>, (accessed 12/12/2015).

Kurdish Globe (2012a), "Exxon Announces 25-Year Oil Deals with KRG," available at <www,kurdishglobe,net/display-article.html?id=C1F203F9EF56C5BC22F8DA5DD D0E3793>, (accessed 05/03/2015).

—— (2012b), "Hawrami Announces KRG Oil and Gas Strategy," available at <www.kurdishglobe.net/display-article.html?id=1542DF665716C1D274B73E32DEFE5 62D>, (accessed 29/09/2016).

—— (2012c), "Iran's Consul in Erbil Describes Trade Relations as Extensive," available at <www.kurdishglobe.net/display-article.html?id=1151D9DFDB21981DCFBEB3 2B0C6C1831, (accessed 16/05/2015).

"Kurdistan Parliament in Session to Address Region's Presidency, Hear Statement from Barzani," *Rudaw*, 29/10/2017, available at <www.rudaw.net/mobile/english/kurdistan/291020175?ctl00_phMainContainer_phMain_ControlComments1_gvCommentsChangePage=2_5>, (accessed 30/10/2017).

Kwrdistani Nwe (2010), "Herem 90% Khorak le Derewe Dehenet" (The Region imports 90% of its food from outside), available at <www.knwe.org/Direje.aspx?Jimare=3287& Cor=11&Besh=Araste>, (accessed 01/02/2015).

Lake, D. A. and D. Rothchild (1998), *The International Spread of Ethnic Conflict: Fear, Diffusion, and Escalation*, Princeton, NJ: Princeton University Press.

Lambert, P. J. (1997), "The United States and the Kurds: Case Studies in United States Engagement," Masters thesis, Monterey, CA.

"Law of Administration for the State of Iraq for the Transitional Period [Iraq]" (2004), available at <www.unhcr.org/refworld/docid/45263d612.html>, (accessed 04/03/2016).

Lawrence, D. A. (2000), "A Shaky De Facto Kurdistan," *Middle East Report* 30(2) (Summer): 24–26.

Lawrence, Q. (2008), *Invisible Nation: How the Kurds' Quest for Statehood Is Shaping Iraq and the Middle East*, New York: Walker Publishing Company.

Layelle, S. (2012), "Erbil Sspires to Be a Regional Hub," *Kurdistan Regional Government Website*, available at <www.krg.org/a/d.aspx?s=02010200&l=12&r=73&a=4536 7&s=010000>, (accessed 29/11/2015).

Leaders-20 Project (2010), "Lesson 8: Failing States," available at <www.l20.org/lessons/Lesson%208%20Failing%20States.pdf>, (accessed 01/07/2016).

League of Nations (1925), "Question of the Frontier Between Turkey and Iraq, report submitted to the Council by the Commission instituted by the Council Resolution of September 30th, 1925," Lausanne, Switzerland: League of Nations.

—— (1932), D. A., Council, Members, A.17.1932.VII (Political.1932.VII.9) 16 August 1932, "Declaration of The Kingdom Of Iraq, made at Baghdad on May 30th, 1932, on the occasion of the termination of the Mandatory Regime in Iraq, and containing the Guarantees given to the Council by the Iraqi Government: article 9," Baghdad, Iraq.

Leezenberg, M. M. (2002), "Urbanization, Privatization, and Patronage: The Political Economy of Iraqi Kurdistan," *Iraq's Economic Predicament*, K. A. Mahdi (ed.), Lebanon: Ithaca Press.

——— (2006), "Urbanization, Privatization, and Patronage: The Political Economy of Iraqi Kurdistan," *The Kurds: Nationalism and Politics*, F. A. Jabar and H. Dawood (eds.), London: Saqi Books, pp. 151–179.

Levy, A. (1990), "The Gulf Crisis in Historical Perspective," *Suffolk Transnational Law Journal* 14: 23.

Lévy, B. H. (2017), "Who Betrayed the Kurdish People?" *Tablet Magazine*, available at <www.tabletmag.com/jewish-news-and-politics/247574/who-betrayed-the-kurdish-people>, (accessed 12/11/2017).

Little, D. (2010), "The United States and the Kurds: A Cold War Story," *Journal of Cold War Studies* 12(4): 63–98.

Litvak, M. (1991), "Iraq," *Middle East Contemporary Survey; (CD-ROM Version), vol. I–XVIII*, O. Bengio (ed.), The Moshe Dayan Center for Middle Eastern and African Studies, Tel Aviv University, Tel Aviv, Israel, 2000.

Loney, J. (2011), "Delicate Balancing Act Required in Iraq's Kirkuk," *The Daily Star*, available at <www.dailystar.com.lb/News/Middle-East/2011/Aug-01/Delicate-balancing-act-required-in-Iraqs-Kirkuk.ashx#axzz2GhRgwybE>, (accessed 01/09/2015).

Lortz, M. G. (2005), "Willing to Face Death: A History of Kurdish Military Forces, the Peshmerga, from the Ottoman Empire to Present-Day Iraq," Masters thesis, Florida State University.

Lukitz, L. (1995), *Iraq: The Search for National Identity*, London: Frank Cass & Co. Ltd.

Lyon, W. (2002), "Kurds, Arabs & Britons: The Memoir of Wallace Lyon in Iraq 1918–44," *Kurds, Arabs & Britons: The Memoir of Wallace Lyon in Iraq 1918–44*, D. K. Fieldhouse (ed.), London: IB Tauris.

Mack, D. L. (2007), "The United State Policy and the Iraqi Kurds," *Kurdish Identity: Human Rights and Political Status*, C. G. MacDonald and Carole S. O'Leary (eds.), Gainesville, FL: University Press of Florida.

Mahdi, O. (2011), "Dulaimi Calls for a Sunni Province," available at <www.niqash.org/articles/?id=2775>, (accessed 28/12/2014).

Mahwi, A. (2012), "Wazareti Samana Srwshtiyekan Asankari bo Nardene Derewey Newt bo Eran Dekat (The Ministry of the Natural Resources Facilitated the Export of Oil to Iran), Hawlati, available at <www.hawlati.co/babetekan/16217>, (accessed 23/11/2016).

Mairakov, M. (1963), "Stop the Atrocities Against the Kurds," *International Affairs* 9(8): 55–59.

Makhmwri, G. (2010), *Bisaraha: Hiwarat Hawla al-Qadhiya al-Kurdiya (Frank Dialogues About Kurdish Issues)*, Erbil, Iraq: Minara Press.

Makiya, K. (1994), *Cruelty and silence: war, tyranny, uprising, and the Arab World*, London: W. W. Norton & Company, Inc.

Malanczuk, P. (1991), "The Kurdish Crisis and Allied Intervention in the Aftermath of the Second Gulf War," *European Journal of International Law* 2: 114.

Mamikonian, S. (2005), "Israel and the Kurds (1949–1990)," *Iran and the Caucasus* 381–399.

Marr, P. (1985), *Modern History of Iraq*, Boulder, CO: Westview Press.

Martini, J., O. Al-Shahery, L. & Hanauer (2011), "Managing Arab-Kurd Tensions in Northern Iraq After the Withdrawal of US Troops," Rand National Defense Research Institute, Santa Monica, CA.

Maruf, N. (1979), "Arrube al-Ulama al-Mansubin ila al-Alacamye fi bilad al-Rum w al-Jazire w Shehrezur we Azerbaijan (The Arab origin of Islamic Scholars in the Rum Land, al-Jazira and Azerbaijan)," Third edition, Wazara al-Fnun wal-Thaqafa al-Iraqiya.

Mathewson, E. (2003), "Rebuilding Iraq: Lessons from the British Military Occupation," *U.S. Policy in Post-Saddam Iraq: Lessons from the British Experience*, M. Eisenstadt and Eric Mathewson (eds.), Washington, DC: The Washington Institute for Near East Policy.

Mazhar, K. (2001), *Chand Laparayak la Mezhwi Gali Kurd (Several Pages in the History of the Kurdish Nation)*, Erbil, Iraq: Mukiryani.

McDowall, D. (1992), "The Kurdish Question: A Historical Review," *The Kurds: A Contemporary Overview*, P. Kreyenbroek and S. Sperl (eds.), London: Routledge.

——— (2004), *A Modern History of the Kurds*, London: IB Tauris.

McDowall, D. and M. Short (1996). *The Kurds*, A Nation Denied, London: Minority Rights Group.

Meiselas, S. (2008), *Kurdistan: In the Shadow of History*, Second edition, Chicago, IL: University of Chicago Press.

Mella, J. (2000), *Kurdistan w al-Kurd: Watan Masruq we Mughtasab we Muqasm; Umma mustbide w Sajine wa Bila Dawla (Kurdistan and the Kurds, a Stolen and Divided Homeland, a Nation Enslaved, Imprisoned and Without a State)*, Third edition, London: Jamiaat Gharb Kurdistan.

——— (2005), *Kurdistan and The Kurds a Divided Homeland and a Nation without State*, London: Western Kurdistan Association Publications.

Memorandum from Jonathan Howe to Secretary of State Eagleburger (1983), "Iraqi Use of Chemical Weapons," Document no. 25, available at <www2.gwu.edu/-nsarchiv/NSAEBB/NSAEBB82/iraq25.pdf>, (accessed 18/01/2016).

Mina, A. Q. (2012), *Amni Stratiji Iraq w Sekuchkay Ba'siyan: Tarhil, Ta'rib, Tab'ith (Iraq's security strategy and the Ba'thists' tripod: Displacement, Arabization and Ba'thification)*, Suleimaniya, Iraq: Kurdistan Centre for Strategic Studies.

Ministry of Higher Education and Scientific Research (2012), "Universities in Kurdistan," available at <www.mhe-krg.org/node/23>, (accessed 25/03/2015).

Minorities at Risk Project (2004), "Chronology for Kurds in Iraq," available at <www.unhcr.org/refworld/docid/469f38a6c.html>, (accessed 11/04/2015).

Miran, R. (2009), *Etnografya w yeketi etniki Kurd (Ethnograpy and the Unity of the Kurdish Ethnicity)*, Erbil, Iraq: Aras Publications.

Mirawdeli, K. (1993), "The Kurds Political Status and Human Rights," Paper presented at The Kurds Political status and Human Rights Conference, Georgetown, Washington, DC.

——— (2003), "Kurdistani Intellectuals Must Unite Now, Lest History Repeat Itself as a Tragic Farce," *KurdishMedia*, available at <www.kurdmedia.com/article.aspx?id=9285>, (accessed 05/06/2015).

Mohammad, K. I. (2006), *Al-Qadhiye al-Kurdiye fi Iraq wjud am Hadud? (Is the Kurdish Issue in Iraq the Issue of Presence or Border?)* Erbil, Iraq: Salahaddin University.

Moore, M. (2006), "The Ethics of Secession and Postinvasion Iraq," *Ethics & International Affairs* 20(1): 55–78.

"More than 168, 000 People Displaced from Kirkuk and Other Areas," *Kurdistan Regional Government*, 25/10/2017, available at <http://cabinet.gov.krd/a/d.aspx?s=040000&l=12&a=55943>, (accessed 05/11/2017).

Muheddin, W. O. (2006), *Danusanekani Bzwtnewey Rizgarixwazi Netewey kwrd u hkwmetekani Eraq 1921–1968 (Negotiations of the Kurdish Liberation Movement with Iraqi Governments 1921–1968)*, Sulaimaniya, Iraq: Centeri Lekolinewey Strategi Kurdistan.

Mukiryani, K. (2008), *Serdemani Zmani Kurdi w Komele Zmanani Erani (Stages of Kurdish Language and the Iranian Group of Languages)*, Erbil, Iraq: Aras Publishers.

Naamani, I. T. (1966), "The Kurdish Drive for Self-Determination," *Middle East Journal* 20(3): 279–295.

Nagel, J. (1980), "The Conditions of Ethnic Separatism: The Kurds in Turkey, Iran, and Iraq," *Ethnicity* 1(3).

Nakdimon, S. (1997), *Al-Mosad fi al-Iraq and Dwal al-Jiwar (Mosad in Iraq and neighbouring countries)*, Amman: Jordan Dar al-Jalil li-Alnashir.

Natali, D. (2000), "Manufacturing Identity and Managing Kurds in Iraq, Turkey, and Iran: A Study in the Evolution of Nationalism," Ph.D thesis, University of Pennsylvania.

——— (2005), *The Kurds and the state: evolving national identity in Iraq, Turkey, and Iran*, New York: Syracuse University Press.

——— (2010), *Kurdish Quasi-State: Development and Dependency In Post-Gulf War Iraq*, New York: Syracuse University Press.

Nawa Newspaper (2012a), "Yasin Majid: Sardanakay Masud Barzani u Kurakay bo Kerkuk Serdanakani Saddam Hussein u Uday babir Dehenetwe" (Yasin Majid: The Visit of Masud Barzani and His Son Reminds Us of Saddam Hussein and His Son)," available at <www.radionawa.com/Detail.aspx?id=2478&LinkID=1#.UMmLBMVUl_A>, (accessed 12/12/2014).

——— (2012b), "Sardanakay Barzani bo Kerkuk Payamaek bu baway Ewan Aamadan bo Shar" (The visit of Barzani to Kirkuk was a message that they are ready to fight), available at <www.radionawa.com/Detail.aspx?id=2456&LinkID=1#.UMmMXMVUl_A>, (accessed 12/12/2014).

Nebez, J. (2001), *Kurdistan w Shorishekey (Kurdistan's Revolution)*, Erbil, Iraq: Aras Publishing House.

——— (2004), *The Kurds: History and Kulture*, London: WKA Publications.

Neff, D. (1991), "The U.S., Iraq, Israel, and Iran: Backdrop to War," *Journal of Palestine Studies* 20(4): 23–41.

The New York Times, 12/6/1962.

——— 24/6/1965.

——— 30/12/1969.

——— 01/04/1974.

Nida' Kurdistan (1956), *"Fi sabil tawhid al-Haraka al-Thawriya fi Kurdistan al-Iraq" (For the Revolutionary Movement in Iraqi Kurdistan)*, Iraq: Nida' Kurdistan.

NIHA, Niha News Agency (2012), "Kurdistan U Qubris le Yari Kotayida (Kurdistan and Cyprus in the Final Game)," available at <www.niha24.com/Direje.aspx?Jimare=6167>, (accessed 09/06/2016).

Nisan, M. (2002), *Minorities in the Middle East: A History of Struggle and Self-Expression*, Jefferson, NC: McFarland & Company, Inc.

Nuri, B. (2001), *Mudhakarat Baha al-Din Nuri: Sikritir al-Lajnah al-Markaziyah lil-Hizb al-Shu'i al-Iraqi (Memoirs of Baha al-Din Nuri: Secretary of the Central Committee of the Iraqi Communist Party)*, London: Dar al-Hikma.

Nuri, F. (2007), *Bzavi Barzani (The Barzani Movement)*, Erbil, Iraq: Aras Publisher.

O'Balance, E. (1973), *The Kurdish Revolt: 1961–1970*, London: Faber and Faber.

Ofteringer, R. and R. Bäcker (1994), "A Republic of Statelessness: Three Years of Humanitarian Intervention in Iraqi Kurdistan," *Middle East Report* (187/188): 40–45.

O'Leary, B. (2007), "Nationalities, Oil, and Land: Kirkuk and the Disputed Territories," Paper for Conference at Chatham House, London, 19/12/2007.

—— (2009), *How to Get Out of Iraq with Integrity*, Philadelphia, PA: University of Pennsylvania Press.
O'Leary, C. A. (2002), "The Kurds of Iraq: Recent History, Future Prospects," *Middle East Review of International Affairs* 6(4): 17–29.
Olson, R. (1987), "The Second Time Around: British Policy Toward the Kurds (1921–22)," *Die Welt des Islams* 27(1/3): 91–102.
—— (1992), "The Kurdish Question in the Aftermath of the Gulf War: Geopolitical and Geostrategic Changes in the Middle East," *Third World Quarterly* 13(3): 475–499.
Omer, A. H. (2007), *Endame Kurdekani Enjwmeni Nwenerani Eraqi le Rozgari Pashayetida (Kurdish Members of the Iraqi House of Representatives During the Monarchy)*, Erbil, Iraq: Chapemeni Shahab.
Omer, S. (2002), *Yeketi Nishtimani Kurdistan: Damezrandn u Dest Pekrdnewey Shorish 1975–1976 (Patriotic Union of Kurdistan: Foundation and Resumption of the Revolution 1975–1976)*, Sulaimaniya, Iraq: Koliji Zanste Mrovayetiyekan.
Omissi, D. E. (1990), *Air Power and Colonial Control: The Royal Air Force, 1919–1939*, Manchester: Manchester University Press.
Özoğlu, H. (2004), *Kurdish Notables and the Ottoman State: Evolving Identities, Competing Loyalties, and Shifting Boundaries*, Albany, NY: State University of New York Press.
Park, B. (2003), "Strategic Location, Political Dislocation: Turkey, the United States, and Northern Iraq," *Middle East Review of International Affairs* 7(2): 11–23.
—— (2004), "Iraq's Kurds and Turkey: Challenges for US Policy," *Parameters* 34(3): 18–30.
Parsi, T. (2006), "Israel and the Origins of Iran's Arab Option: Dissection of a Strategy Misunderstood," *The Middle East Journal* 60(3): 493–512.
Pelletiere, S. C. and D. Johnson (1991), *Lessons Learned: The Iran-Iraq War*, Washington, DC: DTIC Document.
Perry, W. L., et al. (2009). *Withdrawing from Iraq: Alternative Schedules, Associated Risks, and Mitigating Strategies*, Washington, DC: DTIC Document.
Peshang Newspaper (1982), "Kurdistan Democratic Popular Party," no. 1.
Pflüeger, F. (2012), "New Stability and Prospects for Kurdish Oil and Gas," *KGE-Business Alliances*, available at <www.kge-businessalliances.com/new-stability-and-prospects-for-kurdish-oil-and-gas>, (accessed 04/12/2015).
Piremerd, T. (2002), *Diwani Piremerd: Piremerd u Pedachuneweyeki Nwey Zhyan u Berhemekani* (Divan of Piremerd: Piremerd and a Revision of his Life and Writings), O. Ashna (ed.), Erbil, Iraq: Aras Publishers.
"Political Crisis Escalates in Iraq's Kurdistan Region," *Reuters*, 12/10/2017, available at <www.reuters.com/article/us-iraq-kurds/political-crisis-escalates-in-iraqs-kurdistan-region-idUSKCN0S60HX20151012>, (accessed 13/10/2017).
Polk, W. R. (2005), *Understanding Iraq*, New York: Harper Collins.
Pollack, K. M. (2004), "After Saddam: Assessing the Reconstruction of Iraq," Saban Center for Middle East Policy, Washington, DC.
Potter, L. G. (2004), "The Evolution of the Iran-Iraq Boundary," *The Creation of Iraq, 1914–1922*, Reeva Spector Simon and Eleanor H. Tejirian (eds.), New York: Columbia Press.
"President Barzani Addresses the People of Kurdistan," *Kurdistan Region Presidency*, 29/09/2017, available at <www.presidency.krd/english/articledisplay.aspx?id=/99h3O ipowc=>, (accessed 03/10/2017).

"President Barzani Addresses the People of Kurdistan," *Kurdistan Region Presidency*, 29/09/2017, available at <www.presidency.krd/english/articledisplay.aspx?id=/99h3Oipowc=>, (accessed 03/10/2017).

"President Barzani Meets with Kurdistan Region's Political Parties to Set the Date for the Referendum," *Kurdistan regional Presidency*, 07/06/2017, available at <http://presidency.krd/english/articledisplay.aspx?id=/99h3Oipowc=>, (accessed 12/09/2017).

"Press Statement by Heather Nauert," Department Spokesperson 20/10/2017, available at <www.state.gov/r/pa/prs/ps/2017/10/274980.htm>, (accessed 01/11/2017).

"Press Statement by Heather Nauert," Department Press Briefing, 08/06/2017, available at <www.state.gov/r/pa/prs/dpb/2017/06/271653.htm>, (accessed 09/09/2017).

"Press Statement by Rex W. Tillerson," Iraqi Kurdistan Regional Government's Referendum, 29/09/2017, available at <www.state.gov/secretary/remarks/2017/09/274522.htm>, (accessed 02/10/2017).

"Press Statement by Heather Nauert, Iraqi Kurdistan Regional Government's Planned Referendum," Department Spokesperson, 20/09/2017, available at <www.state.gov/r/pa/prs/ps/2017/09/274324.htm>, (accessed 01/10/2017).

Princeton University (2010), "Wordnet," Princeton, NJ.

PUK, Patriotic Union of Kurdistan (1985), *Gftwgoy Shorish Legel Miri (The Revolution's Negotiations with the Government)*, Sulaimaniya, Iraq: Bnkey Chapemeni Asos.

——— (1986), "Haqiqa al-Mwaqif al-Itihad al-watani al-Kurdistani" (Facts About Positions of the Patriotic Union of Kurdistan), Shahid Jaf'ar.

——— (1988), "Rageyandini Mektebi Syasi Yeketi Nishtimani Kurdistan" (A Statement by the Politboro of the Patriotic Union of Kurdistan), available at <www.sbeiy.com/UserFiles/File/NewFiles/Beyani%20Anfal.JPG>, (accessed 12/11/2014).

——— (1992), *Bername u Peyrewi Nawkhoy Yekei Nishtimani Kurdistan: Pesend Krawi Yekemin Kongrey Gshti 1992 (The Constitution of the Patriotic Union of Kurdistan: Ratified by the First General Congress 1992)*, Publisher unknown.

——— (2001), *Bername u Peyrewi Nawkhoy Yekei Nishtimani Kurdistan: Pesend Krawi Yekemin Kongrey Gshti 2001 (The Constitution of the Patriotic Union of Kurdistan: Ratified in the Eleventh General Congress 2001)*, Publisher unknown.

Qadir, A. M. (2007), *Mawqif Majlis al-Nawab al-Iraqi mn al-Qadhiya al-Kurdiya fi al-Iraq 1925–1945 (The Position of the Iraqi Parliament on the Kurdish Question 1925–1945)*, Sulaimaniya, Iraq: Binkey Zhin.

Qaftan, K. (2003), *Al-Intifadhat al-Barzaniya: Safhat mn Tarikh al-Haraka al-Taharruriya al-Kurdiya fi Nisf al-Awal mn al-Qrn al-Ishrin (The Barzanis' Uprisings: Pages in the History of the Kurdish Revolutionary Movement During the First Half of the Twentieth Century)*, Erbil, Iraq: Aras Publisher.

Rabil, R. G. (2002), "The Iraqi Opposition's Evolution: From Conflict to Unity?" *Middle East Review of International Affairs* 6(4): 1–17.

Rajkowski, R. (1946). "A Visit to Southern Kurdistan," *The Geographical Journal* 107(3/4): 128–134.

Randal, J. C. (1997), *After Such Knowledge, What Forgiveness? My Encounters with Kurdistan*, New York: Farrar, Straus and Giroux.

Rebaz (1993), *Qendil Beghday Hejand (Qandil Convulsed Baghdad)*, Erbil, Iraq: Zanko Publishing.

Rebazi Nwe (1982), *Iraqeki Demokrat u Serbekho, Kurdistaneki Autonom (A Democratic, Independent and Autonomous Kurdistan)*, Suleymaniya, Iraq: Patriotic Union of Kurdistan 3(2–3).

Regay Rizgari newspaper (1985), "Shorish le pilanekani dwzhmn be heztre (Revolution Is Stronger than the Enemy's Conspiracy)", *Yeketi Shorishgeriani Kurdistan* 3.
Rengin Newspaper (1988). no. 10, Baghdad.
Resul, I. M. (2008), *Ahmedi Khani: 1650–1707 (Ahmedi Khani: 1650–1707)*, Sulaimaniya, Iraq: Mektabi Bir u Wishiyari Y.N.K.
Reuters (2009), "Kurdish Independence Just a Dream, Talabani Tells Turkey," available at <www.reuters.com/article/2009/03/16/idUSLG519166>, (accessed 01/02/2016).
RI-MI, Republic of Iraq, Ministry of Information (1977), *Law of Autonomy*, Third edition, Baghdad, Iraq: Al-Hurriya Printing House.
Rizgari (1952a), "Le Jezhni Nawrozda" (In Nawroz Feast) 6; (1948).
—— (1952b), "Yadi Roley Nebez Pesheway Netewey Kurd" (In the Memory of a Brave Son and the Leader of the Kurdish Nation), 7.
——(1953), "Kurdistan Democratic Party-Iraq," no. 6.
—— (1954), "Kurdistan Democratic Party." no. 5.
Robinson, L. (2005), *Masters of Chaos: The Secret History of the Special Forces*, New York: Public Affairs.
Romano, D. (2004), "Safe Havens as Political Projects: The Case of Iraqi Kurdistan," *States Within States: Incipient Political Entities in the Post-Cold War Era*, P. Kingston and S. Kingston (eds.), New York: Palgrave MacMillan, pp. 81–97.
Rose, J. (2011), "Defining the Rogue State: A Definitional Comparative Analysis Within the Rationalist, Culturalist, and Structural Traditions," available at <http://jpi-nyu.org/wp-content/uploads/2011/02/Defining-the-Rogue-State-.pdf>, (accessed 23/01/2015).
Roshinbiri News (1989), "Em Hoze Kurdane le Bnecheda Arab" (These Kurdish Tribes Are Originally Arabs), *Roshinbiri News*, no. 124, Baghdad.
Rubin, A. H. (2007), "Abd al-Karim Qasim and the Kurds of Iraq: Centralization, Resistance and Revolt, 1958–63," *Middle Eastern Studies* 43(3): 353–382.
Rubin, M. (2003), "Are Kurds a Pariah Minority?" *Social Research: An International Quarterly* 70(1): 295–330.
Russia Today (2010), "As Long as Iraq Abides by the Constitution, We're Iraqis," Interview with Masud Barzani, available at <http://rt.com/politics/kurdistan-iraq-barzani-election/>, (accessed 18/06/2015).
Saadabad Pact (1937), "Treaty of Nonaggression Signed by Afghanistan, Iraq, Iran, and Turkey on July 8, 1937, at the Saadabad Palace in Teheran," *League of Nations Treaty Series* 190(1938): 21–28.
Sabir, R. (2005), *Iraq: Dimokratizekrdn yan Helwashandnewe?* (Iraq: democratisation or dismemberment?), Publisher unknown.
Sabir, S. A. (2007), *Rafiq Hilmi wa Hayatuho al-Syasa (Rafiq Hilmi and his Political Life)*, Sulaimaniya,Iraq: Mua'assassa al-zhin.
Salih, B. (2006), "Kurds, Safety Valve of New Iraq," *Soma-Digest*, no. 4, available at <http://soma-digest.com/PDFs/soma-digest-06.pdf>, (accessed 09/06/2015).
—— (2012), "PUKmedia," available at <www.pukmedia.com/ansat/lmk.pdf >, (accessed 05/04/2016).
Salih, R. and A. Zangana (2008), "Rabari Rojnamenusi Kurdi" (A Guide to Kurdish Newspapers), Binkey Zhin, no. 4, available at <www.binkeyjin.com/Belgenamekan/1963-1970.pdf>.
Salim, J. N. (2008), *Aya Fedraliyat Wek Kheyareki Syasi le Eraqda Pyade Dekret? (Will Fedralism as a Political Option Will Be Followed in Iraq?)* Erbil, Iraq: Aras Publications.

Sbeiy (2012), "Kishanawy Peshmerga u Dubarebunewey Sinaryokan" (The Withdrawal of Peshmergas and the Repetition of Scenarios), available at <www.sbeiy.com/Detail.aspx?id=14461&LinkID=14>, (accessed 08/12/2015).

Scarritt, J. R. (2008), "Ethnopolitics and Nationalism," *Politics in the Developing World*, P. Burnell and Vicky Randall (eds.), Oxford: Oxford University Press, pp. 111–128.

Schmidt, D. A. (1962a), "Warn U.S. to Give Them Aid or They Will Ask the Soviets," *The New York Times*, 10/9/1962.

—— (1962b), "Kurdish Rebel Chief Says Force Is only Way to Win Autonomy," *The New York Times*, 11/9/1962.

—— (1963a), "Kurds Try to Foil Iraqi Army Drive," *The New York Times*, 2/8/1963.

—— (1963b), "Iraqi Troops Driving on Kurdish Rebels' Centers," *The New York Times*, 13/6/1963.

—— (1964). "Kurdish Rebels and Iraq Agree to Cease Fighting," *The New York Times*, 11/2/1964.

—— (1974), "Kurdish Leader, Facing Possible Civil War, Looks to West for Support," *The New York Times*, 1/4/1974.

Seale, P. (1988), *Asad of Syria: The Struggle for the Middle East*, Berkeley, CA: University of California Press.

Security Council Resolution 687 (1991), "The United Nations Security Council," 3/4/1991, available at <www.casi.org.uk/info/undocs/gopher/s91/4>, (accessed 27/09/2016).

Security Council Resolution 688 (1991), "The United Nations Security Council," 05/04/1991, available at <www.casi.org.uk/info/undocs/gopher/s91/5>, (accessed 27/09/2016).

Security Council Resolution 660 (1990), "The United Nations Security Council," 2/8/1990, available at <www.casi.org.uk/info/undocs/gopher/s90/14>, (accessed 27/09/2016).

Security Council Resolution 661 (1990), "The United Nations Security Council," 6/8/1990, available at <www.casi.org.uk/info/undocs/gopher/s90/15>, (accessed 27/09/2016).

Security Council Resolution 986 (1995), "The United Nations Security Council," 14/4/1995, available at <www.casi.org.uk/info/undocs/scres/1995/9510988e.htm>, (accessed 27/09/2016).

Security Council Resolution 1153 (1998), "The United Nations Security Council," 20/02/1998, available at <www.casi.org.uk/info/undocs/scres/1998/sres1153.htm>, (accessed 27/09/2016).

Security Council Resolution 1483 (2003); SCR1546 (8/6/2004); SCR1637 (11/11 2005); SCR1723 (28/11/2006); SCR1790 (18/12/2007); SCR1859 (22/12/2008).

Seeking Alpha (2009), "Iraqi Kurdistan: One of the World's Most Coveted Oil Fields," *Seeking Alpha*, available at <http://seekingalpha.com/article/145257-iraqi-kurdistan-one-of-the-world-s-most-coveted-oil-fields>, (accessed 26/06/2015).

Serbekhoyi Newspaper, 25/4/1992.

Seymour, M. H. (1983), *The Prince of Power: Kissinger The Nixon White House*, New York: Summit Books.

SFA, Strategic Framework Agreement (2008), "US Department of State," available at <www.state.gov/documents/organization/122076.pdf>, (accessed 08/11/2015).

Shadid, A. (2009), "Kurdish Leaders Warn of Strains with Maliki: Military Conflict a Possibility, One Says," *The Washington Post*, 1/7/2011.

Shakeli, F. (2010), "Kurdish Nationalism in Mam u Zin of Ahmedî Khânî," *Kurdish Globe*, available at <www.kurdishglobe.net/displayArticle.jsp?id=B035657F9D7C0443961A48068F4D6553>, (accessed 03/02/2015).

Shamzini, A. (2006), *Jwlanaway Rizgari Nishtimani Kurdistan (The Kurdish national liberation movement)*, Fourth Edition, Sulaimaniya, Iraq: Senteri Lekolinewey Strategi Kurdistan.

Sharif, A. S. T. (1978), *Ta'arikh al-Hizb al-Thawri al-Kurdistani (The History of the Kurdistan Revolutionary Party)*, Baghdad: Shoreshger.

―――― (2007), *Al-Jamiyat wal-Munadhamat wal-Ahzab al-Kurdiya fi nisf al-Qirn: 1908–1958 (Associations, Organisations and Kurdish Parties in Half a Century 1908–1958)*, Sulaimaniya, Iraq: Dar al-Sardam.

"Shaswar Abdul-Wahid in NRTTV Tawtwe Show," *NRTTV*, 17/09/2017, available at <www.youtube.com/watch?v=0KJeNK6gww8>, (accessed 07/11/2017).

Sherko, B. (1986), *Keshay Kurd: Mezhwi nwe u Estay Kurd (Kurdish Question: Old and Present History of the Kurds)*, Muhammad Hama Baqi (trans.), Kurdistan: Shahid Ja'far Press.

Shields, S. (2004), "Mosul Questions: Economy, Identity, and Annexation," *The Creation of Iraq, 1914–1922*, Reeva Spector Simon and Eleanor H. Tejirian (eds.), New York: Columbia University Press, pp. 50–61.

Simon, S. (1974), "The Hashemite 'Conspiracy': Hashemite Unity Attempts, 1921–1958," *International Journal of Middle East Studies* 5(3): 314–327.

―――― (2004), "The View from Baghdad," *The Creation of Iraq, 1914–1921*, Reeva Spector Simon and Eleanor H. Tejirian (eds.), New York: Columbia University Press.

―――― (2008), "The Price of the Surge: How US Strategy is Hastening Iraq's Demise," *Foreign Affairs* 87: 57–76.

Simonsen, S. G. (2005), "Addressing Ethnic Divisions in Post-Conflict Institution-Building: Lessons from Recent Cases," *Security Dialogue* 36(3): 297–318.

Sinjari, A. (2006), *Al-Qadhiya al-Kurdiye wa al-hizb al-Ba'ah al-Arabi al-Ishtraki fi al-Iraq (The Kurdish Problem and the Arab Socialist Ba'ath Party in Iraq)*, Duhok, Iraq: Haji Hashim Press.

Sky, E. (2011), "Iraq, From Surge to Sovereignty," *Foreign Affairs*, available at <www.foreignaffairs.com/print/67459>, (accessed 19/08/2016).

Sluglett, P. (1976), *Britain in Iraq, 1914–1932*, Beirut: Ithaca Press for the Middle East Centre.

Sluglett, P. and M. Farouk-Sluglett (1992), *Tuttle Guide to the Middle East*, Boston, MA: C.E. Tuttle Co.

Smith, A. D. (1987), *The Ethnic Origins of Nations*, Oxford: Oxford University Press.

―――― (2009), *Ethno-Symbolism and Nationalism: A Cultural Approach*, London: Routledge.

Smith, R. J. (1992), "Dozens of U.S. Items Used in Iraq Arms," *The Washington Post*, 22/7/2002.

SOFA, U.S.–Iraq Status of Forces Agreement (2008), "Agreement Between the United States of America and the Republic of Iraq on the Withdrawal of United States Forces from Iraq and the Organization of Their Activities during Their Temporary Presence in Iraq, U.S. Department of State," available at <www.state.gov/documents/organization/122074.pdf>, (accessed 08/11/2015).

Spokesman (2011), "Jaf'ar Sheikh Mustafa: Jmarey Peshmerga 200,000 u Baghda Deyewet le 70,000 kemtrman Nebet" (Jaf'ar Sheikh Mustafa: The number of Peshmerga is 200,000 and Baghdad claims that we have no more than 70,000), Ministry of Peshmerga, available at <www.witebej.com/K_WitarDireje.aspx?Cor=Chawpekewtin&Jimare=25>, (accessed 23/12/2012).

Stansfield, G. R. V. (2003), "The Kurdish dilemma: the golden era threatened," *Iraq at the Crossroads: State in the Shadow of Regime Change*, Toby Dodge and Steven Simon (eds.), London and Oxford: Adelphi Papers, pp. 131–148.

Stansfield, S. (2006), "The Kurdish Question in Iraq, 1914–1974," *The Middle East Online*, availavble at <www.tlemea.com/iraq/essay5.asp>, (accessed 22/10/2016).

"Statement from Kurdistan Regional Government," *Kurdistan Regional Government*, 24/10/2017, available at <http://cabinet.gov.krd/a/d.aspx?s=040000&l=12&a=55938>, (accessed 25/10/2017).

"Statement from Kurdistan Regional Government," *Kurdistan Regional Government*, 25/10/2017, available at <http://cabinet.gov.krd/a/d.aspx?s=040000&l=12&a=55938>, (accessed 04/10/2017).

Stavenhagen, R. (1996), *Ethnic Conflicts and the Nation-State: United Nations Research Institute for Social Development*, New York: Palgrave Macmillan.

Stromseth, J. E. (2003), "Law and Force After Iraq: A Transitional Moment," American Journal of International Law: 628–642.

Strouse, T. (2010), "Opening of the Turkish Consulate in Erbil," *The Other Iraq*, available at <http://theotheriraq.wordpress.com/2010/03/18/opening-of-the-turkish-consulate-in-erbil/>, (accessed 01/05/2015).

Tabani, H. (2010), *Hawneteweyi Kurd u Mad (The Co-Nationality of the Kurds and Medes)*, Erbil, Iraq: Mukiryani.

Tahiri, H. (2007), *The Structure of Kurdish Society and the Struggle for a Kurdish State*, Costa Mesa, CA: Mazda Publisher.

Talabani, J. (1970), "Kurdistan wa al-Haraka al-Qawmiya al-Kurdiya" (Kurdistan and the Kurdish nationalist movement), Baghdad: Al-Nur.

——— (1988), "Hawla al-Qadhiye al-Kurdiya (About the Kurdish Question)," Ibrahim Ezzo.

——— (2004), *Gft u Goyeki Ciddi Legel Subhi Abdulhamid u Hawrekani (A Serious Dialogue with Subhi Abdul-Hamid and His Colleagues)*, Slemani, Iraq: Sharewani Slemani.

——— (2011), *Erkekani Khabat le Helumerjecki Dizhwarda (The Duty of Struggle in Terrible Circumstances)*, Sulaimaniya, Iraq: Akadimiyai Hoshyari.

Talabani, Q. (2005), "What the Kurds Want," *The Wall Street Journal* – Eastern Edition.

Talabany, N. (2001), *Arabisation of the Kirkuk Region*, Uppsala, Sweden: Kurdistan Studies Press.

——— (2004), "Iraq's Policy of Ethnic Cleansing: Onslaught to Change National/Demographic Characteristics of the Kirkuk Region," 25/12/2010.

——— (2004), *Mantiqat Kirkuk wa Mihawalat Taghir Waq'iha al-Qawmi (Kirkuk Area and the Attempts to Change Its Ethnic Reality)*, Third edition, Erbil, Iraq: Aras Publishers.

Tanter, R. (1999), *Rogue Regimes: Terrorism and Proliferation*, New York: Palgrave Macmillan.

Tejel, J. (2008), *Syria's Kurds: History, Politics and Society*, London: Routledge.

"Tillerson Says Kurdish Independence Referendum Is Illegitimate," *The Washington Post*, 29/09/2017, available at <www.washingtonpost.com/world/middle_east/iraq-bans-flights-to-kurdish-region-as-rift-grows-over-independence-bid/2017/09/29/860e326e-a532–11e7-b573–8ec86cdfe1ed_story.html?utm_term=.113767c2ac41> (accessed 30/09/2017).

Tiron, R. and K. Klimasinska (2012), "No Contract Freeze for 'Committed' Exxon, Kurdish Minister Says," available at <www.bloomberg.com/news/2012-04-02/no-contract-freeze-for-committed-exxon-kurdish-minister-says.html>, (accessed 06/04/2016).

Tomasek, R. D. (1976), "The Resolution of Major Controversies between Iran and Iraq," *World Affairs* 139(3): 206–230.

Totten, S. and W. S. Parsons. (2009), *Century of Genocide: Critical Essays and Eyewitness Accounts*, London: Taylor & Francis.

Tran, M. (2008), "Turkey Withdraws Troops from Northern Iraq, Military Says," *The Guardian*, available at <www.guardian.co.uk/world/2008/feb/29/kurds.turkey>, (accessed 02/03/2015).

Treaty of Sèvres (1920), "WWI Document Archive," available at <http://wwi.lib.byu.edu/index.php/Section_I%2C_Articles_1_-_260>, (accessed 11/9/2015).

Tucker, M. (2006), *Hell Is Over: Voices of the Kurds After Saddam*, Guilford, CT: Lyons Press.

U.S. Senate (1988), "Chemical Weapons Use in Kurdistan Iraq's Final Offensive," Committee on Foreign Relations, Washington, DC.

University of Duhok (2011a), "Faculty of Humanities," available at <www.uod.ac/en/college/3/faculty_of_humatities>, (accessed 10/09/2016).

University of Raparin Website, (2012), available at <www.raparinuni.org/(A(OHJtmjjjzQEkAAAAZDE5MDg2YWMtOGQ1Ny00NWJiLThmMDgtODJjNjc3NWY0NDhknBGh8m6Zv7M2O7bg0vdgv0oMk2c1))/En/>, (accessed 28/53/2015).

University of Sulaimani (2012a), "Mezhwi Nwe u Hawcherkh" (The Modern and Contemporary History), available at <www.univsul.org/K_D_WaneDireje.aspx?Besh=65&Jimare=944>, (accessed 09/07/2015).

University of Sulaimani (2012b), "Course Subjects," available at <www.univsul.org/K_D_Wanekan.aspx?Besh=65>, (accessed 05/07/2016).

Vanly, I. C. (1990), "Kurdistan in Iraq," *People without a Country: The Kurds and Kurdistan*, G. Chaliand (ed.), Michael Pallis (trans.), London: Zed Press, pp. 154–210.

——— (1992), "The Kurds in Syria and Lebanon," *The Kurds: A Contemporary Overview*, London: Routledge, pp. 143–170.

Volcker, P. A., R. Goldstone and M. Pieth. (2005), "Manipulation of the Oil-for-Food Programme by the Iraqi Regime, Independent Inquiry Committee into the United Nations Oil-for-Food Programme," available at <www.iic-offp.org/documents/Final%20Report%2027Oct05/IIC%20Final%20Report%20-%20Cover%20and%20Index.pdf>, (accessed 17/08/2015).

Wagner, J. Q. (1992), *Ethnic Conflict: The Case of the Kurds*, Washington, DC: DTIC Document.

Walker, M. (2003), "The Making of Modern Iraq," *The Wilson Quarterly* 27(2): 29–40.

Waqai' Kurdistan (The Official Gazette of Kurdistan Region), 15/08/2007, Erbil, Iraq.

——— 17/06/2008, Erbil, Iraq.

"War in Iraq: Masoud Barzani, Ex-Kurdish Leader, Says U.S. Knew in Advance About Iraqi Assault on Kirkuk," *Newsweek*, 07/11/2017, available at <www.newsweek.com/iraq-kurds-isis-betrayal-america-barzani-iran-independence-kirkuk-704480>, (accessed 08/11/2017).Weber, M. (1997), *The Theory of Social and Economic Organization*, New York: Free Press.

Weinstock, A. B. (2005), "Using Institutions to Moderate Separatist Tendencies: A Focus on Iraqi Kurdistan," Masters thesis, Massachusetts Institute of Technology.

Wenner, L. M. (1963), "Arab-Kurdish Rivalries in Iraq," *Middle East Journal* 17(1/2): 68–82.

White House (2003), "President Discusses Beginning of Operation Iraqi Freedom," available at <http://georgewbushwhitehouse.archives.gov/news/releases/2003/03/print/20030322.html>, (accessed 23/09/2015).

Whitley, A. (1980), "The Kurds: Pressures and Prospects," *The Round Table* 70(279): 245–257.

Williams, M. W. (2004), *The British Experience in Iraq from 1914–1926: What Wisdom Can the United States Draw from Its Experience?* Washington, DC: DTIC Document.

Wilson, A. (1931), *Mesopotamia, 1917–1920: A Clash of Loyalties*, Oxford: Oxford University Press.

Wimmer, A. (2004), "Democracy and Ethno-Religious Conflict in Iraq," *Survival* 45(4): 111–134.

Woolf, N. (2010) "Is Kurdistan the Next Dubai?" Guardian, available at www.guardian.co.uk/commentisfree/2010/may/05/kurdistan-next-dubai-iraq, guardian.co.uk>, (accessed 12/05/2016).

Wright, C. (1985), "Religion and Strategy in the Iraq-Iran War," *Third World Quarterly* 7(4): 839–852.

Yamulki, A. (2005), *Serjemi Berhemi Abdulaziz Yamulki (The collection of writings from Abdulaziz Yamulki)*, Sulaimaniya, Iraq: Binkey Zhin.

────── (2003), "War and Occupation in Iraq: What Went Right? What Could Go Wrong?" *Middle East Journal* 57(3): 381–399.

────── (2004), "Iraqi Identity After the Fall of Saddam," *Middle East Institute*. available at <www.mideasti.org/publications/publications_transcripts.php>, (accessed 01/09/2015).

Yeketi Tekoshin no. 2 (1944).

────────── no. 3 (1945).

────── (1945), "The Mouthpiece of the Kurdish Branch of the Iraqi Communist League," no. 2.

Zaman, A. (2010), "Turkey and the Iraqi Kurds: From Red Lines to Red Carpets," *The German Marshall Fund of the United States (GMF)*, available at < www.gmfus.org/wp-content/blogs.dir/1/files_mf//galleries/ct_publication_attachments/Amberin_Analysis_Turkey_0510_Final.pdf>, (accessed 28/11/2012).

Zawya (2011), "Iran-KRG Trade to Hit $5b, Zawya Zawya," available at <www.zawya.com/story/ZAWYA20110907050008>, (accessed 03/01/2015).

Zeki, M. A. (2003), *Khulasat Tarikh Kurd wa Kurdistan (A brief history of Kurds and Kurdistan)*, Beirut: Al-Jam'iya al-Kurdiya al-Lubnaniya al-Khayriya.

Zewer, B. (2003), *Diwani Bakhtiyar Zewer (The Divan of Bakhtiyar Zewer)*, Erbil, Iraq: Aras Publications.

Zhiyan Newspaper, 28/8/1930; 21/07/1930; 11/4/1929; 23/02/1928; 16/02/1928.

Zilinskas, R. A. (1997), "Iraq's Biological Weapons," *JAMA: The Journal of the American Medical Association* 278(5): 418–424.

List of news and newspaper sources

AFP (Agence France-Presse)
AKnews
Al-Ahram
Al-Hayat
Al-Iraq
Al-Jamhuriya
Al-Thawra
Al-Waqai' al-Iraqiya
Asharq Al-Awsat
Awene Newspaper
Baghdad
Khabat
Kurdistani Nwe
The New York Times
Rizgari
Rudaw Waqai' Kurdistan
Zhiyan

Index

agha xxii, 37, 38, 76, 77, 79, 80
al-Abadi, Haidar 207
al-Baghdadi, Abu Bakr 200
Algeria Agreement 94, 107
al-Haras al-Qawmi 203
al-Husri, Sati' 39
Allies 151, 153, 154, 155, 156, 157, 159, 160, 161, 162, 163, 164, 171
al-Sistani, Ali 202
al-Watan al-Arabi 39
Ankara 191
Arabic x, 19, 36, 39, 40, 41, 62, 83, 100, 101, 132, 133, 153, 169, 170, 197, 219, 226, 227, 229
Arabisation xv, xxi, 37, 39, 41, 120, 137, 138, 145, 153, 163, 240
Arabised Kurds 37, 72, 73, 82
Arab nationalism 39, 44, 73
Arif, Abd al-Salam 39, 43, 85, 94, 95, 98
assimilation 35, 39, 41, 54, 138, 140
Assyrian 36, 64, 197
Azadi 58, 78, 79, 217, 226
Azerbaijan 22, 50, 62, 190, 233
Azeri xviii

Ba'ath xxi, 26, 38, 39, 40, 41, 42, 43, 45, 62, 63, 94, 95, 109, 110, 112, 116, 121, 131, 132, 133, 137, 149, 156, 175, 214, 239
Baghdad xi, xii, xiii, xiv, 37, 38, 39, 43, 44, 51, 52, 58, 61, 62, 63, 65, 67, 71, 73, 74, 76, 79, 80, 82, 84, 88, 93, 96, 99, 107, 109, 110, 111, 115, 117, 118, 120, 121, 122, 123, 124, 126, 127, 128, 131, 132, 133, 134, 135, 136, 137, 138, 139, 141, 142, 144, 145, 146, 149, 150, 151, 156, 157, 158, 162, 163, 167, 168, 169, 172, 173, 174, 175, 179, 182, 183, 185, 186, 187, 188, 190, 191, 192, 193, 195, 198, 199, 200, 202, 204, 206, 207, 208, 209, 210, 211, 212, 213, 214, 215, 216, 217, 226, 227, 228, 230, 231, 236, 237, 239, 240, 243
Barzani, Masud, xi, xiv, xxv, xxvi, 60, 63, 68, 69, 74, 87, 99, 100, 112, 138, 144, 145, 151, 165, 172, 179, 184, 186, 188, 193, 194, 197, 198, 199, 200, 201, 203, 204, 205, 207, 208, 209, 211, 212, 213, 215, 216, 217, 218, 224, 229, 230, 231, 234, 235, 236, 237, 241
Barzani, Mustafa 43, 45, 55, 56, 57, 58, 63, 67, 71, 77, 78, 79, 80, 81, 85, 86, 87, 88, 90, 95, 96, 102, 104, 105, 108, 109, 113, 152, 165
Barzani, Nechirvan 78, 168, 188, 190, 197, 211
Barzani, Sheikh Ahmad 37, 38, 56, 57, 75, 76, 77
Basra 40, 43, 52
Bilad al-Akrad 49
Bitlisi, Sharafkhan 49, 50, 51, 65, 66, 219
Bolivia 13
Burma 13

Ceyhan 186
chemical weapons 30, 114, 118, 122, 142, 150
christians 41, 90, 138
Coalition Provisional Authority (CPA) xiii, 170, 175, 176, 179, 180, 221, 222
Coalition Task Force 175, 176
communism 77, 111, 224
constitution xi, xii, xiii, xvi, xx, xxvi, 22, 36, 39, 40, 41, 53, 55, 78, 81, 90, 91, 119, 146, 167, 170, 171, 179, 184, 206, 211, 227
Cyprus xvii, 2, 9, 11, 22, 88, 234

Index   245

depopulation vi, xv, xvi, 45, 115, 138, 140, 141, 142, 143, 144
discrimination 25, 26, 140, 164
disputed areas xvi, xiv, xxv, 13, 16, 137, 139, 140, 163, 164, 171, 172, 174, 187, 201, 202, 204, 206, 207, 208, 209, 210, 211
Diyala 139, 174, 215
Diyarbakir 50, 51
Dubai 190, 242
Duhok 88, 91, 94, 112, 133, 134, 139, 170, 210, 215, 239, 241

East Timor xviii
Egypt 95, 98, 99, 103, 215
Erbil xii, xiii, xiv, 28, 36, 62, 63, 64, 65, 68, 83, 88, 91, 92, 95, 99, 100, 101, 115, 120, 128, 131, 134, 138, 139, 143, 144, 145, 162, 167, 185, 187, 189, 191, 192, 194, 195, 198, 199, 201, 202, 210, 211, 214, 215, 217, 218, 220, 222, 225, 227, 228, 230, 231, 232, 233, 234, 235, 236, 240, 241, 242
executive council 90, 91, 132
external sovereignty 4, 10, 11, 26, 29, 30
Ey Reqib x, 47, 93, 152, 153, 214

Fact-Finding Commission (FFC) 70
failed-state 13
Faili-Kurds 139
federalism xii, xiii, 46, 58, 152, 167, 217, 220, 229
Free Kurdistan xv, xxii, 55, 87, 88, 89, 90, 91, 92, 93, 94, 95, 96, 97, 98, 99, 102, 103, 104, 105, 106, 108, 109, 111, 112, 114, 115, 117, 118, 119, 120, 121, 124, 125, 128, 131, 141, 143, 147, 225

Gorran Movement 198, 203

Halabja 118, 125, 148, 168, 220
Hashd al-Shaabi 202, 203, 207, 208, 210
Hawrami 185, 186, 189, 194, 231
Hilmi 78, 79, 226, 237
Hiwa xxii, 45, 55, 67, 73, 74, 77, 78, 79, 80, 81
Hizbullah 193
Human Rights Watch (HRW) viii, 129, 135, 136, 141, 145, 146, 147, 166, 226
Hussein, Saddam xi, 30, 40, 58, 62, 101, 113, 141, 147, 217, 228, 234

imperialism 43, 44, 45
indirect rule xv, 37, 38, 57, 58, 76, 77, 89, 134, 135, 136, 137

integration xv, xvii, xx, xxi, xxii, 14, 25, 27, 55, 72, 73, 97, 122, 134, 148, 178, 183, 190
International Crisis Group (ICG) xiii, 146, 179, 194, 227
international oil companies (IOCs) xxv, 182, 183, 185, 187, 188, 189
Iraq al-Ajam 49
Iraq al-Arab 49
Iraqi Communist Party (ICP) viii, xxii, 61, 73, 77, 81, 84, 106, 127, 217, 226, 234
Iraqi Kurdistan Front (IKF) xiii, 55, 59, 61, 68, 69, 114, 118, 125, 144, 148, 149, 151, 227
Iraqi National Congress (INC) xiii, 162, 227
Iraqi Nation-Building Project (INP) xiii, xix, 32, 35, 39, 46, 41, 42, 43, 44, 61
Islamic State in Iraq and Syria (ISIS) viii, xiii, xiv, 10, 187, 191, 199, 200, 201, 202, 203, 205, 206, 208, 209, 212, 222
Islamic Union of Kurdistan 203
Israel xviii, xxiii, 44, 57, 63, 88, 96, 101, 103, 104, 105, 106, 107, 108, 112, 129, 147, 166, 192, 193, 195, 216, 218, 219, 222, 232, 234, 235

Jash x, xv, 38, 94, 119, 122, 128, 136, 137, 142, 143, 144, 148, 151
Jew 90

Kakays 41, 138
Khabat 49, 65, 66, 67, 68, 100, 129, 179, 195, 218, 228, 240, 243
Khamenei, Ali 193, 196
Khaneqin 87, 88
Khani, Ahmadi 50, 65, 229, 237
Khutba 51
Khuzestan 110
Komalla 54, 55, 58, 59, 65, 66, 67, 68, 69, 100, 128, 129, 146, 214, 229
Komallay Jyanewey Kurd 81
Koyi, Haji Qadir 50, 51, 65, 229
Kurdish liberation movement 47, 55, 62, 152
Kurdish MPs 45, 56
Kurdish Nationalist Movement x, xix, xxi, xxii, xxiii, 35, 44, 61, 74, 80, 81, 114, 116, 125, 133
Kurdish Nationhood Project (KNP) viii, 32, 35, 46, 48, 52, 58
Kurdish quasi-state xii, xiii, xix, xxi, xxii, xxiii, xxiv, xxv, xxvi, 25, 27, 28, 29, 56, 84, 97, 99, 102, 103, 116, 138, 141, 148,

149, 150, 151, 152, 153, 154, 155, 156, 157, 158, 159, 160, 161, 162, 163, 164, 165, 166, 167, 168, 169, 170, 171, 172, 173, 174, 175, 176, 177, 178, 179, 180, 181, 183, 210
Kurdish Urbanites xxii, 53, 73, 74, 77, 78, 79, 80, 86
Kurdistan Democratic Party (KDP) 6, 8, 33, 36, 49, 52, 53, 55, 58, 59, 60, 61, 65, 66, 67, 68, 69, 73, 74, 77, 78, 80, 81, 82, 84, 85, 86, 87, 89, 90, 91, 92, 93, 102, 104, 112, 113, 115, 117, 118, 124, 126, 127, 129, 137, 138, 158, 162, 171, 201, 208, 212, 217, 225, 228, 237
Kurdistan Democratic Party of Iraq (KDPI) vi, 81
Kurdistani xxi, 35, 46, 47, 48, 49, 53, 54, 56, 61, 66, 67, 68, 82, 119, 128, 137, 138, 152, 153, 158, 165, 168, 170, 178, 197, 215, 223, 228, 231, 233, 236, 239, 243
Kurdistan National Assembly (KNA) vi, 46, 64, 65, 149, 152, 153, 165, 166, 229
Kurdistan Regional Government (KRG) xiii, xi, xii, xiii, xiv, 28, 47, 64, 65, 67, 68, 82, 146, 148, 149, 151, 152, 153, 156, 158, 161, 163, 165, 167, 169, 170, 175, 179, 185, 186, 187, 188, 189, 191, 192, 193, 194, 195, 196, 197, 199, 204, 206, 210, 211, 213, 217, 218, 230, 231, 236, 242
Kurdistan Region of Iraq (KRI) xiii, xiii, xiv, xv, xvi, xvii, xix, xx, xxiv, xxv, 1, 27, 28, 29, 55, 88, 141, 149, 151, 153, 155, 156, 158, 159, 161, 162, 167, 168, 169, 170, 171, 172, 173, 174, 178, 179, 182, 183, 184, 185, 186, 187, 188, 189, 190, 191, 192, 193, 197, 198, 199, 200, 201, 202, 203, 204, 205, 206, 207, 208, 209, 210, 211, 212, 229
Kurdistan Revolutionary Army (KRA) viii, 92

Latif, Sheikh 78
League of Nations 48, 49, 54, 56, 58, 59, 70, 71, 72, 75, 82, 231, 237
Lebanon 10, 38, 42, 65, 76, 88, 100, 141, 218, 230, 241
Libya 190

Mahmud, Sheikh 48, 52, 56, 57, 65, 70, 71, 77, 82, 215
Makhmour 137, 138, 205
Maliki, Nuri 168, 179, 200, 231, 238

Mandaly 139
March Manifesto 95, 101, 107, 138
Medes 36, 47, 64, 153, 240
Mediterranean 186, 193
Mem û Zîn 50
Mesopotamia 36, 46, 49, 242
monarchy xxii, 31, 36, 37, 38, 43, 44, 45, 55, 56, 58, 67, 70, 71, 72, 73, 74, 75, 76, 77, 78, 79, 80, 81, 82, 83, 84, 85, 86, 110, 114, 116, 121, 136, 138, 140, 176, 178
Mosul xiii, 43, 49, 51, 65, 70, 85, 86, 88, 91, 92, 118, 126, 133, 137, 138, 139, 172, 174, 200, 205, 218, 226, 239
Mujama'at x, 38, 39, 118, 120, 121, 126, 134, 135, 143
Muslims 40, 200
Mustashar 39, 136

NABACO 186
Nagorno-Karabakh Republic xviii
nation-building xxi, xxii, xxiv, 14, 20, 29, 44, 47, 53, 61, 73, 74, 82, 90, 92, 93, 119, 125, 151, 152, 153, 168, 169, 170, 178
nationhood project xix, xxi, 32, 35, 36, 42, 43, 44, 45, 46, 47, 51, 52, 54, 55, 56, 57, 58, 60, 61, 84
nation without a state xviii, xix, xxi, 32, 35
Nawroz x, 47, 74, 93, 119, 153, 170, 219, 226, 237
Nehri, Sheikh Ubeiydeulla 50
Netanyahu, Beniamin 192, 193, 195
no-fly zone (NFZ) ix, xxiv, 150, 153, 154, 156, 157, 159, 161, 162, 163, 164
No-Man's Land xii, 114, 115, 121
non-nation state (NNS) xvii, xix, xx, xxi, 1, 30, 32, 35
northern iraq 33, 141, 147, 210, 216, 225, 235, 241
North Korea 13

Oil and Gas Law 184, 189, 193, 230
oil contracts 182, 183, 185, 187, 188
Oil- for-Food Program (OFFP) vii, xxiv, 29, 153, 157, 158, 159, 162, 163, 182
Operation Provide Comfort (OPC) 155
Ottoman x, 37, 43, 48, 50, 51, 52, 62, 65, 66, 70, 72, 73, 75, 76, 82, 83, 101, 220, 232, 235

Palestine xviii, 2, 141
pan-Arab 39, 44, 79, 81, 85, 86, 110
parent state xvii, xviii, xxii, xxiv, 13, 14, 15, 17, 18, 19, 20, 21, 26, 29, 94, 96,

102, 119, 124, 126, 149, 151, 159, 172, 173
Pasha, Sharif 51
Patriotic Union of Kurdistan (PUK) ix, xxv, 33, 52, 54, 55, 58, 59, 60, 65, 67, 68, 69, 100, 114, 115, 117, 118, 120, 121, 124, 127, 128, 129, 137, 142, 158, 171, 208, 209, 225, 236
Peace Conference 48, 51, 59, 65, 72
Persian Gulf 50, 110, 111
Peshmerga x, xi, xiii, xiv, xv, xvi, xxii, xxiii, 68, 84, 85, 88, 90, 91, 92, 93, 94, 95, 96, 105, 112, 114, 115, 116, 117, 118, 119, 120, 121, 122, 127, 128, 134, 135, 136, 137, 140, 141, 142, 143, 144, 147, 148, 149, 151, 170, 171, 172, 173, 174, 187, 200, 201, 202, 204, 205, 208, 215
Peshmerga Controlled Area (PCA) viii, xxiii, 119, 124, 125, 126, 136, 137
Production Sharing Contracts 189, 193, 230

Qasim, Abd al- Karim 36, 39, 43, 84, 85, 86, 87, 94, 98, 99, 106, 223, 237
quasi-state 1, 2, 3, 4, 5, 6, 7, 10, 12, 13, 14, 15, 16, 17, 18, 19, 20, 21, 22, 23, 24, 25, 26, 27, 28, 29, 30, 31, 35, 85, 86, 87, 88, 89, 90, 91, 92, 93, 94, 95, 96, 97, 98, 99, 100, 101, 102, 114, 119, 124, 125, 126, 128, 148, 149, 151, 159, 163, 164, 168, 170, 172, 173, 174, 175, 178, 182, 188, 202, 204

Rawanduz 118
recognised quasi-state xvii, xviii, xix, xx, xxiii, xxiv, 5, 12, 97, 99, 125, 128, 164, 175, 178
referendum xi, xiii, xxv, 70, 140, 144, 146, 148, 190, 192, 193, 195, 197, 198, 199, 200, 201, 202, 203, 204, 205, 206, 207, 208, 209, 210, 211, 212, 213
Republic of Mahabad 47, 58, 80, 81, 93, 152
revenue sharing 171, 172, 183, 186
Revolutionary Command Council of Iraq (RCCI) ix, 90, 91, 131, 132, 133, 139
Revolutionary Command Council of Kurdistan (RCCK) ix, 90, 91
Royal Air Force (RAF) ix, 71

safe haven xxiv, 20, 28, 53, 57, 81, 97, 105, 116, 122, 150, 153, 154, 155, 156, 159, 160, 161, 163, 164
scorched-earth 114, 141, 142
Security Council xx, xxiv, 150, 153, 154, 156, 157, 159, 160, 161, 175

self-determination 23, 28, 56, 58, 59, 60, 61, 72, 75, 160
Seljuks 51, 66
semi-autonomous 11, 119
September revolution 66, 67, 87, 92, 228
Shabak 41, 62, 138, 214
Shah, The 104, 108, 109, 110, 116, 117
Shekhan 137
Shia xii, xiii, 5, 25, 28, 116, 139, 149, 150, 168, 173, 174
Sinjar 62, 202, 224
Somalia 2, 9, 13
southern Kurdistan 48, 49
South Sudan xviii
Soviet ix, xxiii, 10, 24, 58, 80, 86, 96, 98, 103, 104, 106, 107, 108, 111
state-building 14, 25, 37, 70, 72, 75, 90, 91, 92, 168, 178
statehood xvi, xvii, xx, xxv, 1, 2, 3, 4, 5, 6, 7, 9, 10, 11, 13, 18, 20, 23, 26, 27, 31, 92, 159, 182, 192, 200, 204
Strategic Framework Agreement (SFA) ix, 177, 178, 181, 238
Sulaimaniya 61, 66, 72, 73, 77, 88, 89, 91, 92, 95, 100, 117, 118, 134, 139, 143, 144, 210, 214, 223, 226, 235, 236, 237, 239, 240, 242
Sunni xii, xiii, 5, 25, 28, 77, 139, 149, 173, 174, 176, 187, 200, 202, 203, 205, 216, 232
Syria ix, xiii, 9, 42, 54, 60, 66, 98, 99, 100, 103, 104, 112, 137, 187, 200, 208, 210, 227, 238, 240, 241

Talabani xi, xii, 48, 54, 59, 60, 61, 64, 65, 66, 67, 68, 69, 77, 83, 89, 92, 167, 224, 237, 240
Tanzimat x, 37, 62, 73, 75, 76, 83, 223
Tehran 105, 109, 111, 207
Tekoshin 58, 69, 82, 242
Tikrit 13, 118, 174, 200
Tillerson, Rex 206, 207, 211, 213, 218, 236, 240
Traditional Autonomous Entities (TAE) ix, 80, 84, 99, 136
Treaty of Sèvres 59, 69, 72, 82, 241
tribal x, 37, 38, 52, 53, 54, 57, 58, 62, 73, 75, 76, 77, 78, 79, 80, 81, 82, 84, 85, 86, 87, 92, 93, 94, 99, 136, 137, 148
tribes 38, 62, 216, 220, 237
Trump, Donald 208
Turkey xiv, xviii, 22, 41, 50, 51, 54, 57, 60, 81, 109, 111, 118, 126, 127, 128, 140, 141, 142, 144, 155, 160, 161, 162,

163, 173, 185, 186, 188, 189, 190, 191, 193, 200, 207, 210
Turkman 90

UN Charter 60, 150, 151, 160
Union of Soviet Socialist Republics (USSR) ix, 86, 87, 98, 99, 103, 104, 105, 106, 107, 108, 111, 112, 113
United Nation (UN) ix, xvii, xx, 28, 55, 60, 106, 123, 144, 150, 151, 153, 154, 155, 156, 157, 158, 159, 160, 162, 163, 164
University of Sulaimani 133, 169, 170, 179, 241
US-Iraq Status of Forces Agreement (SOFA) ix, 177, 178, 181, 239
US-led coalition 176, 205

Vilayet 49, 51
voluntary union xi, xii, 60, 61

Wahbi, Tofiq 59, 72
weapons of mass destruction (WMD) ix, 30, 162
Welati Kurdistan 51
Wilson, Woodrow 59, 69, 72, 82, 241, 242
World War I (WWI) xxii, 28, 49, 52, 69, 82, 241
World War II (WWII) xxii, 52, 57, 71, 76, 77, 79

Yazidi Kurds 41, 62, 75, 138

Zagros 41, 47
Zakho 88, 94
Zionist 45, 226
Zoroastrianism 46, 47, 64, 153
Zuhak 47
Zyiad, Kaka 78